New Trends in Mission

New Trends in Mission

The Emerging Future

*Essays from SEDOS Mission Symposium
October 11–15, 2021, Rome, Italy*

Edited by

PETER BAEKELMANS, CICM, AND MARIE-HÉLÈNE ROBERT, OLA

Maryknoll, New York 10545

Founded in 1970, Orbis Books endeavors to publish works that enlighten the mind, nourish the spirit, and challenge the conscience. The publishing arm of the Maryknoll Fathers and Brothers, Orbis seeks to explore the global dimensions of the Christian faith and mission, to invite dialogue with diverse cultures and religious traditions, and to serve the cause of reconciliation and peace. The books published reflect the views of their authors and do not represent the official position of the Maryknoll Society. To learn more about Orbis Books, please visit our website at www.orbisbooks.com.

Copyright © 2022 by SEDOS.

Published by Orbis Books, Box 302, Maryknoll, NY 10545-0302.

All rights reserved.

No part of this publication may be reproduced or transmitted in any form or by any means, electronic or mechanical, including photocopying, recording, or any information storage or retrieval system, without prior permission in writing from the publisher.

Queries regarding rights and permissions should be addressed to: Orbis Books, P.O. Box 302, Maryknoll, NY 10545-0302.

Manufactured in the United States of America.
Manuscript editing and typesetting by Joan Weber Laflamme.

Library of Congress Cataloging-in-Publication Data

Names: Baekelmans, Peter, editor. | Robert, Marie-Hélène, 1967- editor.
Title: New trends in mission : the emerging future / edited by Peter Baekelmans and Marie-Hélène Robert.
Description: Maryknoll, NY : Orbis Books, [2022] | Includes bibliographical reference | Summary: "An overview of trends in Catholic mission from SEDOS Mission Symposium 2021"— Provided by publisher.
Identifiers: LCCN 2021057748 (print) | LCCN 2021057749 (ebook) | ISBN 9781626984516 (trade paperback) | ISBN 9781608339143 (epub)
Subjects: LCSH: Catholic Church—Missions—History—21st century.
Classification: LCC BV2185 .N49 2022 (print) | LCC BV2185 (ebook) | DDC 266/.2—dc23/eng/20220118
LC record available at https://lccn.loc.gov/2021057748
LC ebook record available at https://lccn.loc.gov/2021057749

Contents

Opening Message   xi
    Pope Francis

Inaugural Address   xiii
    His Eminence Luis Antonio Cardinal Tagle

Preface   xix
    Tesfaye Tadesse Gebresilasie, MCCJ,
    and Mary T. Barron, OLA

Introduction   xxiii
    Peter Baekelmans, CICM

PART ONE
EVANGELIZATION AND MISSION

Introduction to Part One   3
    Michael McCabe, SMA

The "Why" of Mission   7
Biblical Trends in Mission for Our Changing Times
    Rekha M. Chennattu, RA

The "What" of Mission   23
Refining Our Comprehension of Mission
    Joseph Scaria Palakeel, MST

Theological Evolution in Mission 41
A Theology of Mission
    STEPHEN B. BEVANS, SVD

Pope Francis and Mission 55
A Call to Hear the Crying Existential Peripheries
    PAUL BÉRÉ, SJ

The Role of Missionary Religious Institutes 69
A Strange Species of Christians?
    ALOYSIUS PIERIS, SJ

PART TWO
WAYS OF DOING MISSION

Introduction to Part Two 85
    SUSAN K. WOOD, SCL

The "When" of Mission 89
Rediscovering "Initial Proclamation" in Evangelization
    ALFRED MARAVILLA, SDB

The "Who" of Mission 105
We Are Mission
    IDA COLOMBO, CMS, HÉLÈNE ISRAËL SOLOUMTA KAMKÔL, CMS,
    AND MARIA TERESA RATTI, CMS

The "Where" of Mission 123
Fifty Years of Ad Gentes *in Africa*
    ANTHONY AKINWALE, OP

The "How" of Mission 133
Going "Outside the Gates" for the Kingdom's Sake
    PUDOTA RAYAPPA JOHN, SJ

PART THREE
NEW TRENDS IN MISSION

Introduction to Part Three   153
    Bryan Lobo, SJ

Secularization   157
Mission in a Secular Age
    Daniel Patrick Huang, SJ

Mission with Migrants   173
The Roots of "People on the Move"
    Carmen Elisa Bandeo, SSpS

Mission among the Poor   181
"You Always Have the Poor with You" (Mk 14:7)
    Marvi Delrivo, SFP,
    and Licia Mazzia, SFP

Reconciliation   191
The New Face of Evangelization in Africa
    Anne Béatrice Faye, CIC

Mission and Women   199
"Her-Story" of Mission
    Mary T. Barron, OLA

Peacebuilding   209
Peace Promotion as Integral to Evangelization
    James H. Kroeger, MM

Interreligious Dialogue   217
Interreligious Dialogue in the Context of Mission
    Maria De Giorgi, MMX

Islam 227
A Mission of Mercy
    JOHN MALLARE, CICM

Eastern Religions 239
Trusting Christianity's "Incarnational" Thrust
    GERARD HALL, SM

Indigenous Religions 249
Religious Congregations and Indigenous Australians
    ROBYN REYNOLDS, OLSH

African Traditional Religion 257
Working Together to Promote the Culture of Life
    BEDE UKWUIJE, CSSp

Ecumenism 267
Mission and the Search for Unity
    MARIE-HÉLÈNE ROBERT, OLA

Interculturality 277
Culture and the Experience of God
    TIM NORTON, SVD

Media and Mission 287
Staying Connected
    MONIQUE TARABEH, RGS

Medical Mission 295
Mission as Healing
    AGNES LANFERMANN, MMS

Education 305
The Transforming Role of Education
    MARIA ANTONETTA PEREIRA, FMM

Missionary Parishes 313
Growing as a Missionary Parish
    LAZAR T. STANISLAUS, SVD

Laity in Mission 325
The Laity: More than a Lending Hand
    OLIVER AQUILINA, SDC

Youth in Mission 335
Believing in Young People
    TERESA GÓMEZ AND NESTOR ANAYA, FSC

Integrity of Creation 343
Our Work Is Loving the World
    ILIA DELIO, OSF

Conclusion 359
    MARIE-HÉLÈNE ROBERT, OLA

Appendix 369
The Emerging Future in Mission:
Summary of the 2021 SEDOS Mission Symposium

SEDOS Member Congregations 377

Opening Message

Pope Francis

The Holy Father Francis addresses his cordial greetings to the participants attending the international symposium promoted by the Documentation and Study Service of the Global Mission (SEDOS) on the theme "new trends in mission, the emerging future." He hopes that the study days may constitute an intense experience of reflection and communion for the various religious institutes, favoring a renewed apostolic momentum in favor of the proclamation of the Gospel, in the awareness that the mission of the church is a docile and courageous action, and the work of the Holy Spirit. His Holiness encourages proposals and their implementation that, avoiding to impose fixed cultural forms, reflect the nature of the people of God all holy with a thousand faces. And, while assuring union in prayer, His Holiness is pleased to impart his apostolic blessing.

Cardinal Pietro Parolin,
Secretary of State of His Holiness
From the Vatican, 7 October 2021

Inaugural Address

His Eminence Luis Antonio Cardinal Tagle

A warm greeting to everyone. I should like to thank the organizers of this symposium, *New Trends in Mission,* for the invitation to deliver the inaugural address. And thanks to the history of SEDOS and its mission, and the work done to make this symposium possible.

Your exchanges, I am sure, will be based on lived experience, the history of your communities, on intense studies, your struggles, your pains, and also your hope. This symposium will be a great help to the whole church and to the Congregation for the Evangelization of Peoples. I will not give a theological or missiological speech. What I shall do is just to share *some questions and some observations* based on my experience as prefect of the Congregation for the Evangelization of Peoples. I have been in office now for one year and eight months. So, I am learning. By sharing my observations and questions, I hope you can develop them with further reflection and even a critical study.

It's providential that we are opening this symposium on the anniversary of the opening of Vatican II, chosen as the feast day of Saint Pope John XXIII. Propaganda Fide will also celebrate its 400th founding anniversary in 2022, next year. The Congregation for the Evangelization of Peoples focuses mainly on the formation and the growth of local churches, its so-called missionary territories, sometimes referred to as the young churches, and part of that is also the commitment to animate all the members of the church in mission awareness, in prayer for the missions, and in solidarity, especially expressed by the charitable contributions of the World Mission Sunday Collection and of the other Pontifical Mission Societies.

Now for my sharing today, I have three points, not in order of importance and definitely not exhaustive. But you have five days to reflect on it (*smile*).

First, since Vatican II we have been emphasizing the shared dignity of all the baptized in the common priesthood. Rooted in baptism is also the universal call to holiness and the call for all of us to be missionaries, or as Pope Francis would refer to us, *missionary disciples*. We have to admit that for the past sixty years we have seen great progress in the involvement and participation of many Christians in search of holiness, discipleship, and in mission, but we also have to admit that there is still much room for growth in this area.

The word *mission* often carried in many parts of the world a sort of connotation associated with the ordained, with religious men and women. Fr. Aloysius Pieris will have some questions about that: "How should we call them? Societies or Institutes of 'Apostolic Life'? Or otherwise?" And not only that. The word *mission* also classifies some countries and churches—you have countries that are classified as "missionary sending countries" while others are classified as "missionary receiving countries." I think that it is due to the fact that the word *mission* also carried some sort of colonial connotation. Now, I am sure that in past years SEDOS engaged in a critical study and understanding of the word *mission*. In many cases when people hear the word *mission*, they mostly think of the religious men and women who leave their own country in order to embrace the life in another country. Today, we thank the Holy Spirit for the presence also of many lay people, even families, who engage in mission.

Now why am I raising this point? Since the Second Vatican Council's invitation to make mission truly a "project" of all the baptized, how do we in a way free the word *mission* from such stratification and classification by people within the churches, and even the classification of churches? Fr. Peter Baekelmans referred to evangelism, and I would like to support that direction. Could we do an extended study on how *evangelism and mission* could really come together? After all, the congregation of which I am prefect is the Congregation for the *Evangelization* of Peoples. When we talk of evangelization, I remember the first chapter of the First Letter of Saint John, where he says that what they have heard, what they have seen with their eyes, what they have touched with their hands concerning the word of life, they in turn should share with others, and in that sharing communion is generated. And it is not just human communion, for their communion is communion with God. I see in that biblical passage this coming together of what we call evangelization and also mission. It is rooted in a gripping, a life-changing culture that is a gift, a gift of the presence of Jesus in the Spirit to someone: that someone is changed; that someone needs to share that story; that someone knows that it cannot be kept to oneself; that person knows the news, and the experience is so good that it must reach the ends of the earth. But that is true for all.

That is true not only for the ordained, those who made vows, and not only for some countries—it is true for everyone, gifted with the presence, with the encounter with the Lord in the Spirit which changes one's life.

Here, I think we have a fertile area for rethinking mission so that it becomes the domain of all the baptized. Especially with all the fluidity in boundaries of territories, even cultural shifts, when it comes to a strict classification of an evangelized country that now sends missionaries to countries not yet evangelized, or those that receive missionaries. One bishop from Europe visiting the Propaganda Fide shared with us that more than 60 percent of the clergy in his diocese come from Africa and Asia, and he said that "maybe my diocese should move from the Congregation for Bishops to Propaganda Fide?" (*smile*). Even these classifications do not seem to work anymore when we look at the existential reality. And we don't even look at the virtual territories and the virtual spaces. I'm afraid I am confusing you, but you should reflect on this. Perhaps the invitation especially from our Protestant brothers and sisters who are very strong in evangelism could in a way help us.

The second point that I have seen operating in the congregation and which brings much pain also is this: while during the past years we were working toward becoming a more globalized world, globalized humanity—we said the boundaries separating us, the walls, the barriers need to fall so that we can work as one human family—we see in this form of "progressing," in this brand of *globalization*, the world becoming more fragmented than ever. We see a lot of suspicion and fear of the other, and therefore some sort of self-defense, the protection of "who I am." The lowering of barriers and boundaries seems to be a big threat to "who I am." This suspicion and fear of the other, I think, has brought also a lot of loneliness, isolation, both as personal and societal loneliness. *Fear breeds loneliness. And fear also breeds violence.*

SEDOS is also very much into the questions of *inculturation, dialogue of cultures*. And I would encourage SEDOS to continue that and to pursue the reflection and study on the context of globalization that has led to so much fragmentation, violence, suspicion, fear of the other, and even loneliness. I think this is also quite appropriate and timely since the Holy Father Pope Francis calls the whole church to a synodal process. And when we listen to his speeches about the walking together in "synodality" in the church, it is not just for us. It is at the service also of humanity. Humanity now wants to part ways, to refuse to walk with one another, and we find excuses to walk our own way. And so, I think this is part of our *evangelizing mission*: how do we bring the gospel of *Fratelli Tutti* and how Jesus embraces every human being, as Vatican II and Pope John Paul II affirmed in *Redemptoris Missio*, to our generation, which is so fearful, so suspicious, so self-defensive, and yet so lonely?

And I have to say, with a lot of pain in my heart, that within the church *ethnicity*, even a tendency to tribalism, destroys communion and destroys our common witness. We see how even positions in the church are the object of ethnic conflicts. The desire is not to have a competent person or someone with a missionary heart to occupy some position of responsibility. Sometimes, the only consideration is: "It's time for our tribe, or our ethnic group, to shine"; and if someone from another group is put in charge, you see a lot of noncooperation, you see a lot of destruction of the person, even leading to violence.

I think we can learn from the business world. In the business world, when looking for a person to work in a position at the regional or international level, they look for a person with what they call *cultural intelligence*. I don't know if in the church we could provide this as one medium or venue of evangelization where every person is a product of a culture. Our cultures present to us a way of being human. We think, we act, we eat, we prepare food, we celebrate, and we grieve according to our respective cultures. But sometimes the cultures are used in a dehumanizing way, and we judge each other's cultures based on our ignorance of those cultures, based on a lack of appreciation and even of prejudice. I think the gospel must go to the roots of prejudice, of misunderstanding. And when we speak of cultures, most of the cultures of the world are being influenced by religion. So, when we promote the unification of cultures, the encounter of cultures through human encounters, we are also touching on religions.

The gospel is culture based. That is why exegetes spend so much time studying the culture of the original writers so that we can understand what the Spirit is telling us through those cultural media. Now since we can do it with the biblical texts, why don't we spend also more time *studying the cultures* so that we could hear what the Spirit is saying through them, the elements of truth and justice present in them? And then we could promote, not only within the church but in humanity, the gospel of universal love, for God loved the world and Jesus died for all, and the Spirit blows in all. We can learn from Jesus. Jesus was born in a particular culture. But he also had the freedom to bring what I would call *a culture from the One who sent him*. And he did it in a very simple way.

Cultures can be perceived, not only through their rituals and ceremonies, but also through the use of space. When you enter a room, you love the culture of the people who are working there by arrangement. Also the concept of time is very relative. In the Philippines we say, "Let us meet at four o'clock," and then we follow it by saying "Philippine time or European time?" (*smile*). A culture is also formed by the people that we consider to be heroes or heroines, or idols; the system of reward and punishment; the preparation and consumption of food, all of these.

Jesus brought *a new culture* by respecting the use of space. He allowed a woman of ill-repute, a well-known public sinner, to touch his feet, bathe his feet with her tears. He touched a person with leprosy. There is also his use of time: "It is my Father who determines my hour, not the watch" (*smile*); family, not just blood relationship, but obedience, an act of obedience to the will of God in action. Who were the heroes and heroines of Jesus? Outsiders—the Syrophoenician woman, the good Samaritan, the repentant criminals, the centurion. Can you please help us to reflect on this, study this in a world closing in on self, in protection of self, yet becoming lonelier and lost?

And my final point is that we see in our present context a rise in nationalism and populist movements and politicians, and they foment fear of the other. They divide societies; they divide peoples. Now, they are very clever, they thrive on some true and even legitimate frustration and anger of people who have been neglected by the current system, by the current economic, social, and cultural system. People have been forgotten, and these populist movements and politicians go to the angry, the frustrated, the hungry, the desperate. And they present themselves as saviors, as messiah figures, and some of them, with a Christian background, use Christianity, use the gospel for their populist agenda. The poor who have their legitimate protest and cry are further manipulated by such leaders who appear to be bearers of the gospel. Some of these people feel that they are in fact following the gospel by following these populist leaders, and in the end they are further victimized, further manipulated.

So here, I think part of our evangelizing mission is for the church to really walk with the poor, showing them our closeness, our empathy, our genuine words of justice and charity; expressing our interest without any self-interest, making the poor really experience love; helping them to protect themselves from further manipulation. And I include here the gospel of reconciliation and forgiveness, in line with Pope Francis's proposal in *Fratelli Tutti*, a "penitential memory," based on truth, justice, and forgiveness, so that the cycle of violence, the cycle of division would be stopped—but not by ignoring the past. Not by ignoring the demands of justice, but by refusing to be like the oppressor, and refusing to be bearers of a hatred that might dehumanize other people.

As you see, these are scattered thoughts, but I wanted to share them with you: with your expertise, and with your exchanges these coming five days, I hope you could address some of these, and even expand them. Thank you very much.

This talk was given at the SEDOS Mission Symposium, October 11, 2021.

Preface

Tesfaye Tadesse Gebresilasie, MCCJ, and Mary T. Barron, OLA

Since SEDOS published *Mission in Dialogue* in 1982, both the landscape of mission and the membership of the organization have changed remarkably. Today SEDOS (Service of Documentation and Study on Global Mission) boasts a membership of eighty-four organizations, compared to forty-five in 1982. These members are institutes of consecrated life and societies of apostolic life that share a common denominator and are united by a common charism, the mission *Ad Gentes*. In the interim period since the 1982 publication, with an evolution in the *who, what, why, where, when*, and *how* of mission, the language of mission has also progressed. Since 2001 when William Burrows first coined the phrase *Inter Gentes*, missiologists and missionary practitioners generally refer to mission *Inter Gentes* rather than *Ad Gentes*, reflecting the understanding that mission is no longer "to" but rather "among" nations and peoples. This seemingly simple nuance captures a deep shift in the reflections and practice of mission in the intervening forty years. This volume encourages reflection on some of those changes and on the new trends in the *emerging future of mission*.

Each member organization, and indeed every religious missionary organization, is entrusted with a specific charism that flows into the common charism uniting all missionaries. Individually and together these organizations engage in a constant dance of renewal and revitalization, with the goal of being ever more faithful to the charism entrusted to them and of nurturing more fruitfulness in mission. Inspiration for this renewal comes from many sources and, like a great wave, trends emerge and everyone seems to be moving in similar directions, grasping new ways of being, struggling with similar challenges, and experimenting with new forms and new expressions of mission. The Holy Spirit is the ultimate guiding force for this dynamic, with congregations and societies constantly seeking to follow the promptings of the Spirit through ongoing prayer, reflection, and discerned choices, and especially so during a chapter's incentives. Another source of inspiration arises from the ecclesiology in vogue in a particular era, which undoubtedly influences the understanding and expression of mission. In 2015, Walter Kasper noted a number of ways in which modern ecclesiology has had an impact on the understanding of the missionary nature of the Catholic Church. The church, according to Kasper, is becoming a fraternal, dialogical, and communicative church that emphasizes the relational dimension. With Pope Francis we get a practical sense of this relational church, as he seeks to open avenues of dialogue and inclusion. In a similar vein, mission has moved to become more relational and dialogical, with increasing awareness of, and respect for, reciprocal relationships in the context of mission.

Inspiration also emerges from the Magisterium, from the church's formal teachings. The publication of Pope John Paul II's encyclical *Redemptoris Missio* in 1990 gave great impetus to mission toward the end of the twentieth century. This document, on the permanent validity of the church's missionary mandate, renewed the emphasis on the proclamation of Jesus Christ as the universal Savior as inherent to mission, following a period in which the primary sense of mission was expressed as building the reign of God through the service of liberation. *Redemptoris Missio* challenged missionaries to reclaim their specific missionary identity and to understand mission as "a single but complex reality [that] develops in a variety of ways." The pontificate of Pope Francis has undoubtedly influenced the understanding and expression of mission. Marked by a repeated call to missionary discipleship for all of the faithful, he reminds us that we are called to a deep personal encounter with Love, an encounter that engenders the impetus and commitment to share the joy experienced in that encounter (*Evangelii Gaudium*), a call to open the doors and go forth as a missionary church to the peripheries, a call to care for our common home (*Laudato Si'*), and a call to fraternity and social friendship (*Fratelli Tutti*).

When we are open to these layers of inspiration, the single complex reality of mission emerges differently in varying eras and contexts. And the context, both global and local, is deeply influential. In our era there have been—and continue to be—great shifts in mission with a very striking geographical shift. What began as mission "from the West to the rest," to use a very blunt but evocative phrase, has evolved into a global mission on all the continents, with all continents being at one and the same time both mission-sending and mission-receiving realities, in a great missionary project of reciprocity and mutual respect. While mission was previously the prerogative of "professional" missionaries, as it were, those men and women who totally dedicated their lives to mission, mission today is the prerogative of everyone, with Pope Francis challenging all baptized Christians to live out their missionary calling, wherever they may be. Within all these calls to mission there remains the "specific missionary" call to missionaries to resolutely leave home and family behind to cooperate with Jesus, who needs hearts eager to experience vocation as a true love story that urges them to go forth to the peripheries of our world as messengers and agents of compassion.

It behooves missionaries to be vigilant in their reflection and discernment, to be alert to the emerging trends influencing the essence and work of mission today. SEDOS, by its very nature, is instrumental in facilitating such reflection. SEDOS, in its many conferences and seminars in the past years, has tried to address and deepen the reflection around the various trends in the mission of the church, which is basically *missio Dei* and touches all our human life. SEDOS continues to encourage research and the dissemination of information through its bulletin, the annual SEDOS residential seminar (May), as well as the spring session and autumn seminar, the SEDOS website, and other public conferences and workshops, all of which have become increasingly well attended since moving to the online platform. Nowadays missionaries from all continents can meet online for enriching and informative inputs and profound sharing on the call to mission today. The dream of this new volume, a sequel, as it were, to the original *Trends in Mission* in 1991, is to capture the insights of modern missionaries and missiologists that attest to the diversity and complexity of the emerging reality of mission today. Providing a basis for a mission symposium that took place in October 2021, we entrust these reflections and the emerging future to God in the sure knowledge that although as humans we may plan and prepare, it is God, the author of all mission, who decides what will be done (cf. Prov 16:9).

>**Mary T. Barron, OLA,** is SEDOS vice-president and superior general of the Sisters of Our Lady of Apostles.
>
>**Tesfaye T. Gebresilasie, MCCJ,** is SEDOS president and superior general of the Comboni Missionaries of the Heart of Jesus.

Introduction

Peter Baekelmans, CICM

"The frog in the well" is a well-known expression in Japan to refer to those who think they know the world but have only seen a small part of it, their "own" world. Missionaries are graced to have come out of the well and to have seen a wider world, not only as tourists but as those who have shared the language, customs, joys and pains, culture and religion of other people. They are the "frontier missionaries"[1] who set a concrete example to all baptized people to move out of their usual environment to meet people, to be with people, and to help the needy among them. Mission means to live as Jesus did: always on the road, ready to go wherever the Spirit moves them.

Mission is in essence a *missio Dei* (being called and sent by God), and this mission is carried out by way of "prophetic dialogue."[2] Missionaries can therefore never be "self-referential" (Pope Francis), as they will always refer spontaneously to the God they love and the people they were sent to. Mission-minded theologians too will automatically go against every theological "inbreeding" and will seek to integrate their experience and knowledge of the wider world in their theological reflections, as does, for instance, a liberation theologian, a theologian of religions, or a cyber-theologian. However, missionaries also keep a certain "prophetic" stance toward the people they are sent to, because there is a message to be transmitted, the gospel message, which is not only about peace and harmony, but also about justice and respect for the wholeness (and holiness) of Creation.

---

[1] See "The Role of Missionary Religious Institutes: A Strange Species of Christians?" by Aloysius Pieris, SJ, in this volume.
[2] See "Theological Evolution in Mission: A Theology of Mission" by Stephen B. Bevans, SVD, in this volume.

The theme of this symposium on mission, *New Trends in Mission: The Emerging Future*, arose from my experience on the General Committee on Mission I was asked to start for my Congregation, CICM. In our lengthy discussions we always came back to the basic question: "What does mission mean (for you)?" Without that answer we cannot come to a formulation of what a missionary parish is, or a missionary community, a missionary project, and so on. We need to go "back to the roots" of mission and see its task and identity with new eyes, because if we do not see the whole missionary endeavor clearly, we think that mission is in crisis. But if we formulate the task of a missionary well, people will react positively. It is we missionaries, religious and lay, who have to be clear on who we are and what we are doing as missionaries. Mission is basically *ad extra*, even as we have broadened its meaning to *inter gentes*, *intra gentes*, or *missio ad intra*. As missionaries we exemplify the task of mission, going out and meeting people to bring them the joyful message of the gospel. Pope Francis speaks of the "*Chiesa in uscita*" (the outgoing church). This is the core of his missiological message and it makes him a great Jesuit missionary and a missionary pope.[3]

The theme of the mission symposium is titled "New Trends in Mission." The word *new* has two meanings here: one refers to the older book of 1991, which is a collection of talks given at different SEDOS residential seminars; and the other refers to the new ways of doing mission. Although not everything is new in mission, we will however point out the new trends that are coming up, and the challenges we will have to face in the future in doing mission, especially now with all of the ecological problems, the many refugees,[4] and the COVID-19 pandemic. Fr. Chris Chaplin, MSC, a member of the SEDOS Executive Committee, proposed the addition of the subtitle "The Emerging Future" because the future is emerging before our very eyes. We only have to see the signs of the times, judge them, and act upon them. The symposium, and this subsequent book, are guides to this discernment process.

As to the spirit of the book itself, it is not a purely academic study, even though most of the contributors have academic degrees. It wants to be a joint reflection by SEDOS's members on what we as missionaries are doing, or are supposed to do. SEDOS is an inter-congregational organization that serves its eighty-five member congregations on the level of the

---

[3] See "Pope Francis and Mission: A Call to Hear the Crying Existential Peripheries" by Paul Béré, SJ, in this volume.

[4] See "Mission with Migrants: The Roots of 'People on the Move'" by Carmen Elisa Bandeo, SSpS, in this volume.

documentation and study of global mission. SEDOS organizes different kinds of seminars—the main one is the yearly five-day Residential Seminar—and it publishes the bi-monthly *SEDOS Bulletin*. The Mission Symposium in October 2021 was a special seminar and the third of its kind in SEDOS's more than fifty years of existence. This book consists of the written texts of the speakers' interventions at the symposium. Part One and Part Two of the book are the more academic contributions but with a personal touch. Part Three contains the more personal contributions on specific themes elaborated by the SEDOS Executive Committee that most of the member congregations have in common. They represent our "common missions."

Part One of the book deals with the "roots" of mission, especially the "why" (*missio Dei*) and "what" (to embody God's reign) of mission. It offers a renewed understanding of mission, starting from the Bible. We then look back at where we came from—especially as SEDOS—more than fifty years ago, and at how missiology has evolved in this period too. This brings us to Pope Francis's challenging vision of mission. We close with a discussion of the place of missionaries and missionary organizations in current church language and structures.

In Part Two the contributions explore in more detail the different aspects of doing mission: who will do it, when is the best time for it, where should it be done, and, last but not least, how should it be done? The many diverse ways of doing mission are not new phenomena. Already in the Gospels, according to Lucien Legrand, "mission is in the plural" (*la mission au pluriel*): to proclaim the gospel (Mark), to make disciples of Christ (Matthew), to witness the work of the Spirit (Luke), and to bring (a trinitarian) unity (John).[5] The former SEDOS mission symposium came up with four "principal activities" of the church's mission: proclamation, dialogue, inculturation, and the liberation of the poor.[6] But in general we can discern two basic missionary methods, which the World Council of Churches calls *evangelism and mission*: the *evangelizing* method and the more *caritative* method. Protestants and Catholics are in a continuous search for the correct balance between these two.[7] There exists in the

---

[5] Lucien Legrand, *Paul et la mission, Apôtre des temps nouveaux* (Paris: Médiaspaul, 2021), 163–64. See "The 'Why' of Mission: Biblical Trends in Mission for Our Changing Times" by Rekha M. Chennattu, RA, in this volume.

[6] Mary Motte, FMM, and Joseph R. Lang, MM, eds., *Mission in Dialogue, The SEDOS Research Seminar on the Future of Mission, March 8–19, 1981, Rome, Italy* (Maryknoll, NY: Orbis Books, 1982), 634.

[7] For instance, the commission for mission within the World Council of Churches is called Commission on World Mission and Evangelism, and the Pontifical Council for Interreligious Dialogue speaks of "Dialogue and Proclamation."

Catholic Church a certain reluctance to talk about the importance of the "communion between God and human beings,"[8] and instead to view mission in the first place as implanting the church and/or working for God's kingdom on earth, the "caritative mission."[9] In this symposium, however, the role of the Spirit and of God in doing "evangelical mission" has come well to the fore: first, under the important concept of "initial proclamation,"[10] where we create the condition for a miracle or a calling to happen; and second, in the refreshing idea of "synodality" in mission,[11] which declares that we do mission together because Jesus is there where two or more are gathered in his name (Mt 18:20).

The contributors to Part Three were asked to appraise their work and what they see as important evolutions for all those who work, or want to work, in that field, using their own congregation as an example. Most of the twelve themes represented in this part are universal and eternal, but one can also perceive some important evolutions within them. These themes represent our "common grounds of mission" in which we try to discern the "trends" in each of these mission fields. Among these trends, two "new global trends" stand out. To start with, the topic of secularism[12] is addressed first to show missionaries that we should not juxtapose the secular and the religious, as is mostly done in religious (and secular) parlance, but seek how we can be religious in a secular world. Our situation can be compared to that of the people in the Middle Ages (and even today in certain parts of the world), who (vice versa) had to find out how to be secular in a religious world.

The whole world is heading toward a secular and pluralist worldview because of the increasingly intercultural and interreligious reality in which we live. Today, Christianity is everywhere on the globe, as are other religions, nationalities, cultures, and so on. Learning to live and work together in harmony and peace will be—and is already—the great contribution

---

[8] See "The 'What' of Mission: Refining Our Comprehension of Mission" by Joseph Scaria Palakeel, MST, in this volume.

[9] For instance, the first mission symposium organized by SEDOS in 1969 carried the theme "Development and Dialogue." The result of the second mission symposium of SEDOS in 1989 was summarized as "Mission in Dialogue." See also Part One, "Introduction," by Michael McCabe, SMA, in this volume.

[10] See "The 'When' of Mission: Rediscovering 'Initial Proclamation' in Evangelization" by Alfred Maravilla, SDB, in this volume.

[11] See "The 'Who' of Mission: We Are Mission" by Ida Colombo, CMS, Hélène Israël Soloumta Kamkôl, CMS, and Maria Teresa Ratti, CMS, in this volume.

[12] See "Secularization: Mission in a Secular Age" by Daniel Patrick Huang, SJ, in this volume.

of missionary religious institutes. However, this remains a challenge also for these institutes and their members.[13] The book's last article, on eco-spirituality, is surely a new trend in mission that will ask for our special attention and cooperation in the future.[14] The COVID-19 pandemic has placed this eco-friendly effort in danger because of the economic crisis it has caused in the world. On the other hand, thanks to the pandemic, missionaries have started to use the modern ways of communication more intensively, as has SEDOS. For instance, this mission symposium was held fully online, with low cost and high participation. The challenge here, as in every missionary endeavor, is to stay connected in a "Christian" way and not to exclude anyone.[15]

Each of the many articles in this book has its own character. Some can be used for personal reflection, some for group discussion,[16] some for getting the historical background of a certain type of mission,[17] and some even as an evaluation grid[18] or as a guideline in a certain mission field.[19] Many also contain valuable academic material students can use. A sincere thanks goes therefore to the coeditor of this book, Sr. Marie-Hélène Robert, OLA, who helped greatly in evaluating the contributions, and to Philippa Wooldridge from the Roman-Catholic newspaper *L'Osservatore Romano*, who, as a longstanding coworker of SEDOS, has diligently revised all the contributions. During the preparation for the symposium and subsequent book, it was especially Fr. Joseph Palakeel, MST, who guided me throughout this huge undertaking. Special thanks go to him for the unconditional support and advice he has given me.

SEDOS is grateful to Orbis Books for the final edit of the articles by the professional hand of Jill Brennan O'Brien, and for presenting them in a pleasing format. Sincere thanks as well go to all those who have contributed with their precious articles to this rich source of information on mission. A last word of thanks goes to the members of SEDOS who through their annual contribution make all this possible. SEDOS is an

---

[13] See "Interculturality: Culture and the Experience of God" by Tim Norton, SVD, in this volume.

[14] See "Integrity of Creation: Our Work Is Loving the World" by Ilia Delio, OSF, in this volume.

[15] See "Media and Mission: Staying Connected" by Monique Tarabeh, RGS, in this volume.

[16] See Colombo et al., "The 'Who' of Mission."

[17] See "The 'Where' of Mission: Fifty Years of *Ad Gentes* in Africa" by Anthony Akinwale, OP, in this volume.

[18] See "Missionary Parishes: Growing as a Missionary Parish" by Lazar T. Stanislaus, SVD, in this volume.

[19] See Tarabeh, "Media and Mission."

inter-congregational effort for reflection on our mission activities, and this book (and symposium) is one concrete example of what a group of people can do when they combine their efforts toward a common goal.

My term as director has come to an end after six fulfilling years. I feel immensely grateful for this rewarding opportunity, and I am happy to hand the torch over to the next director of SEDOS.

In the name of SEDOS, we wish you all happy reading!

Peter Baekelmans (1960–) is a Belgian Catholic theologian (STD), member of the Congregation of the Immaculate Heart of Mary, CICM, and was a missionary in Japan for twenty years. He holds an MA in Comparative Religions (Int. Univ. of Lugano), an MA in Buddhist Studies (Koyasan Univ.), and a PhD in Theology of Religions (Nanzan Univ.). He is at present director of SEDOS in Rome, Italy, and guest professor at the Faculty of Theology and Religious Sciences of Catholic University of Louvain (KUL), Belgium.

PART ONE

EVANGELIZATION AND MISSION

Introduction to Part One

Michael McCabe, SMA

The vision of evangelization and mission that inspired the great missionary movement of the nineteenth century—a movement that lasted up to the middle of the last century—was thoroughly ecclesio-centric. It was concerned with the expansion of the Church. Mission meant that particular activity of the Church whereby it brought its deposit of revealed truths and means of salvation to new peoples and places. The chief purpose of this activity was to save souls for the glory of God. The agents of this activity were called missionaries. They were mostly groups of priests and religious, commissioned by Rome,[1] to go to places where the Church had not yet been established. The methods they employed to carry out their task were: the preaching of the gospel; the conversion of individuals to Christ and their baptism into the Church; and the building up of the structures of the Church (as these had developed in their home countries) and the administration of the sacraments. Evangelization meant promoting the reign of the Church, viewed as identical with the reign of God, everywhere in the world. This vision dominated Catholic thought and practice up to the time of the Second Vatican Council, by which time it was beginning to lose much of its shine and motivational power.

The Second Vatican Council (1962–65) set out to examine and rethink the nature of the church and its mission in the world. This led to a significant deepening of the church's understanding of its mission. Perhaps no statement of the Council expresses better this renewed understanding of mission than the assertion that "the pilgrim Church is essentially missionary."[2] This means that mission is not some extraordinary task that the church undertakes in addition to its normal business. Mission is

---

[1] Via *Propaganda Fide*, now known as the Congregation for the Evangelization of Peoples.
[2] See Vatican Council II, *Ad Gentes (Decree on the Mission Activity of the Church)* (1965), no. 2.

rooted in the being of the church. It is something the church is, before it is something the church does. In its evangelizing work the church is expressing its very nature as God's pilgrim people.

While the council sowed the seeds of a missionary ecclesiology, it also made it clear that mission begins with God, not with the church. The triune God of Christianity is a missionary God, whose loving concern embraces all people and every aspect of their lives, and indeed the entire order of creation. This universal outreach of God's love is the context in which the church's mission must be situated. The church, and all who belong to it, is called to participate in a project that comes from God and is directed by God's Spirit. The biblical foundations of this understanding of mission as "God's project" and its practical implications for our time are developed in the first article in this section, "The 'Why' of Mission: Biblical Trends in Mission for our Changing Times," by Dr. Rehka M. Chennattu.

Setting the evangelizing mission of the church in the context of God's mission broadens, as well as deepens, the mission of the church in the world. God's mission embraces all human beings and all the creatures on earth with whom we are inextricably connected. Today within the church there is widespread acceptance of this broad understanding of God's loving concern for, and involvement with, all creatures. Mission is God's turning toward the world in creative love, redemptive healing, and transforming power, and the church is invited to participate in this outreach—an outreach that takes place in ordinary history and is not confined to the activity of the church. Pope John Paul II, in his encyclical letter *Redemptoris Missio,* speaks of the universal and unlimited presence and action of God's Spirit which affects "not only individuals but also society and history, peoples, cultures and religion" (*RM,* no. 28).

Despite the deepening and broadening of the church's understanding of its mission, initiated and stimulated by the Second Vatican Council, the post–Vatican II years witnessed a discernible diminishing of the church's missionary spirit, a development that Pope John Paul II sought to address in *Redemptoris Missio.* The second article in this section, by Joseph Scaria Palakeel, "The 'What' of Mission: Refining our Comprehension of Mission," wants to refine our comprehension of mission by defining church from a "missional" perspective as "the universal sacrament of salvation" (*LG,* no. 48), wherein church exists as the continuation of the *missio Dei* to invite all to communion with God and with one another and thus to establish the reign of God.

Participating in God's mission, the church never starts from scratch, so to speak. It inhabits a world in which God's Spirit is already present and active from the dawn of creation. We are invited to discover a treasure we have yet to open. This viewpoint sets mission in a perspective that takes a great deal of the anxiety and aggressiveness out of it. God is already present before us, gracing all creatures with God's love, in ways unknown to us. The first challenge of missionaries is to attend, to look, to listen, to discern, and to collaborate with what God is already doing in the world among peoples of all nations and cultures. We must not impose our agendas on them. Mission is a giving and receiving across cultural and religious frontiers. When it descends into cultural or religious domination, as has unfortunately happened in the past, it no longer deserves the name Christian. In the past, missionaries tended to get engrossed in doing things for people. But too much activity may block rather than facilitate the action of God's Spirit. A more contemplative and dialogic style of missionary presence is an essential prerequisite for missionaries. Mission cannot be separated from dialogue. Indeed mission is, as Stephen B. Bevans puts it, "prophetic dialogue." The contours of this dialogue are developed by him in the third article of this section, "Theological Evolution in Mission: A Theology of Mission."

The main concern of Pope Francis throughout his pontificate has been to reawaken the missionary spirit of the entire church and give a clear focus to its missionary outreach. With great clarity he has articulated his vision of a church "with a pastoral goal and a missionary style" (*Evangelii Gaudium,* no. 33). This is a church of missionary discipleship "that goes forth to meet God in others, especially the poor and oppressed, the despised and overlooked" (*EG,* nos. 39, 48); a church "that accompanies people on a journey of openness to God" (*EG,* no. 44); a church that "is bruised, hurting and dirty because it has been out on the streets, rather than a Church which is unhealthy from being confined and from clinging to its own security" (*EG,* no. 49). In the fourth article, "Pope Francis and Mission: A Call to Hear the Crying Existential Peripheries," Paul Béré, SJ, develops Pope Francis's vision of a missionary church in which all of its members are true disciples of Christ, witnessing to God's loving concern for all, especially those who are oppressed and live on the margins of society.

While all the members of the church are called to missionary discipleship and to the service of the gospel, some members are called to be "frontier missionaries," among whom are the members of missionary religious institutes. The members of these institutes commit themselves to those "new and bold endeavors" (*RM,* no. 66) that will always be required if the church is to become what it claims to be: the sacrament of God's universal love. These bold endeavors will always involve a movement out beyond the existing edges of the church, into the world of the other. There still exist many new worlds to which the gospel of God's reign has yet to be proclaimed as the liberating good news that it is. It will take no less courage and skill to enter into, and engage with, these new arenas of mission (for example, the world of migrants and refugees; the world of the youth; the world of the media; the exploited and wounded earth) than it did, in former times, to cross barren deserts and raging waters to reach far-flung regions of the globe. Only by reviving and creatively reinterpreting their pioneering charisms will the members of these religious institutes become catalysts in the ongoing transformation of the church and the world it serves. Aloysius Pieris, SJ, underlines the continuing relevance and significance of the role of these "frontier missionaries" in the final article of this part, "The Role of Missionary Religious Institutes: A Strange Species of Christians?"

Michael McCabe, SMA, is a member of the Irish Province of the Society of African Missions and currently director of the Mission Department of the Province. He holds a PhD in theology from Pontifical Gregorian University; taught for many years in Zambia, Liberia, and Kenya; and has a particular interest in the challenges of mission today.

The "Why" of Mission

Biblical Trends in Mission for Our Changing Times

Rekha M. Chennattu, RA

The COVID-19 pandemic has gripped the entire world in fear and uncertainty. I am personally amazed at how, within a few days, the entire human family started to observe social distancing, use face masks, and get used to working from home, participating in online lectures, and attending virtual liturgies. Many things in our way of life will be different in the post-pandemic era. When we think of the world today, other deadly viruses come to mind, such as corruption, poverty, forced migration, dehumanizing discrimination, human trafficking, economic exploitation, unfolding tragedies in war-torn nations, frequent natural calamities, religious conflicts, and scandals and abuses in the church. This moment of crisis is an opportune time for change, and believers are looking for a new way of being God's people. This is a call for a return to our biblical sources and a re-appropriation of the church's identity and mission.

The word *mission* comes from the Latin *missus* ("sent"), and the notion of being chosen and sent by God is at the heart of the biblical understanding of mission. In this essay I hope to offer insights from the biblical narratives that may help us deepen and broaden the horizons of the church's mission for our changing times. Within the limits of a paper like this, it is not possible to attempt a detailed study of all the biblical texts that speak about mission. It is my hope that insights from selected texts will help us revisit and renew our understanding of the church's mission and make it more relevant for today. These reflections are neither exhaustive nor conclusive.

Mission as God's Project

What do the biblical narratives teach us about mission? The Bible is a very complex work, containing seventy-three books, written in three languages over a period of more than a thousand years, in a great variety of social, cultural, religious, and political contexts. It is understandable that different biblical writers presented diverse perspectives on mission. The different life contexts of the biblical authors demanded different approaches to mission.[1] There is, however, an overarching unity as the biblical authors gradually and progressively revealed the experience of a God who is active in the history of human beings and the cosmos. The biblical story begins with God's creation of "the heavens and the earth" (Gen 1:1) and ends with the appearance of "a new heaven and a new earth" (Rev 21:1). Mission in the Bible begins with God's creation of the universe, human beings, and gradually unravels the mystery of their evolution toward the fullness of life. Salvation history shows that mission begins in the mind of God, and it is God's project of creation, liberation, redemption, and the eschatological hope of a new creation. Mission as God's project thus refers to God's ultimate purpose for the whole of creation, and it refers to all that God has sent—Israel, prophets, Jesus, the apostles, and the entire church—for the realization of that purpose.[2] Our mission is thus to participate in the project of God.

Israel as God's People of Blessing

We begin our survey by exploring the identity and mission of Israel as the people of God.[3] The foundation of God's people is signalled by the call of Abram (Gen 12). The narrative reveals five important aspects of the identity and mission of Abraham and his descendants (later known as Israel) as God's Chosen People (12:1–20):

1. Israel is invited to be a pilgrim people of God. Abram is asked to set out on a journey, to leave his familiar place and people. It is a call to be a migrant in an unknown place and among unknown peoples (12:1, 20).
2. Israel is chosen to be a blessing (12:2).
3. Israel is called to become a blessing for other nations: "All the families of the earth will be blessed in you" (12:3). Abraham and

---

[1] See George M. Soares-Prabhu, "Missiology or Missiologies?" *Mission Studies* 3, no. 2 (1986): 85–87.

[2] See also the discussion in Christopher J. H. Wright, *The Mission of God: Unlocking the Bible's Grand Narrative* (Downers Grove, IL: InterVarsity Press, 2006), 61–69.

[3] See the discussion in Christopher J. H. Wright, *The Mission of God's People: A Biblical Theology of the Church's Mission* (Grand Rapids, MI: Zondervan, 2010), 114.

his descendants will be God's instruments through which all the families of the earth shall be blessed.
4. Israel is called to obey God and walk in God's ways. They are expected "to keep the way of the Lord by doing righteousness and justice" (12:19). The subsequent chapters reveal that the obedience of Abraham and his household to God's command is requisite for the fulfillment of these covenant promises (see Gen 18:18–19; 22:18; 26:4–5; 28:14). The covenant with God was possible "because Abraham obeyed my voice and kept my charge, my commandments, my statutes, and my laws" (Gen 26:5). Being a blessing implies a life that manifests God's blessings for all the families of the earth by walking in God's ways.[4]
5. God will be with them on their journey—"I will be with you" (Gen 12:20). God assures Abraham and his descendants (Israel) of God's guiding presence and invites them to be a pilgrim people who adopt the way of the Lord that makes God's righteousness and justice visible in the world. Israel is chosen to become God's instrument of blessings for all the nations of the earth.

Moses is another important figure through whom God continues the divine mission of liberation. In the story of his "missionary vocation," Moses was minding his own business, taking care of his father-in-law's flock in Midian (Ex 3:1–21), when suddenly a bush burst into flame, and Moses heard a voice calling him by name: "Moses, Moses." This summons is followed by a long monologue by God. God reveals God's identity and continues: "I have observed the misery of my people who are in Egypt; I have heard their cry on account of their taskmasters. Indeed, I know their sufferings, and I have come down to deliver them from the Egyptians" (Ex 3:7). God sees the suffering of God's people and God wants to liberate them. So, God takes the initiative to talk to Moses, and it is God's project to deliver the people. But then comes a surprising turn, when God says to Moses: "So come, I will send you to Pharaoh to bring my people, the Israelites, out of Egypt" (Ex 3:10). Moses is sent by God to accomplish God's mission of delivering God's people. He is assured of God's support and accompaniment: "You will not go empty-handed" (Ex 3:21). Like Abraham, Moses must leave his comfortable and safe place with his father-in-law to face the oppressor, the powerful pharaoh of Egypt. Moses becomes God's instrument through whom God liberates God's suffering people and leads them to the promised land.

---

[4] See also the discussion in Dean Flemming, *Recovering the Full Mission of God: A Biblical Perspective on Being, Doing, and Telling* (Downers Grove, IL: InterVarsity Press, 2013), 22–26.

Another important aspect of God's mission is the election of Israel as a chosen people (Deut 7:6–8). God has set apart Israel as God's "treasured possession" (*segullah*), as a people holy to God (Deut 7:6). The text does not refer to holy individuals, but to a holy people that belongs entirely to God. Israel's identity and mission is primarily to be God's covenant community.[5] It is important to keep in mind that the election of Israel is not based on its virtue or strength, but on God's love and faithfulness (Deut 4:37; 7:7–8). As we have already seen, God chose Israel not for Israel's own sake, but for a special purpose: to become a blessing for other nations. Israel becomes a holy people, a people of blessing, by walking in God's ways in response to what God has done for it. Walking in God's ways, obeying God's commands, and doing what is right and just (Gen 18:18–19; Deut 10:12) is participating in God's mission. God's ways must become the way of life of Israel; God's dream for humanity is to be realized through the life witness and commitment of Israel.

As Israel belongs to God, the community is distinct and different; it cannot be like other nations (Num 23:9; cf. 1 Sam 8:4–22). Israel is a community chosen to fulfill God's mission of building up a new society in which there should be "no one in need (*ebion*)" among them (Deut 15:4).[6] It was with this new community of justice and equality that God established the Covenant with Israel and made it the Chosen People (Ex 6:6–7; Deut 7:6; 14:2).[7] God gave Israel the Law (*torah*) as a means of revealing God's dream for humanity. The Law was meant to provide structures that took care of the security and well-being of all, especially the weak, the poor, and the disadvantaged sections of the community.[8] The people of Israel are also asked to "love the stranger (*ger*)" (Deut 10:19).[9] The memory of their exodus experience, their experience of being oppressed by the Egyptians, and God's gracious deliverance should enable them to be kind toward outsiders. As God's possession, an uncompromising commitment to become a covenant community (not like other nations) was demanded of Israel. A way of life marked by unconditional obedience to God's commands and thus

---

[5] See Rekha M. Chennattu, *Johannine Discipleship as Covenant Relationship* (Peabody, MA: Hendrickson, 2006), 50–65. See also Flemming, *Recovering the Full Mission of God*, 28–29.

[6] The Hebrew word *ebion* means "poor or impoverished."

[7] See Rekha M. Chennattu, "Religious Life: A Call to Be a Contrast Community in the World—Consecrated Life as Mission: Biblical Perspectives and Practical Implications," *Kristu Jyoti* 27 (2011): 22–24.

[8] Bruce C. Birch, W. Brueggemann, T. E. Fretheim, and D. L. Petersen, *A Theological Introduction to the Old Testament* (Nashville, TN: Abingdon Press, 1999), 131–67.

[9] The Hebrew word *ger* means "a sojourner or an outsider."

mirroring God's righteousness was mandatory for Israel to maintain its identity as God's covenant people.

Prophets as Reminders of God's Ways

The biblical narrative tells us that Israel failed to be a covenant community because they wanted to become like other nations and have a king (1 Sam 8:19–20). As Gerhard von Rad pointed out, it is in Israel's failure to be a covenant community "that prophecy first begins to make its voice heard" with the vigorous activities of Elijah and Elisha.[10] The prophets revealed God's radical concern for social justice, righteousness, and the integrity of the universe (see Hos 12:6; Am 5:15, 26; Isa 11:9; 14:7). Just as God showed passionate concern for the poor and needy, prophets spoke up for the powerless and oppressed with passion and integrity (Am 2:7; 5:11; 8:4–6). The mission of the prophets was to remind the people of Israel of their covenantal relationship with God and to restore their status as God's people. They experienced a dynamic energy from within to communicate God's message with conviction and commitment. They condemned idolatry, social injustice, and the exploitation of the poor and the marginalized (Isa 58:6–7; Jer 2:20–28; 22:13; Hos 10:13; Am 2:6–9). The Indian biblical scholar George Soares-Prabhu described it as "the dharma of the biblical prophet."[11] The prophets brought the challenges of God into the history of Israel, thereby generating a powerful movement of renewal and social reform.

Prophets are men and women on fire. Take the examples of Jeremiah and Judith.[12] Jeremiah speaks of his inability to be silent: "If I say, 'I will not mention him, or speak any more in his name,' then within me there is something *like a burning fire* shut up in my bones; I am weary with holding it in, and I cannot" (Jer 20:9). For Jeremiah, to know God or to have faith in God is to dare to proclaim God's message. Similarly, Judith's

---

[10] Gerhard von Rad, *Old Testament Theology*, 2 vols. (Edinburgh: Oliver and Boyd, 1965), 2:6.

[11] See George M. Soares-Prabhu, "The Dharma of the Biblical Prophet," in *Biblical Spirituality of Liberative Action, Collected Writings of George Soares-Prabhu*, 4 vols., ed. Scaria Kuthiralkkattel (Pune: Jnana-Deepa Vidyapeeth, 2003), 3:105–25. See also Chennattu, "Religious Life," 24–26.

[12] I consider Judith among the "prophets of the Lord," as someone who dared to speak on behalf of God and reminded the people of Israel of God's ways and delivered them from their enemies. See also Rekha M. Chennattu, "Biblical Women as Agents of Justice and Peace," in *Word of God: Source of Justice and Peace*, ed. A. Peter Abir (Tindivanam: Catholic Biblical Federation, 2008), 124–58.

abiding relationship with God empowered her to challenge the decisions of the elders of her community.[13] She rebuked them for their lack of commitment to the covenant relationship with God and reminded them of what God had done for them (Jdt 8:9–27). Judith understood God's ways and was certain that God would be with her to accomplish her mission (8:33). She became an agent of God's mighty works in saving Israel from its enemies (16:25). She receives, like Mary in the New Testament, the honorary title of "blessed above all other women on earth" (13:18). In sum, the life and message of the prophets reminded the people of Israel of their covenant obligations and helped them to remain faithful. Through the prophets, God thus continues God's mission in the history of salvation.

Jesus as the Embodiment of God's Reign

The Gospels proclaim the salvific mission of God by narrating the story of Jesus, his life and mission. Although all four Gospels focus on Jesus's mission, each Gospel emphasizes one aspect of his mission.[14] But one can summarize Jesus's mission in the New Testament as doing the will of God, revealing God's love, and announcing and embodying the reign of God in the world. In what follows, I focus on the mission of Jesus as presented by the four Gospels (Mark, Matthew, Luke, and John), with a reference to the mission of his disciples and to that of the church today.

The Markan Jesus begins his mission by announcing the arrival of God's reign (Mk 1:14–15) and then by performing powerful redemptive actions (1:21–45). The multidimensional ministry of Jesus—teaching with authority, healing diseases, forgiving sins, raising the dead, expelling demons, and overpowering nature—demonstrated and validated the presence of God's reign. Jesus committed himself fully to be at the service of humanity: "For the Son of Man came not to be served but to serve, and to give his life as a ransom for many" (10:45). The Markan Jesus is the beloved Son of God who embodies the loving, saving mission of God that was fulfilled in his suffering and sacrificial death (15:39).[15] Mark's striking focus on the passion of Jesus (8:31; 9:31; 10:31) underlines the fact that

---

[13] See also the discussion in detail in Rekha M. Chennattu, "Biblical Women as Models of Theologizing," *Vidyajyoti* 73, no. 9 (2009): 673–76.

[14] See also the section titled "La mission au pluriel," in Lucien Legrand, *Paul et la mission: Apôtre des temps nouveaux* (Paris: Médiaspaul, 2021), 163–64.

[15] See Francis J. Moloney, *Witnesses to the Ends of the Earth: New Testament Reflections on Mission* (Sydney: St Paul's Publications, 2020), 27–52.

the mission entails suffering, sacrifice, and self-giving service. Mark thus reveals Jesus as the beloved Son of God (1:11), whose divine power is coupled with loving compassion and sacrificial death for the salvation of humanity (10:45; 14:22–24). The Markan Jesus relativized his family ties and identified those who do the will of God as his mother, brothers, and sisters (3:31–35). Like Jesus, the disciples must deny themselves, take up their cross, lose their lives, endure suffering, and become servants of all (13:9–13; 10:39). Like Jesus, who has come to serve and not to be served (10:45), the church lives for others and is at the service of the reign of God.

The Matthean understanding of the mission is distinguished by the mission discourse in Matthew 10:1–42 and the great commission in 28:19–20. Matthew 10 is addressed to the twelve disciples, who are sent out by Jesus to the "lost sheep of Israel" to proclaim the good news of the dawning of God's reign (vv. 6–7). The following verses articulate the way of life of the disciples of Jesus (vv. 8–42). They are to follow Jesus by taking up their cross and losing their life for the sake of the reign of God. The theocentric vision of the mission is absolutely clear in the mission discourse. On the other hand, the great commission is addressed to the eleven, and it is very Christocentric, making disciples of the risen Lord, and teaching them all that Jesus has taught them (28:19–20). Based on the teachings of Jesus elsewhere addressed to the disciples in general (5:13–16), George Soares-Prabhu rightly argued that the Matthean presentation of mission is not merely Christocentric but theocentric, and that it is not merely an individual proclamation but a prophetic community witness.[16] The sayings of Jesus such as "You are the salt of the earth" (5:13); "You are the light of the world" (5:14); and "let your light shine before others, so that they may see your good works and give glory to your Father in heaven" (5:16) justify this claim. The first thing we observe here is that these commands are addressed not just to the twelve disciples but to the whole Christian community. As the evangelist Matthew indicates elsewhere, there is an intimate relationship between giving glory to God, doing the will of God, and the coming of God's reign (6:9–10). One glorifies God's name by doing the will of God, which in turn makes God's reign visible in the world. The inference thus follows that the church's mission is determined by the "primacy of God's reign" and that it should lead people to give glory to God. The church's mission thus embraces all the manifold—cosmic, historical, and spiritual—dimensions of the reign of

---

[16] George M. Soares-Prabhu, "The Church as Mission: A Reflection on Mt 5:13–16," *Jeevadhara* 24 (1994): 280.

God.[17] In short, the church's mission is to help advance human history to its full realization of the reign of God in the cosmos.

Luke's Gospel, sometimes described as the "Gospel of the poor" or the "Gospel of mercy," highlights the liberation and salvation that come from living in right relationship with God, with oneself, with others, and with the entire creation.[18] The evangelist Luke presents Jesus as the one *anointed* by God to preach the gospel to the poor, the one fulfilling the prophecy of Isaiah 61:

> "The spirit of the Lord is upon me,
> 	because he has anointed me
> 		to bring good news to the poor.
> He has sent me to proclaim release to captives,
> 	and recovery of sight to the blind,
> 		to let the oppressed go free,
> 	to proclaim the year of the Lord's favor." (Lk 4:18–19)

In this quotation from the Book of Isaiah, the words "captives," "blind," and "broken" reveal his radical commitment to the poor, outcast, oppressed, and marginalized. Jesus's way of life is marked by stark confrontation with the rich and the powerful, as he was an itinerant preacher who had "nowhere to lay his head" (9:58). The Lukan Jesus has compassion on the poor, women, Samaritans, sinners, tax collectors, and outcasts of all sorts. Jesus eats with sinners (5:30); his teaching focuses on the dangers of wealth and the need for social justice (16:13; 18:24); he defends the woman who weeps at his feet (7:36–50); and he praises the Samaritan leper who returns to give thanks (17:11–19). Like the Old Testament prophets, Jesus was committed to bringing Israel back to God and was in search of the lost sheep of Israel—sinners and those who lived on the margins of the Jewish community (4:16–21; 15:6). Jesus's extraordinary outreach to those on the fringes of the community, as well as his powerful protest and fearless resistance to all forms of evil, should be the heartbeat of the church's mission today.

John's Gospel presents Jesus as someone who abides in God's love. The evangelist applied the verb "abide" (*menein*) for the first time in the context

---

[17] See also George M. Soares-Prabhu, "Following Jesus in Mission: Reflections on Mission in the Gospel of Matthew," in *Bible and Mission in India Today*, ed. J. Kavunkal and F. Hrangkhuma (Bombay: St. Paul's, 1993), 64–92; Moloney, *Witnesses to the Ends of the Earth*, 53–78.

[18] See also Chennattu, "Religious Life," 27–28.

of Jesus's baptism to reveal the divine origin and identity of Jesus as the one in whom the Spirit abides (Jn 1:31–34). The abiding of the Spirit in Jesus is the sign of his identity as the Incarnate Word of God (1:14), the one who baptizes with the Holy Spirit (1:33), the one who is constantly in communication with God (1:1–2, 18).[19] Through the Samaritan episode the Johannine Jesus announces a world in the process of a dynamic movement from alienation to communion, from exclusion to integration, that transcends sectarian boundaries of social and religious discrimination (4:4–42).[20] The Johannine Jesus presents himself as someone *consecrated, sent by God* to accomplish God's work, and emphasizes his obedience to the Father (10:36; see also 4:43; 5:17). God was the source of his life and mission, and his God experience enabled him to speak on behalf of God and to do the work of God (5:19–30). Jesus maintains an intimate relationship with the Father, as he defines his mission as "doing the will of the Father who sent him" (5:30) and "accomplishing God's work" (4:34). The Johannine usage of "work" (*ergon*) stems from the Jewish theological background, and it is used to refer to the creative activity of God (Ps 8:3) or the liberating activity of God on behalf of the people of Israel (Ex 34:10). In the fifth chapter of the Gospel of John, when Jesus was accused by the Jews for breaking the Sabbath laws, Jesus defended himself by saying: "My Father is still working, and I also am working" (5:17). In John 5 the use of the verb "to work" reflects Jesus's cooperation in the creative and liberating acts of God. That Jesus performs a healing on the Sabbath is a clear indication of the fact that the divine "life-giving" and liberating activities are shared by Jesus.

In short, Jesus's mission was to make God's loving presence visible: God's work accomplished in the world. In John's Gospel, the disciples are sent out on the Father's mission by the Son in the power of the Spirit (Jn 20:21). No one denies the centrality of the love command in John's Gospel.[21] Reciprocal love is the identity mark of the disciples (13:34–35). Abiding in God's love, loving one another as friends and covenant partners in God's mission, and doing the will of God are characteristics of Johannine discipleship.[22] Just as the disciples, the church is called and commissioned

---

[19] See Chennattu, *Johannine Discipleship as a Covenant Relationship*, 112–15. See also D. A. Lee, "Abiding in the Fourth Gospel: A Case-Study in Feminist Biblical Theology," *Pacifica* 10 (1997): 123–36.

[20] Chennattu, "Biblical Women as Models of Theologizing," 679–84.

[21] See the detailed discussion in Francis J. Moloney, *Love in the Gospel of John* (Grand Rapids, MI: Baker Academic, 2013), 99–133; 161–89. See also Moloney, *Witnesses to the Ends of the Earth*, 109–27.

[22] Chennattu, *Johannine Discipleship as a Covenant Relationship*, 111–18.

by Jesus to build up communities of disciples and friends whose life and actions will glorify God and reveal God's life-giving presence in the world.

Paul as God's Instrument

Paul's ministry was a mission of love in building communities of faith and love. Biblical scholars have studied and presented Paul's missionary vision, activities, experience, principles, and strategies as models for the church's mission today.[23] Paul understood himself as "an apostle set apart to proclaim the Gospel of God" (Rom 1:1), the "God-appointed apostle to the Gentiles" (Gal 1:15–16), and an "ambassador for Christ" (2 Cor 5:20). In Paul's own words, "For Christ's loves compels us" (2 Cor 5:14). As Raymond Brown points out, the self-sacrificing love of Christ was "the driving factor of Paul's life."[24] Paul's apostolic ministry was inspired, grounded, and shaped by his Damascus encounter—his personal experience of God's redeeming love in Christ. Paul's apostolic ministry was a holistic mission of love, building up communities of love and manifesting the salvific love of Christ in the world.

Paul's mission and miraculous works stand in continuity with Jesus's own mission in the history of salvation.[25] As Dean Flemming puts it, "Paul carried out a holistic mission that in many ways mirrored that of his Lord. Like Jesus, he preached and taught, performed mighty deeds, cared for people in need, suffered for the benefit of others, practiced intercessory prayers, embodied the good news."[26] Like Jesus, Paul was a man of prayer and considered prayer an integral part of his mission.[27] Paul was committed to founding as well as nurturing his newly founded believing communities in order that they "walk worthy of God" (1 Thess 2:10–12). Establishing Christian communities in every region that he visited was the goal and purpose of his missionary endeavors. In the words

---

[23] Eckhard J. Schnabel, *Paul the Missionary: Realities, Strategies, and Methods* (Downers Grove, IL: InterVarsity Press, 2008); Trever J. Burke and Brian S. Rosner, eds., *Paul as Missionary: Identity, Activity, Theology, and Practice* (London: T&T Clark, 2011). For a recent study, see also Legrand, *Paul et la mission*, 119–93.

[24] Raymond E. Brown, *An Introduction to the New Testament* (New York: Doubleday, 1997), 449.

[25] See, for example, Rom 15:18–19; 2 Cor 12:12; Gal 3:5; also Acts 13:9–12; 14:8–10; 16:16–18; 20:9–12.

[26] Flemming, *Recovering the Full Mission of God*, 79–80.

[27] Paul prays for the salvation of his fellow Jews (Rom 10:1). He prayed constantly (Phil 1:4) that the love of the Philippians might overflow with insight and they be found blameless on the day of Christ (Phil 1:9–11).

of W. Paul Bowers, "A distinguishing dimension of the Pauline mission is that it found its fullest sense of completion neither in an evangelic preaching tour nor in individual conversions but only in the presence of firmly established churches."[28] Paul's missionary work was to establish Christian communities—loving, caring, holy, and fruitful communities of faith. The mission aims at the transformation of believing communities in such a way that they might be found "blameless on the day of Christ" (1 Thess 5:23; Phil 1:10).

Among the metaphors used by Paul to describe Christian communities, the image of a loving family stands out. Paul addressed the believing communities in general as God's beloved (Rom 1:7; 1 Thess 1:4), Paul's beloved (Rom 12:19; 1 Cor 15:38) or Paul's beloved children (1 Cor 4:14). When referring to the Christians, another image used by Paul is "God's building" (1 Cor 3:9), or the "temple of God," the building par excellence as the dwelling place of God (1 Cor 3:16–17). Paul writes: "We are the temple of the living God; as God said, 'I will live in them and walk among them, and I will be their God, and they shall be my people'" (2 Cor 6:16b). The temple symbolism highlights the holiness of life that the members should have as a visible sign of God's presence in the world. Both metaphors, family and God's building/temple, underscore the centrality of love (*agape*) and fellowship (*koinonia*) that manifest themselves in concrete acts of service that the members should render to the world.[29]

Paul's option for the poor was evident in his ministry of compassion, which took priority over other works of evangelization. Paul was even ready to delay his trip to Rome in order to deliver the collection for the poor in Jerusalem first (Rom 15:23–25).[30] That collection was an integral part of his missionary trips and it became a passion for Paul, because it expressed (1) his own personal concern for the poor; (2) the church's unity and solidarity that foster communion among the Jews and Gentiles; and (3) a way of living out the new life Christ modelled after the self-sacrificing love of Jesus Christ.[31]

Paul's vision of a new life in Christ marks the end of discrimination of every kind and establishes full equality among the members in the

---

[28] W. Paul Bowers, "Mission," in *Dictionary of Paul and His Letters*, ed. Gerald F. Hawthorne, Ralph P. Martin, and Daniel G. Reid (Downers Grove, IL: InterVarsity Press, 1993), 610.

[29] Chennattu, "Religious Life," 31–32.

[30] Paul mentioned this in four letters: Rom 15:25–31; Gal 2:10; 1 Cor 16:1–4; 2 Cor 9:1–15.

[31] See a detailed study in Scot McKnight, "Collection for the Saints," in Hawthorne et al., *Dictionary of Paul and His Letters*, 143–47. See also Flemming, *Recovering the Full Mission of God*, 176–78.

church (Gal 3:28).³² Christ has set us free for a life in the community; our freedom is for the building up of a "new creation" (Gal 6:15). Paul asserts, in the context of the new creation brought into being through God's work in Christ, that Christians are called to become "the righteousness of God (*dikaiosyne theou*)" (2 Cor 5:21). The text deals with reconciliation between God and human beings in and through Christ. Paul claims that those who are reconciled are called to become the righteousness of God. Paul describes the righteousness of God as God's response to an ever-failing people (Rom 3:21–26) and as designating those acts of God that restore the broken relationship between God and human beings. It thus refers to God's forgiving love and redemptive interventions in human history. So, when Paul says that the believers are called to become "the righteousness of God," it would imply that we are called to become active agents in God's ongoing reconciling work among humans and to become instruments in restoring harmony in God's creation.³³ As the whole universe is in a dynamic process of evolving and becoming a new creation, the commitment to the integrity of creation is fundamental to God's work as well as to that of the church today.

God's Reigning Presence in the New Jerusalem

The climax of the biblical story is found in the visions of "a new heaven and a new earth" and "the holy city, the new Jerusalem" in the Book of Revelation, chapters 21–22. These visions portray the ultimate victory of God's reign over all of creation. The author takes his readers into the messianic era of God's reigning presence in the risen Lord, the Lamb, so that they can see their present history, experience, and mission from the perspective of God's ultimate purpose for which human beings and the cosmos were created. I do not consider the new Jerusalem mentioned here (21:10) as a reference to some "future" reality that will come into existence at the end of the world.³⁴ The new Jerusalem here symbolizes

---

³² Rekha M. Chennattu, "Reciprocal Partnership and Inclusive Leadership: Exploring Paul's Attitudes to Women," in *Learning from St. Paul: Reflections for the Pauline Year*, ed. Shaji J. Puykunnel and Jose Varickasseril (Shillong: Vendrame Institute Publications, 2008), 139–57.

³³ For a detailed discussion, see K. L. Onesti and M. T. Brauch, "Righteousness, Righteousness of God," in Hawthorne et al., *Dictionary of Paul and His Letters*, 827–37.

³⁴ For this new interpretation, see the paradigm-shifting work of Francis J. Moloney, *The Apocalypse of John: A Commentary* (Grand Rapids, MI: Baker Academic, 2020), 325–62. See also Eugenio Corsini, *Apocalypse: The Perennial Revelation of Jesus Christ*, trans. Francis J. Moloney (Wilmington, DE: Michael Glazier, 1983).

the church as it should be in the here and now, the fruit of the death and resurrection of Jesus, the slain and risen Lamb (21:9–14). The church does not have to wait for an eschatological future. As Francis Moloney maintains, "God, through the resurrection of the Lamb, has established a blessed era that is experienced and witnessed to in their day-to-day lives, enjoying the gift of light and life, available in the new Jerusalem."[35] The vision of the new Jerusalem embodies an alternative social reality and it sets the agenda for the church's mission today.

The description of the new Jerusalem in chapters 21–22 furnishes us with a vision of a new society, emulating God's reigning presence. As Flemming argues, "The new creation provides an utterly stunning picture of what God is about in our world—and consequently, what the church should be about as well."[36] So, by way of inference, the mission of the church includes reconciling and restoring the broken relationship with God, with other human beings, and with all of creation (21:3; 22:1–54); healing the sick and lessening pain and misery in the world (21:4; 7:15–17); and working for social and economic justice (18:11–17). The vision of the new Jerusalem in Revelation beckons the church to be a mirror of this new Jerusalem here and now, in the present moment of human history—in today's trying times. If we are open to what the Spirit is saying to the churches, we are summoned to bear witness to the "new creation" envisaged by God. The church will then be able to offer a distinctive model of a believing community to the peoples and cultures around them. The church becomes "the light of the world" (Mt 5:14), or as Isaiah puts it, Christians become a "light to the nations" (Isa 42:6; cf. Rev 21:22–24).

The Church's Mission Today—Biblical Insights and Challenges

The biblical story is all about God's mission of creation and its journey toward the eschatological time of a new heaven and a new earth. Mission begins with God, and it flows out of God's immense love in order to restore and bring fullness of life to all of creation. The church is called to become a community of God's people, the temple of God, a foyer of love that builds up communities of faith where everyone can experience God's reigning presence and enjoy the fullness of life.

Our participation in God's mission is inspired by the self-sacrificing love of Jesus, by the passion and commitment of the prophets, and the

---

[35] Moloney, *The Apocalypse of John*, 362.
[36] Flemming, *Recovering the Full Mission of God*, 246.

life witness and innovative missionary zeal of the apostles; it is impelled by the Holy Spirit and made concrete in our response to the emerging realities of life.

In the light of the above survey, the *why* of the people of Israel, of the church, and consequently *the why of mission*, is God's love. The church's very being is the fruit of God's love and exists for God's mission, which is to embody God's loving presence in today's world. The church does not simply have a mission; the church is *apostolic* by nature. Like the people of Israel, the church needs to be reminded of its identity as God's pilgrim people, a holy people who walk in God's ways and exist not for their own sake but for God's mission. Since God's love is the foundation of God's choices, it is likewise the heartbeat of Israel's mission and the church's mission.

As for *the how of mission*, I would like to emphasize two things. The first is that our mission is rooted in a personal encounter with God. Biblical stories demonstrate that mission is always based on a personal experience of God. They impel us to return to God's interventions in our life. The mission of the apostles was a spontaneous proclamation and joyful communication of their encounter with and experience of God. As Flemming rightly observes, "Mission flows from our relationship *with* God, not what we do *for* God."[37] The second is that our personal experience of God includes a personal conversion (*metanoia*) that goes hand in hand with our work of social transformation. A life that manifests God's forgiveness should be an integral part of our mission to liberate people from unjust and oppressive social systems. While we continue to proclaim the Gospel to nonbelievers, the primary focus of our mission today is to evangelize ourselves. We hope to attract others to Christ by living a distinctive social life committed to gospel values. Always and everywhere, we are called to live out the compassionate love of Christ and to care for one another as a visible sign of God's reign in the world. Our mission is therefore a full-time commitment in communion with God.

Our choices and commitment, witnessing to the values of God's reign, trigger misunderstanding, conflicts, and hardships. Just as suffering was an essential aspect of Jesus's mission on earth, difficulties and adversities will be our lot as well. Our mission inevitably entails redemptive suffering and includes taking up our cross, dying and rising daily to a newness of life. This task is not easy, but the resurrection of Jesus, the victory of Jesus over sin and death, gives us the hope and grace to fulfill our mission. We are also assured of God's accompaniment through the gift of the Holy Spirit.

---

[37] Flemming, *Recovering the Full Mission of God*, 129.

The "Why" of Mission 21

What might we discern as biblical trends in mission—*the "what" of mission*—for our changing times? I offer a few thoughts.

Transformed by our personal experience of God's grace, the church is called today to be a catalyst for spiritual renewal and social transformation. The way of life of the church should mirror God's ways, revealing them in righteousness as well as in social and ecological justice.

> When we deepen our faith through daily personal conversion and renewal,
> when we reclaim our contemplative tradition and embrace diversity,
> when we truly become God's covenant community from which no one is excluded,
> when we make synodality a way of life and bridge the gap between clergy and laity,
> when we give women their rightful place in the life and mission of the church,
> when we accompany young people searching for meaning and purpose of life,
> when we forgive and break down divisive walls, and seek justice for the oppressed,
> when we respect the dignity of every human person, and care for the sick and elderly,
> when we welcome migrants and outsiders, and help resettle refugees,
> when we become a voice for the voiceless, a face for the many faceless peoples,
> when we earnestly foster communion among churches through ecumenical dialogue,
> when we build up just and humane societies through socio-economic-political commitments and interreligious dialogue,
> when we strive to bring about lasting reconciliation between war-torn nations and work for sustainable peace,
> when we protect the cosmos through networking with world leaders and joining hands with indigenous and tribal communities,
> when we become channels of the joy and hope of the risen Lord,

then I believe, we, the church, will be faithful to our identity as well as to God's mission; we will be a blessing for the universe, and we will contribute to the creation of "a new heaven and a new earth."

As Moloney once commented: "What makes practicing Christians different? If there is no difference, we have a problem."[38] Or as Eugene Boring asked, "Are we out of step with what God is ultimately doing in the world?"[39] Let me conclude by asking: Does the church embody God's love in today's world? Do the ministries of the church contribute to the mission of God? Is the church's identity and mission validated by the integrity of her life-witness?

Rekha M. Chennattu, RA, holds a PhD in biblical studies from the Catholic University of America. She was a participant at the Synod on New Evangelization (2012). She is a member of the Federation of Asian Bishops' Conferences—Office of Theological Concerns, and the superior general of the Congregation of the Religious of the Assumption (France).

---

[38] Francis J. Moloney, *Gospel Interpretation and Christian Life* (Adelaide: ATF Theology, 2017), 366.

[39] Eugene Boring, "Revelation 19–21: End without Closure," *Princeton Seminary Bulletin*, Supplementary Issue 3 (1994): 80.

The "What" of Mission

Refining our Comprehension of Mission

JOSEPH SCARIA PALAKEEL, MST

Our conception of mission is constantly being reformed and refined. The documents of Vatican II are eloquent on the missionary nature of the church and impart a new mission theology in tune with the emerging self-understanding of the church. In response to the questions raised by differing interpretations of the mission documents of Vatican II, Pope Paul VI, in his 1975 apostolic exhortation *Evangelii Nuntiandi*,[1] clearly laid out the theological principles to guide Catholics in understanding evangelization. The new mission theology was received with much enthusiasm by Catholics worldwide. However, on the occasion of the twenty-fifth anniversary of the conciliar decree on mission (*Ad Gentes*), in 1990, Pope John Paul II promulgated an encyclical on mission, *Redemptoris Missio*,[2] revealing his concern that "difficulties both internal and external have weakened the church's missionary thrust toward non-Christians" and hence that "missionary activity specifically directed 'to the nations' (*ad gentes*) appears to be waning, and this tendency is certainly not in line with the directives of the Council and of subsequent statements of the Magisterium."[3] The "what" of mission thus began to crop up as a relevant and important question.

What were the "internal and external difficulties" that John Paul II believed had diminished the missionary spirit of Catholics, despite twenty-five years of intense theological enquiry into mission? Was he hinting at a wrong or deviated interpretation of the conciliar missiology when he

---

[1] Pope Paul VI, apostolic exhortation *Evangelii Nuntiandi (Evangelization in the Modern World)* (1975), hereinafter *EN*.

[2] Pope John Paul II, encyclical *Redemptoris Missio (On the Permanent Validity of the Church's Missionary Mandate)* (1990), hereinafter *RM*.

[3] *RM*, no. 2.

wrote that "this tendency is certainly not in line with the directives of the Council?" Or, did he mean that Catholic missiology was still looking for convincing answers to the core questions of what, why, who, and how of mission? During the period in question, we noticed ambivalence in mission theology directly linked to a shift in the church's self-understanding. While *Evangelii Nuntiandi* was inspired by the people of God's ecclesiology, *Redemptoris Missio* delineates mission from the "communion" ecclesiology, as recommended by the Synod of Bishops in 1985. Missiologies, shaped by ecclesiologies, naturally led to ideological debates that served only to weaken the missionary thrust. It is in this context that Pope Francis, in his 2013 apostolic exhortation *Evangelii Gaudium*,[4] recommends the "Church's missionary transformation"[5] as "the first step" to "embark upon a new chapter of evangelization."[6] It is a call to rethink the church's self-understanding from a missionary perspective,[7] summoning up the original missionary resolve of the Second Vatican Council.

The Shifts in the Missionary Spirit of Vatican II

The Missionary Intent of the Council

Vatican II can be considered to be the second *missionary* council, after the Council of Jerusalem, because of its missionary goal and spirit. The primary concern of Pope John XXIII in convoking the Second Vatican Council was to bring "the modern world into contact with the vivifying and perennial energies of the Gospel,"[8] *not* "modernizing" the church, as is commonly believed. The contemporary society of the period was devastated by the world wars and overwhelmed by the scientific and technological developments promoting material progress without moral, spiritual, and religious foundations. Pope John XXIII believed that the church could

---

[4] Pope Francis, apostolic exhortation *Evangelii Gaudium (The Joy of the Gospel)* (2013), hereinafter *EG*.

[5] *EG*, nos. 19, 27.

[6] *EG*, nos. 24, 1.

[7] The popes' proclivity for using the terms "mission" and "evangelization" in these three documents indicates their ecclesiological underlining. *Redemptoris Missio* marks the reappearance of the word "mission" in place of "evangelization" (which had been popularized by *Evangelii Nuntiandi*). *Evangelii Gaudium* uses both terms with equal emphasis, interpreting mission as evangelization.

[8] Pope John XXIII, apostolic constitution *Humanae Salutis (The Bull of Indiction of the Second Vatican Council)* (December 25, 1961), nos. 3 and 11.

address the problems by teaching the contemporary world to seek God. The unambiguous missionary intention rang out loud and clear in his opening speech as well as at the council: "So that they, to whom it has been said: 'Subdue the earth and dominate it' (Gen 1:28) do not forget that very strict command: 'Worship the Lord your God and only worship him' (Mt 4:10; Lk 4:8)."[9] The council had a profoundly missionary intent.

The missionary spirit is discernible in all the major documents of Vatican II, including *Lumen Gentium*,[10] *Gaudium et Spes*,[11] and *Ad Gentes*.[12] The very first sentence of *Lumen Gentium* enunciates the "inner nature and universal mission" of the church as "proclaiming the Gospel to every creature, to bring the light of Christ to all men."[13] "Christ is the Light of nations" and the same "light [is] brightly visible on the countenance of the Church." Hence, "the Church is in Christ like a sacrament or as a sign and instrument both of a very closely knit union with God and of the unity of the whole human race."[14] All disciples participate in divine life through baptism and are called to be missionaries by sharing it with others. Thus, every Christian in particular and the church in general are entrusted with the duty to reach out to all and communicate the love of God. *Ad Gentes* outlines the missionary nature and vocation of the church: "Divinely sent to the nations of the world to be unto them 'a universal sacrament of salvation,' the Church, driven by the inner necessity of her own catholicity, and obeying the mandate of her Founder (cf. Mark 16:16), strives ever to proclaim the Gospel to all men."[15] The Second Vatican Council generated much missionary enthusiasm among Catholics worldwide, especially in the traditional missionary territories and the young churches, where indigenous missionaries had begun to replace European missionaries.[16]

---

[9] "Address of the Holy Father John XXIII at the Solemn Opening of the Vatican II Ecumenical Council" (October 11, 1962), nos. 5, 6.

[10] Vatican II, *Lumen Gentium (The Dogmatic Constitution on the Church)* (1964), hereinafter *LG*.

[11] Vatican II, *Gaudium et Spes* (Pastoral Constitution on the Church in the Modern World) (1965), hereinafter *GS*.

[12] Vatican II, *Ad Gentes (Decree on the Mission Activity of the Church)* (1965), hereinafter *AG*.

[13] *LG*, no. 1.

[14] *LG*, nos. 1, 48.

[15] *AG*, no. 1.

[16] For instance, in the case of Asia, the Missionary Society of St Thomas the Apostle (India, 1968), the Heralds of Good News (India, 1984), Mission Society of the Philippines (1965), and the Korean Missionary Society (1975) were started exclusively for mission *ad gentes*, in response to Vatican II; similarly, indigenous religious congregations and dioceses also took up organized missionary work.

Ecclesiology Shapes the "Mission Trends"

This vigorous missionary *ad gentes* disposition of the council was soon inundated by debates over the *ad intra* aspects of the church, which hallowed ecclesiology as the hermeneutical key to the council and rendered mission theology acquiescent to ecclesiology. The dominant self-understanding of the church prevalent on the different continents became the operational model for missionary reflection and action of the church.[17] Although the dominant ecclesiologies within the council were "church as mystery" and the "mystical body of Christ," the "people of God" ecclesiology stood out as the most popular vision of the church after the council. Countless pastoral, missionary, and liturgical reforms during this period were inspired by the self-understanding of the church as the new people of God. However, two decades after Vatican II, the Synod of Bishops in 1985 hailed communion ecclesiology as the authentic ecclesiology of the council and the church. The post–Vatican II mission trends can be broadly classified under the "people of God" ecclesiology or the "communion" ecclesiology, with divergent goals and focus.

The "People of God" Ecclesiology and the Regno-centric Missiology

Much of the euphoria over Vatican II was an outcome of the new vision of the church as the people of God with a relevant mission to accomplish in the modern world, as envisioned by Pope John XXIII. The church, with a divine origin and a historical existence and mission, seemed like the most perfect vision of the church for the twentieth century. In the words of the International Theological Commission, "The expression 'the New people of God' has come to stand for the ecclesiology of the Council, because it renders better the divine origin, election and mission of the Church and indicates that the church is a historic subject and an agent with a mission in the world to bring all human beings into communion with God."[18] As both "mystery" and "historical subject," the new people of God "is a community composed of men . . . who, united in Christ and guided by the Holy Spirit, press onward toward the Kingdom of the

---

[17] See Avery Dulles, *Models of the Church* (Dublin: Gill and Macmillan, 1988).

[18] See International Theological Commission, *Select Themes of Ecclesiology on the Occasion of the Twentieth Anniversary of the Closing of the Second Vatican Council* (1984), II.1, hereinafter ITC. See also *LG,* no. 9: "Christ instituted this new covenant . . . , calling together a people made up of Jew and gentile, making them one, not according to the flesh but in the Spirit. This was to be the new People of God."

Father and are bearers of a message of salvation intended for all men."[19] This new vision of the church, bolstered by the emerging historical consciousness (*aggiornamento*) in the church, paved the way for ecclesiological and missiological thinking in the decades following the council.

Catholic mission theology found new vigor and vitality from this vision of the church. Called and commissioned by Jesus Christ as a sacramental community "to proclaim and communicate [the good news] in the remembrance and expectation of Jesus Christ," the mission of the church is to be a pilgrim community that remains always "on the way" and "in commitment to mission."[20] As a people who have come to know the good news of salvation and to experience the mysteries of salvation through the word of God and the sacraments, all the baptized are missionaries "in the ordinary circumstances of social and family life."[21] By "the witness of their life, resplendent in faith, hope, and charity, they must manifest Christ to others,"[22] and "being led by the spirit of the Gospel, they may contribute to the sanctification of the world, as from within like leaven, by fulfilling their own particular duties which constitute their very existence." Thus, chosen from among the whole of humanity to be witnesses and agents of transformation to the reign of God, their mission is to "lend embodiment to the Kingdom of God" and to "humanize" the world.[23]

In the 1974 Synod of Bishops, the ensuing apostolic exhortation *Evangelii Nuntiandi* by Pope Paul VI espoused the church's new mission theology. *Evangelii Nuntiandi* defines evangelization[24] as "bringing the Good News into all the strata of humanity, and through its influence transforming humanity from within and making it new."[25] The document clarifies further that "it is a question not only of preaching the Gospel in ever wider geographic areas or to ever greater numbers of people, but also of affecting and as it were upsetting, through the power of the Gospel, mankind's criteria of judgment, determining values, points of interest,

---

[19] ITC, IV.1.

[20] ITC, III.3 and 4.

[21] See *LG*, no. 31.

[22] *LG*, no. 31.

[23] ITC, III.4.

[24] See the preferential use of the term *evangelization* instead of mission in *Evangelii Nuntiandi* (and later) by Pope Francis. The Congregation for the Doctrine of the Faith considers it equivalent to *mission:* "The term evangelization has a very rich meaning. In the broad sense, it sums up the church's entire mission: her whole life consists in accomplishing the *traditio Evangelii*, the proclamation and handing on of the Gospel" (Congregation for the Doctrine of the Faith, *Doctrinal Note on Some Aspects of Evangelization* [2007], no. 2).

[25] *EN*, no. 18; cf. *EN*, no. 4.

lines of thought, sources of inspiration and models of life."[26] Missionaries are called to bring the power of the Gospel into the very heart of culture and purify and elevate it. The goal of the mission is to make the good news of the kingdom a reality by building that ideal community of justice and righteousness that Christians refer to as the kingdom of God. Here we find the emergence of a regno-centric mission—with the goal of establishing the reign of God, through the proclamation of the kingdom values, in dialogue with religions, cultures, and the poor. Inculturation and interreligious dialogue and the preferential option for the poor thus came to be defined as "paths of mission" in official documents like *Evangelii Nuntiandi* and *Redemptoris Missio*, not to mention in the episcopal conferences, seminars, and publications on mission. All the major international conferences on mission during the first decades after Vatican II treated the themes of dialogue, development, and inculturation as the core of mission theology.[27]

Missionaries were always promoting education, health, and human development, especially in the developing world. The new kingdom-centered (*basileological*) vision of mission gave a new impulse to all forms of humanitarian work toward empowerment of the poor as well as engagement in inculturation and interreligious dialogue. Liberation theology is the paramount expression of the people of God ecclesiology and kingdom-centered mission theology. But while the regno-centric mission itself is quite in tune with the incarnational dynamics of Christianity, forgetting the deeper spiritual dimension of human redemption and slighting the transcendental dimension of the kingdom of God proved to be counterproductive,[28] in that wherever mission was equated with

---

[26] *EN*, no. 19; cf. *LG*, no. 13.

[27] These included (1) SEDOS Symposium on "Mission Theology for our Times," held in Rome in March 1969, published in French as "Salut et Development," *Spiritus* 10, no. 39 (1969): 327–528, and published in English as *Foundations of Mission Theology* (Maryknoll, NY: Orbis Books, 1972); (2) *All India Seminar: Church in India Today*, Bangalore, 1969 [Report] (New Delhi: CBCI Centre, 1969); (3) International Theological Conference, Nagpur (India), 1971, published as Mariasusai Dhavamony, ed., *Evangelization, Dialogue, and Development: Selected Papers of the International Theological Conference, Nagpur (India), 1971* (Rome: Gregorian University, 1972). See also the SEDOS research seminar on the future of mission held March 8–19, 1981, in Rome, published as Mary Motte and Joseph R. Lang, eds., *Mission in Dialogue: The SEDOS Research Seminar on the Future of Mission, March 8–19, 1981, Rome* (Maryknoll, NY: Orbis Books, 1982); William Jenkinson and Helene O'Sullivan, eds., *Trends in Mission: Toward the Third Millennium: Essays in Celebration of Twenty-Five Years of SEDOS* (Maryknoll, NY: Orbis Books, 1993).

[28] *Instruction on Certain Aspects of the "Theology of Liberation"* (1984), by the Congregation for the Doctrine of the Faith, speaks of "the temptation to reduce the Gospel to an *earthly gospel*" (VI.4, VI.5), italics added.

humanizing the world, evangelization became pure humanitarian work.[29] The lament of *Redemptoris Missio* echoes this concern, and the adoption of communion ecclesiology is attributable to a critique of the predominantly "immanentist" interpretation of church and kingdom sparked by the people of God ecclesiology. This in no way denies the value of dialogue and *diakonia* in mission for the realization of the reign of God, and the regno-centric mission continues to be the dominant mission theology worldwide.

Communion Ecclesiology and Ecclesio-centric Missiology

The Synod of Bishops in 1985 distanced itself from the horizontal and anthropological stress of the people of God ecclesiology and sought to promote the ecclesiology of communion as "the central and fundamental idea of the Council's documents."[30] This view was supported by the Congregation for the Doctrine of the Faith, which said that the communion ecclesiology is "very suitable for expressing the core of the Mystery of the Church, and can certainly be a key for the renewal of Catholic ecclesiology."[31] With its emphasis on "the *vertical* (communion with God) and the *horizontal* (communion among men)," the communion ecclesiology expresses well the nature of the church as the mystery of "the new relationship between man and God that has been established in Christ and is communicated through the sacraments."[32]

Communion ecclesiology understands the church as the locus of this divine-human communion, willed by the Father, established by Christ, and rendered sacramentally available in the church by the Holy Spirit and, thus, serves as a foundational ecclesiology for the church's self-understanding

---

[29] See Joseph Palakeel, "Anthropological Grounding of Evangelization: From Mission *ad Gentes* to New Evangelization," in *Evangelizing Mission: The Role and Relevance of Missionary Societies and Congregations in Evangelization and New Evangelization* (Bangalore: ATC, 2018), 59–81.

[30] See Synod of Bishops, Second Extraordinary Assembly (1985), *Relatio finalis*, Section II: Particular Themes of the Synod, C: The Church as Communion, no. 1. Cardinal Ratzinger was instrumental in this communion ecclesiology.

[31] Congregation for the Doctrine of the Faith, *Letter to the Bishops of the Catholic Church, On Some Aspects of the Church Understood As Communion* (1992), 1, hereinafter CDF. See also *The Ratzinger Report: An Exclusive Interview on the State of the Church* (San Francisco: Ignatius Press, 1985), which considerably influenced the synodal discussions on the reception of Vatican II; and Joseph Ratzinger, "The Ecclesiology of Vatican II," Conference of Cardinal Ratzinger at the Opening of the Pastoral Congress of the Diocese of Aversa (Italy) in 2001.

[32] CDF, 3, 4.

and ecumenism among the churches, as well as dialogue and communion with people of other religions and ideologies. Nonetheless, it is often given a narrow interpretation as "the visible communion in the teaching of the Apostles, in the sacraments and in the hierarchical order," "into which each individual is introduced by faith and by Baptism, and has its root and center in the Blessed Eucharist."[33] Such a basically Augustinian communion ecclesiology based on the visible union of the eucharistic community under a bishop tends to be a refurbished version of the Tridentine perfect society, with a hierarchical-sacramental monopoly over salvation. Thus, in overemphasizing the vertical dimension of the church in an effort to counterbalance the horizontal leanings of the regno-centric mission, communion ecclesiology appears to be ecclesio-centrism.

This is discernible in *Redemptoris Missio*, which was issued in the context of the emergence of communion ecclesiology to official status. It declares that "just as the risen Lord gave the universal missionary mandate to the College of the Apostles with Peter as its head, so this same responsibility now rests primarily with the College of Bishops, headed by the Successor of Peter."[34] Chapter 6 of *Redemptoris Missio*, entitled "Leaders and Workers in the Missionary Apostolate,"[35] makes pope and bishops "primarily responsible for missionary activity" and categorizes all others—diocesan priests, consecrated persons, laity, Catechists, and all those in different ministries[36]—as "workers."[37] This way of restricting the missionary responsibility to ordained and consecrated persons prevents the authentic and full expression of the missionary nature of the entire church. All the Vatican II and post–Vatican II documents on mission unmistakably declare that all the faithful are "missionaries by baptism"[38] and that "the mission

---

[33] CDF, 4, 5.

[34] *RM*, no. 63. This follows closely Chapter IV of *Ad Gentes* (nos. 23–27), dedicated to "Workers" of mission. Interpreting *Ad Gentes* no. 1 and *Lumen Gentium* no. 23, *Redemptoris Missio* states that "the charge of proclaiming the Gospel throughout the world belongs to the body of shepherds, to all of whom in common Christ gave the command." In contrast we find that *Evangelii Nuntiandi* speaks of a kingdom-centered evangelization as the responsibility of the whole church, with institutional-hierarchical and sacramental links (*EN*, nos. 59–60).

[35] *RM*, nos. 61–76.

[36] *RM*, nos. 67, 69–70, 71–72, 73.

[37] *RM*, nos. 63ff.; cf. *AG*, nos. 23, 38; *RM*, nos. 65–66. This is a continuation of the Tridentine church in which the pope had to mandate missions directly; later on, this task is delegated to the Propaganda Fide. With Vatican II, bishops are vested with pope-like juridical power in the diocese, and all missionary activities are to be mandated by the bishops (see Edith Bernard, "Leaders and Workers in the Missionary Apostolate," *International Review of Mission* [July 1, 2001]).

[38] *RM*, no. 71.

ad gentes is incumbent upon the entire People of God."[39] Further, it is stated that "the need for all the faithful to share in this responsibility is not merely a matter of making the apostolate more effective, it is a right and duty based on their baptismal dignity, whereby 'the faithful participate, for their part, in the threefold mission of Christ as Priest, Prophet and King.'"[40] An inclusive interpretation of the essentially missionary nature of the church[41] necessitates an ecclesiology based on mission, rather than a mission theology based on ecclesiology.

Reclaiming the Mission-centered Ecclesiology

The above analysis shows that we need to look for an integral ecclesiology and mission theology capable of expressing the vertical and horizontal communions that have been established in Christ within the universal salvific will of God. Thus, an ecclesiology based on mission can better explain the role of the church as the universal sacrament of salvation *within* the economy of the universal salvific will of God, as both are intimately linked. Mission is, above all, an attribute of God,[42] and the church is missionary because the work of God is entrusted to the church. *Missio ecclesiae* is deeply rooted in *missio Dei Trinitatis*. As the new people of God, the church is the visible communion on earth sacramentally embodying the kingdom of God proclaimed by Jesus. Mission is, hence, foundational to the self-understanding of the church: "Missiology trumps ecclesiology."[43]

Missio Dei Trinitatis

Mission is largely traced to Jesus's great commission to go to the ends of the earth to proclaim the good news.[44] However, Jesus is the not the prime source of mission. Mission originates from the "fountain-like love of God the Father," who has created us and calls us to share in his

---

[39] *AG*, no. 2; *RM*, no. 62.

[40] *RM*, no. 71. See also *AG*, nos. 35–36, 41; Pope John Paul II, *Christifideles Laici (The Lay Members of Christ's Faithful People)* (1988), nos. 14, 35.

[41] *AG*, no. 1; *LG*, no. 48.

[42] The concept of *missio Dei* was introduced by Karl Barth as early as 1935 in the first volume of his *Church Dogmatics* as part of the sketch of his systematic theology.

[43] Peter C. Phan, "The Church: Towards a Common Vision: A View from the Asian Churches," *Journal of World Christianity* 7 (2017): 91.

[44] Mt 28:20; Mk 16; Lk 24; Acts 1:8.

Life, generously poured out through the Son and the Holy Spirit.[45] The trinitarian mission of the Father, accomplished by the Son and the Holy Spirit, was entrusted to the Apostles and through them to the church and to every Christian. Mission is not the work of the church for God. Instead it is the work of God on behalf of humanity, and the church is a participant, agent, or coworker commissioned by Jesus and empowered by the Holy Spirit. Mission is the work of God (*missio Dei*), who is revealed as a "missionary Trinity."

In the *missio Dei Trinitatis* perspective, Jesus is the first evangelizer. *Evangelii Nuntiandi* states that "Jesus himself, the Good News of God, was the very first and the greatest evangelizer."[46] And *Tertio Millennio Adveniente* calls for "a renewed appreciation of Christ, Savior and Proclaimer of the Gospel."[47] The Gospel of John speaks of the sending of the Son into the world by the Father as the first mission[48] to become the way, the truth, and the life of humanity. The Epistle to the Hebrews explicitly calls Jesus "the Apostle,"[49] which is to say "one who is sent." The entire life of Jesus was a response to a missionary vocation.[50]

After his resurrection and ascension, Jesus sends the Holy Spirit to continue his mission: the Spirit will bear testimony to Jesus[51] and empower the disciples to proclaim the Gospel.[52] The Spirit (of the risen Lord) is also present and active in the universe and in all religions and cultures as part of the trinitarian economy of salvation. Thus the work of the Holy Spirit (*missio Spiritus*) in creation, redemption, and eschatological salvation is central to Christian mission theology. From the mission of the Spirit is born the church, and the Spirit carries out the mission in the name of God the Father and the risen Lord. Thus "the mission was not entrusted to the Church, but the Church was entrusted to the Mission of the Spirit. The one who carries out the mission is not primarily the Church; rather the Church, and of course the Holy Spirit, are their ally."[53] The mission is the mother of the church and the church is the "visible" earthly part-

---

[45] See *AG*, no. 2.

[46] *EN*, no. 7.

[47] Pope John Paul II, apostolic letter *Tertio Millennio Adveniente (On Preparation for the Jubilee of the Year 2000)* (1994), no. 40. Cf. Lk 4:18–21; Lk 1:69, 72–73a; cf. also Gen 3:15 and 12:1–3.

[48] 1 Jn 4:9–10, 14; Jn 3:17; Jn 3:34; Jn 5:36–38.

[49] Heb 3:1.

[50] Jn 4:34.

[51] Cf. Jn 14:26.

[52] Jn 15:26–27.

[53] José Cristo Rey García Paredes, "The Challenge of Religious Leadership: A Theological and Practical Vision for Our Times," *UISG Bulletin* 149 (2012): 25–26.

ner, not the author or owner of the mission. The church originates from the mission and perpetuates it. Here we have a definitive move from an ecclesio-centric concept to a theocentric or trinitarian-centric concept of mission.

Missio Ecclesiae: Universal Sacrament of Salvation

The mission of the church, *missio ecclesiae*, is to be *the universal sacrament* of the *missio Dei Trinitatis*. It means that "The pilgrim Church is missionary by her very nature, *since it is from the mission of the Son and the mission of the Holy Spirit that she draws her origin*, in accordance with the decree of God the Father."[54] She herself is "the first beneficiary of salvation" won by Christ, and the church is made "a part of his plan of salvation" and "his co-worker in the salvation of the world. He carries out his mission through her."[55] This is best expressed by the Second Vatican Council with the notion of the church as "the universal sacrament of salvation."[56] Although this concept best describes this mission of the church *ad extra* within the context of the universal salvific will of God to save everyone,[57] this notion is often understood in the *intra ecclesia* context of the actual sacraments of the church as the means of salvation.

The church affirms the possibility of salvation *extra ecclesia*: "The universality of salvation means that it is granted not only to those who explicitly believe in Christ and have entered the Church, [but] . . . is offered to all, [and] must be made concretely available to all."[58] Yet the church has a role as the locus and mediator of human salvation: "To this catholic unity of the people of God, therefore, . . . all are called, and they belong to it or are ordered to it in various ways, whether they be Catholic faithful or others who believe in Christ or finally all people everywhere [the whole of humankind] who by the grace of God are called to salvation."[59] How shall we then explain the *sacramental function* of the church in relation to universal salvation? It is best done by borrowing biblical imagery.

The church as "the messianic people" constitutes "a small flock" "set up by Christ as a communion of life, love and truth" as "a sign lifted up

---

[54] *AG*, no. 2, italics added.
[55] *RM*, no. 9.
[56] *LG*, no. 48; *GS*, no. 43; *AG*, nos. 7, 21.
[57] Cf. 1 Tim 2:4; *LG*, nos. 13–17; *RM*, no. 9.
[58] *RM*, no. 10.
[59] *RM*, no. 9; *LG*, no. 13.

among the nations"⁶⁰ to serve as "a lasting and sure seed of unity, hope and salvation for the whole human race."⁶¹ As the instrument of salvation for all, the church is sent on a mission to the whole world as "the light of the world and the salt of the earth."⁶² *Lumen Gentium* opens with the same assertion that "Christ is the Light of nations . . . a light brightly visible on the countenance of the Church."⁶³ Another New Testament image used in this context is leaven: "Being Church means being God's people, in accordance with the great plan of his fatherly love. This means that we are to be God's leaven in the midst of humanity."⁶⁴ Evangelization is, thus, the work of enlivening the world with the light, salt, and leaven of the Gospel. The *missio ecclesiae* is to make *missio Dei Trinitatis* sacramentally present to the ends of the earth and the end of time because the economy of salvation "will attain its full perfection only in the glory of heaven, when there will come *the time of the restoration of all things* . . . [when] the human race as well as the entire world, . . . will be perfectly reestablished in Christ."⁶⁵ Till then the church is a sign and sacrament of the saving action of God.

Toward a "Missional" Ecclesiology

The missionary revamping of the church that motivated Pope John XXIII to call the Second Vatican Council did not materialize, because the post–Vatican II debates got embroiled in the hierarchical-sacramental aspects of ecclesiology and fell "prey to a kind of 'ecclesial introversion.'"⁶⁶ We find a welcome change with Pope Francis, who writes in *Evangelii Gaudium*: "I dream of a 'missionary option,' that is, a missionary impulse capable of transforming everything, so that the Church's customs, ways of doing things, times and schedules, language and structures can be suitably channeled for the evangelization of today's world rather than for her

---

⁶⁰ Cf. Isa 11:12.

⁶¹ *LG*, no. 9; *RM*, no. 9.

⁶² Mt 5:13–16.

⁶³ *LG*, no. 1; see also *AG*, nos. 1, 24.

⁶⁴ *EG*, no. 114; see also *AG*, no. 15; *EG*, nos. 278 and 237.

⁶⁵ *LG*, no. 48. It is important to note that *Lumen Gentium* no. 48 appears in chapter 7 of *Lumen Gentium*, which speaks of "the Eschatological nature of the Pilgrim Church and its union with the Church in heaven."

⁶⁶ John Paul II, post-synodal apostolic exhortation *Ecclesia in Oceania* (2001), 19: *AAS* 94 (2002), 390. Quoted in *EG* no. 27 as "all renewal in the Church must have mission as its goal if it is not to fall prey to a kind of ecclesial introversion." Pope Francis states that since the church is primarily the community of missionary disciples, all renewal should be "part of an effort to make them more mission-oriented" (*EG*, no. 27).

self-preservation,"⁶⁷ so that the church can be "permanently in a state of mission."⁶⁸ Pope Francis believes that preaching the gospel is "the first task of the Church"⁶⁹ and "must remain foremost."⁷⁰ His call for "the Church's Missionary Transformation"⁷¹ is based on the conviction that "missionary outreach is paradigmatic for all the Church's activity."⁷²

Missional ecclesiology⁷³ traces its origin to a "renewed appreciation of Baptism as the basis of Christian living"⁷⁴ and holds that "Baptism constitutes the foundation of communion among all Christians, including those who are not yet in full communion with the Catholic Church."⁷⁵ In the words of Pope Francis, "In all the baptized, from first to last, the sanctifying power of the Spirit is at work, impelling us to evangelization,"⁷⁶ and, "All the members of the People of God have become missionary disciples."⁷⁷ "The mandate given by the Risen Jesus at Easter is inherent in Baptism" and "touches us personally: I am a mission, always; you are a mission, always; every baptized man and woman is a mission."⁷⁸ His assertion that "we no longer say that we are 'disciples' and 'missionaries,' but rather that we are always 'missionary disciples'"⁷⁹ stands in sharp contrast to *Redemptoris Missio*'s distinction of "leaders and workers" of mission. Mission is entrusted to each Christian in particular and to the church in general because the Holy Spirit gives charisms to every believer and every Christian community to share in the trinitarian life and mission.

Missional ecclesiology is also linked to the recovery of the primary meaning of the *apostolicity* of the church. The *apostolic* and *catholic* properties of the church in the Nicene Creed are closely connected to mission. In the words of Yves Congar, "The original sense of *apostolicity* is always

---

⁶⁷ *EG*, no. 27.
⁶⁸ *EG*, no. 25.
⁶⁹ *EG*, no. 15, quoting *RM*, no. 34.
⁷⁰ *EG*, no. 15, quoting *RM*, no. 86.
⁷¹ *EG*, no. 19; *EG*, nos. 25, 27–33.
⁷² *EG*, no. 15.
⁷³ J. Palakeel, "Missional Ecclesiology: Reflections on the Church as the Universal Sacrament of Salvation," in *Studies in Ecclesiology*, ed. J. Kudiyiruppil (Mumbai: St. Pauls, 2021), 306–33.
⁷⁴ John Paul II, *Tertio Millennio Adveniente*, no. 41.
⁷⁵ John Paul II, *Catechism of the Catholic Church* (1992), no. 1271.
⁷⁶ *EG*, no. 119.
⁷⁷ *EG*, nos. 120, 27.
⁷⁸ Pope Francis, "Baptized and Sent: The Church of Christ on the Mission in the World," Message for World Mission Day 2019 (in the context of the Extraordinary Missionary month in commemoration of the hundredth anniversary of the promulgation of the apostolic letter *Maximum Illud* [*On Mission*]).
⁷⁹ *EG*, no. 120.

connected with the *Apostolic mission* and it consists in the continuity of a unique mission from the Father, through the Son and through the Apostles."[80] However, over the centuries the *apostolic* property of the church came to be used primarily to signify the Apostolic See and the primacy of Peter and his successors, and in establishing the hierarchical and ministerial succession and legitimacy of the bishops.[81] *Apostolic* property is definitely useful in determining authenticity of doctrine and succession of bishops. However, the centralization of apostolicity solely on ecclesial hierarchical ministries and institutional aspects limited mission to those in the hierarchical-sacramental order, leaving out the vast majority of the faithful.[82] Apostolicity entails the entire people of God and not just those with a hierarchical, ministerial function. All are missionary disciples.

Mission as a Call to Communion

The triune God, who is a communion of persons, created man and woman in God's own image to be in communion with their Creator, with one another, and with the entire creation.[83] All religions in the world seek communion with God through contemplation, prayer, and rituals and promote communion among their members. The Christian faith teaches perceptibly that by creation all are children of God—and destined to

---

[80] See Yves Congar, *L'Église une, sainte, catholique, et apostolique* (Paris: Editions du Cerf, 1970), 185–89. Moltmann also considers this *apostolic* property of the church as vital to the missionary nature of the church. See Jürgen Moltmann, *The Church in the Power of the Spirit: A Contribution to Messianic Ecclesiology* (New York: Harper and Row, 1977), 358.

[81] By analyzing the usage of this notion in the history of the church, Louis-Marie Dewailly determines four different norms of usage: (1) the primitive sense in relation to the apostles, apostolic period, and apostolic churches; (2) the Roman sense in relation to Peter and the Apostolic See of Peter; (3) the medieval sense in relation to the apostolic life; and (4) the modern sense in relation to an apostolic work in the spirit of the apostles (Louis-Marie Dewailly, "Mission de l'Église et apostolicité," *Revue des Sciences Philosophiques et Théologiques* 32 [1948]: 148, 150–51).

[82] The Greek term *apostolos* (a derivative from the verb *apostello*), means "one who is sent," in the formal sense of a messenger or an ambassador. The Aramaic term *Shaliah* has the same meaning as *commissioning*. That could be the reason for reserving *apostolic* property to the church to pope and bishops only. The word *apostle* has also in the New Testament a larger meaning and denotes some inferior disciples who, under the direction of the apostles, preached the gospel or contributed to its diffusion.

[83] Gen 1:26, 27; 2:15.

communion with God. Sin disrupted the communion[84] and God sent his Son to restore the (vertical) communion with God and the (horizontal) communion among human beings[85] through his passion, death, and resurrection.[86] As Son of the Father sent into the world to reestablish the relationship between man and God, Jesus revealed "the Face of Mercy" (*Misericordiae Vultus*) of the Abba-Father, in sharp contrast to "God's judgment" preached by John the Baptist or the prophets before him. Jesus inaugurated the reign of God and invited all to enter the communion through repentance and the forgiveness of sins.

"Evangelization will always contain—as the foundation, center and at the same time the summit of its dynamism—a clear proclamation that, in Jesus Christ . . . salvation is offered to all people, as a gift of God's grace and mercy."[87] The risen Lord commissioned his disciples "that repentance and forgiveness of sins should be preached in his name to all nations."[88] To the Jews they proclaimed "the Messiah!"[89] and to the Gentiles "the Father's action" of love and mercy made visible in Jesus Christ[90] and the availability of forgiveness of sins (salvation) in "his name." Mission introduces man "into the mystery of the love of God, who invites him to enter into a personal relationship with himself in Christ."[91] This is the good news "which reveals and gives access to the mystery hidden for ages and made known in Christ"[92] and "changes man and his history, and which all peoples have a right to hear."[93]

The church is constituted as the universal sacrament of salvation, namely, a sign and instrument of communion with God and of unity among peoples of all nations, languages, and cultures. The church is God's servant in the world to manifest the mystery of God's gracious purpose for the whole of humanity and of the divine plan to gather all things together in Jesus Christ.[94] When the gospel is proclaimed and empowered by the Spirit, people who recognize the saving action of God in Jesus come to

---

[84] Gen 3:4; 11:1–9; Rom 8:18–22.

[85] 1 Pet 2:24; 1 Jn 2:1, 2.

[86] Mt 27:51; Eph 2:14–18; Jn 19:30; Rom 4:25.

[87] *EN*, no. 27; *RM*, no. 44.

[88] Lk 24:47. The great mission commission in Matthew (Mt 28:19–20), however, defines mission as "making disciples of nations," baptizing and teaching the commands of Jesus.

[89] Jn 1:41; 4:26, 39–42; Acts 9:20; cf. 22:6–21 and also *EG*, no. 120.

[90] 1 Jn 4:7–8.

[91] *AG*, no. 13; *RM*, no. 44.

[92] Cf. Eph 3:3–9; Col 1:25–29.

[93] *RM*, no. 44.

[94] Eph 1:9–10.

the mystical body of Christ in fellowship with Christ and through him with the Father[95] and with the Spirit.[96] Fellowship with Christ also brings fellowship with one another, all members of the one body,[97] expressed in common faith and worship, and in the sharing of meals and resources.[98] The church is thus the locus of visible communion, formalized through baptism, fully manifested in the Eucharist, as the destiny and vocation of all human beings according to the universal salvific will and plan of God. The Christian mission is to proclaim this truth that all human beings are people of God called to communion until all human beings enter the reign of God in an eschatological communion in the new heaven and new earth.

Conclusion

The pre–Vatican II church was assured of mission: Mission simply meant sending out missionaries to a foreign land, preaching Christianity, converting and baptizing the Gentiles, and establishing churches wherever they did not exist. In the post–Vatican II period the rise of historical consciousness and the positive recognition of other religions and cultures led to the disavowal of the dictum *extra ecclesia nulla salus* in favor of "the universal salvific will of God." The great commission still inspires missionaries, and mission is forging new paths of dialogue, inculturation, and development in the midst of the struggle to reconcile exclusivism and inclusivism, christocentrism and theocentrism, ecclesio-centrism and regno-centrism. This ambivalence is paralleled by the church's self-understanding. While the people of God ecclesiology favored a regno-centric approach with an overarching anthropological focus, communion ecclesiology returned to a modified ecclesio-centric approach with an emphasis on the hierarchical-sacramental dimensions of mission. Both these trends are discernible in church documents as well as church praxis. We are progressively aware of the limits of missiology rooted in ecclesiology in all areas of the church *ad extra,* in ecumenism as well as in relation to other religions and cultures. In this sense, neither regno-centrism nor ecclesio-centrism captures the full

---

[95] 1 Jn 1:3.
[96] 2 Cor 13:14.
[97] Rom 12:5; Gal 3:28.
[98] Acts 2:44–7; 2 Cor 8:1–15.

richness and depth of *missio Dei Trinitatis*. The way forward is to adopt a mission-centered ecclesiology, or a *missional* ecclesiology.

The comprehension of mission in Catholic theology has undergone a major shift from *missio ecclesiae* to *missio Dei Trinitatis* in the post–Vatican II period. *Missio Dei Trinitatis* relativizes the mutually exclusive dyads of exclusivism/inclusivism, ecclesiocentrism/regno-centrism, and christocentrism/theocentrism, and renders meaningless the looming dispute over how to name mission: *missio ad gentes* or *inter gentes* or *cum gentibus*. Mission is not merely an activity of Christians toward non-Christians (*ad gentes*), but the perpetuation of the trinitarian mission directed to the whole of humanity. Salvation is a free gift of God in Jesus Christ to all human beings. "The mandate given by the Risen Jesus at Easter is inherent in Baptism: as the Father has sent me, so I send you, filled with the Holy Spirit, for the reconciliation of the world."[99] The whole of humanity constitutes the people of God called to the communion designated by Jesus as the reign of God. *Missio Dei Trinitatis* integrates well the universal salvific will of God with the role of the church as the universal sacrament of salvation: "What in the Christian is a sacramental reality—whose fulfillment is found in the Eucharist—remains the vocation and destiny of every man and woman in search of conversion and salvation."[100]

The church, as "the chosen people of God" and the "visible communion," is entrusted with the task of making the reality of the reign of God present through witness, dialogue, development, and inculturation. And every Christian, as a person who has heard the good news, has the responsibility to share it with others out of charity so that all human beings can have fellowship with the Father through the economy of the Son and the Spirit: "By proclaiming God's Word, bearing witness to the Gospel and celebrating the life of the Spirit, they summon to conversion, baptize and offer Christian salvation, with respect for the freedom of each person and in dialogue with the cultures and religions of the peoples to whom they are sent."[101] However, the church often gets stuck on the "paths of mission,"[102] vacillating between ecclesial and anthropological fixations rather than empowering men and women to realize their vocation to be adoptive children of the Father. Consequently, there exists among missionaries and among missionary congregations a reticence to

---

[99] Pope Francis, *Baptized and Sent: The Church of Christ on Mission in the World* (Message for World Mission Day, 2019), 1; cf. Jn 20:19–23; Mt 28:16–20.

[100] Pope Francis, *Baptized and Sent*, 2.

[101] Pope Francis, *Baptized and Sent*, 3.

[102] *RM*, nos. 41–60 (chapter V, "The Paths of Mission").

talk about the importance of the communion between God and human beings. Mission is a call to come into communion with God and with one another by accepting the reign of God.

Joseph Scaria Palakeel, MST, is a member of the Society of Saint Thomas the Apostle and director of studies at the Ruhalaya College of Theology, Ujjain, India. He holds a doctorate in theology from the Gregorian University, Rome. His latest publication is *Evangelizing Mission: The Role and Relevance of Missionary Societies and Congregations in Evangelization and New Evangelization* (editor, 2018).

Theological Evolution in Mission
A Theology of Mission

Stephen B. Bevans, SVD

When the director of SEDOS, Fr. Peter Baekelmans, CICM, contacted me about this SEDOS mission symposium, he wrote: "We would like to invite you to write an essay on 'Theology of Mission,'" and the tentative overview of the program he sent me had in parentheses "Mission theological evolutions." I hope what I offer here will answer this request adequately. What I present will not be *the* theology of mission—something definitive—but rather *a* theology of mission, one that I think has evolved in the last several decades, and one that in these last years has had the imprint of the thought of Pope Francis. It is also one that I personally espouse.

I believe that the way the theology of mission has evolved is still rooted in the theology of the *missio Dei* or the mission of our triune God, but that the content of that mission needs to be imagined within a context of cosmic and biological evolution that offers the promise to change all our theology very profoundly. Because of this context, mission has to be understood and practiced in a radically holistic way, for the goal of mission has to be the completion of creation as the full flourishing of humankind and other kinds alike. Mission has to touch the spiritual yearning of humankind, but it also has to embrace human bodies, many of which are oppressed and suffering, as well as the bodies and reality of all creatures—living and inanimate. We Christians have been called and chosen by God to share in this mission as transforming, missionary disciples of the Word that share the stuff of creation, and we are called to do it by the practice of a continuing prophetic dialogue, deeply rooted in spirituality and contemplation.

The first part of my essay, therefore, focuses on mission as the completion of creation, as Christians are caught up in the missionary life of God through faith in God's Word made flesh by the power of the Holy Spirit.

The second part reflects on the diverse ways in which mission needs to be practiced. Mission, though one single reality, has many different dimensions, all of which are constitutive of it. The third part sketches out an understanding of transforming, missionary discipleship, and the fourth and final part lays out the basic shape and method of prophetic dialogue. This is, to my mind, one way that the theology of mission has evolved in the last several decades, and certainly since the renewal of mission thinking marked by the Second Vatican Council.

Mission as the Completion of Creation

The theology of mission today must begin with the mission of the triune God, and God's mission begins at the very first moment of the creation of the universe. Ultimately, as we shall see, Christian mission is about human partnership with God in the completion of creation, working with God to realize God's dream of the harmony and radical kinship of every creature, every particle of creation, with one another.

To be God is to be totally self-emptying. This is the point of—in our stuttering theological language—the "processions" in trinitarian theology. The Mystery at the center of Reality eternally empties Godself into the Word, who responds with self-emptying as well. The mutual love of Mystery and Word breathes forth the Holy Spirit, who in turn breathes that love back to both. We only know this, however, because these processions empty themselves out in creation—in mission—as God "makes space" for otherness, and fills it with the Spirit and the Word. Some theologians conceive of this divine self-emptying as a kind of "voluntary limitation" of divine power. With Elizabeth Johnson, however, I argue that God's power is expressed most fully in God's ability to "stand back" and empower creation through the inviting, prodding, pushing, pulling, luring power of the Spirit and the Word *within* creation. God acts with the omnipotence of love. As God begins and continues God's mission, "not the monarch but the lover becomes the paradigm."[1]

Mission, therefore, God's self-emptying and gifting of freedom to creation as God, through the Spirit and the Word, works toward the full freedom and mutual relationship of all that exists and is coming to be. This is what we see in the history of salvation. From the first nanosecond

---

[1] Elizabeth A. Johnson, *Ask the Beasts: Darwin and the God of Love* (London: Bloomsbury, 2014), 159. These sentences summarize Johnson's argument on pages 154–69.

of creation, God's Spirit and Word have been present in God's universe. This is beautifully expressed in the biblical narrative of creation, as the Spirit of God blows over the waters of chaos, broods over them like a mother bird over her nest, and out of the chaos God speaks, bringing all into order (Gen 1:1–3).

The Genesis passage, of course, summarizes in beautiful, mythic poetry what science identifies as billions and billions of years of cosmic and then biological evolution. From the perspective of Christian faith, Australian Denis Edwards writes,

> As particles of hydrogen and helium separated out from radiation and formed the first atoms, as the clouds of gas composed to form the first generation of galaxies, as the universe was lit up by the first stars, it was the Spirit of God who breathed life into the whole process.[2]

The Spirit "was at work as Earth began to form around the young Sun 4.5 billion years ago, as the first bacterial life emerged on the new planet 3.8 billion years ago, as simple cells became more complex and multicellular creatures emerged, as life forms developed wonderfully in the seas, as life moved onto the land, and as mammals and then hominid species evolved."[3] The Spirit was at work, too, together with the Word (the *Logos*) as a "secret presence," when emerging humans began to question and experience transcendence in their lives, and the first forms of religion began to appear among various peoples.[4]

One of these peoples was God's Chosen People, Israel, which had its origin in God's call to Abraham and Sarah (as they were eventually named[5]), who promised them that in them "all the families of the earth shall bless themselves."[6] In the sacred writings of this people, the Spirit of God is described in several graphic but illusive images, such as a breath and wind that brings life to living creatures[7] and dramatically to a valley

---

[2] Denis Edwards, *Breath of Life: A Theology of the Creator Spirit* (Maryknoll, NY: Orbis Books, 2004), 172.

[3] Ibid.

[4] Vatican Council II, *Decree on the Church's Missionary Activity (Ad Gentes)* (hereinafter *AG*), in Austin Flannery, ed., *Vatican Council II: Constitutions, Decrees, Declarations*, nos. 9, 4. See also John Paul II, *Redemptoris Missio*, nos. 28–29.

[5] Gen 17:5, 15.

[6] Gen 12:3.

[7] Gen 2:7; Job 33:4.

of dry bones;[8] oil that anoints prophets to speak God's word;[9] water that gives refreshment and vitality;[10] and Lady Wisdom, who gives people understanding,[11] and who roams through the streets of cities, calling for repentance.[12] Wisdom—*sophia*—is often connected with Word—*logos*—as the Spirit and the Word continue to be intertwined. Their close connection would be expressed in the prologue to the Gospel of John. In these images we see God emptying Godself in mission: "the gracious, furious mystery of God engaged in a dialectic of presence and absence throughout the world, creating, indwelling, sustaining, resisting, challenging, guiding, liberating, compelling."[13]

Then, "in the fullness of time,"[14] the self-emptying mystery that is God took on a human face in the Person of Jesus of Nazareth. In him, the Word became flesh.[15] Not *although* he was God but *because* he was God, he emptied himself, as Michael J. Gorman argues.[16] And so he was conceived through the power of the Holy Spirit,[17] the same Spirit that would anoint him at his baptism "to preach good news to the poor . . . to proclaim release to the captives . . . recovery of sight to the blind . . . to set at liberty those who are oppressed, and to proclaim the year of the Lord's favor."[18] These words from the Gospel of Luke are expressed by Mark in terms of the kingdom or reign of God.[19] Jesus after his baptism calls women and men to repent—not to feel bad, but to think differently. The reign of God is about reimagining the world, relationships, and God. It is an invitation to "radical kinship," "radical intimacy" with sisters and brothers, and with a merciful and loving God.[20] It is God's dream for the completion of creation. It is the purpose of God's mission.

---

[8] Ezek 37:1–14.

[9] 1 Sam 16:13; Isa 61:1–2.

[10] Isa 33:21; 35:6–7; Ezek 47:1–12.

[11] Wis 9:17.

[12] Prov 1:20–33.

[13] Elizabeth A. Johnson, *She Who Is: The Mystery of God in Feminist Theological Discourse* (New York: Crossroad, 1992), 133.

[14] Gal 4:4.

[15] Jn 1:14.

[16] Michael J. Gorman, *Becoming the Gospel: Paul, Participation, and Mission* (Grand Rapids, MI: Eerdmans, 2015), 107n.6.

[17] Lk 1:35.

[18] Lk 4:18–19.

[19] Mk 1:15.

[20] Gregory Boyle, *Barking to the Choir: The Power of Radical Kinship* (New York: Simon and Schuster, 2017); and Willie James Jennings, *Acts* (Nashville, TN: Abingdon, 2017), 29.

Jesus's mission was to embody, demonstrate, proclaim, and illustrate this radical kinship and intimacy.[21] He was, in the words of theologian Mark Oakley, "God's body language,"[22] revealing God and God's mission by his Spirit-led life of inclusion and table fellowship, his love of the poor and the marginalized, and his leadership of a community of equals.[23] He demonstrated the power of God's reign by his acts of healing and exorcism, revealing God's healing and liberating grace as both spiritual and physical. He proclaimed and illustrated the message of God's reign in language of striking paradox (*the grain that dies to live*[24]) and lively, consoling, and challenging parables that spoke of God's extravagance in forgiving[25] and inclusion.[26]

But Jesus's mission was dangerous. Israel was an occupied country, and Jesus's call for conversion in the light of the kingdom's radical intimacy and equality caught the eye of the Romans, no doubt, and certainly the authorities like Herod, and the religious leaders in Galilee and Jerusalem, who were cooperating with them. Jesus's kingdom message, notes Elizabeth Johnson, did not explicitly call for an open rebellion against Rome, but this did not mean that Jesus's personal behavior, healing ministry, and subversive teaching were not perceived as menacing. On the contrary, "preaching the hope of God's coming kingdom with its new order of peace and justice put the current order under threat."[27] Particularly when Jesus entered Jerusalem,[28] such a threat, in the eyes of the occupiers and their collaborators, became a clear possibility.

> The crowds heralded Jesus as the hoped-for messiah. What a challenge to imperial dominion. . . . Any Roman colonial governor worth his salt would want to discourage the possibility.[29]

---

[21] For a fuller description of what follows, see Stephen B. Bevans, SVD, "Committed to His Mission," in *Becoming Intercultural: Perspectives on Mission*, ed. Lazar T. Stanislaus, SVD, and Christian Tauchner, SVD (Sankt Augustin, Germany: Steyler Missionswissenschaftliches Institut / New Delhi, India: ISPCK, 2021), 37–47.

[22] Mark Oakley, *The Collage of God*, 2nd ed. (Norwich, UK: Canterbury Press, 2012), 25, 27.

[23] See Antonio M. Pernia, *The Eucharist and Our Mission*, Following the Word 7 (Rome: SVD Publications, 1996), 38; Elisabeth Schüssler Fiorenza, *In Memory of Her: A Feminist Reconstruction of Christian Origins* (New York: Crossroad, 1983).

[24] Jn 12:24.

[25] Lk 15.

[26] Lk 10:25–37.

[27] Elizabeth A. Johnson, *Creation and the Cross: The Mercy of God for a Planet in Peril* (Maryknoll, NY: Orbis Books, 2018), 93.

[28] Mt 21:1–11; Mk 11:1–11; Lk 19:28–38; Jn 12:12–19.

[29] Johnson, *Creation and the Cross*, 91.

And so in the "tinderbox" in which Jesus lived, getting Jesus out of the way would be a "prudent Roman response."[30] And so they killed him—a brutal state execution that was both shameful and excruciatingly painful. In the process of his arrest and trial all his disciples deserted him. Only John recounts that Jesus's mother, Mary, the "beloved disciple" (John), and a few other women were standing by the cross.[31] Matthew and Mark record that only women looked on from a distance;[32] Luke reports that "all his acquaintances" as well as women looked on—but also from a distance.[33] God's mission in Jesus seemed to end in a sad and sorry failure.

But in faith, we know it did not. Days after Jesus's death and burial his scattered, discouraged disciples experienced him as alive, offering them the same mercy, despite their desertion, that he had offered to so many others during his life. But not only that. He was now sharing that mission of mercy and inclusion with them, as he lavished the same Spirit lavished on him at his baptism:

> Peace be with you. As the Father has sent me, even so I send you.
> . . . Receive the Holy Spirit. If you forgive the sins of any, they are forgiven; if you retain the sins of any, they are retained.[34]

The same Spirit's coming, as Luke narrates in Acts 2, comes upon them in power, and the whole of the Acts of the Apostles is the story of that Spirit transforming the community in ways they never expected, and even at first resisted. Luke's aim in Acts is to show that the Jesus community after the resurrection is empowered by the Spirit to share and continue Jesus's mission of embodying, demonstrating, and proclaiming the reign of God's "radical intimacy" in all cultures and nations until the end of time.[35] The church becomes the church as it opens up to the Spirit's guidance in mission. The church is indeed "by its very nature missionary," a "community of missionary disciples."[36] Like the triune God in whom its

---

[30] Paula Frederiksen, *From Jesus to Christ* (New Haven, CT: Yale University Press, 2000), 125, quoted in Johnson, *Creation and the Cross*, 93.

[31] Jn 19:25–27.

[32] Mt 27:55–56; Mk 15:40–41.

[33] Lk 23:49.

[34] Jn 20:21, 23.

[35] For a detailed narrative of how this transformation comes about, see Stephen B. Bevans and Roger P. Schroeder, *Constants in Context: A Theology of Mission for Today* (Maryknoll, NY: Orbis Books, 2004), 10–31.

[36] *AG*, no. 2; See also, Pope Francis, *Evangelii Gaudium* (hereafter *EG*), no. 24.

mission is rooted, the church becomes the church as it empties itself in service to the world, partnering with God in the completion of creation.

Mission as a Single but Complex Activity

Understanding the mission as sharing in God's dream for the completion of creation opens it up to much more than working to expand the church, saving women and men from eternal damnation, or calling them to conversion to Christianity. Reading Vatican II's *Decree on the Church's Mission Activity (Ad Gentes),* about how mission combines the two classic schools of missiology, seems out of date today. Mission is more than "the evangelization and the implanting of the church among peoples or groups in which it has not yet taken root."[37] These activities are not futile or mistaken ones, but they are not at the heart of what participating in God's mission is all about. Mission is about sharing and continuing Jesus's mission of embodying, demonstrating, and proclaiming God's reign, and as Pope Paul VI argues, that work cannot be reduced to any one single activity.[38] In his great apostolic exhortation *Evangelii Nuntiandi*, Pope Paul VI certainly emphasizes the clear and confident witnessing to and preaching of Christ, but he also includes the importance of what the Vatican calls "human promotion" and even action for human and societal liberation, and for an evangelization that pays close attention to human cultures.

In 1981, a landmark meeting of this body—SEDOS—noted four "principal activities" of the church's mission: proclamation, dialogue, inculturation, and the liberation of the poor.[39] In other statements by Roman Catholics, Conciliar Protestants, and even Evangelicals, mission began to be understood more widely to contain a number of elements, many of which pointed to a more holistic understanding.[40] My colleague Eleanor Doidge and I, and then later and more expansively, Roger Schroeder and I, offered a synthesis of missionary thinking and practice at the end of the twentieth and beginning of the twenty-first centuries: mission was about witness and proclamation; liturgy, prayer, and contemplation; justice,

---

[37] *AG*, no. 6.

[38] Pope Paul VI, *Evangelii Nuntiandi*, no. 17.

[39] Mary Motte, FMM, and Joseph R. Lang, MM, eds., *Mission in Dialogue: The Sedos Research Seminar on the Future of Mission, March 8—19, 1981, Rome, Italy* (Maryknoll, NY: Orbis Books, 1982), 634; see also, "Agenda for Future Planning, Study, and Research in Mission," in *Trends in Mission: Toward the Third Millennium*, ed. William Jenkinson and Helene O'Sullivan, 399–414 (Maryknoll, NY: Orbis Books, 1991).

[40] See Bevans and Schroeder, *Constants in Context*, 350–51.

peace, and the integrity of creation; interreligious, ecumenical, and secular dialogue; inculturation; and reconciliation.[41] Pope Francis has certainly confirmed this multifaceted idea of mission in his writings, especially in his great apostolic exhortation *Evangelii Gaudium*, and we find that many of these themes are treated in the present SEDOS mission symposium.

While proclaiming the gospel is still the "foundation, summit, and center of evangelization,"[42] it can only be done faithfully and effectively "wherever God opens a door of speech"[43] and when the church that proclaims it is truly credible in a particular context. The church grows only "by being attractive."[44] This is why, when we reflected on the mission of Jesus earlier in this presentation we began with Jesus's Person, his embodiment of the gospel/kingdom message. "The Witness of an authentically Christian life," insists Pope Paul VI, is "the first means of evangelization"[45]—individually, communally, institutionally. But that witness is included and bolstered up by a real demonstration of what God's dream is and can be: a community dedicated to prayer and beautiful liturgy, Christians committed to, and willing to, suffer for justice and peace in the world, learning from and being evangelized by the poor,[46] and ready to sacrifice themselves to preserve our "common home,"[47] women and men dedicated to dialogue with other religious people, other Christians, and unbelievers of good will, people convinced of the possibility and necessity of reconciliation at the personal, societal, and ecclesial levels. In Pope Francis's stunning phrase, mission is truly about getting our shoes "soiled by the mud of the street."[48] As we do all this, we tell the world the amazing story of God emptying Godself in love, showing divine omnipotence best in mercy,[49] revealing Godself in the "leftovers" of this world,[50] revealing Godself fully in an innocent man crucified between two thieves. We do this with a

---

[41] Stephen Bevans and Eleanor Doidge, "Theological Reflection," in *Reflection and Dialogue: What Mission Confronts Religious Life Today?* ed. Barbara Kraemer (Chicago: Center for the Study of Religious Life, 2000), 48; Bevans and Schroeder, *Constants in Context*, 348–98.

[42] Pontifical Council for Interreligious Dialogue and Pontifical Congregation for Evangelization, *Dialogue and Proclamation*, in *Redemption and Dialogue: Reading* Redemptoris Missio *and* Dialogue and Proclamation, ed. William R. Burrows (Eugene, OR: Wipf & Stock, 1993), no. 10.

[43] AG 13.

[44] *EG*, no. 14.

[45] *EG*, no. 41.

[46] Cf. *EG*, no. 198.

[47] Pope Francis, *Laudato Si'*, no. 17.

[48] *EG*, no. 45.

[49] *EG*, no. 37, quoting Thomas Aquinas, *Summa Theologiae* II.II, 30, ad 4.

[50] *EG*, nos. 37, 53.

sensitivity to context and culture, with the conviction that God's Spirit is already present in every place and people to which missionaries go and among whom missionaries live.[51] We do this with deep respect, with imagination, and with "daring prudence."[52]

Empowered by the same Spirit and divine Word present and spoken at creation, Christians empty themselves in service to God's world, working with God to bring it to completion.

Mission as Discipleship

Drawing on his experience at the Latin American Bishops' Conference 2007 meeting in Aparecida, Brazil, Pope Francis has spoken of the church as "a community of missionary disciples."[53] Drawing on Pope Francis's phrase and reflecting on the implications of its 2013 document on mission, *Together towards Life*, the World Council of Churches' (WCC) Conference on World Mission and Evangelism dedicated its 2018 world mission conference in Arusha, Tanzania, to the theme of transforming discipleship. At this conference, the assembly issued a document entitled "The Arusha Call to Discipleship," and several documents afterward deepened the notion of discipleship in significant ways.[54] In his important commentary on the "Arusha Call," Kenneth Ross spoke of discipleship as the "game changer" that could bring about the transformation that mission needs today.[55] Discipleship—Transforming / Missionary Discipleship[56]—has emerged as a way of naming how Christians can partner with God in bringing about the completion of the creation of radical kinship in God's reign.

Pope Francis emphasizes that all Christians are missionary disciples in virtue of their baptism:

---

[51] *AG*, no. 11; Vatican Council II, *Pastoral Constitution on the Church in the Modern World (Gaudium et Spes)*, in Flannery, *Vatican Council II*, no. 22.

[52] Pope Francis, Homily at the Opening of the Pan-Amazonian Synod, October 6, 2019.

[53] *EG*, no. 24.

[54] Conference on World Mission and Evangelism, *Together towards Life: Mission and Evangelism in Changing Landscapes*, ed. Jooseop Keum (Geneva: WCC, 2013). See also "The Arusha Call to Discipleship" and "Conference on World Mission and Evangelism Report," *International Review of Mission* 107, no. 2 (December 2018): 542–43, 547–60. The entire issue offers further reflections on the conference and on the notion of transforming discipleship.

[55] Kenneth Ross, *Mission Rediscovered: Transforming Disciples, A Commentary on the Arusha Call to Discipleship* (Geneva: WCC and Globalethics.net, 2020), 10.

[56] See Stephen Bevans, "Theologies of Mission," in the *Oxford Companion to Mission Studies* (Oxford: Oxford University Press, 2022).

> All the baptized, whatever their position in the Church or their level of instruction in the faith, are agents of evangelization, and it would be insufficient to envisage the plan of evangelization to be carried out by professionals while the rest of the faithful would simply be passive recipients.[57]

This coincides with the thinking of several contemporary theologians who emphasize the idea of discipleship as a way of speaking about the fundamental equality of all Christians, and their call to ministry and mission. Kathleen Cahalan, for example, in her brilliant book on ministry, writes about how all disciples are followers, worshipers, witnesses, neighbors, forgivers, prophets, and stewards. To be a disciple, in other words, is to be engaged in the "single but complex reality" of the church's mission that we outlined above.[58] Discipleship is the foundation for ministry, but ministers of any kind, including those ordained, never lose their identity as disciples and are always responsible for the growth and development of their fundamental missionary identity. Discipleship might hold the promise of getting away from the dichotomy created by the terms *lay* and *clerical*.[59] A deeper understanding of discipleship might be a key to develop the sense of synodality that Pope Francis and the October 2022 synod on synodality is calling for. To be a true community of missionary disciples, the church must be a listening church, listening to all the voices of gender, generations, responsibilities, both in and outside itself. Working to become a true community of disciples might be a way to witness the radical intimacy that God is dreaming of for creation.

The report on the WCC's Arusha Conference reflected on three ways in which discipleship is transforming. In the first place, it says, "the very idea of discipleship needs to be transformed." It is far from being a cozy relationship with Jesus, but "a matter of being actively engaged in continuing Jesus's mission in the world." In this regard it is close to Pope Francis's idea of missionary discipleship. Second, being disciples means being persons who are committed to transformation as the Spirit guides them in new and perhaps surprising ways. Discipleship is *personally* transforming. Discipleship means living within a community of faith that shapes its

---

[57] *EG*, no. 120.

[58] Kathleen Cahalan, *Introducing the Practice of Ministry* (Collegeville, MN: Liturgical Press, 2010), 1–23.

[59] This is what I proposed in an essay on priesthood. See Stephen Bevans, "Ordained Discipleship," in *Priestly Ministry and the People of God,* ed. Richard R. Gaillardetz, Thomas Groome, and Richard Lennan (Maryknoll, NY: Orbis Books, 2022).

members by liturgy, prayer, challenge, and support. The Arusha Conference, the report notes, spoke of discipleship as being "Christ-connected"—a novel, rather controversial expression, the newness of which might open our eyes in new ways to discipleship, with strong overtones of being a member of Christ's body, and points to our mutual relationship with him as well. Discipleship connects us to Christ, but it also connects Christ to us. A third aspect of discipleship that surfaced at Arusha was that it is a call to transform the world. "True discipleship creates a movement of resistance and hope, countering the death-dealing forces of our time and discovering the fullness of life."[60]

A transforming, missionary discipleship sheds a guiding light on how we as Christians can participate in the self-emptying, freedom-respecting mission of God to bring creation to completeness. We are *partners*, but partners who are disciples—disciples of Jesus who are transformed by the Spirit to share in God's missionary life, disciples of Jesus who grow in our connectedness to him and his mission, disciples of Jesus who "re-present" him in transforming the world.

Mission as Prophetic Dialogue

We exercise our discipleship through the practice of prophetic dialogue. "Prophetic dialogue" is a phrase that had its origin in the General Chapter of my religious congregation, the Society of the Divine Word, in the year 2000, but over the last two decades it has caught on as a fresh and powerful way to speak about missionary thinking and practice.[61]

As I have developed it in the last few years, prophetic dialogue arises out of a deep spirituality and habit of contemplation. *It is a way that disciples discern what God is doing in the world and joining in*, to allude to a wonderful

---

[60] Conference on World Mission and Evangelism, *Together towards Life*, 551–52.

[61] See, for example, Bevans and Schroeder, *Constants in Context*; José Antunes da Silva, *Prophetic Dialogue: Identity and Mission of the Divine Word Missionaries* (Siegburg, Germany: Franz Schmitt Verlag, 2021); Rosalia Meza, *Toward a New Praxis-Oriented Missiology: Rediscovering Paulo Freire's Concept of* Conscientizaçao *and Enhancing Christian Mission as Prophetic Dialogue* (Eugene, OR: Pickwick Publications, 2020); Bradford E. Hinze, *Prophetic Obedience: Ecclesiology for a Dialogical Church* (Maryknoll, NY: Orbis Books, 2016); Tim Noble, *Mission from the Perspective of the Other: Drawing Together on Holy Ground* (Eugene, OR: Pickwick Publications, 2018); Cathy Ross and Stephen Bevans, eds., *Mission on the Road to Emmaus: Constants, Context, and Prophetic Dialogue* (Maryknoll, NY: Orbis Books, 2015); Bevans, "Theologies of Mission."

phrase of former Archbishop of Canterbury Rowan Williams.[62] It can be done by a disciple alone, but it is best done in community, in a spirit of mutual trust where everyone is convinced that "everyone has a piece of wisdom," a different piece, but an important piece.[63] Through reflecting, praying, and discussing—even arguing—together, a community engages in a real exercise of contextual theologizing, examining a particular situation or locality, connecting the situation with the theological tradition and missiological insights, and then coming to a decision for action. This dialogue is the first step in the process of prophetic dialogue. The goal of this dialogue is to discover what kind of prophetic action needs to be taken in the light of what God is already doing or is calling to be done.

It may be that the community's dialogue would result in a decision to engage in an attitude or a practice of dialogue—a truly prophetic act in some situations. Such a decision might be to initiate or continue a "dialogue of life," in the context of where the community does mission—being present and available to the people among whom it works. Or it might mean a dialogue of action as the community works with people of other faiths or no faith in meeting the needs of the local community—food banks, clinics, counseling services, for example. Or it might mean discovering together the riches of one another's beliefs and spirituality.

But other decisions of prophetic action might be the result of the basic dialogue of reflection and discernment. It might be offering words and actions of hope in almost hopeless situations, like those in areas of violence, or after natural disasters, or in times like the current COVID-19 pandemic. It might mean making sure people receive accurate information—a real service in some situations where misinformation or a narrative of the lie is prevalent. It might mean standing up to injustice and greed, or working for a more equitable distribution of wealth, or, today, working for the equitable distribution of vaccines. Perhaps in some situations, if the Spirit "opens a door" to the proclamation of the gospel, this may be the prophetic action in which the community decides to engage. When we do this, however, we have to make sure that the message we offer is contextually relevant and faithfully expressed. As we dialogue together, we will discern where God's Spirit is working so we can join in, and the Spirit will guide us in our participation. In what was probably his last written article, Robert Schreiter, CPPS—a participant in many of these SEDOS

---

[62] Rowan Williams, cited in Kirsteen Kim, *Joining in with the Spirit: Connecting World Church and Local Mission* (London: Epworth Press, 2009), 1.

[63] Mary Benet McKinney, *Shared Wisdom: A Process for Group Decision Making* (Valencia, CA: Tabor, 1987).

seminars—emphasized that prophetic dialogue was more than trying to reconcile two ways of doing mission, where some emphasize a dialogical stance and others emphasize either an evangelistic or prophetic liberation stance. Rather, he writes, prophetic dialogue "represents something that must characterize any missionary discourse when living between the times in search of deep transformation."[64] Such times, certainly, are our own.

Conclusion

A theology of mission for today must be rooted in God's mission, God's dream of bringing to completion the creation of God's world. That mission, the work of the Spirit and the Word made flesh, is shared in a particular way with Christians, as they take up the mantle of Jesus of Nazareth as his disciples. Discipleship is a transforming, missionary discipleship, rooted in a spirituality of discernment and contemplation, searching for faithful and relevant prophetic action in union with the missionary God.

> **Stephen Bevans, SVD,** is a priest of the Society of the Divine Word and professor emeritus of mission and culture at the Catholic Theological Union in Chicago. He has edited and written some twenty books, many of which Orbis Books has published. He is a member of the World Council of Churches' Commission on World Mission and Evangelism.

---

[64] Robert J. Schreiter, "Locating European Mission in a Wounded World in Deep Transformation," *Mission Studies* 37 (2020): 342.

Pope Francis and Mission

A Call to Hear the Crying Existential Peripheries

Paul Béré, SJ

As leader of the Catholic faithful, Pope Francis has been calling the whole community to become missionary disciples. The call to mission rings somehow unusual for some parts of the world. The gospel message has reached almost the whole world. Western churches with ancient Christian traditions, and fewer human resources to send abroad, have thus far accomplished a great deal. For younger churches, as in Africa in particular, St. Paul VI's address in Kampala, in July 1969, still resounds as a relevant call: "By now, you Africans are missionaries to yourselves." For all, the growing phenomenon of secularization in some parts of the world signals that the faith experience should not be taken for granted. The inflation of popular religious practices in the Global South calls for depth. In response, Pope Benedict XVI convened a synod of bishops in 2012 to reflect on the "new evangelization for the transmission of the Christian faith." But a few months later, comes on the scene Pope Francis, a member of a missionary religious institute, the Society of Jesus. He repeatedly invited the church to "go out," to become a church in mission. What does it mean? What is the understanding of mission the pope proposes in his frequent use of the term? Is this the real and most important issue for the Catholic Church of our times?

In order to unpack the significance of Pope Francis's insistence on leading the whole church on the path of mission discipleship, I propose that we consider his voice as a prophetic one, recognized as such by his fellow bishops who chose him for the seat of Rome. By *prophetic* I mean that Francis's call to mission resonates with the expectations and needs of a church that entered the twenty-first century with wounds and in need of healing. *Mission* thus becomes the means. To illustrate my point, I would like to tell the story of a young religious in crisis. He went to a senior fellow Jesuit to share his pains and suffering in his experience of community life, apostolic activities, and so on. As a response, the senior Jesuit invited him to visit the sick in a nearby hospital. When they came back, he asked his young fellow: "What have you seen? How do you feel about what you have seen?" The young man confessed that this experience de-centered him from himself and re-centered him on those most in need. He felt his spirit replete with strength and energy. This real life story could work as a parable to understand Pope Francis's "mission appeal."

In order to spell out the elements of that call, I suggest that we first take a close look at the state of the church on the eve of the new pontificate, and with the eyes of Cardinal Jorge Bergoglio. Second, I examine Pope Francis's understanding of mission as a solution to a church meant to be journeying. Third, I contemplate the church of missionary disciples as Pope Francis dreams it.

The Church in Search of a New Breath

During the first decade of the twenty-first century, the Catholic Church was walking on a *via dolorosa*. The eruption of the scandals on sexual abuse weakened a faith community that was struggling against secularism and relativism. The challenge became even daunting when papal confidential documents were seemingly leaked to the press by Vatican insiders. Amid the turmoil came the renunciation of Pope Benedict XVI, which ushered in a new dawn for the papacy.[1]

Who Will Lead through the Whirlwind?

On the cusp of the 2012 synod on the "new evangelization," not only was the relation of the church with the world shaken by scandals (sexual abuse, the butler's "Vatileaks" trial, and so on), but the preparatory document's declaration that "now is the time for a new evangelization in the West" seemed to have frustrated other parts of the church. The issues on the agenda were to some extent pertinent to the global church: secularism and relativism, fundamentalism, sects, the economy, politics, migration, and so forth. The institution had actually entered a storm or a whirlwind, and the synod preparatory documents were calling for "the courage to speak out against infidelity and scandal which arise in Christian communities

---

[1] Pope Francis has been described as the "first" in many aspects (first from Latin America; first Jesuit; first pope to be called Francis after the Italian saint of Assisi; and so on).

as a sign and consequence of moments of fatigue and weariness in the work of proclamation. Other fruits include: the courage to recognize and admit faults; the capacity to continue to witness to Jesus Christ, while recounting our continual need to be saved."[2]

Meanwhile, Pope Benedict XVI had to lead an institution under the fire of both the media and politically motivated groups of oppression with their own agenda. Within the church there were those who clung to their traditions and those who were asking for an institution apace with the world.[3] The leaks seemed to have been the straw that broke the camel's back. The pope did not feel strong enough to sail the church through waves that spread the overall impression of a confusion. The words of the preparatory documents of the synod pointed to the right direction, judging from today's perspective. And yet, the synod was not effective enough to appease the world. The collegial body's "failure" meant that the wound was deeper. Then comes the renunciation of Pope Benedict XVI on February 10, 2013, expressed in the following words:

> After having repeatedly examined my conscience before God, I have come to the certainty that my strengths, due to an advanced age, are no longer suited to an adequate exercise of the Petrine ministry. I am well aware that this ministry, due to its essential spiritual nature, must be carried out not only with words and deeds, but no less with prayer and suffering. However, in today's world, subject to so many rapid changes and shaken by questions of deep relevance for the life of faith, in order to govern the barque of St. Peter and proclaim the Gospel, both strength of mind and body are necessary, strength which in the last few months, has deteriorated in me to the extent that I have had to recognize my incapacity to adequately fulfill the ministry entrusted to me. For this reason, and well aware of the seriousness of this act, with full freedom I declare that I renounce the ministry of the Bishop of Rome, Successor of St. Peter, entrusted to me by the Cardinals on 19 April 2005.[4]

The last words of Pope Benedict in office captured well enough the dramatic situation in which the church has to "proclaim the gospel." The question arises: Who will take the lead?

---

[2] Synod of Bishops, XIII Ordinary General Assembly, *Lineamenta*, no. 17.
[3] See Benedict XVI, *Light of the World, The Pope, the Church, and the Signs of the Times. A Conversation with Peter Seewald* (San Francisco: Ignatius Press, 2010).
[4] Pope Benedict XVI, "Declaratio," February 10, 2013.

Cardinal Bergoglio's Proposal

During the meetings preceding the election, the cardinals discussed issues pertaining to the state of the church in today's world. The interventions were not intended to be published, but luckily Cardinal Jorge Bergoglio's speech struck a chord with (at least) the archbishop of San Cristobal of La Havana (Cuba), Cardinal Jaime Ortega, who requested a written form from the speaker and permission thereafter to publish it.[5] The text gives us access to what was running through the mind of Pope Francis on the eve of his election. In addition, the four-point note can serve as a hermeneutical tool to understand Francis's insistent call to become a church in mission.

On the specific question of the profile of the new leader, in the current circumstances of the church, Cardinal Bergoglio shared the following words:

> Thinking of the next Pope: a man who, through the contemplation of Jesus Christ and the adoration of Jesus Christ, may help the Church to go out from itself toward the existential peripheries, that may help it to be the fecund mother who lives "by the sweet and comforting joy of evangelizing."[6]

Two elements stand out in Bergoglio's vision to help the church to weather the storm waves: (1) the need to help "the Church to go out from itself toward the existential peripheries"; and (2) the need to "help it to be the fecund mother who lives 'by the sweet and comforting joy of evangelizing.'" These can be narrowed down to the following expressions: "go out," "existential peripheries"; "joy of evangelizing"; and "fecund mother." Can this solution really save the church from the issues in which it seems to be taken up? Thinking back to the parable in my introduction, I would say that there is a deep meaning in Bergoglio's insight. It likely resonated with what the cardinal-electors wanted; selecting him to be pope meant his solution was worth trying to help lead the church through the storms of the moment. An inward-looking or self-referential church cannot but suffer. As in the case of the young Jesuit, the way out is not just to go out. This first step is important but not sufficient. The church should go to the suffering world that Cardinal Bergoglio calls the "existential peripheries."

---

[5] The manuscript was published in the magazine *Palabra Nueva* of the Archdiocese of Havana on March 26, 2013. For the English version, see Sandro Magister, "The Last Words of Bergoglio before the Conclave," *Chiesa Espresso* (March 27, 2013).

[6] Ibid.

Before describing the ideal next leader of the church as discussed above, Cardinal Bergoglio's intervention outlined the required elements to heal the church. His proposed ecclesiology for the church's situation was sketched out in the following claims or convictions:
- *Not self-referential but outreaching*: "When the Church does not come out from itself to evangelize it becomes self-referential and gets sick (one thinks of the woman hunched over upon herself in the Gospel). The evils that, in the passing of time, afflict the ecclesiastical institutions have a root in self-referentiality, in a sort of theological narcissism. . . . The self-referential Church presumes to keep Jesus Christ within itself and not let him out."
- *Outward looking church*: "There are two images of the Church: [1] the evangelizing Church that goes out from itself; that of the 'Dei Verbum religiose audiens et fidenter proclamans' [the Church that devoutly listens to and faithfully proclaims the Word of God—editor's note], or [2] the worldly Church that lives in itself, of itself, for itself. This should illuminate the possible changes and reforms to be realized for the salvation of souls."
- *Sent to existential peripheries*: "The Church is called to come out from itself and to go to the peripheries, not only geographical, but also existential: those of the mystery of sin, of suffering, of injustice, those of ignorance and of the absence of faith, those of thought, those of every form of misery."[7]

Read against the past years of Francis's pontificate, we realize that this vision of the church shared during the pre-conclave conversation among the cardinals has been fleshed out in an extensive way by the papal speeches, homilies, and documents. What was then given in a nutshell can now be deeply understood through a close look at Pope Francis's magisterium. We have a better idea of what he is calling for when he talks about mission.

The Francis Solution: A Call to Care for the Wounds of the World

One expected that Francis would at once attend to the burning issues of the church itself, and kneel down to take care of them. Pope Francis instead has chosen to call the church to care for others by becoming missionary. By now, we have become familiar with Francis's language inviting the church "to go out from itself toward the existential peripheries." I

---

[7] Ibid.

would like to explore his major initiatives and tease out the components of that appeal to mission. He started with a missionary action (a visit to Lampedusa, the Italian island), then committed into writing his thoughts on mission in *Evangelii Gaudium*, the "Magna Carta" that he offered as a compass to guide the Catholic community under his leadership. The third aspect of his appeal to mission I invite us to look at is "for a synodal church" that aims to create a culture of synodality in the Catholic Church. He thus calls the Catholic community to go out of the way things are usually done, and to become creative in learning a new manner of journeying together.

A Call to Go Out

Pope Francis oftentimes invites the church to "contemplate" the world, and even to "contemplate the problems."[8] Strange as it may look at first sight, the expression is in fact rooted in the Ignatian way of grounding theologically the *missio Dei*. For those familiar with the *Spiritual Exercises*, Ignatius proposes to the person doing the retreat an exercise called the "Incarnation." This exercise is meant to transform the imagination of disciples by teaching them to look at the world with the "eyes" of God. St. Ignatius makes the retreatant see from God's point of view how "all humans were going down to hell," and thus the Trinity decided "that the Second Person shall become human to save the human race, and so, the fullness of times being come, they sent the Angel St. Gabriel to Our Lady."[9] The whole prayer, called an exercise in contemplation, invites the retreatant to "see" the world, to "hear" God's inner conversation, and to "look at the divine actions."

When Pope Francis invites the church to contemplate the world and its problems, he is using an Ignatian frame. The incarnation as a movement "out of" the divine realm becomes the theological foundation of mission. The Son enters the human realm because he is sent to save humanity. The capacity to see and to hear the sufferings of the world stems from the ability to contemplate the problems with the eyes of God. As a Jesuit, Francis has been practicing this form of prayer, and even taught others to do so. Contemplation as a dimension of life prepares one for mission-action. Ignatius did not just imagine it. It is

---

[8] See Pope Francis, *Amoris Laetitia* (2016), no. 4 (on contemplation, see nos. 128, 323); see also General Audience, September 16, 2020, and General Audience, May 5, 2021.

[9] St. Ignatius, *Spiritual Exercises*, "The first day and first contemplation is on the Incarnation" (nos. 101–9). I have replaced "men" with inclusive language.

rooted in the scripture. Let's think of God calling Moses to send him to save his people:

> The Lord said, "I have observed the misery of my people who are in Egypt; I have heard their cry on account of their taskmasters. Indeed, I know their sufferings, and I have come down to deliver them from the Egyptians, and to bring them up out of that land to a good and broad land, a land flowing with milk and honey. . . . I have also seen how the Egyptians oppress them. So come, I will send you to Pharaoh to bring my people, the Israelites, out of Egypt."[10]

Contemplation turns the eyes outward. It serves to determine the horizon of mission and to prepare for action. Thus, the first step is to "see" and to "hear" the sufferings of humanity, places where people are crying for help. Francis's idea of mission starts from a contemplation that moves to action, but more than that it is a way of being that transforms the heart.[11] He will exemplify it in responding to the scourge of migration.

Lampedusa: The Wound of Migration

Amid the criticism against the church on sexual abuse, and while the leaders of the nations seemed to be watching with indifference the migrants swallowed by the sea, the new pontiff took action. He went to Lampedusa to celebrate mass for the migrants "gone before us"; it was his first official travel out of the Vatican. This action struck the imagination of the world as Francis presided over a ceremony of funerals for those who had no dignity in the eyes of the world. Thousands of migrants had died in those waters, but the world declared its incapacity to protect them. Against the timid European response to the crisis, Francis went out of his residence to show care and humanness.

Lampedusa symbolizes Francis's vision of the church's mission in today's world. Those who have died in these waters are most of the time coming from countries suffering from wars, economic exploitation, corruption, ill governance, and so on. Worse, the migrants' countries of origin, mostly African, can potentially provide a better life for their population. These women, men, and children are born in lands where all kinds of minerals are of interest for energy and technology (oil, cobalt, coltan, diamonds, gold, and so forth). All these riches are taken away to develop a decent

---

[10] Ex 3:7–10.
[11] See Pope Francis, General Audience, May 5, 2021.

life in other lands. To control the wealth generated by this business, leaders and rebels in Africa wage war against each other. The consequences are well known: migration. Left in despair, the youth are forced out of the lands. A close look at the whole phenomenon reveals how connected are the exploitation of the land and migration. Later, in *Laudato Si'*, Francis calls the world's attention to the "interconnectedness" of social and environmental crises. Lampedusa therefore becomes a symbol of the consequences of a crisis wrought by the exploitation of the environment and human beings. Migrants make visible the existential periphery Pope Francis calls the church to care for. With the publication in 2013 of his first major papal document, *Evangelii Gaudium (EG)*, we get a better grasp of his action to the peripheries.

Evangelii Gaudium as Francis's Vision of Mission

Right at the beginning of his pontificate, Francis's apostolic exhortation *Evangelii Gaudium (On the Proclamation of the Gospel in Today's World)* presents his pastoral program. *Evangelii Gaudium (EG)* offers a conceptual vision of what Francis intends to convey to the whole church when he speaks of mission. In this section I point out some key passages that define the understanding and significance of mission. One fact should not be forgotten: *Evangelii Gaudium* is not post-synodal, even though it integrates the material of the 2012 synod on the new evangelization for the transmission of the Christian faith.[12] Francis widens the scope of his exhortation to encompass the entire life of the church. The call to mission in *Evangelii Gaudium* enters into conversation with a good variety of other local churches, particularly episcopal conferences.[13] The style or tone becomes dialogical, and shows the path towards listening to the voices of other local churches.

The papal document strongly emphasizes the need to "go out" (*exodus*). It clearly does not mean from one geographical location to the other but from the current mindset to a renewed one. It requires a conversion that drives the faithful from their comfort zone to becoming missionaries. For that to happen, "Each Christian and every community must discern the path that the Lord points out, but all of us are asked to obey his call to go

---

[12] *EG*, no. 14.

[13] The Bishops of Latin America and the Caribbean; the United States Conference; the Episcopal Conferences of Brazil, France, the Philippines, DR Congo, and India; the apostolic exhortations on Africa (*Ecclesia in Africa*), on Asia (*Ecclesia in Asia*), and on America (*Ecclesia in America*); among others.

forth from our own comfort zone in order to reach all the 'peripheries' in need of the light of the Gospel."[14] For "every Christian is a missionary to the extent that he or she has encountered the love of God in Christ Jesus: we no longer say that we are 'disciples' and 'missionaries,' but rather that we are always 'missionary disciples.'"[15]

Becoming a missionary disciple is not just an individual journey; it involves the community as well. Francis considers a Christian community to be a collective subject of mission.[16] Thus, the "Church which 'goes forth' is a community of missionary disciples," he says. The Shepherd of that community is the Lord. "An evangelizing community knows that the Lord has taken the initiative, he has loved us first (cf. 1 Jn 4:19), and therefore we can move forward, boldly take the initiative, go out to others, seek those who have fallen away, stand at the crossroads and welcome the outcast."[17]

Such a change cannot take place without the help of the Spirit of the Lord in a process of conversion and renewal at all levels of the whole church, including the papacy.[18] The life of a missionary disciple begins with the rejection of spiritual worldliness that appears when people "look on from above and afar," "reject the prophecy of their brothers and sisters," "discredit those who raise questions," "constantly point out the mistakes of others," and "are obsessed by appearances." The way out of it, asserts Francis, is "by making the Church constantly go out from herself, keeping her mission focused on Jesus Christ, and her commitment to the poor."[19]

The above considerations have tried to sketch out Pope Francis's thoughts on mission as a journey with the Lord and as a process of bringing the experienced joy of the gospel to others. It is indeed an experience that should push the disciples and communities out of their comfort zones, out of themselves, and out toward the needy. Francis is aware that it cannot happen unless a discerned decision is taken to change, to convert, to reform, to go through the experience of purification. He boldly invited the church to embark on such a journey because the Lord has taken the lead.

For a Synodal Church: A New Way of Being in Mission

Walking together in mission stems from the gospel indeed. For our times, the Second Vatican Council (1962–65) renewed our understanding of

---

[14] *EG*, no. 20.
[15] *EG*, no. 120.
[16] *EG*, nos. 30, 129, 239.
[17] *EG*, no. 24.
[18] *EG*, no. 32.
[19] *EG*, no. 97.

mission for the church by pointing out the communal, participatory, and missionary dimensions. The reception of this ecclesiology is still in process. Pope Francis repeatedly asserted, as I have said, that the collective subject of mission is the community of missionary disciples. How does it relate to the culture of synodality that the pope wants the church to develop? The practice remains a challenge, but the theological ground is solidly established,[20] even though it has not sufficiently trickled down to the grassroots.

The International Theological Commission's document on the matter concludes that

> Pope Francis teaches that "to walk together is the constitutive way of the Church; the figure that enables us to interpret reality with the eyes and heart of God; the condition for following the Lord Jesus and being servants of life in this wounded time. The breath and pace of the Synod show what we are, and the dynamism of communion that animates our decisions; only in this way can we truly renew our pastoral ministry and adapt it to the mission of the Church in today's world; only in this way can we address the complexity of this time, thankful for the journey accomplished thus far, and determined to continue it with *parrhesia*."[21]

By way of illustration, I consider the case of the church in Africa. It has been moving from being "a mission church" to "a church in mission," in response to Pope Paul VI's Kampala address of 1969. In the newly decolonized countries of the continent, this call resonated with many Catholics' deep sense of belonging. The notion of being "missionaries to yourselves" reoriented the understanding of mission, but it also raised a question as to what it meant for Africans themselves to be "a community of disciples." At the 1994 synod for Africa, the bishops responded that it meant to be the church as the "family of God."[22] To understand the family of God in an ecclesiological perspective, one obviously needs a good grasp of the doctrine of the Trinity as a divine family, but that alone would not suffice. We should also bear in mind the socio-anthropological

---

[20] See International Theological Commission, *Synodality in the Life and Mission of the Church* (March 2018).

[21] Ibid., no. 120. The word *parrhesia* is defined in early Christianity as "freedom of speech or frankness in speaking, excluding slander, defamation, or disinformation."

[22] John Paul II, *Ecclesia in Africa* (1995), no. 85.

experience of "being a family" in the African mindset/context.[23] I would like to highlight one such aspect in relation to acting as one family, as this pertains to our conversation.

Based on the philosophy of *Ubuntu*, family issues are discussed in the *baraza* (the Swahili word that refers to both the meeting place and the meeting/conversation itself). It is a place and a way of proceeding in finding solutions to problems. For Sub-Saharan Africans, therefore, when the church, the family of God, engages in a synodal process, it should be the "normal" way of dealing with community affairs. Family should "meet" (*baraza*) to undertake any collective mission-action. No voice should be silenced. While some perceive an opposition between a "church in mission" and a "church in meetings," a deep grasp of what *ecclesia* stands for cannot oppose the two notions. Coming together is part of the mission, as it reminds us of what Jesus said: "By this everyone will know that you are my disciples, if you have love for one another."[24] A church that sits together, where people speak to one another and listen to one another, opens itself up to the Holy Spirit, and such a way of living proclaims already the good news. The challenge for a synodal church in Africa will definitely be to "inculturate" synodality by authentically listening to one another, irrespective of age, state of life, origin, sex, and so on. All the voices must be heard, because, as St. Benedict wrote in his *Rule*, "All are to be called to council because it is often to a junior that the Lord reveals what is best."[25]

At this moment in history the church Francis has been called to lead seems to be like that of the disciples of Emmaus. Desperate, they split apart from the community and were on their way to return home. On the way, Jesus joined them, journeyed with them, shared the meal with them, and as a result they defeated the night and came back to Jerusalem where they gathered together with the others. The encounter with the Lord reunited the disciples,[26] before the Holy Spirit sends them again away to all the corners of the world.[27] Thus, the way of being in mission,

---

[23] See Idara Otu, "Rediscovering the Teachings of the First and Second African Synods: Renewal of the Church in Africa," in *African Theology in the 21st Century: A Call to Baraza*, ed. Elias O. Opongo, SJ, and Paul Béré, SJ (Nairobi: Paulines Publications Africa, 2021), 305–29. For a developed link to Vatican II, see Friedrich Bechina, *Die Kirche als "Familie Gottes," Analecta Gregoriana* (Rome: G&B Press, 1998).

[24] Jn 13:35.

[25] St. Benedict, *Rule*, chap. III.

[26] Lk 24.

[27] Cf. Acts 1:8; 2.

or even "being mission,"[28] being sent wherever the Lord wills his disciples, starts first with being with him[29] and with one another as a discerning community for the mission.[30] Francis invites the church to be mission in "synodality,"[31] in journeying together.

Francis's "Church in Mission" Outlook

In this last section, I look at Pope Francis's use of the expression "I dream of . . . "[32] What does the church-in-mission dreamt by Francis look like? In *Evangelii Gaudium* he boldly asserts:

> I dream of a "missionary option," that is, a missionary impulse capable of transforming everything, so that the church's customs, ways of doing things, times and schedules, language and structures can be suitably channelled for the evangelization of today's world rather than for her self-preservation. The renewal of structures demanded by pastoral conversion can only be understood in this light: as part of an effort to make them more mission-oriented, to make ordinary pastoral activity on every level more inclusive and open, to inspire in pastoral workers a constant desire to go forth and in this way to elicit a positive response from all those whom Jesus summons to friendship with himself.[33]

In order to put and keep the church in a "permanent state of mission,"[34] not only does Francis's dream involve the whole Catholic community, but it also envisions all levels of church life and its activities as mission oriented. The call to mission entails a new way of living in the world in the footsteps of Jesus. Any activity should proclaim the good news. No dichotomy should be found between a disciple's personal life and the *kerygma*. What is at stake therefore, I believe, is authenticity, the wholeness of a life rooted in Christ. Such a life, either personal or communal, should be catalytic and transform human societies with the seed of the gospel values.

---

[28] Pope Francis affirms: "I am a mission on this earth" (*EG*, no. 273).
[29] Cf. Mk 3:14.
[30] Acts 15.
[31] The three-stage synod beginning in October 2021 and ending in 2023 will certainly help launch that movement.
[32] *EG*, no. 27.
[33] *EG*, no. 27.
[34] *EG*, no. 25.

Such an understanding of the church in mission dreamt by Francis can be further highlighted by his own expressions mentioned here and there. When we examine them, or at least some of them, one notices that they all characterize a church in the midst of "existential peripheries." Pope Francis encapsulated his vision of the church in mission, for instance, in the following expressions, which I sometimes reformulate:

A poor church for the poor: poverty here is not sociological, but anthropological and theological in the sense that it describes any disfigured humanity found in concrete women or men;

A field hospital that cares for the sick: the image of the Good Samaritan would be most fitting here to translate the vision of that church. The church leaves nobody on the side of the road, wounded without attendance;

A joyous community of missionary disciples: the joy of the gospel recalls the experience of the first Christians who were persecuted during the first centuries. Amid their sufferings, their joy meant the strength of their faith and hope in the risen Lord;

A herald of the gospel message who brings it down to the essentials: faith seeking understanding has yielded a good amount of theological production, but the gap between the simplicity of the language of the Gospels and the current "church parlance" seems to have obscured the message and its freshness. Francis calls for a new way of crafting the message;

A creative and audacious community of disciples: clinging to the comfort zone appears when Christians, both as individuals and as communities, are not willing to change, are closed up to new challenges. A church that dares should move out and invent new forms, styles, methods, and so forth;

A community that "goes out" and departs from being "self-referential": threatened by a rampant secularization, mainly in the West, or torn inside by groups clinging to past forms of worship, the global church leadership focused on ensuring the right doctrine of faith and morals. Francis instead has been calling the church to heal itself by moving out and caring for others, particularly those whose lives are broken.

The successor of Peter is aware that the implementation of his vision or program and the transformation of the church's current culture will take time. But he also speaks of launching processes. It cannot be a leap, but a gradual growth into the depth of our Christian self.

Conclusion

Pope Francis's call to become a missionary disciple community looks backward and forward. To deeply understand his notion of missionary discipleship, we need to go back to St. Paul VI's Magna Carta on evangelization, *Evangelii Nuntiandi*, which, in turn, takes root in Vatican Council II. The pope writes, "The Second Vatican Council recalled [*Ad Gentes,* nos. 5, 11–12] and the 1974 Synod vigorously took up again this theme of the Church which is evangelized by constant conversion and renewal, in order to evangelize the world with credibility."[35] Renewal and mission form an essential dimension of the church. The evangelizer should first be evangelized. Yet, for Francis, if the church wants to renew itself, it has no other option but to reach out to the world, especially the suffering one. The church self-evangelization appears as a precondition to evangelize the world, but actually both are linked in such a way that the second makes the first possible. It is by bringing the joy of the gospel to those most in need that the missionary disciples reach the state of authenticity.

Beyond the principle of continuity to which I referred in the preceding paragraph (beginning with Vatican II and then *Evangelii Nuntiandi*), we are witnessing the emergence of a new ecclesial paradigm. The election of Cardinal Bergoglio (Pope Francis) ushered in a new way of being church coming through his personal experience rooted in the Jesuit missionary tradition. And that tradition was grown in the Latin American ecclesial soil. The result can be compared to a tributary running into the long river of the Catholic tradition. Pope Francis's calling to mission echoes the faith legacy of the Latin American Catholic community, trained through the struggles of its martyrs, guided by its theologians and pastors, and strengthened by the unyielding commitment of its faithful. Maybe the whole church should look to that region to learn more about missionary discipleship.

Paul Béré, SJ, born in 1966, is a Jesuit from Burkina Faso. He is on a teaching mission at the Pontifical Biblical Institute (Rome), and he is a member of the Pontifical Biblical Commission and of the Anglican–Roman Catholic International Commission (ARCIC). He serves as a consultant to the Pontifical Council for Culture and sits on the Theological Commission of the 2021–2023 Synod.

---

[35] Pope Paul VI, *Evangelii Nuntiandi* (1975), no. 15.

The Role of Missionary Religious Institutes
A Strange Species of Christians?[1]

ALOYSIUS PIERIS, SJ

The Search for a Proper Name

Until the 1950s they were regarded as men and women living in the so-called states of perfection, as if the other ways of following Christ were mired in imperfection. Then they came to be called religious, implying that the rest of the church and even non-Christians were all a bunch of irreligious people! They were also once known as the regulars (those living under a *regula,* Latin for "rule") and were contrasted with the seculars (regardless of the fact that the latter, too, were governed by ecclesiastical rules). The more recent appellation, consecrated life, seems to insinuate that no consecration occurs in the sacrament of holy matrimony that gives birth to the household church, or in the sacrament of holy orders that creates presbyteral and episcopal ministers. Does not the Holy Spirit anoint and consecrate every Christian for a specific mission at his or her baptism? As for the frequently mentioned "evangelical counsels," we seem to have forgotten that every Christian is called at his or her baptism to be evangelically poor, obedient, and chaste, each within his or her particular vocation, while, on the other hand, church law recognizes the consecrated life of virgins who do not profess the three vows!

My conclusion from the above is that we are dealing with a form of *sequela Christi* ("following Christ," Mt 19:21) that cannot be pigeon-holed in the *currently accepted* theological and legal framework.

---

[1]This is a slightly modified version of an article on the so-called religious life or *vita consecrata* (originally titled "Freaks in the Church?"), which first appeared in *Vagdevi: Journal of Religious Reflection* 18 (July 2015) (the year dedicated to Religious Life). It presupposes what the author has discussed in detail in the articles and books mentioned at the end of the article.

John Paul II's apostolic exhortation *Vita Consecrata* has captured the essence of the discussions and conclusions of the synod of 1996. There it is insisted that consecrated life is "an intimate part of her [church's] life . . . and mission," and that it refers to "states of life willed by the Lord Jesus Christ for his Church," something that the Spirit has raised and that is very different from lay life. On the other hand, the same document falls back into the old habit of referring to this specific mode of life with *words and phrases that express the vocation of all Christians*, as for instance that [the so-called] religious life is a baptismal participation in the paschal mystery or conformation to the image of Christ, and so on. Sometimes the document gets around this problem by adding that religious life is a "specific" or "special" way [of living what every Christian is called to live]. Twice the document repeats the synodal opinion that consecrated life is "objectively superior" to the vocations of other Christians—introducing, unhappily, a hierarchical gradation into what Vatican II had clearly described as a "universal call to holiness" in which different categories of the baptized participate in mutual complementarity rather than in a pyramidal arrangement. I think this papal document comes closer to the target only when it refers to the "consecrated ones" as *charismatic* vis-à-vis the institutional leadership of the hierarchy.

Though the bishops felt they were dealing with something essentially belonging to the church (*de re nostra agitur*), they did not seem to capture an image that could portray the distinctive features of this unique category of people. The church has not yet discovered a theologically justifiable name to identify their calling but does describe in various ways their mission within and outside the Christian community. The church acknowledges the undeniable fact that without them it would suffer a severe shortage of shepherds and shrink in stature and in service.

My conclusion from the foregoing is that we are dealing here with a strange species of Christians who defy definition and yet demand recognition. Will *that* conclusion finally help us to decipher who these "strange species of Christians" are?

Thinking outside the Canonical Framework and within History

As long as our theology is based on (or biased by) ancient Rome's jurisprudential mindset that lurks beneath the traditional church law, we shall never find a slot for these seemingly unaccountable members of the Roman Communion. This is not an aspersion cast on canon law or on the role of canonists, both of which are absolutely necessary for governing a complex body of people such as the church; I merely caution against cramping the mission and ministry of the church into the canonical framework that is characterized by a non-scriptural and even anti-scriptural bisection of the people of God into "secular and religious" as well as "clerical and lay." As long as these two *canonical* dichotomies are allowed to dominate the church's *theological* parlance, we shall never find the word we are searching for.

Who are they? What is their origin? What is their role? Are they indispensable? To answer these questions one must consult the history of the church rather than limit our search exclusively to canon law, which itself is a later product of history.

Note first that the history of Christianity in its earliest stage recognized two categories of married people. The first group consisted of presbyters and bishops, who shepherded the local churches; they were all married males. In addition, the flocks they shepherded were also families much like those of today. These two sets of people—the shepherds and their flocks—had never been referred to, respectively, as *clergy* (a class of priestly leaders) and the *laity* (a mass of non-priestly people) as we do today in ecclesiastical parlance. Let us formulate this principle as the first clarification required:

> (1) In the nascent church there was no priest class called clergy that stood apart from a supposedly non-priestly sector known as the laity. For the whole church was a *communitas sacerdotalis*, a "priestly community," to use the language of Vatican II. The leaders (shepherds) were chosen from the *all-priestly-community* and were known as *prebyteroi* (elders) or *episcopoi* (overseers).

In other words, some priests selected from this all-priestly-community were variously known as presbyters and bishops. These men were priests by baptism and already married, and preferably not remarried after the death of the spouse as Paul had advised. Hence, it was not a question of them celebrating mass and the rest participating in it. Rather, the whole community was concelebrating the Eucharist while the local leader (bishop or presbyter) *presided over* the service. Their servant leadership was neatly expressed by the title shepherd ("pastor" in Latin). As church leaders they usually presided over the community also during the Eucharist, which is the church's most intense moment of communion.

The terms *presbyters* (elders) and *bishops* (overseers) were two terms borrowed from Judaism, more precisely from the Essenes. Note that these two designations were alternatively employed by New Testament writers for the same leadership function, with *no difference in social or ecclesiastical status between them*. They were local pastors, who, on the basis of the People's consent, were appointed (ordained) to their leadership office.

Who ordained them? Could these have been the *frontier missionaries* known as the apostles (*apostoloi*)? For it was these frontier missionaries who preached the gospel beyond the confines of the existing ecclesial boundaries, starting with the twelve apostles, and all those who followed in their footsteps. In the apostolic period (33–180 CE) they eventually established new local churches over which they could be presumed to have appointed bishops or presbyters after consulting the flock. Celibates like Paul and Barnabas, perhaps including some women, were among the frontier missionaries or "apostles" who exercised this *trans-local leadership*. There were celibates among them; their celibacy, just like that of Jesus, should not be seen as a Christian innovation, for there were Jews in the Second Temple Period who greatly valued and practiced celibacy, as Philo, a first-century Jewish witness, has informed us. Hence our next principle:

(2) The celibates among these leaders who were exercising a mobile and missionary type of frontier ministry—the *apostoloi*—never regarded themselves as "religious" in contrast to, say, the local leaders known as bishops and presbyters; nor were these latter ever thought to be "secular."

For Roman jurisprudence, the pagan division of labor had not yet fully penetrated the administration of the earliest churches. The distinction was solely between sin and grace, and between mammon and God; for the belief that God created all things with the power of God's Word and that this Word, who is Christ, permeates all creation, and that Christ had further sanctified humanity and infra-human nature with his redemptive act, left no room for early Christians to admit a division between secular and religious. All that was secular was also sacred. Then Roman jurisprudence (which no doubt had guaranteed governmental efficiency to the leaders of an increasingly unwieldy church structure) introduced the distinction of secular and sacred into ecclesiastical parlance, which obscured the role of the frontier ministers, who were actually the forerunners of what current canon law designates as religious!

The Three Frontier Ministries in the Nascent Church

The aforementioned frontier missionaries (*apostoloi*) of the nascent church were flanked by at least two other groups in the same trans-local ministry: the teachers (*didaskaloi*, the forerunners of theologians); and the prophets (*prophetai*, announcers and interpreters of the word of God, corresponding to today's spiritual guides). These three non-presbyteral and non-episcopal ministries are performed today mostly (but not exclusively) by those in the so-called religious life. Unfortunately, the gradual hierarchization of the church that accompanied its incipient Romanization in the post-apostolic period resulted not only in bishops acquiring a higher status than presbyters—despite St. Jerome's vehement rejection of that pyramidization as a scripturally unwarranted innovation attributable to the devil—but also in the bishops' attempt to absorb all other ministries into their episcopal office. The episcopal phobia of theologians (former *didaskaloi*) seems to have had an early start, as can be inferred from the earliest history of the church attributed to Eusebius. There was an attempt on the part of the bishops to eliminate the role of the teachers (theologians) and to absorb their ministry into the episcopate, too.

This unhealthy process eliminated the three types of trans-local ministries that were originally independent of, and even antecedent to, the sedentary ministries of the episcopate and presbyterate. Thus, the neo-testamentary complementariness between the itinerant and sedentary ministries was eliminated and, in its place, a pyramidal monolith (with bishops at the apex, laity at the base, and presbyters in-between) became the order of the day. The appearance of this pyramid was first detected in the second-century writings of Ignatius of Antioch and Irenaeus. It was only after this hierarchical monolith had crystallized as the structure of the church that the jurisprudential framework developed over the centuries into what we call today the canonical framework.

Reemergence of Frontier Ministries as the So-called Religious

One of the earliest protests against this monolithic structure of the church was the *desert movement*, which could be interpreted to have originated as a wild search for the authentic Christian life that seemed to have disappeared after the period of persecution, the Age of Martyrs (33–300 CE). This experiment, which is associated with many names such as Paul of Thebes, Antony, Pachomius, Evagrius, and so on, took a variety of forms;

some were monastic fraternities, while others were *anchoritic*, often taking extreme forms such as ascetics standing on one leg (*stationarists*), living on top of high pillars (*stilites*), grotto dwellers, and *dendrites* (those living under a tree). Basil and the two Gregory's in the East and Benedict in the West reorganized this movement into a *coenobitic* (communitarian) form as *integral but peripheral* to the hierarchical church.

With this process a new principle of church-renewal emerged: when the leadership shows signs of decadence, there is a centrifugal movement (a stampede to the periphery of an institution) in search of authenticity, which often succumbs to extremism, only to be followed by a centripetal return (in a modified form) to the church as a renovative current led by charismatics. Some of what we call religious congregations originated in that way. I have already illustrated this principle with concrete examples in other places.[2] Many other congregations originated as a response to needs that the hierarchy could not handle—for example, the Marist Brothers and the Brothers of the Christian Schools who, as evangelical educationists (*didaskaloi*), rescued and safeguarded the faith of Christian youth from the adverse effects of the *laïcité* that followed the French Revolution.

A retrospective analysis indicates that most of these new apostolic or spiritual movements that ended up canonically as religious congregations not only followed this pattern but also restored some dimensions of the early church's frontier missions. The innovation, if there was any, was that these new forms of ministries were not exercised singly or in pairs, as in the nascent church, but within the framework of monastic or apostolic *communities* or *coenobia* that projected the image of *ecclesiolae* (mini-churches). In fact, they proffered a possible exemplar that the local church would do well to emulate, namely, a Jesus community animated by Love which is a Divine Person.

St. Augustine's laudable effort to turn his *presbyterium* into a *coenobium*, gathered round the bishop, seems to have inspired the formation of the medieval communities of canons regular, which, in their present form, entered canon law under the heading of *Religious Institutes* together with clerics regular such as the Jesuits. Since we are formed in the image of God, who is a triune community of love, all ministries must bear the communitarian dimension like the local churches, and yet canon law does provide a slot for individual hermits as well as for individual virgins.

---

[2] See the reference material at the end of this essay.

The religious communities classified under canon law have all restored the lost charismatic ministries as the patrimony of the incipient church. They produced *prophetai*, or spiritual guides, who (like Philip's virgin daughters mentioned in the New Testament) interpreted the word of God, that is, helped others to discern the will of God. Among these monks, specially the Benedictines, great theologians or teachers arose who doctrinally explained the word of God, thus resuming the work of the *didaskaloi* mentioned in the New Testament (such as Priscilla, who taught Apollo the profound truths of Revelation). They also produced frontier missionaries, the *apostoloi*, who traveled to the far ends of Europe to preach the word, baptize the converts, and establish local churches, which they gradually handed over to local pastors. They became the pioneer missionaries of Northern Europe (as were Paul, Barnabas, and other apostles in the early decades of the church).

From the Middle Ages onward we see the three ministries— *apostoloi*, *didaskaloi*, and *prophetai*—reappearing in a much diversified manner: Cistercians producing great spiritual masters, for instance, and the mendicant orders taking over the frontier missions as well as developing universities to teach the Christian doctrine. The women, who originally pursued a monastic model, very soon began to invade the whole church with a variety of apostolic congregations, some continuing the healing ministry of Jesus (like the Camelians or the Medical Missionaries) and others in the teaching profession (*didaskalia*), which included primary, secondary, and even tertiary levels. And, in the nineteenth century, many male missionary societies[3] also gave birth to a new generation of *apostoloi* or frontier missionaries.

Note, however, that all these ministries, like the frontier ministries of the nascent church, were not subjected to episcopal jurisdiction because they arose as new versions of the early church's trans-local ministries that predated the appointment of the bishops or presbyters. Canon law, it should be noted, respects the relative autonomy of these renewalist movements (known as religious congregations). Theology accepts—and *should* accept—what history reveals about them: that they are not mandated by the hierarchy but raised by the Spirit and the Spousal Love of Christ, as Bishop (now cardinal) Vincent Nichols declared at the synod on *vita consecrata* (religious life) in 1996.

---

[3] Such as the Pontifical Institute for Foreign Missions (PIME), the Paris Foreign Mission Society (MEP), the Society of the Divine Word (SVD), the Missionaries of the Sacred Heart (MSC), and the Congregation of the Immaculate Heart of Mary (CICM), known in the United States as the Missionhurst Fathers.

How Should They Be Named?

These men and women became labeled as religious in the earlier canon law that had introduced the lay-clerical and secular-religious categories into Christian parlance. In the current canon law, they are listed under *Institutes of Consecrated Life*. These titles are ambiguous, as mentioned above. History invites us to recognize them—at least provisionally until we find a better name—as *charismatic leaders*, in contrast to institutional leaders or local ordinaries, as John Paul II's *Vita Consecrata* called them;[4] or as *mobile ministers* cutting across diocesan structures and distinct from the sedentary ministers (such as the bishops and presbyters); or more accurately as *frontier missionaries* as opposed to intra-ecclesial pastors (or the hierarchy). In other words, we should not be misled by canonical terminology. Rather, we should recognize the mission of these men and women for what it is has always been:

> (3) *A frontier ministry* of preferably *coenobitic* men and women, liberated from conjugal ties and family obligations in order to be free to move *across church frontiers,* working neither under nor against the episcopate but as the episcopate's dialectical counterpart.

Those who are proclaiming the gospel directly and indirectly through dialogue, inculturation, or humanitarian and charitable work, primarily among non-Christians, are *apostoloi* or frontier missionaries proper. Their charismatic leadership, as we mentioned above, does not originate from the episcopate. It is the Spirit of the risen Lord that raises men and women to work in the periphery of the church's structures in response to ever new challenges and the unforeseen needs of God's people. For instance, the Jesuits existed as a mobile community engaged in the ministry of the word long before the pope (in the name of the whole church) *recognized* their legitimate and necessary role in the church.

Others are called to walk on the fringes of the church's doctrinal framework, seeking a deeper and contextually determined understanding of our faith. Thus, for example, many doctrinal positions that were regarded as beyond doubt have been questioned and recast by theologians (*didaskaloi*), who, inspired by the Spirit, walked on the margin of orthodoxy. For example, the long-held theory of static creationism and monogenism based on a literalist interpretations of Genesis 1 and 2 was abandoned, and a more dynamic evolutionary approach characterized by polygenism

---

[4] Pope John Paul II, *Vita Consecreta* (1996), no. 48.

was accepted by recent popes; though one of its early propounders, Pierre Teilhard de Chardin, was censured and silenced initially. The credit goes to great theologians like Henri de Lubac, Karl Rahner, Yves Congar, and many others belonging to the transcendental neo-Thomist school, who were *thinking "for" the church and thinking "ahead of" the church.*

Thus, charismatic leadership has to be exercised in the *periphery* of the church, where one is in touch with the extra-ecclesial reality. This type of center-periphery dialectics is inherent in the very nature of the papacy itself:

(4) The analogy between Peter, who exercised an institutional leadership conferred by the historical Jesus (Jesus in the day of his flesh), and Paul, who was summoned to a charismatic and itinerant leadership by the risen Lord (Christ as we know him now) are both represented in the person of the bishop of Rome, whose original title was not Vicar of Christ but Vicar of Peter and Paul. As Peter's vicar he tends the sedentary ministry of the episcopate/presbyterate, and as Paul's vicar he has responsibility for the frontier mission of the itinerant ministers (whom today we call the religious).

Formation of "Trans-local" Ministries

The two sets of ministries—the local and the trans-local—are so radically different, both with regard to the services rendered and the skills required, that their recruitment as well as their ongoing training demands entirely different procedures and entirely different locations. The Jesuits at their 31st General Congregation recommended that apostolic centers also serve as a locus of formation, implying that there should be greater collaboration between houses of formation and places of apostolic activities in the training of ministers. The Asian Institute of Theology, an initiative of the Oblates and Claretians in Sri Lanka, is a laudable effort in this direction despite the inattention and indifference shown by other congregations.

Pope Francis has gone further by comparing a well-formed religious to a table with four legs. A table cannot stand if even one leg is missing. The four legs function *simultaneously*. They are *study, spirituality, apostolate,* and *community life*. Frontier ministers, male or female, must be formed in such a way as to allow them to grow into persons who have integrated all four of these dimensions. This means that these four areas of formation are to be provided, *not successively* (as is done often and almost everywhere), *but simultaneously*. And unless the formators, too, have integrated these dimensions, they cannot impart this holistic formation to the young.

We hope and pray that these Franciscan thoughts about the current papacy will inspire the missionary religious institutes in every country to train frontier missionaries who can stop being mere "caretakers" of a weary church and venture out to the periphery to expand the church's kingdom-horizons, so that it may become what Vatican II summoned it to be: "a universal sacrament of salvation."[5]

A word of caution: since Vatican II has summoned the church to ceaseless self-renewal in agreement with Luther's famous dictum, *ecclesia semper reformanda* (the church is in need of continuous reform), the frontier communities must also submit themselves to a ceaseless renewal lest they fail in their mission to be the leaven of reform in the wider Christian community and become, instead, mere replicas of an irrelevant church—as history has amply demonstrated. The salt can lose its flavor.

Hence, I like to offer, for the consideration of the church as a whole, and also for those who are the subject of this discussion, a possible model, one that would redeem them from being irrelevant and impotent and would strengthen their identity as the charismatic and pioneering leaders of the church.

An Embodiment of the Marian Charism?

Perhaps the nameless men and women religious could discover their identity by recognizing the Marian character of their charism in keeping with the Mariology of Vatican II. The council was struggling with the question of identifying the role of Mary within the mission of the church—just as the church (in *Vita Consecrata*) is straining to find a designation to categorize the *charismatic leaders*, such as the religious are called to be. Let us take a clue from Vatican II, which managed to identify the *ecclesiastical role* of Mary in *Lumen Gentium (Dogmatic Constitution on the Church)*; there we might find a hint as to how to define the ecclesiastical role of the so-called religious.

From the discussion that led to the inclusion of Mariology as a chapter in the council's ecclesiology[6] rather than in a separate document, we can infer that Mary, like Peter, is *not above* the church but *within* the church—with only Christ being the *Head* of the church and standing *above* the

---

[5] Vatican II, *Lumen Gentium (Dogmatic Constitution on the Church)* (1964), no. 48.
[6] *Lumen Gentium,* chap. VIII.

church. But at the same time, Mary is not only a *member of the church*, like Peter, but also a *"forerunner" of the church*, like Paul. Paul follows the Marian model and hence is a precursor of the so-called religious members. It is this Marian model and mission that the so-called religious can spell out through their unique service both within, and in the forefront of, the contemporary church.

The Catholic Church believes that Mary was conceived without original sin through the anticipated merits of her Redeemer Son. This means that she did not need baptism to become a member of the church established by Christ; in other words, she was already "a single-member church" long before Christ instituted the church. *Thus the church, even before its establishment, was already identified with Mary*. For she was the church that brought forth the founder of the church. Hence, we see her *anticipating* (in her person) whatever would happen to the church later. What took place at Pentecost—the Holy Spirit descending on Jesus's followers and transforming them into the church or the mystical body of Christ—was anticipated in Mary, who became one body with Jesus when overshadowed by the Spirit; just as the church on receiving the Spirit went forth bringing the word to the world, so also Mary, after the Spirit had formed her into a Christ-bearer, hastened to bring the incarnated Word to Zecharia's house and assisted at the birth of her Son's precursor.[7] She followed Christ as a disciple (one who heard the word and kept it), while those who claimed to be his disciples had abandoned him at the crucial moment of his death. She fore-owned the sacerdotal character of the whole church when she stood by the cross where, in her Son, *her own flesh and blood was offered to the Father* as the priest-victim of the New Covenant. She was present at the formation of the church in the upper room. By her glorious assumption, she is the *risen church in advance*, anticipating the future glory of the eschatological church. In short, she anticipated in her life and deeds what the church would and should be later in its life and deeds.

Mary, therefore, is the model for those summoned by the Lord to be *active and faithful members "within" the church* and yet *walk "ahead" of the church*, pointing to what the church *should be* in the future. While the church is commissioned to walk ahead of the world, pointing to the world's own redeemed future, Marian Christians are called to be in the forefront of the church, helping the church to fulfill that mission. This Marian charisma defines the role of these nameless ministers who are looking for a name. They cannot stop at "thinking *with* the church" (*sentire cum ecclesia*); rather, they are called to "think *for* the church" (*sentire pro ecclesia*) and to

---

[7] Lk 1:39–56.

walk *ahead* of the church, that is, even outside the physical boundaries of church, opening the church's "kingdom horizons," as they have done in the past at all periods of the church, especially in times of crisis.

Obviously, we need to master the art of discernment in order to serve the church in the Marian mode. Here, Ignatius's legacy is quite useful and necessary. Whatever the meaning of the *hierarchical church,* that Ignatius had in mind when speaking of discernment—a discussion which is still in process among Jesuits, as for instance, in Fredrik Heiding's *Ignatian Spirituality at Ecclesial Frontiers*—we learn from Vatican II that Christ's *prophecy, priesthood, and servant-leadership* are first given to his body, *the whole church as the "people of God,"* from whom the hierarchy derives its threefold function (*munus triplex*), namely, being a priest, a prophet, and a king to its people. Those summoned to a Marian mission, therefore, must think *with* the church, understood in its primordial sense of "believing people." The Marians have to be trained to be sensitive to the *sensus fidelium,* the pulse of the faithful as a totality, which is infallible (*in credendo falli nequit*).[8] It is that experience that qualifies the Marian emissaries to *think for* the hierarchical church by moving *ahead* of them, facing the risks and clearing the path.

> (5) This Marian mission calls for *profound humility* to accept opposition from institutional leaders without giving in to resentment and rancor so that, equipped with the *spiritual stamina* that flows from *deep faith,* they would walk in the dark, as Mary did. The Marians do not serve the hierarchy; they serve the church as the people of God in a dialectical collaboration with the hierarchy.

Pope Francis has urged the religious to step out of themselves and walk to the fringes without being intimidated by the fear of making mistakes or being censured by the institutional leadership. This presupposes a *Marian formation given in the frontier for service in the frontier.* We hope this special Marian formation will see an awakening of the Marian spirit and the Marian thrust in their recruitment and formation as well as in their discipleship (vocation) and apostolate (mission), so that they may be equipped in every way to serve the people of God as the "charismatic" counterpart of the hierarchy and as an indispensably vital part of the church's life and mission (as stated in the teaching of John Paul II in *Vita Consecrata*).

---

[8] *Lumen Gentium,* no. 12.

Conclusion

We can now provisionally name the charismatic leaderships as *leadership ministries* that are
- (a) itinerant,
- (b) trans-local,
- (c) frontier,
- (d) charismatic,
- (e) pioneering, and
- (f) witnessing to the Marian character of the church.

Reference Material Written by Fr. Aloysius Pieris, SJ

"Monkhood: Sociological Analysis and Theological Perspectives" (review article). *Dialogue* NS 1, no. 3 (1974): 93–99.

"Monkhood: Some Elementary Facts about Its Origin and Its Place in a Buddhist-Christian Dialogue." *Dialogue* NS 1, no. 1 (1974): 4–10. Reprinted in *Tjurunga* 10 (1975): 67–74.

"The Spirituality of the Buddhist Monk in Sri Lanka." *Inter Fratres* (Fabiano) 27 (1977): 121–32. Reprinted in *Tjurunga* 17 (1979): 31–48; in Italian in *Il monchesimo nel terzo mondo* (Rome: Paoline, 1979), 190–203; in French in *Bulletin de AIM* (Vanves) 27 (1980): 56–69.

"Monastic Poverty in the Asian Setting." *Dialogue* NS 7, no. 3 (1980): 104–18. Reprinted in *Tjurunga* 26 (1984): 5–16. Extract in French in *Mission d'Eglise* (Paris) 59 (1983): 36–40. Summary in *Theologie im Kontext* 3 (1982): 120.

"The Recruitment Policy of Religious Congregations and Diocesan Clergy." *Aquinas Journal* 6, no. 1 (June 1989): 45–60.

"A Priest-Uncle's Letter to a Niece on the Day She Entered the Great Carmel." *The Missionary Oblate* 10 (July-December 1994): 2–6.

"Chastity as Total Consecration to Service." *Vidyajyoti Journal of Theological Reflection* 58, no. 9 (September 1994): 545–58. Spanish summary in *Seleziones de Teologia* 138, no. 35 (1996): 153–59.

"The Jesuits as Frontier Men." *Ignis* 3 (1996): 6–17.

Fire and Water. Maryknoll, NY: Orbis Books, 1996. 172–214.

"The Responsibilities of the CMRS in *Sri Lanka Today.*" *Vidyajyoti Journal of Theological Reflection* 61, no. 9 (September 1997): 577–84.

"Prayer in Contemplative Monasticism and Apostolic Activism." *Asia Focus* (March 9, 2001): 3.

"The Mission of the Contemplatives." *Journal of Religious Reflection* (Kandy) (April-May 2001): 17–23.

"Give Vatican II a Chance." *Kelaniya* (2010): 88–90.

"Our Unhidden Agenda: How We Jesuits Work, Pray, and Form Our Men." *Kelaniya* (2012).

"To Love Is to Serve: The Biblical Core of Ignatian Spirituality." *Vagdevi 17,* vol. 9, no. 1 (January 2015): 35–43. A shorter version was published in *Prabodhanaya* (July-August 2014): 6–8.

Aloysius Pieris, SJ, is the founder-director of the Tulana Research Centre for Encounter and Dialogue in Kelaniya, Sri Lanka, and editor-in-chief of *Dialogue NS* and *Vagdevi, Journal of Religious Reflection*. He is the author of twenty-three books and 270 articles, and has lectured as Indologist-cum-theologian in more than twenty universities around the world.

PART TWO

WAYS OF DOING MISSION

Introduction to Part Two

Susan K. Wood, SCL

Part Two discusses ways of doing mission: the where, who, what, and how of mission. As is often repeated, the church does not have a mission; it is missionary by its very nature since "it draws its origin from the mission of the Son and the mission of the Holy Spirit, in accordance with the plan of the Father."[1] Indeed, missionary outreach is "paradigmatic of all the Church's activity."[2] Even though the church in its evangelizing mission proclaims a gospel offering a salvation that is both transcendent and eschatological, this mission and gospel must also reach into and influence societies, cultures, and political and social orders. While the essays that follow will treat these themes in more detail, the following gives a thumbnail sketch of the themes of this section.

The "Where" of Mission

Mission, as one aspect of the new evangelization, addresses an *ad intra* audience of those people who have already heard Christ proclaimed, "countries with ancient Christian roots, and occasionally in the younger Churches as well, where entire groups of the baptized have lost a living sense of the faith, or even no longer consider themselves members of the Church, and live a life far removed from Christ and his Gospel."[3] Mission *ad intra* addresses primarily lukewarm Christians, former Christians, or secular societies that were once Christian.

---

[1] Vatican Council II, *Ad Gentes (Decree on Missionary Activity)* (1965), no. 2.

[2] Pope Francis, apostolic exhortation *Evangelii Gaudium (The Joy of the Gospel)* (2013), no. 15, hereinafter *EG*.

[3] Pope John Paul II, *Redemptoris Missio (On the Permanent Validity of the Church's Missionary Mandate)* (1990), no. 33, hereinafter *RM*.

As John Paul II notes in *Redemptoris Missio,* missionary activity proper, namely the mission *ad gentes,* primarily addresses an *ad extra* audience, "'peoples or groups who do not yet believe in Christ,' 'who are far from Christ,' in whom the Church 'has not yet taken root' and whose culture has not yet been influenced by the Gospel." In other words, it is "addressed to groups and settings which are non-Christian because the preaching of the Gospel and the presence of the Church are either absent or insufficient."[4] *Redemptoris Missio* cautions, however, that there are no clear boundaries between the new evangelization, pastoral care of the faithful, and missionary activity, and notes that there is a real and growing interdependence among these various saving activities of the church. Each of these activities, both *ad intra* and *ad extra,* should be a credible sign and stimulus for the other.[5]

The "Who" of Mission

The entire people of God—inclusive of the laity, clergy, and religious—are called to the mission of witness and proclamation that the world may be transformed into the reign of God and that the human community may be formed into the universal community of brothers and sisters in Christ and sons and daughters of God the Father through the power of the Holy Spirit. Mission is an outgrowth of the prophetic anointing received at baptism and at confirmation. As Pope Francis reminds us, we are all *missionary disciples.*[6] Yet, mission is "first and foremost the Lord's work."[7] We are privileged to participate in this endeavor guided by the Spirit.

The "What" of Mission

The missionary mandate is found in Matthew 28:19–20: "Go therefore and make disciples of all nations, baptizing them in the name of the Father and of the Son and of the Holy Spirit, teaching them to observe all that I have commanded you." The "what" of mission is the preaching of the *gospel,* the *good news.* Mission is an activity on the part of those who

---

[4] *RM,* no. 34.
[5] *RM,* no. 34.
[6] *EG,* no. 119.
[7] *EG,* no. 12.

have encountered the love of God in Jesus Christ and go out and give witness to that love.[8]

The "How" of Mission

The "how" of mission is as varied as those who engage in mission, ranging from simple accompaniment to high-level theology, to give two examples. Examples of mission as accompaniment include the Little Brothers of Jesus, an outgrowth of the work of Charles de Foucault, who was killed in 1914 without having built up a community during his lifetime. The brothers work a full day in the mines, on the docks, and in various similar places of labor, live in communities of two or three, and have the Blessed Sacrament in their simple dwellings. There is also a community of sisters who do the same. This witness is similar to the priest-worker movement originated by Fr. Jacques Loew, who started working on the docks in Marseille in 1941. A similar initiative was begun in England in the 1960s. These endeavors have resonances also in the Catholic Worker Movement founded by Dorothy Day and Peter Maurin in 1933 in the United States during the Great Depression. The "how" of mission for such groups consists in radical Christian living among the poor to witness to those who may not have contact with Christianity through more traditional avenues.

To move from the "how" of simple accompaniment to the "how" of high-level theology, we have the example of two well-known German Catholic theologians, Karl Rahner and Walter Kasper, who framed their theology to respond to a secular culture. Kasper begins his book *The God of Jesus Christ* with sixty pages of natural theology rather than with revelation, since natural theology does not depend upon faith or revelation to argue for the rationality of belief in God.[9] Similarly, Rahner gives an account of the human being as "hearer of the word" and as "spirit in the world" in order to argue for the human, grace-given capability to receive God's gift of God's self to us in "uncreated grace."[10] Both theologians address secular culture in the light of faith, trying to make sense of that faith in a contemporary context marked by pluralism of all kinds. One rarely thinks of Rahner and Kasper as being missionaries, but they both

---

[8] *EG*, no. 120.

[9] Walter Kasper, *The God of Jesus Christ* (New York: T & T Clark International, New Edition, 2012; German original Freiburg im Breisgau: Verlag Herder GmbH, 2008).

[10] See Karl Rahner, SJ, *Theological Investigations*, vol. 1, *God, Christ, Mary, and Grace* (London: Darton, Longman and Todd, 1961).

witness to faith and offer theologies directed to those who have not heard or received the gospel.

The many ways of doing mission only multiply with the contemporary awareness that mission is not the esoteric activity of a few in exotic lands, but the activity of all the people of God called to radiate the fruits of their personal encounter with God in witness and action.

Susan K. Wood, SCL, is academic dean of Regis College at the University of Toronto, Canada, and professor emerita of theology at Marquette University in Milwaukee, Wisconsin. She was president of the Catholic Theological Society of America from 2014 to 2015. She is author of *One Baptism: The Ecumenical Implications of the Doctrine of Baptism* (2009).

The "When" of Mission
Rediscovering "Initial Proclamation" in Evangelization

Alfred Maravilla, SDB

In our present historical moment when the evangelizing activity of the church focuses on stirring up the faith in nonbelievers and reviving it in all the baptized, there is a renewed appreciation of initial proclamation's relevance and importance. Actually, this is a new term for an old reality.

Two personal encounters of Jesus in the Gospel of John are wonderful examples of initial proclamation. In his conversation with Nicodemus,[1] Jesus guides the development of the dialogue by helping him to make a leap from his narrowmindedness toward the totally new and transcendent. The other is Jesus's encounter with the Samaritan woman.[2] With a simple request for a drink, Jesus opens the woman to a dialogue that not only dissipates ethnic hatred and widens her horizons, but also leads her to enter herself and face the truth she finds there. This encounter enabled the Samaritan woman to recognize Jesus as the Messiah and to transform her to become a bearer of the good news to her country folk.

The Acts of the Apostles shows that the lifestyle of the early Christian communities was a living witness to how the gospel changed their lives. At the Areopagus,[3] Paul tried to explain to the citizens of Athens, as concisely as possible, the characteristics of this new religion, and he used various means to deal with his listeners and immediately to feel in tune with them. Paul touched on their fundamental philosophical presuppositions; he showed great familiarity with their significant literary and historical traditions; he appealed to natural revelation where it dealt with universal norms. Although many left him when he started talking about the resurrection of the dead, some did listen to him and believed in Jesus Christ.

---

[1] Jn 3:1–42.
[2] Jn 4:5–42.
[3] Acts 17:16–34.

The apologists at the end of the second century underlined the role of culture in the history of salvation. Through dialogue and a comparison with the Jews and the Gentiles the apologists sought to stir up an interest in the Person of Jesus Christ and his gospel. Instead, Saints Cyril and Methodius tried to learn more about the inner world of the Slavic people, created an alphabet for the Slavonic language, and translated the Bible and liturgical books into their language. This enabled them to proclaim the word of God using images and concepts that were familiar to Slavs and easily aroused their interest. Much later, upon their arrival in the Philippines in 1521, the Spanish missionaries wrote the grammar of the local languages that became the basis of the catechetical materials in the local languages. Meanwhile, Matteo Ricci (1552–1610) sought to explain Christianity by using *Confucian* values and Chinese concepts. St. Justin de Jacobis (1800–1860) wore the local style of dress, learned the Ethiopian language, and celebrated in the Coptic Rite following the Ethiopian liturgical calendar. These are just a few of the countless missionaries who have fostered initial proclamation in various ways among the peoples and nations of every continent.

Rediscovery of Initial Proclamation

There are two different ways of understanding evangelization in the two important documents of the magisterium of the church: *Ad Gentes* (1965) and *Evangelii Nuntiandi* (1975). The conciliar decree *Ad Gentes*, no. 7, presents evangelization as a specific moment in the missionary activity of the church, aimed at bringing about conversion and initial acts of faith, which in turn leads to the catechumenate. Instead, Pope Paul VI's apostolic exhortation *Evangelii Nuntiandi* was a turning point in the definition of evangelization. In no. 24, it identifies evangelization with the very mission of the church; hence, it includes various complementary and mutually enriching elements: the renewal of humanity, witness, explicit proclamation, inner adherence, entry into the community, acceptance of signs, and apostolic initiative. Although *Evangelii Nuntiandi* helped gain a deeper comprehension of evangelization, it paradoxically brought about some difficulties because while presenting evangelization with a wider perspective it never entirely abandoned its restricted understanding.

To reconcile these two concepts of evangelization many forms have been developed by adding adjectives and prefixes, for example, *pre*-evangelization, *first* evangelization, *re*-evangelization, and *new* evangelization.

This multiplication of terms has not clarified the term *evangelization,* and instead has brought about a divergent understanding and interpretation. For some, evangelization already includes an initial encounter with Jesus that leads to conversion, while others consider it identical with *kerygma* (Greek for "proclamation"), and not a few consider the three concepts of *kerygma,* initial proclamation, and evangelization to be interchangeable.

Pope Paul VI's *Evangelii Nuntiandi* was the first pontifical document to use the term "initial proclamation" as directed to those who do not know Christ and his gospel, as well as to the baptized who do not live their faith or have abandoned it (nos. 51–53). Initial proclamation was to appear gradually in other papal documents, albeit with varying nuances. At the beginning of his pontificate, Pope John Paul II's exhortation *Catechesi Tradendae* (1979) emphasized that catechesis is based on initial proclamation, describing it as "missionary preaching through the *kerygma* to stir up faith" (no. 18). He later underlined in his missionary encyclical *Redemptoris Missio* (1990) the central and irreplaceable role of initial proclamation because it leads the person to a personal relationship with Jesus, which opens the way to conversion (no. 44). In the light of *Catechesi Tradendae*. nos. 19–21, and following the *General Directory of Catechesis* (1997), no. 51, the post-synodal exhortation *Ecclesia in Europa* (2003) introduced a new distinction between "initial proclamation" and "renewed proclamation." The former is used to refer to unbaptized persons, while the latter is used to refer to the baptized who do not live their faith conscientiously (nos. 46–47).

The rediscovery of the initial proclamation has given rise to a different understanding of its place in the process of evangelization, especially regarding its identity as well as its relationship with *kerygma* and catechesis. In fact, initial proclamation is often confused with *kerygma* and catechesis. The Aparecida Document of CELAM V in 2007 stressed, for instance, the importance of kerygmatic proclamation as a way to develop a personal relationship with Christ and discipleship, but at the same time referred to *kerygma* as initial proclamation. Without clearly defining initial proclamation, Aparecida opened up the possibility of variety in its understanding, particularly on the American continent.

Pope Francis's two latest post-synodal exhortations emphasize the importance of initial proclamation: *Amoris Laetitia* (2016), no. 58, speaks of the family as the privileged setting of initial proclamation, while *Christus Vivit* (2019), no. 210, sees young people as agents of initial proclamation. Unfortunately, the term gets lost in the translation. While the official translations in the European languages speak of "primer anuncio," "première annonce," and "primo annuncio," it is poorly translated in English as "the gospel message" and "the seed of the message." The recently published *Directory for Catechesis* (2020) distinguishes three phases and aspects in the first stage of evangelization: first, *witness*; second, *initial proclamation*; and third, *pre-catechumenate*, which leads to an initial response and conversion (no. 33).

Initial Proclamation as "Falling in Love"

When two people from different backgrounds meet and, in some way, sense a feeling for each other, their initial curiosity turns into a desire to know each other better. It all starts from the feeling level, from the experiential plane. Love evolves only when the two people learn to accept each other's uniqueness and become capable of considering their differences as mutual enrichment.

Although there is no precise plan as to when to actually make one's feelings known to the beloved, the lover is constantly on the lookout for the right moment to declare his or her love to the beloved. Similarly, living one's Christian life permanently in a constant state of mission, always on the lookout to grab any opportunity for initial proclamation, is like a sentinel ever ready to give a reason for the hope that is within oneself. There is no set schedule or plan to reveal the lover's personal feelings to the beloved; yet, having this thought always in mind, the lover is always vigilant to seize the opportune time to make his or her declaration of love freely.

After getting to know each other better, there is a magic moment when the lover finally tells the beloved, "I love you." Such a trite declaration is actually the result of the preceding timid and sometimes clumsy steps to get to know the other better. For the lover this expression is not a mere cliché. Instead, it unveils, reveals, and brings to life the deeper meaning of all the previous beautiful moments they have shared. Although this is an overused expression, which risks losing its meaning, for these two, the phrase "I love you" becomes a challenging invitation they can really respond to. Obviously, the initial "I love you" is not the end but the beginning of a process that leads to courtship, engagement, and marriage. In fact, it is the foundation of a happy and lasting marriage.

Just as two people do not plan to fall in love, the initial proclamation is not planned or organized. It is not a program, or a method, or an activity, or a celebration. Hence, we do not *make* an initial proclamation. It takes place especially in the "everyday moments of ordinary daily life lived with Christian charity, faith, and hope," in season and out of season,[4] in various forms depending on the culture, context, rhythm of life, and socio-historical situations of those to whom it is directed. In the same way that love develops only when the lovers learn to accept each other's uniqueness as well as to consider their differences as mutual enrichment, initial proclamation always implies inculturation. It comes about through awareness and the understanding of the language, culture, needs, and potential of those to whom initial proclamation is intended, as well as the capacity to discern "the seed of the word" of God in their context.

A Definition of Initial Proclamation

The adjective *initial* is not to be understood in a strictly linear or chronological sense as being the first moment of proclamation, because that would actually impoverish its richness. Rather, it is initial in the sense that the term *arché* was understood by ancient Greek philosophers—as the principle or the fundamental element from which everything has its origin, or that from which all things are formed. It is in this sense that in English the term *initial proclamation* is preferable to *first proclamation* or *first evangelization*.

When we use a lighter or strike a match, there are usually several sparks before we get the spark that finally lights the flame. Similarly, initial proclamation could be likened to that spark which becomes the principle, the foundation, of the initial act of personal faith in Jesus Christ. It is initial because it is at that moment, but preceded by other indispensable conditions, through which the power of the Holy Spirit has ignited an initial interest in the Person of Jesus Christ or has stirred up questions concerning the place one reserves for God in one's life. It fascinates, attracts, and makes the heart burn as it did for the disciples at Emmaus.

Consequently, the primary concern of the initial proclamation is not to proclaim *who* Jesus is, as expressed in the christological formulas or catechism, but rather *how* to lead others to discover and be fascinated by the Person of Jesus Christ who alone leads them to faith. At this moment it gives primacy not to words but to the experience that stirs up an interest, not to dogmatic formulas but to the work of the Holy Spirit. This allows people to engage in a profound and transforming relationship with Jesus, as it was for Bartimaeus, the Samaritan woman, Nicodemus, and Zacchaeus.

---

[4] 2 Tim 4:2.

Faith is not the outcome of an educational program or scientific study. It is only the result of an encounter with God in Jesus Christ. Hence, it is necessary, first of all, to create the environment, the atmosphere, through personal contact and to discern the right moment and the most appropriate means that could spur and foster a person's desire to know more about Jesus Christ. The witness of life and interpersonal relationships prepare the heart for the initial proclamation and establish a kind of relationship like that of Jesus in the gospel. They become a free and respectful invitation to the dialogue partner, who decides to accept or reject it, exemplified by the encounter of Jesus with the Samaritan woman at Jacob's well.[5] Initial proclamation is effectively fostered if the faith journey follows a gradual pedagogy, which is attentive to the cultural, historical, and social context of the dialogue partner.

Hence, the initial proclamation may be defined as the witness of every Christian and of the whole Christian community or any activity or group of activities that fosters an overwhelmingly exhilarating religious experience, which then, through the Holy Spirit, inspires a search for God and arouses an interest in the Person of Jesus Christ that, ultimately, leads to an initial adhesion to him, or to a revitalization of faith in him.[6]

Those Involved in Initial Proclamation

Unlike the concept of pre-evangelization, which seeks to predispose and open people to the gospel, initial proclamation is much richer and more encompassing because it focuses on four actors:
- the *human person*, considering the socio-cultural-religious context and routine of ordinary daily life, because initial proclamation takes place in the heart of the dialogue partner;
- the *Christian believer*, who practices the faith and lives a committed Christian life as a missionary disciple; the focus is *not* on a person's qualities or on "techniques" for fostering initial proclamation;
- a *personal encounter with God*, which touches the most intimate fabric of one's being and puts one in front of the living God in absolute immediacy so that one may dialogue with, love, and enter into

---

[5] Jn 4:3–42.
[6] Xavier Morlans, *El Primer Anuncio: El Eslabon Perdido* (Madrid: PPC, 2009), 29–31; Serge Tyvaert, "De la Première Annonce à la Nouvelle Évangélisation," *Cahiers Internationaux de Théologie Pratique* 10 (2012): 97–99.

personal communion with God; it is this profound contact that gives birth to faith;
- the *Holy Spirit,* who is the true protagonist of initial proclamation, not the Christian, the missionary, or the preacher. It is the power of the Holy Spirit, who "blows where it wills,"[7] that opens the door of the human heart so that the way of life of every Christian and every activity of the Christian community at any time and place may stir up an interest in Jesus.

It matters less, therefore, whether one is in a school, university, vocational training center, parish, mission station, in the forest, in an urban center, in one's own country, or away from one's homeland, or whether one is involved in education, in pastoral ministry, in health ministry, or in human promotion and development. What matters most is to live the Christian life in a permanent state of mission. When there is a conscious intention to foster the initial proclamation, every Christian, and every Christian community, is always and everywhere a radiating center of Christian mission.

To Whom Is It Addressed?

By its very nature, initial proclamation is primarily addressed to
- those who do not know Jesus Christ;
- those who have known Jesus and then abandoned him;
- those who have a weak and vulnerable Christian identity;
- those who believe that they already know Jesus enough, call themselves Christians or Catholics, but live their faith as a routine, or simply as a part of their culture, yet do not practice it at all; and
- those who are looking for someone or something they perceive but to which they are unable to give a name; and
- those who live a meaningless daily life.

For those who do not know Christ, *initial proclamation* is that spark which could lead to conversion, and then the process of *evangelization* can begin. For the baptized who have become lukewarm, or no longer practice their faith, or live it as something cultural or as mere routine, initial proclamation triggers the revitalization of faith and helps them to renew their initial adhesion to Jesus Christ. This "renewed initial proclamation"

---

[7] Jn 3:8.

is a second free invitation to discover the Person of Jesus Christ on whom the new evangelization is founded anew.[8]

Kerygma and Initial Proclamation

Like the "I love you" expressed by two lovers that leads to a deeper knowledge of each other, initial proclamation leads to *kerygma*. Although initial proclamation precedes *kerygma*, it is also intimately connected to it. While the initial proclamation focuses on the *means* to invite people to faith in Jesus, *kerygma* focuses on Jesus Christ, the *content* of the Christian faith.

The *kerygma* was a response to the memory of Jesus that consisted of his life, teachings, and resurrection. This was pondered upon, accurately formulated, proclaimed, celebrated, and lived as testified by various formulas found in the New Testament.[9] At the propitious moment, the Spirit opens the door of the heart. This consists of no more than a brief, joyful, intelligible, and respectful invitation to know Jesus Christ and his gospel, such as "Jesus is Lord,"[10] or "God has made both Lord and Christ, this Jesus whom you crucified."[11] Inversely, there can be no *kerygma* without the narration of the memory of the Person, life, and teachings of Jesus Christ. It could give birth to faith[12] with its consequent radical conversion, *metanoia*,[13] and commitment to follow and imitate him.[14]

Oriented toward the Process of Evangelization

Expressing one's love to the beloved is not enough. Falling in love is just the beginning that needs to be followed up by an engagement, a marriage proposal, and a lifelong commitment in marriage. Similarly, initial proclamation needs to be deepened through the process of evangelization

---

[8] Enzo Biemmi, *Il Secondo Annuncio* (Bologna: EDB, 2011), 37.
[9] See Mt 28:6; Mk 16:6; Lk 24:6:34; Acts 2:24; 1 Thess 4:14.
[10] Rom 10:9; Phil 2:11.
[11] Acts 2:36.
[12] Rom 10:17.
[13] Acts 5:31; 11:18.
[14] Phil 2:1–12. Jean Audussean and Xavier Léon-Dufour, "Prêcher," in *Vocabulaire de Théologie Biblique,* 2nd ed., ed. Xavier Léon-Dufour (Paris: Cerf, 1970), 1106–11; Cesare Bissoli, "Il Primo Annuncio nella Comunità Cristiana delle Origini," in *Il Primo Annuncio tra "Kerygma" e Catechesi,* ed. Cettina Cacciato (Turin: Elledici, 2010), 13–22; Colin Brown, "Proclamation," in *New Testament Theology,* ed. Colin Brown III (Grand Rapids, MI: Zondervan, 1978), 44–68.

(conversion, catechumenate, baptism, sacramental initiation, and lifelong catechesis). When someone decides to get to know the Person of Jesus Christ, the content of the faith is explained by a pedagogy that introduces the person step by step to the mystery of Jesus Christ, the Son of God. Thus, the initial proclamation cannot be considered in isolation, because it is necessarily linked to and oriented toward the process of evangelization.

The initial grace that, through initial proclamation, has sowed the seed of faith, has to develop into an explicit faith in Jesus Christ through the process of evangelization. There is a progression from an option to follow Christ through conversion, to begin a Christian initiation or catechumenate (or a renewal of initiation for lapsed and lukewarm Christians), to the rites of Christian initiation, the sacramental life, catechesis, and ongoing integral formation, in order to live one's Christian life to the full and share it with others.[15]

A Renewed Missionary Catechesis

We know from experience that making known one's love for the beloved is not enough. The initial "I love you" needs to be regularly renewed on different occasions and different seasons of life. Catechesis is, in fact, keeping oneself enamored of one's first love.[16] This reinforces the mutual love that will enable the person to face the adversities of life. A baptized person whose initial proclamation was inadequate lacks the foundation of a strong faith. Without this initial step that leads to conversion and initial personal faith, catechesis is likely to become sterile. Inversely, initial proclamation needs to be fostered again and again in different ways to ensure an effective lifelong catechesis. In the light of this even Catholics, who attend our parishes, courses of catechesis, and religious instruction, as well as all Christians, need initial proclamation in view of deepening their faith and their personal adherence to Jesus Christ.

A truly missionary catechesis is intimately connected to the experience of human life, because experiences are its reference points in order to encounter those who seek God today, not in ecclesial settings but in the context of daily life and in the situations of present-day society. It is not structured in the sense that it is based on a planned curriculum, but on the experience of every person who accepts the invitation to a second initial proclamation. In this light the catechesis of children and young

---

[15] Tyvaert, "De la Première Annonce à la Nouvelle Évangélisation," 104.
[16] Rev 2:4.

people is seen as a preparation for adult and family catechesis because adults make faith options that affect the family and society.

In lifelong missionary catechesis the initial and renewed initial proclamation are not like a continuous refrain. Rather, they are like a love song accompanied by an appropriate melody: when one falls in love, during engagement, at the birth of a child, at the baptism of children, at peer meetings of adolescents and in the social networking of young people, in the journey of the migrant, in the struggle of workers, and in moments of sickness and old age. Every experience or occasion in life becomes an appeal, an action of grace, and a profession of faith, in the presence of God in the particular stage of life.[17]

Practice of Charity and Witness of Life as Initial Proclamation

The initial proclamation focuses on the practice of charity and witness of life as a primary *means* of inviting people to faith in Jesus Christ. Hence, importance is given to personal contact, interpersonal relationships and dialogue, all of which are preceded, accompanied, and followed by *charity*, because the witness of charity, through the action of the Holy Spirit, inspires, questions, and challenges. Besides, proclaiming Christ is above all an act of charity in making known God's love for each one of us. Thus, wherever the church is engaged in helping the sick, the suffering, the poor, and the marginalized, wherever the church is working for justice, peace, and integrity of creation, the virtual world and social communications provide a propitious setting for initial proclamation. The danger is losing sight of the initial proclamation as the ultimate goal of our dialogue of life and action. Without the overriding concern to foster initial proclamation, our social work would be reduced to philanthropy, and we would become mere social workers. Yet, the church is not an NGO, but God's people sent to share the gospel!

The practice of charity goes hand in hand with a credible *style of life* of individual Christians, of the Christian family, and of the whole Christian community, in its singular expression, in the context of cultural expressions of important moments of human existence, or in all its relational or sociopolitical expressions in daily life. This implies that the whole Christian community lives in a state of constant conversion as it journeys

---

[17] Enzo Biemmi, "La Prospettiva Missionaria come Forma della Chiesa e Figura del Cristianesimo," *Catechesi* 84, no. 1 (2014–15): 9–15.

toward holiness. This journey starts primarily in the family, the domestic church. The parents' witness of life is an initial proclamation that fosters the growth and development of the faith of their children. The educational environment in the family stirs up the interest of the children to know Jesus Christ better and to live up to his teachings and, ultimately, to become his credible witnesses themselves.

A credible witness may be an attractive invitation to learn about the motive and the ultimate reason for such a style of life. The Spirit can inspire and challenge one to examine one's own lifestyle, values, and priorities Thus, it becomes a preliminary path to faith. Hence, particular care and attention ought to be given to the way that the church presents itself as an institution, starting from its public events and its "traditional" pastoral activity (celebration of the sacraments, especially of baptism and marriage; pilgrimages; popular religiosity) because they reflect the ecclesial life that the public perceives. Similarly, it is necessary to face the possibilities and challenges presented by the new frontiers (for example, the digital continent, migration, multicultural and multireligious settings), as well as the new situations brought about by cultural changes (such as cultural fluidity and secularism) because they influence the *style of life* of Christians. It is also important to find and create occasions or places of encounter where people can feel free to talk about existential and religious questions and feel understood and listened to.[18]

The celebration of faith through the liturgy and expressions of popular religiosity also provides opportunities to foster initial proclamation. On the one hand, when these celebrations are carefully prepared, they could foster a fascination of faith that could arouse an interest in the Person of Jesus Christ among those present. On the other hand, they could inspire the deepening of the gospel way of life as well as nourish and strengthen the hope of the participants. The institutional and collective image of the church at its public events are all forms of initial proclamation or, unfortunately, a hindrance to it. The importance of the Christian style of life at the initial proclamation also helps to overcome the danger of reducing Christianity or Catholicism to a mere set of doctrines.[19]

---

[18] Ferruccio Ceragioli, "Le Onde del Vangelo. Dalla Testimonianza di Gesù alla Testimonianza dei Cristiani," *Gridare il Vangelo con la Vita*, ed. Ferruccio Ceragioli and Roberto Repole (Bologna: EDB, 2021), 40–45.

[19] André Fossion, "Proposta della Fede e Primo Annuncio," *Catechesi* 78, no. 4 (2008–9): 30; Luca Bressan, "Quali Esperienze di Annuncio Proporre?" *Notiziario dell'Ufficio Catechistico Nazionale* 36, no. 1 (2007): 61–68.

Storytelling as Initial Proclamation

Anyone can foster initial proclamation by sharing the story of one's personal encounter with Jesus the Savior. Unlike direct proclamation, which might appear in secularized and multireligious contexts as a culturally insensitive and religiously disrespectful monologue, one could tell and retell one's faith experience in the context of a web of relationships among friends. Surely it is only from the strength and fervor of one's faith that one feels the urge and necessity to tell and retell others about one's personal experience of Jesus, without any intention to force it on the listeners. When a story is woven to search for meaning in the life of the listeners, it may foster an encounter with an event, a Person, who gives life a new horizon and a decisive direction that inspires hope and strength in them to face the daily struggle of life.

In multireligious contexts the use of symbols or images drawn from daily life could bring Jesus Christ closer to their existential reality and concerns. Obviously, any image, symbol, or formulation expressed in myths, folklore, and other narratives can be found on analysis to be consistent with the Christian faith by "examining how they incorporate the biblical witness of Jesus and how they make use of the historical Christological traditions."[20] This gradual and dialogical process does not deny, hide, or dilute the complete truth of Jesus Christ; rather, it prepares for the personal reception of his Person and message. The Holy Spirit, the Great Weaver, who works in the depths of every conscience, could trigger by means of stories, symbols, or images, the existential questions in a person, which could lead to the unveiling of the truth and values profoundly longed for by the human heart and spark an interest in the Person and message of Jesus Christ.[21]

Challenges and Opportunities for Initial Proclamation

The first challenge for initial proclamation today is that in our post-truth society the notion of *objective truth* has been banished in favor of

---

[20] Peter C. Phan, "Jesus the Christ with an Asian Face," *Theological Studies* 57 (1996): 428.

[21] Ricardo Tonelli, *La Narrazione nella Catechesis e nella Pastorale Giovanile* (Turin, Leuman: LDC, 2002), 54–64; Johann Baptist Metz, "Breve Apologia del Narrare," *Concilium* 5 (1973): 864–68.

self-serving versions of reality. Truth is not discovered but constructed through language, ethnicity, hopes, fears, and other social elements, according to what suits one. Hence, the use of the very common expression of approval, "I'm comfortable with that," or of disapproval, "I'm not comfortable with that." Thus, truth is reduced to what is externally verifiable or to scientific truths, hence depriving the human person of the capacity to recognize and reach higher truths. Consequently, not only is there no felt need to pursue the truth, but no one also worries about objective truth all together! Similarly, freedom is often reduced to the arbitrary and subjective capacity of choosing among several options.

Since a plausible religious discourse needs to be reasonable, it is important to foster the widening of the horizons of human reason as a profoundly personal capacity to arrive at practical judgments and use a more existential logic. Reason is enabled to go beyond the empirical spheres so that it can confront the existential question of truth without equating it with external objectivity. This, in turn, gives space to imagination, which makes St. John Henry Newman's insight extremely helpful here: "the heart is commonly reached not through reason but through the imagination."[22] For him, imagination "connects our thinking about God first and foremost, not with the physical world, but with the internal world of a man's personal life."[23] It is the keystone in the interpretation of the data of experience and of prompting decisions. Through a reason that leaves space for imagination the human person arrives at the truth in a personal and profound matter. Imagination becomes a vehicle to reach the Truth of God, which could not be ever sufficiently expressed in words.[24] This, consequently, leads to the discovery of the human dimension in the search for truth and opens the mind to think by means of stories and metaphors that, ultimately, reach the heart. Indeed, the reason of the heart is not governed by logical deductions but by subtle spontaneous logic.[25] This perspective opens numerous opportunities for initial proclamation!

---

[22] John Henry Newman, *Grammar of Assent* (Cambridge: Cambridge University Press, 2010), 89.

[23] In Edward A. Sillem, "Cardinal Newman's 'Grammar of Assent' on Conscience as a Way to God," *Heythrop Journal* 5, no. 4 (1964): 400.

[24] Michael Paul Gallagher, "Allargare l'Intelletto verso l'Amore," in *La Carità Intellettuale: Percorsi Culturali per un Nuovo Umanesimo,* ed. Lorenzo Leuzzi (Vatican City: Libreria Editrice Vaticana, 2007), 22–23, 24; Michael Paul Gallagher, "Newman on Imagination and Faith," *Milltown Studies* 49 (2002): 88–91, 95–96.

[25] Michael Paul Gallagher, *Free to Believe: Ten Steps to Faith* (London: Darton Longman and Todd, 1987), 47–49.

The second challenge is that the absence of religious discourse causes *an ever-waning openness to the Transcendent and to supernatural realities*. In an app-dependent and materialistic consumer society the radical openness to the Transcendent, the desire of the human heart to search for answers to the fundamental questions of life, the meaning of things and their existence, and the search for meaning and direction in life is obscured. Similarly, the logic of technology, business, and profit dominate, and people live without hope and direction. This absence of openness to the Transcendent makes initial proclamation not only ineffective, but faith itself and its transmission impossible.[26] With the impoverishment of truth and freedom and their interaction there is no way to arrive at charity. Faith, then, becomes impossible because faith is essentially recognition of love as gift and response to the Giver. What we are experiencing, then, is not only the incapacity to believe in God (*crisis of faith*) but especially the incapacity of the heart to perceive the mediations of faith (*crisis of imagination*). Thus, it is no surprise that there is a growing number of those who identify themselves as atheists or agnostics.

Social media and the internet reveal the innate human desire for personal encounters, friendship, sharing, communion, and meaning. This means that the globalized interconnected and multicultural world of social communications offers us tremendous opportunities to keep alive the spiritual yearning in hearts and the quest for truth in consciences that reveal the human desire for transcendence and authentic witness.[27] However, although the plethora of religious apps could easily lead the present generation to view religion in "app" terms, where one concocts one's own religious brew, apps, and the digital world in general, have fostered the development of some form of virtual religiosity that opens people of the digital continent to the religious discourse. This, in turn, gave birth to cyber-theology or reflections regarding the manner in which the logic of the network can promote the understanding of faith and its reception in a digital culture.[28] Thus, the means of social communications are not mere instruments to enter the digital continent but means of creating and

---

[26] Jose Chunkapura, "An Ever-Waning Openness to the Transcendent, a Key Issue for New Evangelization," *Salesianum* 75 (2012): 57–64.

[27] Domenico Pompili, "La Narrazione della Fede nell'Era della Comunicazione Globale," in *Reti Sociali: Porte de Verità e di Fede; Nuovi Spazi di Evangelizzazione,* ed. Fabio Pasqualetti and Cosimo Alvati (Rome: LAS, 2014), 23–28.

[28] Antonio Spadaro, *Cyberteologia: Pensare il Cristianesimo al Tempo della Rete* (Milano: Vita e Pensiero, 2012), 32–36.

fostering a new culture in order to be a prophetic presence that reflects the face of Christ.

The third challenge consists of those who claim to be religious yet maintain a certain distance from institutions of their religion or believe in an impersonal divine Being rather than a personal God. Actually, they reflect postmodern religiosity, which is *a disjunction among believing, behaving, and belonging*. They do not automatically behave and belong even if they believe; or they do not believe or belong but behave; or they do not believe or behave yet belong because belonging is more strongly asserted than actually believing. Inversely, the existence of a subconscious religiosity is a precious opportunity for initial proclamation. Hence, it is important to rediscover the desire for the Absolute as well as the desire to hear the voice of God that resounds in their consciences in order to arouse interest in the discourse about God. This helps in overcoming the distorted images of God in our society today that give rise to irrational popular religiosity and fundamentalism.[29]

Finally, the phenomenon of *human mobility*, particularly the continuous flow of people from the southern hemisphere to the northern hemisphere, is a challenge that has caused a humanitarian crisis and the rapid and disordered expansion of urban centers which are often unprepared for such masses of people.[30] Coming from a setting where religiosity was expressed in a culture shared by the majority of the inhabitants of a village or country, human mobility causes people to suffer the cultural impact caused by technology, social communications, and the post-truth culture. These expressions of popular religiosity that derive from the inculturation of the Catholic faith in their home countries are also a public proclamation of their faith as well as their active support in maintaining it.[31] Regardless of their particular religious affiliation, people turn to their religion and its institutions for emotional and social support as well as a way of affirming their cultural identity. The witness of life through their commitment to their religion becomes a challenge to lapsed or lukewarm Christians. On

---

[29] Carlos Maria Galli, *Dios Vive en la Ciudad* (Barcelona: Herder, 2015), 157–61; Charles Taylor, *The Secular Age* (Cambridge: Belknap Press, 2007), 507–22.

[30] Pontifical Council for the Pastoral Care of Migrants and Itinerant People, *Erga Migrantes Caritas Christi* (Vatican: Libreria Editrice Vaticana, 2004), nos. 4–10.

[31] Daniel Cuesta Gomez, *Luces y Sombras de la Religiosidad Popular* (Bilbao: Mensajero, 2021), 81–92; Andrés Gallego Garcia, "Evangelizar en la Ciudad: Pequeñas Reflexiones desde América Latina," *Misiones Extranjeras* 253 (2013): 212–13; Bernardo Lindner, "¡Dios Presente en Todo! Vivir y Aprender la Fe en al Mundo Andino," *Páginas* 229 (March 2013): 54–56.

the other hand, the witness of Christian life could challenge followers of other religions to redefine their attachment to their religion and arouse an interest in Jesus.[32]

A Dream

I dare to dream that the rediscovery of the relevance of initial proclamation will open up a new and promising horizon and rekindle our missionary zeal. I dare to hope that it may transform every believer to be "on fire with the love of Christ and burning with zeal to make him known more widely, loved more deeply and followed more closely." Indeed, "a fire can only be lit by something that is itself on fire."[33] Let us not give in to faith fatigue and slide back to the comfortable but joyless and ardorless maintenance mode of Christian life!

Alfred Maravilla, SDB, was born in Silay City, Negros Occidental-Philippines. He was sent as a missionary to Papua New Guinea, where he worked in the Missions Department at the Generalate from 2008 to 2017, and was then elected superior of the Vice-Province of Papua New Guinea–Solomon Islands. At present, he is the general councilor for the Salesian Missions.

---

[32] Jocelyne Cesari, "Religion and Diasporas: Challenges of the Emigration Countries," in *Migrant Integration between Homeland and Host Society,* vol. 1, ed. Agnieszka Weinar, Anne Unterreiner, and Philippe Fargues (New York: Springer International Publishing, 2017), 173–99; Rebecca Y. Kim, "Religion and Ethnicity: Theoretical Connections," *Religions* 2 (2011): 317–18; Galli, *Dios Vive en la Ciudad,* 260–65.

[33] John Paul II, *Ecclesia in Asia* (1999), no. 23.

The "Who" of Mission

We Are Mission

IDA COLOMBO, CMS, HÉLÈNE ISRAËL SOLOUMTA KAMKÔL, CMS, AND MARIA TERESA RATTI, CMS

The Beauty of Witnessing Together

We are three Comboni Missionary Sisters who have had the joy of taking part in a joint project shared within the branches of the Comboni Family.[1] Officially constituted on June 26, 2019, the Social Ministry Commission of the Comboni Family set out its main objectives: (1) to map all social ministries of the Comboni Family; (2) to elaborate common criteria, modalities, and principles in existing collaborative experiences, framing them in an institutional perspective; and (3) to evaluate how the various ministries have an impact of social transformation on reality, and how our ministerial presence responds to the real needs of the signs of the times.[2]

During these two years, we have experienced the beauty of being on a journey together, while attempting to find shared answers to complex and rapidly changing situations. Being part of a common family—the Comboni Family—facilitated the realization of the path in its individual stages, and a shared charismatic vocabulary has surely catalyzed with renewed energy the contents realized along the way.

In addition to the realization of the social ministry map, our central administrations entrusted us with two more tasks: the publication of a second

---

[1] Formed by Comboni Missionary Sisters (CMS), Secular Comboni Missionaries (SCM), Comboni Missionaries of the Heart of Jesus (MCCJ), and Comboni Lay Missionaries.

[2] Official document signed by the General Councilors Sr. Ida Colombo, CMS, and Bro. Alberto Lamana, MCCJ, with the names of the members of the commission and the objectives entrusted to the same (Rome, June 26, 2019).

volume, as a follow-up to the first,[3] and the planning for our participation at the 2020 World Social Forum (WSF) along with the organization of the Comboni Family Forum on Social Ministry. The pandemic caused by COVID-19 greatly affected our roadmap, forcing us to envision ways of participation not contemplated before.[4]

A Path of Many Steps and Events

The most recent historical development that kindled in the Comboni Family the need to highlight social ministry in its missionary methodology was the participation of several Comboni men and women at various meetings of the WSF. Started in 2001 in Porto Alegre (Brazil), the WSF became a platform for networks, movements, organizations, and interested groups to get to know one another, reflect, listen, report, weave, and dream of ways to make *another world really possible*.[5] From 2007, with the WSF held in Nairobi (Kenya), the Comboni Family began to accompany these events as the Comboni Social Forum, and, with the passing of time we better grasped the urgency to embrace ministerial cooperation as a sine qua non condition that would give our evangelical witness the flavor of leavened bread baked within the Comboni synodality.

Our "recent" journey of witnessing mission together has now reached the threshold of twenty years, but our common history comes from much earlier times. For instance, seven years before Porto Alegre 2001, the Comboni Family had been quite involved in founding the Institute of Social Ministry in Mission at Tangaza University College in Nairobi,

---

[3] Fernando Zolli and Daniele Moschetti, eds., *Be the Change You Wish to See in the World—The Comboni Family and Justice, Peace, and Integrity of Creation*, Comboni Network for Justice, Peace, and Integrity of Creation (2018).

[4] Originally scheduled to take place in Rome, on July 18–22, 2020, the Comboni Family Forum on Social Ministry was to be hosted at the Generalate of the Comboni Missionaries. COVID-19 forced us to plan, alternatively, two webinars: December 4–5, 2020, and March 5–6, 2021, hoping for a "real" gathering July 3–7, 2021. The complex situation did not change, so we opted for a third webinar, held on June 25–26, 2021. We greatly rejoiced at the turn of events, since the opportunity to participate was extended to many more people.

[5] Usually, the WSF is organized at the same time as the World Economic Forum, which meets in Davos, Switzerland. Here, the "very rich and powerful of our world meet to work out their strategies to promote growth and maximize profit at almost any cost" ("The Wind of Pentecost Moves Our Struggles," in Zolli and Moschetti, *Be the Change You Wish to See in the World*, 51–57).

Kenya.[6] The inspiring root of this commitment—which over the years has grown to a large tree transplanted into the most varied human terrains where the Comboni Family is present—is contained in the becoming of a divine plan in the life of a very special human being. A vocation, which Providence entrusted in the hands of a young missionary whose life found its meaning in the very middle of an intense dialogue between the two great loves of his life: the love of God and the love of Africa.

A Charism among Continents, Cultures, and Communities

To whom are we referring? Our founder, St. Daniel Comboni (March 15, 1831, Limone sul Garda, Italy–October 10, 1881, Khartoum, Sudan). In his "Plan for the Regeneration of Africa with Africa" (1864), this great apostle of the gospel in the Vicariate of Central Africa understood that reality can be renewed whenever people are involved in the transformation processes of their history. The church in Africa is today a living testimony to his prophetic stance. It is from this charismatic threshold that we shall share our understanding of the "who" of mission.

It is our belief—certainly shared by many people—that at the heart of the missionary experience the "subject"—the "who"—is never a singular entity, but always a plural reality. This is simply because that is the very essence of what we have come to name *mission*.

Ours is a call to witness to the *missio Dei*, which has the Most Holy Trinity as its source and ultimate goal. We are convinced that telling the "who" of mission, according to the modalities that surfaced during our shared exercise, is a testimony to the call that sees us as coworkers of God in the realization of God's mission in every time and in every place.

The weaving of the Comboni dream within continents, cultures, and communities should be welcomed as the background and goal of the growth of a "who" made tangible by the many processes initiated in order to accompany a true social transformation. To experience ministry in its social dimension was the motivation for, as well as the perspective within which the various initiatives took shape. What we shall try to share will echo, in a symbolic-interpretative form, the "who" of mission recounted

---

[6] Officially founded in 1994 by Fr. Francesco Pierli, MCCJ, the Institute of Social Ministry in Mission has systematically contributed to contextualizing a new missionary methodology centered on social transformation. From an initial diploma program, the institute now offers a doctorate, with various fields of specialization. On the twenty-fifth anniversary of its foundation (2019), it adopted a new name: The Institute of Social Transformation.

in the book *We Are Mission*,[7] by some Comboni women and men in Africa, the Americas, Asia, and Europe. Along with them, we shall recount the efforts of other missionary disciples—each striving to find ways and means to communally witness the joy of the gospel.

The "Who" of Mission from Africa
(by Sr. Hélène Israël Soloumta Kamkôl)

In the *mare magnum* of mission, Africa has its own word to say for a better understanding of the precious vitality that envelops the "who" at the heart of missionary witness. However, it is essential to make clear first of all what we understand by the word *mission*. Some biblical examples, in particular, help us to better express what we, in Africa, mean as we approach the ever-burning bush of mission. I am well aware that here we can express only a few understandings, within an immensely broader vision and experience surrounding the wonderful theme that the term *mission* contains.

Our Understanding from the Scriptures

"I have seen the affliction of my people and have heard their cry; I know its sufferings. . . . Come! I will send you to Pharaoh that you may bring my people . . . out of Egypt!"[8] God is a direct witness to the deep experience of suffering the enslaved people are undergoing in Egypt. Sure enough, God chose not to remain silent and safe in some celestial residence. Rather, God made a move to free the people. The command imparted to Moses, "Bring my people out of Egypt," shows that God is ready to fight for justice. God does not want to make the situation bearable, for example by saying, "I am sorry," "Be patient," "Pray a lot," "This time will pass," or "Ask Pharaoh to adjust matters." No! Here, an operative, imperatively definitive exit from oppression was required—a very strong sociopolitical decision that Moses had to face; *not* an ecclesiastical office Moses was called to perform!

---

[7] Fernando Zolli and Daniele Moschetti, eds., *We Are Mission: Witnesses to Social Ministry within the Comboni Family*, Comboni Network for Justice, Peace, and Integrity of Creation (2020), 285. Printed in English, French, Italian, and Spanish, this volume offers a variety of editorial analyses, and describes thirty-one ministerial experiences lived out in various collaborative modalities.

[8] Ex 3:7–10.

God takes the initiative—"Go!"—and spurs Moses into action, inviting him to intercede before Pharaoh. Through Moses, God sets out on a mission to free an abused people, like the Suffering Servant in Isaiah.[9] God observed the suffering, and descended, bending over wounded humanity. This lowering toward people is fully accomplished with and through Jesus. "The Spirit of the Lord is upon me, he sent me to proclaim a happy message to the poor, to proclaim liberation to prisoners, to give sight to the blind, to set free the oppressed, and to preach a year of the Lord's grace."[10] Yes, Jesus's mission has the same rhythm as his Father's.

And within Everyday Life

The Africa that has sprung, at all levels, from the impoverished and the prisoners, the blind and the oppressed, looks at this message of Jesus with hope. This is simply because the integral liberation of the human being also passes through physical, mental, spiritual, moral, and even cultural health. Different African theologians have grasped this very well when they try to express the impact of the liberating action of Jesus on the condition of the people.

Father Jean-Marc Ela, from Cameroon, was a theologian and sociologist (1936–2008). In his synthesis regarding African theological research, seen from the perspective of liberation and commitment, he sought to give a new meaning to the revelation of God in Africa. Quite often, people living in difficult conditions question the significance of the Divine in their situations. Father Ela's reflections, based on his experience among farmers facing famine, drought, and disease, show how the gospel can still nourish the hope of the most disadvantaged.[11] Of course, injustice, exploitation, and oppression show that people, in all walks of life, tend to lose their human dignity.

Theologian Mercy Amba Oduyoye,[12] starting from the African culture—which can also be a source of oppression for women—confirms

---

[9] Isa 53:4–7.
[10] Lk 4:18–19.
[11] Jean-Marc Ela, *Repenser la théologie africaine, le Dieu qui libère*, Chrétiens en liberté–Karthala (2003).
[12] Born in Ghana, Mercy Amba Oduyoye is regarded as the mother of African women's theologies. Director of the Institute of Women in Religion and Culture at Trinity Theological Seminary in Legon, Accra, Oduyoye has worked tirelessly to address issues of poverty, healthcare, youth empowerment, women's rights, destructive cultural and religious practices, and global unrest.

that a concept such as human dignity is often threatened due to its many violations:

> At the center of the culture there is an ideology that has absolute priority: the corporate personality of the family, clan or nation is always preferred to the personality of the individual, especially when this individual is a woman.[13]

Though keenly aware of the role of the culture, Oduyoye is concerned to find that in the many books she had read, African women come through mainly as wife, mother, witch, and so on. So much so that she wondered whether women could be considered part of the human family! Yet, as a famous Akan proverb states: *All human beings are children of God.*

Notwithstanding these dehumanizing and oppressive aspects, Oduyoye knows that African women, who read the Bible with a critical eye, discover in it the trinitarian God as liberator of the oppressed, savior of the marginalized and of all those who live daily in pain, uncertainty, and scarcity.[14]

Furthermore, this great sister of ours states that there must be full humanity and participation in religion and society, because the gospel of Jesus is indeed the gospel of life in its fullness. A gospel that embodies a transformative quality. Hence, it is always important to shape and reshape educational approaches that promote the total liberation of all human beings.

A Non-singular "Who"

The triune God, the source of mission, needs collaborators, men and women, as conscious and convinced instruments capable of realizing God's dream: "As the Father has sent me, so I send you."[15]

In Africa, the Comboni Family—like so many other ecclesial entities—is committed to transforming the dehumanizing system that continues to oppress and imprison the people who know that, as the proverb says, "to raise a child takes an entire village."

---

[13] M. A. Oduyoye, *Introducing African Women's Theology* (Sheffield, England: Sheffield Academic Press, 2001), 15.

[14] See M. A. Oduyoye, "Calling the Church to Account: African Women and Liberation," *Ecumenical Review* 47, no. 4 (1995): 479–89.

[15] Jn 20:21.

On this immense continent, whenever a human being comes into the world, he or she learns that "I am because we are,"[16] thus embodying the strong sense of solidarity that unites family and community. As stated at various times by Cardinal Dieudonné Nzapalainga, who shepherded God's people in the suffering Central African Republic, "For me, wherever men, women, and children are found, they are children of God, and I have the obligation to go out to meet them."

Transformation: The Horizon of Oppressed People

Various charisms of founders and foundresses clearly point to the importance of educational action as a fundamental part of promoting the regeneration of a society in the light of the gospel. This is a truly charismatic area for a qualified preparation of the African people in the name of the Comboni charism. Our journey as social ministers speaks volumes in this regard.

With this mindset, one almost automatically thinks of the establishment of technical and professional schools, of university centers for the formation of people, as places for people to fully embrace their liberation.[17] The objective is to develop the intellectual, human, moral, and religious personality, and to inculcate local and universal knowledge, aiming at promoting the values necessary to ensure a healthy interpersonal relationship and peaceful coexistence in society.

A Journey Together

The many types of "who" in mission in Africa often confuse people. This happened to me when I was about sixteen years old. Thus, I asked to understand better the difference between the mission of the *peacekeepers* and that of the *church* people. Both groups had come from the northern hemisphere.

---

[16] Many languages in Africa express this concept. For instance, the Bantu-Swahili expression is *Sisi tuko pamoja,* stressing the consciousness of belonging to a greater-than-self reality. A person, strengthened by such a vast self-identity, is willing to encounter and serve other people. The *Ubuntu* view focuses on the fact that a person becomes a person through other people. Every human being suffers when other human beings are belittled, humiliated, oppressed, marginalized, tortured, and so on. On this topic we refer to the conference Agbonkhianmeghe E. Orobator, SJ, gave during the recent Rimini Meeting, August 20, 2021 (see A. E. Orobator, SJ, "Io sono perché noi siamo," *L'Osservatore Romano* August 23, 2021).

[17] Daniel Comboni, *Plan for the Regeneration of Africa through Africa,* September 15, 1864.

From my perspective the peacekeepers' mission seemed to have the result that "the fish thinks the fisherman is coming to save it; but in reality it dies." This is because the fisherman looks for food, and certainly not to save the life of the fish. What is preserved with weapons is war, not peace. This is also a strategy for anesthetizing the consciousness of people in order to keep them oppressed.

On the other hand, the true "who" of the evangelical mission is the one who is involved in the process of liberating the people so that they may have life, and life in abundance. That "who" is for us the fruit of the cooperation of all the forces that interact in favor of justice, where humanity suffers the continuous pangs of a woman in childbirth.[18]

The Trinity, who is the source of mission—together with the missionaries, the people, the objectives, and the initiatives—expresses the great intuition already mentioned, namely, that of *Ubuntu-tuko pamoja,* the strong unity that envelops all. Ultimately, it is the unity of the whole—the *plural* "who"—as the members of a single body[19] that aims to forcefully denounce unjust situations, and to proclaim, with renewed joy and hope, the jubilee of grace of the Lord, always and everywhere!

America:
The People as Protagonists and Agents of Transformation (by Sr. Ida Colombo)

By listening attentively—both with the head and with the heart—to the missionary experiences of the Comboni Family we collected during our journey in the Americas, I strongly perceived that people's action and impact stand very much at the center and clearly define the "who" of mission on that vast continent.

The starting point always flows from St. Daniel Comboni's methodology of saving Africa with Africa, which means working *with* people, *for* the people, and *by* the people. In this way we can perceive, in its wholeness, the beautiful influence of the gospel at every latitude and in all cultures.

In my own missionary experience, enriched by years of encounters with humanity and reciprocal welcome in Peru and Ecuador, I have understood that, in God's mission among us, the protagonist is always the

---

[18] Cf. Ps 48:6 and Rom 8:19–24.
[19] 1 Cor 12:12.

people, the little ones who live in the many wounded peripheries of life. They are the agents of change, of transformation through cooperation and networking.

In July 2021, I had the opportunity to visit some of our communities in Mexico, Costa Rica, and the United States. I have seen—especially in Tapachula (Chiapas) and in San Antonio (Texas)—both in the Comboni Sisters and in other women religious engaged in the difficult reality of migration, a great commitment and desire to listen to one another, geared toward facilitating the enormous task of welcoming and accompanying women, children, men, young people, and unaccompanied minors, all of whom were forced to leave their lands in search of a better future.

This is truly a huge challenge, which requires an immense capacity for synergy and apostolic synodality. The presence of these consecrated women, strong in their authority as sisters, where humanity suffers most, is in itself a denunciation of the various governments and leaders, who, in different ways and places, wash their hands of their responsibilities. By so doing, they refuse to acknowledge their complicity in the uncertain futures of so many anguished people.

The city of Tapachula, for example, has been turned into a permanent "waiting area" for thousands of migrants seeking asylum. This waiting time can last six months, a year, or even longer. For this reason the Comboni community in Mexico saw an urgent need to start a presence in this area, one that would be open to collaboration with other associations committed to the defense of human rights. In such precarious conditions the migrants are offered a space where their human dignity is respected, while being assisted in the juridical process for the recognition of their status, and in their search for a better standard of living.[20]

In recent years, on visiting various Comboni communities in countries and continents where we are present, I truly felt the suffering of the population of Haiti, of Uruguay, of San Salvador, together with the suffering of many people from some African countries. They were all immersed in situations of social, political, and cultural uncertainty and tension.

It is impossible not to remember the warning of Pope Francis:

> People are deprived of being the protagonists of their history. When people are discarded, they are deprived not only of material well-being, but also of the dignity of acting, of being the protagonist of

---

[20] Zolli and Moschetti, *We Are Mission*, 175–79.

their history, of their destiny, of expressing themselves with their values and culture, of their creativity, of their fecundity.[21]

Love for the People and Their Life

One of the basic attitudes in missionary work is love for the people and for the life of the people. This requires contact, empathy, compassion, and above all, the ability to consider the people as a subject in their own right, helping them to seek their autonomy and freedom. We must not put ourselves above or outside the people's life, but be always at their service, without pretense, without arrogance, without paternalism/maternalism, without antagonism.

The disciples of Jesus—men and women alike—were sent to be salt, yeast, and mustard seeds. They must express with concrete choices the beauty of witnessing that the good news is an experience to be lived with hands, arms, and hearts open to all the realities they encounter along the path of missionary discipleship.

The Comboni priest Daniele Zarantonello echoed this beautiful vision of the church through a life lived with the impoverished people in Tumaco, Colombia:

> Over the years, we have defined our presence as a "house with the open door," to let physically—and mainly spiritually—the life, the pain, and the struggles of our people walk into our lives. For many years, we have lived in two different houses: we used to call it "a community with two wings" and we tried to live in proximity with people as much as we could through work, pastoral, and community organisation.[22]

In various Latin American countries, the formation of small basic communities is often perceived as the foundation of a large house, where the word of God—always kept at the center—is returned to the people as the result of an overall reflection, which supports and deepens the understanding of the meaning of one's existence.[23] In this regard it is essential

---

[21] Video message of Pope Francis to the participants at the international conference on the theme "A Politics Rooted in the People," organized by the Centre for Theology and Community, April 15, 2021. The event was meant to deepen the themes published in Pope Francis and Austen Ivereigh, *Let Us Dream: The Path to a Better Future* (New York: Simon and Schuster, 2020).

[22] Zolli and Moschetti, *We Are Mission*, 142.

[23] Ibid., 135–40.

to ensure a certain continuity, a "continuous process of development of capacities that allow people not only to be protagonists of their own history, but that they are themselves capable of developing all programs at the community level."[24]

Like a Midwife, a Farmer, a Physician

I find very engaging the words of Brazilian theologian Clodovis Boff, when he argues that the grassroots agent must be like a midwife who helps the mother to give birth, a farmer who cares for the earth to bear good fruit, and a physician who treats the body to maintain or recover health. The missionary fights *with* the people, knows how to arouse, awaken, stimulate, serve, strengthen, assess, share, and coordinate them. The missionary sustains their action, and, immersed in reality, animates the people in the midst of it all.[25]

Likewise, cooperation and networking are transmitted through the significant experience lived out by the Asociación Hermanas Latinas Misioneras in América (AHLMA). The vision that supports the effort of these women's religious communities is to be a human, cultural, and faith bridge among the various populations who migrate from Latin and Central America to the United States of America in search of work, security, and fullness of life. At the core of AHLMA's mission is the desire to accompany women religious in their process of insertion and service in a completely new environment. Together, these religious communities nourish the culture of encounter as an essential part of their identity, which is reflected in their genuine community-centered witness.[26]

In this regard, it is impossible not to mention the experience of the Leadership Conference of Women Religious (LCWR), which, in the United States, gathers the dreams, hopes, efforts, creativity, and evangelical witness of many communities of consecrated women in the most varied areas of life. Its mission statement explains that its primary aim is to accompany members, individually and in community, in collaboratively carrying out service of leadership as a path to fulfill Christ's mission in today's world.

Furthermore, the LCWR seeks to create operational models to enhance the ability of its members in developing relational modalities with other groups interested in social change. In this way, dialogue

---

[24] Ibid., 156.
[25] Gianfranco Masserdotti, *Misioneros por el Reino: Meditaciones de Espiritualidad Misionera* (Madrid: Mundo Negro, 1989), 102.
[26] Zolli and Moschetti, *We Are Mission*, 170–74.

and cooperation, both in the ecclesial and social spheres, benefit from the vital, synergic contribution that animates the LCWR. The existing collaboration between AHLMA and LCWR is an important result of witnessing together.

Europe-Asia: Continents Seeking (New) Life
(by Sr. Maria Teresa Ratti)

Europe has become an "old" continent, and not only in relation to the birth and longevity rate of its respective countries. Besieged by sociocultural, political, economic, and ecclesial issues that require an extra dose of humanity in solidarity, today's Europe must rediscover an extra dose of prophecy—along with trust in knocking again at its doors—if it is to secure a future that honors the best part of its history.

As we write, the dramatic exit of the Western forces from Afghanistan is taking place, and, in a broader spectrum, the whole world is facing the enormous consequences of the COVID-19 pandemic, which is one of the many humanitarian-ecological emergencies of our time.

How to Witness Together?

A missionary mosaic of immense proportions and great opportunities is before our very eyes, challenging us both personally and communally. Such complexity might tempt us to feel incapable, if not even irrelevant. Surely, we must keep well away from this temptation, so as to avoid falling into the trap of feeling like helpless victims. Such an attitude, more than anything, would reveal the weak side of various missionary hermeneutics and methodologies.

How should we move on? Comboni Sister Fernanda Cristinelli, who has delved into the complexity of missionary ministry in Europe, points out:

> The focus on God's activity becomes a source of hope in the face of the smallness of our work and the magnitude of the problems that seem to overwhelm our ability to make significant changes. There we recognize our limitations, and that the work of transformation is first of all the work of God.[27]

---

[27] Fernanda Cristinelli, CSM, "La Ministerialità vissuta nella Famiglia Comboniana," *La Missione Comboniana in Europa—Quaderni di Limone* 6 (April 2013): 110.

Recognizing God's transforming action within reality is an essential step toward ensuring life on our journey. A question then becomes paramount: Within so much complexity, how can we bear witness, both to the proclamation of peace and joy, of sorority and fraternity, of justice and reconciliation for every person and for the whole creation, while expressing the beauty of a "plural who" that this mission in Europe requires of us?

A significant response comes from the inter-congregational missionary community of Modica, in the Province of Ragusa (Sicily, Italy), Diocese of Noto. Starting from the dream, long cradled by the Conference of Missionary Institutes in Italy and implemented during a forum organized in Trevi, Perugia (Umbria, Italy) in 2013, this community began to build upon a two-pillar foundation:

1. Encourage inter-congregational work, with the participation of lay people, fostering processes of common learning (learning to reflect and plan in a style of communion);
2. Enhance as much as possible relations with immigrants in Italy, particularly—but not only—through personal contact, by meeting them wherever they live.[28]

Learning together as ministerial teams, and promoting personal contact with those who experience systemic marginality imposed by racist, xenophobic, and fundamentalist ideologies are models of missionary synodality in Modica. There, the members of the community are currently trying to put into practice the commitment envisioned in this missionary perspective.

The very composition of these teams—made up of men and women coming from various missionary institutes and their lay associates—is a laboratory in which to learn the ABCs of mission here and now.

Sr. Albertina Rosa Correte Marcelino, a Comboni Sister from Mozambique, who this past summer 2021 lived for some weeks in the community of Modica, was enthusiastic about the experience. She felt deeply touched by the group's commitment to be an active and significant presence among the people:

> They work as a bridge between the different migrant peoples and the people of Italy, and between migrants of different backgrounds, cultures, and religions. With other institutions, they prepare many social gatherings where the challenges and opportunities of migration are discussed, in order to sensitize people to welcome migrants as brothers and sisters, and not as foreigners. I will remember with joy

---
[28] Sr. Giovanna Minardi, MDL, "Come tutto è cominciato," CIMI 4 Modica (April 4, 2019), in Italian.

the warmth of the population, very affectionate and friendly; women and children, and all those I met and with whom I exchanged a look, a word, and ate together.[29]

This is a beautiful missionary witness that contains a multiplicity of elements without which it would not be possible to make the joy of the gospel visible!

Proximity, Care, Conviviality

At Camarate, Portugal, a team of Comboni Family members, in collaboration with other ecclesial and social entities, carries out the project Jovem Despertar (Young Awakening). The group takes care of girls and boys from families, often single-parent families, who have migrated into the area. In this ministry closeness and good care express efforts to bear ministerial witness by this sign of cooperation and communion.

In exploring these various missionary ministries in Europe, what touches us most is the awareness that sustains the missionaries: they perceive the call to have been summoned to be human bridges through whom migrant people can experience the beauty of encounter and of care. The missionaries in Camarate are aware that their presence is an opportunity to bring together the different cultures that live in vulnerable situations and contexts. Such an attitude demands a truly welcoming missionary capacity.[30]

Becoming crossroads to build conviviality while promoting collaboration, creativity, and competence expresses well the plural "who" of mission as lived by the Comboni community in Castel Volturno (Caserta) in the south of Italy. It is a strip of land where the lack of legal representation puts an awful strain on the resilience of the people who live a very difficult daily life there. In such a context what is most essential is to work in a network, collaborating with all those who are ready to commit themselves, and to promote knowledge of the social doctrine of the church and missionary formation in all the people of God.[31]

A Favorable Time for Conversion

In the complex missionary mosaic already mentioned, a time for renewal has finally come for the missionary church in Europe. Tempted from the

---

[29] Sr. Albertina Rosa Correte Marcelino, "My Experience in Sicily," *Vita Nostra*, internal Comboni publication (July-August 2021): 17–18.
[30] Zolli and Moschetti, *We Are Mission*, 226–29.
[31] Ibid., 211–19.

beginning to feel like a foundational custodian of the faith to be shared with "mission lands," the church in Europe must reimagine its missionary stance.

In particular, for congregations and missionary institutes of ancient foundation, this is a favorable time to purify all those forms of language and practice—with the related symbolic universe—which for too long have marred the beautiful face of the gospel, *ad intra* and *ad extra*.

In this regard the field of social communication is certainly an *areopagus* that can contribute to a significant change of mentality. We must and can do more and better in this area by using a narrative that respects the dignity and rights of people and of cultures.[32] Today, prophetic missionary ministry calls us to commit ourselves to dismantle the fortresses that various religious congregations and institutes in Europe have been, in some ways, in their past, to overcome all the barriers that have stifled the circular dynamism of mission. Full participation will then be a reality for their membership, and such commitment will make "charismatic citizenship"[33] a concrete experience to be enjoyed and shared at any latitude.

Remain in God's Love

A final word from Asia–Middle East encourages us to continue on our journey with hope. We are aware that, even in these countries, missionaries face challenges every day to make visible a credible testimony able to engage in dialogue with the people and the multiple cultural riches of which they are custodians.

A characteristic, for example, which well defines the style of the missionary presence in Israel-Palestine, is that of fostering interreligious and ecumenical dialogue among the various confessions of faith present in the area. This attitude demands an intense spiritual life rooted in a prayer of intercession. In Bethany, the Comboni Sisters feel a particular responsibility to intercede, in prayer, for the reconciliation of peoples. Today, they are also committed to incarnating and witnessing to the presence of Christ and the values of the "kin-dom" in this holy and tormented land.[34]

---

[32] See Chiara Piaggio and Igiaba Scego, eds., *Africana: Raccontare il Continente al di là degli stereotipi* (Milan: Feltrinelli, 2021).

[33] Elisa Kidane, CMS, often sets this concept at the center of her presentations when interacting with religious congregations on the topics of charism, spirituality, culture, and so forth.

[34] Zolli and Moschetti, *We Are Mission*, 237–41.

On the Feast of the Sacred Heart—June 11, 2021—which was celebrated while more hostility was taking place between the various elements of the human, political, and religious fabric of the Middle East, Sr. Alicia Vacas Moro, provincial superior of the Comboni Sisters in Asia–Middle East, said:

> In our accompanying the peoples of the Holy Land on this long Via Crucis, we find the raison d'être of our presence in the contemplation of the Cross we embraced on the day of our First Religious Profession. Given to us as a sign of our consecration, it bears the invitation of Jesus: manete in dilectione mea ["Remain in my love"—Jn 15:9].

Remaining in the love of Jesus is the living symbol that supports our dedication to the gospel proclamation. All missionary disciples of the kingdom carry the cross and the resurrection of Jesus in their life. Assuring us that he would be with us until the end of time, the glorified Lord is the rock on which we can build the tent of mission that still seeks a home in every corner of the world.

Conclusion: We Are Mission

Through these words we have recounted in a synthetic and certainly partial way the wonderful adventure of being a "who" of mission within the web of a communal journey. We have shared hopes and experiences, challenges and dreams. This opportunity has blessed us with immense possibilities, precisely because of the joy that flows from witnessing together in communion, through collaboration and creativity, and always with a great deal of synodal creativity.

> **Ida Colombo, CMS,** is from Italy, has ministered in the suburbs of Lima, Peru, and in Granada, Spain, and is committed in the field of immigration. As general councilor, she coordinates at present the sector on Evangelization-JPIC.
>
> **Hélène Israël Soloumta Kamkôl, CMS,** from Chad, studied theology and religious sciences in Cameroon, and sociology at Gregorian University. After serving in Sudan, she returned to Rome to study at the Pontifical Institute for Arabic and Islamic Studies, and she currently teaches Arabic and assists in the administration department at the Dar Comboni Institute for Arabic Studies, Cairo, Egypt.

Maria Teresa Ratti, CMS, has served as nurse, mission-vocation promoter, and social communicator. She has lived ten years in the United States, seventeen years in Kenya, and one year in Zambia. Later on, she worked at the *Combonifem* Communication Centre in Verona, Italy. Presently she lives in Rome and collaborates with various editorial entities.

The "Where" of Mission

Fifty Years of Ad Gentes *in Africa*

Anthony Akinwale, OP

The purpose of this reflection on the "where" of mission is first, to retrieve the conciliar vision of the church's identity and mission; second, to evaluate what the church in Africa has accomplished since the publication of *Ad Gentes*, the decree of the Second Vatican Council on the church's missionary activity; and third, to give four proposals to what is left to be done so as to continually make concrete the vision of the Second Vatican Council.[1]

Where Pentecost Overcomes Babel

Ad Gentes begins by referring to *Lumen Gentium (Dogmatic Constitution on the Church)* of the same council. According to *Lumen Gentium*, "the Church, in Christ, is in the nature (*veluti*) of sacrament—a sign and instrument, that is, of communion with God and of unity among all men."[2] This statement of *Lumen Gentium* is to be considered the most important of the statements of the Second Vatican Council because it provides a key to understanding the nature and mission of the church, and indeed every other teaching of the council. Consistent with the scholastic dictum *agere sequitur esse* ("doing follows being"), it is to be asserted that the mission of the church flows from its nature. The church's nature is communion, and its mission is to bring all into communion with God and unity among

---

[1] This article is based on a talk given at the Pan African Missiological Congress, Ikeja, Lagos, Nigeria, on October 27, 2016.

[2] Vatican II, *Lumen Gentium (The Dogmatic Constitution on the Church)* (1964), no. 1, hereinafter *LG*.

human beings. It is in the light of this consistency of mission with nature that we are to understand *Ad Gentes*.

In the first article of *Ad Gentes*, indeed in the opening words of the article, the mission of the church is articulated thus: the church "is divinely sent to the nations that she might be 'the universal sacrament of salvation.'"[3] For its part, the church assumes this mission in obedience to "the mandate of her founder." In fidelity to this mission, imitating Christ and "following the footsteps of the apostles," "she strives to preach the Gospel [the word of truth]" to the whole world, to give birth to new churches.[4] These churches are instances of communion *ad intra* and *ad extra*. In each of the local churches there is an assembly of men and women in communion with God and in unity with one another.

The church's nature as communion makes it possible to assert that the church is "missionary by its very nature."[5] Its origin is the communion of the triune God made manifest in the mission of the Son and the Holy Spirit. The eternal, fountain-like love of the Father is made manifest in time in the mission of the Son and the Holy Spirit.

> As the principle without principle from whom the Son is generated and from whom the Holy Spirit proceeds through the Son, God in his great and merciful kindness freely creates us and moreover, graciously calls us to share in his life and glory. He generously pours out, and never ceases to pour out, his divine goodness, so that he who is creator of all this might at last become "all in all" thus simultaneously assuring his own glory and our happiness. It pleased God to call men to share in his life and not merely singly, without any bond between them, but he formed them into a people, in which his children who had been scattered were gathered together.[6]

Sin led to a break in communion between God and human beings, and this break in communion is manifested in unbelief, apostasy, blasphemy, and heresy. It led to division among human beings, a division that is manifested in all manner of conflicts: interpersonal, intercommunal, international, and gender related. Sin brought about a disharmony between

---

[3] Vatican II, *Ad Gentes* (*Decree on the Missionary Activity of the Church* (1965), no. 1. hereinafter *AG*. Here one sees in the very beginning of *Ad Gentes* a clear reference to the beginning of *Lumen Gentium*.
[4] *AG*, no. 1.
[5] *AG*, no. 2.
[6] *AG*, no. 2.

human beings and the rest of creation, as can be seen in the environmental degradation that afflicts our planet today. In this respect, the church is where Pentecost overcomes Babel,[7] where the wound of division that tears humanity apart is treated with the word of God and sacraments. And this explains its mission.

The mission of the church is to be a sign and instrument of communion, overcoming the different conflicts afflicting our world. Given this understanding of the missionary activity of the church, it is important that we inquire fifty years after the publication of *Ad Gentes*: Where are we with the mission of the church in Africa? How far has the church traveled on the journey of communion and unity? How far does it still need to travel on this journey? In other words, what have we done about mission and what still remains to be done? I deliberately frame the questions this way—that is, looking at what has been done before looking at what is yet to be done—so as to avoid a self-flagellating exercise that would begin by looking at what we have failed or are yet to do to the point of overlooking what the Holy Spirit has been doing in the life of the church since the publication of *Ad Gentes*. But it is important to begin by describing the situation in which the decree *Ad Gentes*, and indeed other conciliar documents, found us Africans, that is, the horizon in which our reading and reception of the council took place.

When the council ended on December 8, 1965, some African countries were either in turmoil or about to be in turmoil.[8] There was already ethnic strife and political instability in the Democratic Republic of the Congo. In Nigeria, on January 15, 1966—exactly one month and one week after the closure of the council—Nigeria witnessed its first military coup. That and the countercoup of July 29, 1966, plunged Nigeria into a thirty-month civil war. It is a well-known fact that bitter memories of that war are still evoked today. In 1966, the African continent witnessed a wave of military interventions and the attendant installation of totalitarian regimes noted for their violation of fundamental human rights. The consequence was that, instead of reading conciliar documents in view of their interpretation and reception, Africans were preoccupied with wars. But that does not tell the whole story. Fruits of the council were not completely absent from Africa.

---

[7] J.-M.R. Tillard, *Church of Churches: The Ecclesiology of Communion* (Collegeville, MN: Michael Glazier/Liturgical Press, 1992), 7–9.

[8] Anthony Akinwale, *The Congress and the Council: Towards a Nigerian Reception of Vatican II* (Ibadan: Michael Dempsey Centre for Religious and Social Research, 2003), 5–7.

Fruits of Mission

It is to be noted that even in this situation, this was an era when the church in Africa experienced tremendous growth. Without citing statistics, we can note with gratitude to divine Providence that the number of dioceses and parishes increased by leaps and bounds. Whereas at the time of publication of *Ad Gentes*, Africa was ministered to by bishops, priests, and religious—missionaries from the Western world—today, Africa is sending priests and religious to work as missionaries in local churches in the Western world. One cannot leave out of this narrative the founding in 1979 of the Missionaries of St. Paul in Nigeria, whose members can now be found as missionaries on virtually every continent on the planet. We have witnessed, and we are still witnessing, a vocation boom. It is such that many religious institutes originating in the West would have gone into extinction by now if there were no Africans joining them. In fact, Africa is the only continent where some of these religious institutes still flourish. It can be said, therefore, without any fear of contradiction, that in this respect, the goal of mission—the preaching of the gospel and the begetting of local churches, local instances of communion—has been attained in Africa. And these churches, though young—perhaps one should say *because* they are young—are quite vibrant.

In the past fifty years there have been giant strides taken to ensure the Africanization of Christianity. This is seen in greater attention to liturgical inculturation—the proclamation and celebration of the Christian faith using African modes of communication. The ground for this was already prepared by the publication in 1956, nine years before *Ad Gentes*, of *Des prêtres noirs s'interrogent*.[9] The publication of *Ad Gentes* was followed by the visit of Pope Paul VI to Kampala, Uganda, where he made the famous declaration: "You can and you must have an African Christianity."[10]

The establishment of theology faculties in Abidjan, Port Harcourt, and Nairobi in 1979, twenty-two years after the establishment of the faculty of theology in Kinshasa, should be acknowledged as signs of maturity of the church in Africa. The intellectual output of these faculties assisted the church in Africa for the first and second African synods and has nourished the pastoral life of the church in Africa and beyond. The publication of two post-synodal exhortations—John Paul II's *Ecclesia in Africa* and Benedict XVI's *Africae Munus*—count among the fruits of

---

[9] Présence Africaine, *Des prêtres noirs s'interrogent* (Paris: Ed. du Cerf, 1956).
[10] Pope Paul VI, Eucharistic Celebration at the Conclusion of the Symposium Organized by the Bishops of Africa, Kampala (Uganda), July 31, 1969.

Ad Gentes. Theologians and pastors trained in these theological faculties now provide theological and pastoral services in places even far beyond the African continent. Indeed, the church in Africa has come of age since the publication of *Ad Gentes* fifty years ago.

Challenges

At the Second Vatican Council the church opened its arms to embrace all within the church. This could be seen in the way *Lumen Gentium* described the relationship between papal primacy and episcopal collegiality, between the local bishop and the local church, and between the clergy and the lay faithful. This openness is also to be seen in the ecumenical tone, turn, and content of conciliar documents like *Lumen Gentium*, *Orientalium Ecclesiarum*, and *Unitatis Redintegratio*. The church's openness to the modern world is visibly demonstrated in *Gaudium et Spes*, and its goodwill to other religions is made manifest in *Nostra Aetate*. However, whereas *Nostra Aetate* explicitly bore signs of goodwill toward the Jewish religion and to the religion of Islam, it is not so clear if those who inspired and wrote *Nostra Aetate* had African ancestral religions in mind. Perhaps it is in *Ad Gentes* that one can see the council's concern for Africa and Asia.

Fifty years after *Ad Gentes* the challenge of mission remains. It is the challenge of gathering God's children scattered by sin and wounded by division into the assembly of charity, an assembly whose mission is to be in Christ a sign and instrument of communion with God and of unity among human beings. This challenge is multiform in its manifestation. But it can be described in a nutshell as an alliance of materialism and exploitation of diversity. It is the exploitation of ethnic and religious diversity for materialistic purposes. This calls for explanation.

In order to explain how the alliance of materialism and exploitation of diversity pose a challenge to mission, I shall fall back on a statement made by Thomas Aquinas in his account of concupiscence. According to Aquinas, all the wars among animals are over food and sex.[11] In other words, animals go to war because their appetite for pleasure is disconnected from the leash of rationality. This explanation could be applied to human beings, too.

Disconnected from the good use of reason, the human appetite for pleasure runs riot. This is what plays out in materialism: power is sought in order to acquire riches, and riches are acquired in order to maximize

---

[11] Thomas Aquinas, *Summa Theologiae* I, 81.2.

pleasure. In order to win wars waged to attain power and to maximize profit and pleasure, the strategy of exploitation of diversity is deployed through a divide-and-rule tactic. Thus, religious and ethnic diversity is exploited for the sake of narrow political interests, in the violation of fundamental human rights, and in the absence of authentic development. This is not just an African problem but a human problem. What makes it worse in Africa is the absence of democratic institutions designed and operated to defend the citizen's right against aggression by the state or by fellow citizens.

The reign of strong men has militated against the establishment of strong institutions. The quest for power, riches, and pleasure at the expense of others, and the manipulation of diversity to divide and rule run counter to the very purpose of mission by promoting disharmony. The very purpose of mission, spelled out in *Ad Gentes* as God's design of establishing a relationship of peace and communion with himself and bringing about union among human beings, is radically contradicted by exploitation of ethnic and religious diversity.

The issue here is not that people are of diverse ethnic origins, for, as Jean-Marie Tillard would say, the church is not an abolition but a communion of difference. Neither is it their love of ethnic affiliation. The issue is not ethnicity but ethnocentrism, that is, a malicious ethnic solidarity that works against the interests of members of other ethnic communities. It is seen in the ethnic disharmony that afflicts many African societies and that rears its head even within the church. There is an ever-present and increasingly urgent need to grasp the profound meaning of the words of St. Paul to the Galatians: "There is no longer Jew or Greek, there is no longer slave or free, there is no longer male and female; for all of you are one in Christ Jesus."[12]

Since *Ad Gentes* Africa has witnessed ethnic cleansing in the Congo, in Nigeria, and in Rwanda, to mention only a few instances. The fact that Christians were involved in some of these cases points out that there is still a long distance to travel if we are to live up to the evangelical ideal that inspired the Second Vatican Council to espouse an ecclesiology of communion reflected in mission, as articulated in *Ad Gentes*. Ethnic and religious diversity in Africa, mismanaged in precolonial, colonial, and postcolonial eras of the continent, thus leading to sterile, bloody, and debilitating conflicts, challenge the church to be a sign and instrument of communion with God and of unity among Africans.

---

[12] Gal 3:28.

Coming with ethnocentrism are the challenges of human rights violations and political instability. Ethnocentrism turns a blind eye to the fact that what makes me human is what makes the man or woman of a different ethnic affiliation human. Not recognizing the humanity of the other person, my desire to dominate collides with the resolve of the other person not to be dominated. The consequence of this collision is further fragmentation, often degenerating into hatred and violence. In the ensuing struggle for control of the state in countries where the state controls the wealth of the people, the desire of members of one ethnic or religious community to appropriate the state so as to appropriate the wealth of the land manifests itself in the desire to dominate members of other ethnic or religious communities. This is how ethnic diversity and religious diversity are used and abused to divide peoples and to attain political advantage. It is manifest in the strain of intolerant Islam preached by Boko Haram in Nigeria.

The struggle for power and resources like land and minerals that occasions this manipulation of diversity gives rise to the use of state apparatus to violate fundamental human rights. State officials run affairs of the state in ways that place the state at the vanguard of human rights violations and political instability. The state and its officials become impediments to solidarity, a solidarity that is needed for the actualization of individual and collective potentials. In the absence of solidarity, Africans assume the unfortunate distinction of being impoverished peoples inhabiting an enormously enriched continent.

But it is not only Islam that is being manipulated. Christianity is, too. Its gospel is instrumentalized to seek political and economic advantage, and the gospel has been materialized and commercialized. I speak here of the challenge of the gospel of material prosperity by aggressive Pentecostalism and its biblical literalism. There is no doubt that we live in an era of further fragmentation of Christianity, doctrinal cacophony, and absence of common witness, a time in need of ecumenical reawakening when we ought to recall the words of *Ad Gentes* that "the division of Christians is injurious to the holy work of preaching the Gospel to every creature, and deprives many people of access to the faith."[13] These echo the words of *Unitatis Redintegratio*, the decree on ecumenism: "Such division openly contradicts the will of Christ, scandalizes the world, and damages that most holy cause, the preaching of the Gospel to every creature."[14]

---

[13] *AG*, no. 6.

[14] Vatican II, *Unitatis Redintegratio (Decree on Ecumenism)* (1964), no. 1.

Proposals for a More Fruitful Mission

I would like to conclude with a number of proposals. First, the challenges I have just itemized and discussed call us to a rediscovery and rereading of conciliar ecclesiology of communion. There is a need for *a reawakening of ecclesial consciousness*, a renewed understanding of why we are a church, a retrieval of ecclesiology of communion by re-reading conciliar and post-conciliar documents. Without a retrieval of this ecclesiology we may not have an adequate understanding of mission, since, as I pointed out at the beginning, the mission of the church, as envisioned by *Ad Gentes*, is rooted in its very nature as *communion*.

Second, since every text is read in a particular light, our rereading of the ecclesiology of communion of *Lumen Gentium*, indeed, our rereading and reception of the sixteen documents of the Second Vatican Council, must be done in a new light. By a new light, I mean the changing circumstances of our time. In this respect *Ad Gentes* speaks of a singular and unchanging mission in changing circumstances. There is no doubt that the circumstances of mission have largely changed from what they were fifty years ago. Ours is no longer a continent receiving missionaries who have come to implant churches but a continent where so many have been baptized. It is an open secret that Africa is where the church is currently enjoying its greatest growth. Yet, we must not seek comfort in numbers. For there are many people today who claim to believe in Christ but who are either afraid or unwilling to bear witness to a gospel way of life. We are not short of people who go by the name of Christians; we are short, rather, of those who would be Christians in name and in deed. It is therefore clear that the time has come to *lay more emphasis on implantation of gospel values* in the hearts of men and women of our time than on the implantation of the church among those who do not yet believe in Christ.[15]

We must go beyond the four walls of the church and of the parish, and go out to implant values of the gospel in the hearts of men and women found in every sphere of human endeavor. The church has a mission of implanting values of the gospel in the hearts of politicians and business people, lawyers and judges, intellectuals and journalists. The task here is not to impose, but to propose the gospel with ecumenical and interreligious sensitivity. This is where the importance of the corpus of the church's social doctrine is to be appreciated. It promotes ways of transforming the

---

[15] *AG*, no. 6.

society to which people may subscribe without necessarily sharing our faith. Its appeal to reason, its principles of natural law, and its respect for human dignity, subsidiarity, and solidarity, provide a common ground for us and for men and women who are not members of our Catholic faith community. Today's agent of evangelization must be well schooled in the social doctrine of the church. That leads me to the third proposal.

In responding to the challenge of mission, *adequate formation is indispensable*. By this I mean formation of the whole church—bishops, priests, consecrated persons, and laity—for evangelization. There is need for a formation that reflects patristic sensibilities, that is, formation that is a meeting point of spiritual, intellectual, and pastoral dimensions of the Christian tradition, formation in holiness, intelligence, and competence. I propose a formation that bears such patristic traits for at least three reasons:

1. Like fathers of the early church, we in Africa are carrying out our mission in an era of political turbulence and doctrinal cacophony.
2. We need to overcome a trichotomy that is becoming increasingly promoted even as it is inappropriate and disturbing. With regard to agents of mission, there is an increasingly concerning tendency to trichotomize among the spiritual, the intellectual, and the pastoral. Each of the three is necessary, but none is of itself sufficient.
3. The convergence of the three reflects the threefold office of Christ, which should be reflected in the life and mission of the church, his body. The spiritual corresponds to the priestly, the intellectual to the prophetic, and the pastoral to the kingly—this is the threefold inseparable office of Christ. Efforts to provide formation devoid of the trichotomy I am referring to must be intensified in our seminaries, faculties of theology, and catechetical schools.

My fourth and final proposal—not to be confused with the three reasons I have just used to justify the need for a formation of patristic inspiration—is this: fifty years after *Ad Gentes* the challenges of mission *call for increased zeal and increased patience*. As we try to make the church present in the world, we must take to heart these words of *Lumen Gentium* that the church is already present even as we await its glorious completion:

> Already present in figure at the beginning of the world, this church was prepared in marvelous fashion in the history of the people of Israel and in the old Alliance. Established in this last age of the world, and made manifest in the outpouring of the Spirit, it will be brought to glorious completion at the end of time. At that moment, as the Fathers put it, all the just from the time of Adam, "from Abel, the

just one, to the last of the elect" will be gathered together with the Father in the universal church.[16]

These words teach us that the mission of the church, already being accomplished, will be fully accomplished only at the eschaton. For now, together we patiently and prayerfully carry on this mission as pilgrims who walk by faith and not by sight. From this faith comes the consciousness that the communion we seek is, to use the wisdom of St. Augustine in his *Confessions* and in *City of God*, in the eternal peace of the Sabbath when we shall rest in God even as God now works in us.

> **Anthony Akinwale, OP,** is professor of systematic theology at the Dominican University Ibadan, Nigeria, where he is also vice-chancellor. He holds master's and licentiate degrees in theology from the Collège Universitaire des Dominicains in Ottawa, Canada, and a doctorate in theology from Boston College. He has recently founded with some of his colleagues the Patristic Association of Nigeria (PATRAN).

---

[16] *LG*, no. 2.

The "How" of Mission

Going "Outside the Gates" for the Kingdom's Sake

PUDOTA RAYAPPA JOHN, SJ

A Telugu[1] folk song by Anand Gurram captures the cry and angst of the agitating peasants in India:

> Yeddu gudda podisi nenu, yevasam edho chesthunte,
> gittu baatu nattivirigi, yaparam cheyamnte,
> ye angadi poyedi, ye retuku ammedi
>
> (I am cultivating my land by kicking the back of my oxen,
> but if I am compelled to do business without being paid
> even the production cost, how can I survive?
> Where can I go and sell my produce and at what price?)[2]

This cry reminds me of the famous phrase, "Please, Sir, I want some more," from *Oliver Twist* by Charles Dickens, a sharp critique of public policy toward the poor in the 1830s. As I write this article, some hundreds of thousands of peasants—men, women, youth, and children—have been camping for months (from September 2020 onward) at the entry points to India's capital, Delhi, demanding the scrapping of three farming laws.[3] This

---

[1] Telugu is a language used in the southern part of India.
[2] Neeraja Murthy, "Telugu Song '*Ye Angadi Poyedi*' Raises Its Voice against the New Farm Bill 2020," *The Hindu*, October 13, 2020.
[3] "The laws are: (1) The Farmers' Produce Trade and Commerce (Promotion and Facilitation) Act, which allows a barrier-free trade of farmers' produce outside the physical premises of the markets specified under the various state Agricultural Produce Marketing Committee laws (APMC Acts); (2) the Essential Commodities (Amendment) Act makes provisions for the removal of items such as cereals and pulses from the list of essential commodities, to attract foreign direct investment to the sector; and (3) the Farmers (Empowerment and Protection) Agreement on Price Assurance and Farm Services Act." See

agitation protest is the longest in Indian history, probably in world history.[4] So far, "three lakhs, thirty thousand [330,000] farmers committed suicide in India," Palagummi Sainath reports.[5] "We will fight over and over again and generation upon generation, but we will not let our land go," a poster at the camp site reads.[6] Besides being an excruciatingly painful reality, it pricks the conscience of the nation's brutal insensitivity and inhuman apathy toward the farmers who were close to the heart of Mahatma Gandhi, the Father of the Nation. In the 1920s, Gandhi supported the farmers' agitation at Champaran, Bihar. The "Champaran agrarian movement was the inaugural event of a Gandhian Movement of *Satyagraha* [*satya,* truth, reality; *agraha,* firm grasping, to hold on]. It had the transformative power to rewrite [India's] history," says eminent sociologist Shiv Vishvanathan.[7]

The aim of this essay is to look at this agrarian crisis in the light of God's liberating word, and to help the church in India and elsewhere abroad understand its mission. "Context-sensitive" realities are the *loci theologici* together with the Christian sources of scripture and tradition, affirms the FABC (Federation of Asian Bishops' Conferences):

> However, as Asian Christians, we do theology together with Asian realities as resources, insofar as we discern in them God's presence, action and the work of the Spirit. We use these resources in correlation with the Bible and the Tradition of the church. Use of these resources implies a tremendous change in theological methodology. The cultures of peoples, the history of their struggles, their religions, their religious scriptures, oral traditions, popular religiosity, economic and political realities and world events, historical personages, stories of oppressed people crying out for justice, freedom, dignity, life, and solidarity become resources of theology, and assume methodological importance in our context. The totality of life is the raw material of theology; God is redemptively present in the totality of human life.[8]

Bretton Woods Project, "India's New Farm Laws Mirror International Financial Institutions' Vision of Agriculture," March 23, 2021.

[4] See YouTube video, "We're So Proud of the Indian Farmers"—American Farmers in Support of the World's Largest Protests.

[5] Palagummi Sainath, "Sagubaguku Annadatalu Udyaminchali," *Eenadu* August 30, 2021, https://www.eenadu.net.

[6] Navsharan Singh, "Agrarian Crisis and the Longest Farmers' Protest in Indian History," *Online Sage Journal,* August 12, 2021.

[7] Shiv Vishvanathan, "Champaran as 'Open Work,' Colours of Imperialism: Memory, Diversity and Champaran," unpublished talk, September 28, 2017, IIC Delhi.

[8] FABC Office of Theological Concerns, "Methodology: Asian Christian Theology: Doing Theology in Asia Today," paper no. 96 (January 2000), no. 3.1, para 1.

The history of humanity has always been filled with joy and hope,[9] pain and protests. The history of agrarian agitation on Indian soil can be traced back to the early twentieth century, with the Champaran Satyagraha in Bihar, Kheda; the Bardoli Peasant Struggle in Gujarat; the Moplah Rebellion in Malabar; the Peasant Revolt in Telangana; the Tebhaga Movement in Bengal; and many others. Although the Government of India, headed by the right-wing Prime Minister Narendra Modi, claims to serve the interests of the farmers, all three of the farming laws in question focus not directly on farmers' welfare but on improving the "ease of doing business" for supply-chain actors, especially the nontraditional private players, such as agrotech companies and retailers. In short, this robs the fundamental respect and dignity of the farmer who tills the land, sows the seed, and cultivates the produce. Why should the food-supply chain come under greater control of the corporations? Why should working peasants lose landholdings? And how do we, as Christians, understand our calling in this scenario? What is our mission? How would Jesus read this situation? Is he, a farmer, in the midst of the protesting farmers? Did he ever speak in agrarian language when confronted with the "savage" political and corporate Roman colonial powers? What should be the mission of the church in India and elsewhere as it witnesses the plight of the farmers or similar sinful and oppressive structures and places?

In this essay I first present briefly how the land is the source and identity of the community and relate it to the biblical notion of the land: "The earth is the Lord's."[10] Then, I argue how the current peasant agitation is not being waged by farmers alone but is also humanity's hope of partaking in the mission of God. Finally, I unearth the agrarian language of Jesus Christ as a gift and task beckoning the Christian community to go forth[11] for the kingdom's sake along the lines of the clarion call given by *Laudato Si'*.

The Land as the Source and Identity of a Community

Human beings in various cultures refer to the land as the source and identity of a community. The land is closely associated with that community's

---

[9] Vatican II, *Gaudium et Spes (Pastoral Constitution on the Church in the Modern World)* (1964), no. 1.

[10] Ps 24:1.

[11] Pope Francis, apostolic constitution *Veritatis Gaudium (On Ecclesiastical Universities and Faculties)* (2018), no. 4.

personal names, family, religion, nationality, race, skin color, taste, and language. Thus, one's identity, as an individual or a community, is intrinsically interwoven with one's land. The word *culture* is related to *agriculture*, and it suggests the cultivation of land. Greek writers like Theophrastus of Eresos (371–287 BCE) and Xenophon (after 362 BCE) paid attention to the specifics of land and agriculture, and Romans like Cato the Elder (234–149 BCE), Varro (117–27 BCE), Virgil (ca. 38 BCE), Celsus (first century CE), and Pliny the Younger (27–79 CE) held agriculture in high esteem.[12] The ancient Tamil text *Thirukural* (200 BCE) speaks of the importance of land and agriculture as the source and identity:

- "World spins around many industries. All such industries spin around agriculture."
- "Farmers alone live an independent life; others worship them and are second to them."
- "If farmers stop cultivation, even rishis (sages) cannot survive."
- "If land is ploughed deep and soil allowed to dry to one fourth weight, even manuring is not necessary."
- "Manuring is more important than ploughing: crop protection is more important than irrigation."
- "If the farmer does not regularly visit his field, the crop will not grow."[13]

Peoples and cultures attribute sacredness to the land and celebrate it meaningfully through the harvest festivals in India. Tamils, one of the ancient peoples called the Dravidians, divide the land into five groups: *Mullai* (forest), *Kurinji* (hills), *Marudham* (cultivable lands), *Neithal* (coastal areas), and *Paalai* (dry and arid land). Their harvest festival is called *Pongal*. The same festival is celebrated as *Sankranthi* in Andhra Pradesh, *Batukamma* in Telengana, *Onam* in Kerala, and *Biasaki/Lohri* in Punjab, and among the tribals as *Navakhani/Sohari*. These festivals bring out the intimate relationship of human beings with God, human beings, and nature (earth). The celebration expresses their gratitude to God and ancestors. On these occasions, games, competitions (boat races, *jallikaatu*[14]), cultural programs with music, dance (*Bharatanatyam, Kathakali, Kathak, Manipuri, Kuchiudi, Odissi,* and a variety of dances by the subalterns), and dramas are performed to celebrate the "interrelatedness" of God, humans, and the earth.[15]

---

[12] See Luke Timothy Johnson, *The Revelatory Body: Theology as Inductive Art* (Grand Rapids, MI: Eerdmans, 2015), 159.

[13] Thiruvalluvar, *Thirukural*, trans. M. Rajaram (New Delhi: Rupa Publications, 2012), 210.

[14] *Jalli* means coins and *kattu* means package; *jallikattu* is a sport that involves bull taming.

[15] See P. R. John, "'Laudato Si': Challenges Faced Today for an Integral Ecology," *Vidyajyoti Journal of Theological Reflection* 80, no. 1 (2016): 27.

There are innumerable texts in these languages that celebrate the land as gift and human stewardship as a responsibility. The ancient Hindu text *Atharva Veda* says: "Whatever I dig up of you, O! earth, may you of that have quick replenishment" (12.1.64); "The earth is the mother, and I the son/daughter of the earth" (12.1.2); and "The earth is a garden, the Lord its Gardner, cherishing all, none neglected" (Sikhism, *Adi Grath, Majh Ashtpadi*, J, M3, J 18).

The development of the human person, his or her physical and mental gifts and talents, art and literature, and the sciences and technology are closely related to the land. A community's narrative is woven according to the characteristics of its territory and land. For example, the identity of *Adivasis* (tribals/original dwellers/indigenous people) in India depends on the historical, geographical, ethnic, sociocultural, and linguistic features that give them a distinct character. Land forms a major part of their being, culture, religion, health, and so on. For an *Adivasi* to claim that he or she is a *Munda, Oraon, Kharia, Ho,* or a *Santhal* means that the person has a definite, particular "location" (spatial implication). Another major group of *Adivasis* with a great cultural history, tradition, and distinct characteristics

> live near the Sahyadris, in the hilly forests of Satpura and Gondwana. . . . Many are nomads, Bhils, Gonds, Koli, Mahadevs, Warlis, Koknas, Thakrs, Andhs, Maria Gonds, Kolams. Tilling the earth in the hills and forests where the *adivasis* farm is the hardest task of all. It has taken them generations to penetrate the rocks and gravel to turn the soil into fodder for the plough.[16]

Land denotes first and foremost the identity of a people. It gives them a feeling of security as a group. The *Adivasis* believe that "the Supreme Being created heaven and earth,"[17] and they refer to the "land" or "earth" as the "mother."[18] It is the symbol of the unity of all living creatures, the spirit, and the Supreme Being. *Jal, Jangle,* and *Jameen* (the water, the forest, and the land) belong to them, and their worldview (*Weltanschauung*) revolves around these existential realties. The land is not mere space to be exploited but a place that owns people and gives personhood and identity to the community.

---

[16] Anita Agnihotri, *The Sickle*, trans. Arunava Sinha (New Delhi: Juggernaut Books, 2021), 227.

[17] A. Wati Longchar, *An Emerging Asian Tribal Theology* (Assam: TSC Jorhat, 2000), 7.

[18] Thomas D'Sa, *The Church in India in the Emerging Third Millennium* (Bangalore: NBCLC, 2005), 202.

It is this filial relationship and its intrinsic bond that make these farmers fight for their future. Unfortunately, we hear many reports of people forced to leave their land due to drought, war, pandemics, and natural calamities. Social and human rights activist Stan Lourduswamy, who fought relentlessly on behalf of the tribals and in defense of their land, and passed away in detention on July 5, 2021, observed:

> A well-planned state action to forcibly acquire indigenous land, forest, water sources and subsoil minerals has been in operation. The constitutional, legal, judicial provisions protective of indigenous people and their rights are being diluted or done away with. Poverty is deepening in rural areas and dozens of indigenous people have died of starvation in the past few years.[19]

Freelance journalist Palagummi Sainath notes that 40 percent of India's agricultural laborers are landless and asks pertinent questions like: "What do the poor do in the some 200–240 days during which there is no agriculture in their areas? How do they survive? What are their coping mechanisms? What is their identity?"[20] India's farmers are grappling with these questions.

Stewardship of the Land: A Divine Mandate

The Christian God is a pilgrim God[21] and the land belongs to him: "The earth is the Lord's and everything in it, the world and all who live in it";[22] "You have visited the land and watered it; you greatly enrich it";[23] "The Lord God formed man from the dust of the ground, and breathed into his nostrils the breath of life."[24] The Bible affirms that humanity is closely linked with land (Adam is formed out of the soil). Human beings

---

[19] Stan Lourduswamy, "Jesuit Social Action amidst Indigenous Peoples of Central India during the Past Five Decades," *Promotio Iustitiae* 128 (2019): 45.

[20] Palagummi Sainath, *Everybody Loves a Good Drought: Stories from India's Poorest Districts* (New Delhi: Penguin Books, 1996), xi. A 2018 census indicates that the percentage has risen to 47 percent (Harry Stevens, "Seven Decades after Independence, Most Dalit Farmers Still Landless," *Hindustan Times* (February 13, 2018).

[21] Jn 1:14.

[22] Ps 24:1.

[23] Ps 65:9.

[24] Gen 2:7.

are to "care" for the land.[25] "The Lord God took man and put him in the garden of Eden to till it and keep it."[26] The biblical narratives clearly state that the peoples' journey with God is shaped through a covenantal relationship with the Creator, with the land and its people, and their ownership. Therefore, we are to return the land to its original owner[27] because it belongs to the Lord.

Land is not a tradable commodity because, given by God, it is closely related to people. This relationship goes back to creation itself. As God's possession, the sacred land has a certain closeness to God. Thus, "You shall not defile the land in which you live."[28] This land is promised by God as a gift to humanity[29] and to all living creatures on earth.[30] The quest for land finds expression in the great experience of the exodus journey.[31] Later, again at the command of the Lord, Joshua takes possession of the land and gives it to the tribes as an "inheritance."[32] Wisdom literature mentions "the profit of the earth is for all"[33] and "the Spirit . . . fills the earth."[34] Prophets in the Israelite tradition, challenged the shaping of the community. The prophets Hosea and Amos denounced the bloodshed, robbery, lying, and false swearing in relation to God and Land: "There is no faithfulness or kindness. . . . Therefore, the land mourns, and all who dwell in it languish"[35]; "They . . . trample the head of the poor into the dust of the earth."[36]

Jesus, in the New Testament, sums up the egalitarian project of the kingdom: "The Spirit of the Lord is upon me, because he has anointed me to preach good news to the poor. He has sent me to proclaim release to the captives and recovery of sight to the blind, to set at liberty those who are oppressed, to proclaim the year of the Lord's favor."[37] In this project

---

[25] Gen 1:28–29.
[26] Gen 2:15.
[27] Lev 25:10.
[28] Num 35:34.
[29] Gen 12:1.
[30] Walter Brueggemann, *The Land: Place as Gift, Promise, and Challenge in Biblical Faith* (Philadelphia: Fortress Press, 1977), 3–6; see also Christopher J. H. Wright, *God's People in God's Land: Family, Land, and Property in the Old Testament* (Grand Rapids, MI: Eerdmans, 1990), 10–12.
[31] Ex 3:7–9; 6:5–8.
[32] Josh 13–19.
[33] Eccl 5:9.
[34] Wis 1:7.
[35] Hos 4:1–3.
[36] Am 2:6–8.
[37] Lk 4:18–19; Isa 61:1–2.

the peasant and the worker become partakers. Such a line of thought can be deciphered in Mary's song of high revolt.[38] Origen of Alexandria wrote the following in the third century: "God causes the grass to grow for the cattle and herbs for the service of man; that he may bring forth fruit out of the earth, and that wine may gladden man's heart and that his face may shine with oil, and that bread may strengthen man's heart."[39] And John Paul II declares: "Man, created in the image of God, shares by his work in the activity of the Creator." The work of the human person is treated as "the gospel of work."[40] The phrase, "subdue it, and have dominion"[41] is not to be interpreted as to "exploit and destroy" but to show "reverence and love," as *Evangelium Vitae* suggests: "To defend and promote life, to show reverence and love for it, is a task which God entrusts to every man, calling him as his living image to share in his own lordship over the world."[42] Luke Timothy Johnson aptly summarizes this idea: "Making a living from the land means observing and creatively responding to the rhythms imposed by nature rather than imposing my will on nature. I need to learn when to plant, when to weed, when to harvest."[43]

Our Involvement as Christ's People: A Missiological Perspective

Involvement in the People's Movement as Mission

Pope Paul VI in his apostolic exhortation *Evangelii Nuntiandi* notes: "People today listen more willingly to witnesses than to teachers, and if they do listen to teachers, it is because they are witnesses,"[44] and this witness of Christian life is, according to *Redemptoris Missio*, "the first and irreplaceable form of mission."[45] Certainly one is affected deeply by daring witnesses in God's mission. I met one such girl at the agitation site during the Christmas season. Her name was Ravneet Kaur (Punjabi), a Sikh by faith who was studying law at a Jesuit School in Bangalore. She

---

[38] Lk 1:50–53. Kurien Kunnumpuram, *The Mission of the Church: Christian Reflection on Evangelization in India Today* (Mumbai: St. Pauls, 2013), 138.

[39] Origen, *Contra Celsum* 4.75.

[40] Pope John Paul II, *Laborem Exercens (On Human Work)* (1981), nos. 25, 26.

[41] Gen 1:28.

[42] Pope John Paul II, *Evangelium Vitae (The Gospel of Life)* (1995), no. 42.

[43] Johnson, *The Revelatory Body*, 157.

[44] Pope Paul VI, apostolic exhortation *Evangelii Nuntiandi (In Proclaiming the Gospel)* (1975), no. 41.

[45] Pope John Paul II, *Redemptoris Missio (On the Permanent Validity of the Church's Missionary Mandate)* (1990), no. 42.

told me that she had come to Delhi for three days to take part in the farmers' protest and would then return to Bangalore, since she was to play the role of Mother Mary at the Christmas celebrations. But to her surprise, she stayed on for almost three months on the road at Ghazipur, Delhi. Her reasons were these:

1. As a student of law, she was interested in learning from the simple agitating farmers and to experience their life;
2. She was shocked to see (in the media) "so many women" at the protest site. Hence, she had many questions: Why had so many women gathered for a cause? How were the farmers managing? Did they have sufficient washrooms? Where were they sleeping? What about their security?
3. She wanted to observe how the Sikh faith community was targeted and labeled as *Khalistanis* (separatists), a term which she had only heard as a child;
4. She wanted to study how the protest was shaping the young minds of her country and what impact it would have on society, on government, and on the lives of people sitting on the road in bone-freezing cold.

In the initial days of Kaur's stay she found it difficult to adjust to the biting winter. In spite of the cold, however, she noticed that the women were increasing in number at the protest site. Many generous people from various faiths—Hindus, Muslims, Sikhs, and Christians—came forward to help the farmers. The atmosphere was one of sharing, and resulted in a *Lungar* (common meal).

Kaur was disappointed to see that the women at the protest were living in a small tent. She offered her services to coordinate "*mahila*-block" (women-block) at the site, and a larger tent was put up for the women in three days' time. There were other questions of how to manage issues women struggle with, such as availability of sanitary pads, undergarments, and so forth. Hence, she initiated a "*mahila*-store" (women-store) in which women could get all their essential items. Then she and her husband thought of setting up a library cum teaching center at the site. This idea was welcomed by all. The library not only had books, but also drawing facilities for kids, discussions on various topics, and at night the library was turned into a cinema hall where everyone sat together and watched patriotic and religious movies. Finally, she said, even though they were living on the road, they spent time in common worship, reading and meditating on *Adi Grant* (Sacred Scripture of the Sikh faith).

I ended my dialogue with Kaur with the following words: "Ms. Kaur, what you have contributed to the farmers' protest is the real meaning of the birth of Jesus—'incarnation.'" The conversation with her reminded me of the work of Nikki Guninder Kaur Singh, *The Feminine Principle in the Sikh Vision of the Transcendent*, which refers to the Divine as *meera*—a female friend or lover—implying a relationship of mutual esteem, dialogue, and bearing witness. Serving humanity in this world means we will be welcomed in the court of God, the Sikh faith declares. Sikhism also believes that while truth is high, higher still is truthful living.

Women like Ravneet Kaur, and many others at the farmers' protest site, enlightened me as to the new understanding of the Christian mission and the "how" of mission.

First, I realized that there was something deeply spiritual about the farmers' agitation. As Christians, we believe that mission is the intervention of God in history, and the farmers' protest is one such intervention of God, who hears the cry of the poor and reaches out to liberate them. God's involvement in history was made concrete in Jesus of Nazareth, who read the signs of his time with the optic of the poor. The "how" of mission, informed by Jesus's pedagogy, has the same prophetic and "bold humility," to use David Bosch's words, to actualize the intervention of God here and now.[46]

Second, I observed that the farmers' protest is fully spearheaded by the *hoi polloi* of diverse faiths—let us say laity, in a broader sense. They can even be aptly called lay missionaries and lay prophets. This is a new way of doing mission theology. A Christian has to mingle with the people of other faiths in the proclamation of the gospel and the work of justice, which are integrally interwoven.[47] Kaur might have missed playing Mary in the play, but her prophetic presence on the roads for the people was not all that different from the Mary of the *Magnificat*.

Third, the farmers' protest is indeed the very *locus* of an "eruption of God"; the hearing, smelling, and tasting of these protests "show the way to God through discernment" and beckon one "to walk with the poor/farmers, the outcasts of the world, those whose dignity has been violated in a mission of reconciliation and justice."[48] This triggers several

---

[46] David J. Bosch, *Transforming Mission: Paradigm Shifts in Theology and Mission* (Maryknoll, NY: Orbis Books, 1991), 17.

[47] George Kudilil and Alex Pandarakappil, *Mission and Contextual Formation* (Satna: St. Ephrem's Publications, 2017), 72.

[48] Society of Jesus, "Universal Apostolic Preferences" (2019–29). This document is the fruit of a two-year process of discernment by the members of Society of Jesus. Fr. Arturo Sosa, the superior general of the Jesuits, promulgated this document on February 19, 2019, in a letter inviting the Jesuits to resolve to concentrate and concretize their vital apostolic energies during the next ten years in the form of four preferences: (1) showing the way to God through the *Spiritual Exercises* and their practice of discernment; (2) walking with

questions: How can I respond to the farmers' protest through my shared responsibility of being a contemplative in action? Am I not supposed to view the vulnerable farmers as privileged among the people? Pope Francis speaks of the church "incarnate in the peoples of the earth, each of which has its own culture,"[49] which must go out into "new sociocultural settings"[50] and reach the "peripheries."[51] Therefore, the cry of the farmers calls into question the integrity of the Christian profession of faith that does justice. Am I prepared to respond? I am indebted to the farmers (love of neighbor)!

Outside the Gate: God Shares the Insult

The farmers are out on the streets, in the peripheries, at the borders, outside the capital—in short, "outside the gate." I think that the parallels are obvious. Noted theologians like Samuel Rayan and Orlando E. Costas have spelled out this obvious allusion in the titles of their works "Outside the Gate: Sharing the Insult"[52] and *Christ outside the Gate, Mission beyond Christianity*,[53] respectively. As we read in the Book of Hebrews, "And so Jesus too suffered outside the gate in order to sanctify the people through his own blood."[54]

The agitation screams out for existence, dignity, and freedom. Herein one hears, sees, smells, tastes, and touches Jesus "outside the gates of Delhi" in the ongoing protests of the farmers. The farmers and other oppressed groups, the *anawim*, are burdened with an affliction as excruciatingly painful as the Hebrew slaves in Egypt. One sees and hears them weeping on account of their oppressors.[55] The crucified guru Jesus is present in their midst with "a mysticism of open eyes," to use the German theologian Johann Baptist Metz's words. Highlighting the spirituality of the Beatitudes in the Synoptic Gospels, Metz writes:

---

the poor, the outcasts of the world, and those whose dignity has been violated, in the mission of reconciliation and justice; (3) walking together with young people, to build a hope-filled future; and (4) working together to care for the earth, our common home.

[49] Pope Francis, apostolic exhortation *Evangelii Gaudium (The Joy of the Gospel)* (2013), no. 115, hereinafter *EG*.

[50] *EG*, no. 30.

[51] *EG*, no. 20.

[52] Samuel Rayan, "Outside the Gate: Sharing the Insult," *Jeevadhara* 11, no. 63 (1981).

[53] Orlando Costas, *Christ outside the Gate: Mission beyond Christendom* (Eugene, OR: Wipf & Stock, 1982).

[54] Heb 13:12.

[55] Ex 3:7.

In the end Jesus did not teach an ascending mysticism of closed eyes, but rather a God-mysticism with an increased readiness for perceiving, a mysticism of open eyes, which sees more and not less. It is a mysticism that especially makes visible all invisible and inconvenient suffering, and—convenient or not—pays attention to it and takes responsibility for it, for the sake of a God who is a friend to human beings.[56]

The question is, do the people living next door see their pain and hear their cry? The cozy middle class in Delhi, the media, the religious-cultural institutions who maintain the status quo, and the government of the country that promises to be for the people, with the people, do not see and hear it very often.

With Jesus's death "outside the gate" a new privileged location of liberation (*mukti*) and salvation (*moksa*) is offered to the human community. Similarly, "outside the gates of Delhi," on the roads where the farmers are sitting in, protesting, singing, praying, prophesying, and making bread, ought to be the very location of liberation and salvation. It is there one is called to be at the service of others.

What does the Christian community do about the plight of the farmers? What is the "how" of our response? Jesuit sociologist Prakash Louis, speaking about the Christian involvement in the farmers' agitation, says:

> What is extremely disturbing and painful is that the Indian Church pretends that it has nothing to do with this protest of the farmers. Even if the official leadership does not join the protest, it must issue a statement that the church is deeply disturbed by seeing the plight of the protesting farmers on the road in the severe winter of Delhi. . . . The church cannot remain a mute spectator, nor pretend to be safe. If this opportunity is lost, the people of this country will not stand by the Christians when an authoritarian and autocratic government would try to wipe out a meagre 2.3 percent of its population. Christ Jesus is sure to say about the Indian church, "Truly, I say to you, as you did not do it to one of the least of these, you did not do it to me."[57]

---

[56] Johann Baptist Metz, *A Passion for God: The Mystical-Political Dimension of Christianity*, ed. and trans. J. Matthew Ashley (New York: Paulist Press, 1998), 163.

[57] Prakash Louis, "Farmers' Protest: A Missed Opportunity for Church," *Matters India*, December 16, 2020, https://mattersindia.com.

There is a need to understand the context and content of the farmers' cry ("faith seeking understanding" of the life of farmers). The farmers' cry is for justice and for liberation/salvation from cultural domination, economic exploitation, police repression, social marginalization, and political imperialism. The powerless and vulnerable farmers' call for *truth* (*satyameva jayate*) is social and theological. An urgent *missiology of protest* (rightful protest is not the same as violence) strongly grounded in the nonnegotiable principles of *ahimsa* (nonviolence), *satyagraha* (holding on to truth), and *sadbhavana* (feeling of goodwill) is the need of the hour; it is crucial, vital, and pressing, and not without its share of hope, as noted by Satyendra Ranjan:

> In recent times, farmers, workers, students, and certain religious and regional minorities have had a clear vision/idea of the India they want to see. Actually, credit goes to them for presenting an antithesis to the ideology of the present ruling arrangement. Though there might not be immediate solutions on the horizon, the recent peoples' movements have definitely proposed certain templates of tactics and strategies, ways of communication as well as politics and ideas for future protests. Their importance should not be underestimated as these movements are the only source of hope amid the continuing onslaught of communal authoritarianism on Indian democracy.[58]

The Goal of Mission Is the Kingdom

An All-India seminar, "The Indian Church in the Struggle for a New Humanity," observes: "Her (the church's) mission requires that she herself embody in her own life and structures of the Kingdom values of freedom, fellowship and justice. It also requires that she contribute to the promotion of those values in the ordering of society."[59] This is beautifully reflected in Pope Francis's invitation to today's evangelizing church to be "a church which goes forth, from our own comfort zone in order to reach all of the 'peripheries' in need of the light of the Gospel."[60]

The kingdom concern that one witnesses in the powerlessness and vulnerability of the Indian farmers at the borders of Tikri, Singhu, Gazipur,

---

[58] Satyendra Ranjan, "Farmers' Protest: A Roadmap for the Opposition," *Economic and Political Weekly* 56, no. 18 (2021).

[59] As quoted in S. Devaraj, "Witness of Life: Our Mission Today," *SEDOS Bulletin* 45, nos. 11–12 (2013): 252.

[60] *EG*, no. 20.

and Shajahanpur is not a problem but instead offers a creative hope of being for others. The powerlessness (cross) and vulnerability (death) that exist alongside great beauty (resurrection), wisdom, insight, and humility are what these farmers give to our nation and the world mission of the church.

Jesus and His Agrarian Missionary Diction

Jesus preached God and the kingdom of God using agrarian language: vine and vineyard, fig and sycamore trees, fruits and roots, digging and pruning, seed and sowing, generation, barn and chaff, winnow and plough. Camels, sheep, bird, dog, viper, wolf, dove, fish, and moth from the animal world feature in Jesus's homiletic world. His parables and preaching revolved around his observation of earth and nature. To his worried disciples, he said, "Consider the lilies, how they grow: they neither toil nor spin; yet I tell you, even Solomon in all his glory was not arrayed like one of these."[61] He went to solitary places (on the top of a hillock, a garden, and so forth) to commune with his Father. Stones, caves, sand, and wilderness, rivers, seas, reeds, grass, foxholes, flowers, nesting, watering, sun, moon, stars, clouds, winds, lighting, and rain create a mosaic of his kingdom. A new humanity and a dream of a new earth is the clarion call. It's no wonder his song was one of revolt.[62]

Going Green for the Kingdom's Sake

Going green for the kingdom's sake is the need of the hour. The dangers that humanity could face in the twenty-first century were clearly stated in the 1972 *Limits to Growth Report*:

> If the present growth trends in world population, industrialization, pollution, food production, and resource depletion continue unchanged, the limits to growth on this planet will be reached sometime within the next one hundred years. The most probable result

---

[61] Lk 12:27.
[62] Samuel Rayan, "Prophet and Poet in One," in *Jesus Today*, ed. S. Kappen (Madras: Aicuf Publication, 1985), 173.

will be a rather sudden and uncontrollable decline in population and industrial capacity.[63]

In 2001, the Canberra Conference that approved the *Global Greens Charter* envisioned "that greener politics ought to be based on the principles of ecological wisdom, social justice, participatory democracy, nonviolence, sustainability and respect for diversity."[64] Pope Benedict XVI, who came to be known as the first "green pope," addressed the issues of ecology.[65] Pope Francis's *Laudato Si'* presents the gift of God's creation and invites everyone to care for and protect the environment. *Laudato Si'* is interdisciplinary in its approach and engages critically with the environmental and cultural issues that threaten the relationship among human beings and nature and between human beings themselves. It also explores the degradation caused by our materialistic society. While supporting the environmental and farmers' movements all over the world, Pope Francis challenges the modern mentality and its "throw-away culture" that contributes to the ecological crisis. He invites the human community to an ecological transformation and to have a passionate heart to protect the world by engaging in "a dialogue with all people about our common home."

> The intimate relationship between the poor and the fragility of the planet, the conviction that everything in the world is connected, the critique of new paradigms and forms of power derived from technology, the call to seek other ways of understanding the economy and progress, the value proper to each creature, the human meaning of ecology, the need for forthright and honest debate, the serious responsibility of international and local policy, the throwaway culture and the proposal of a new lifestyle.[66]

One can't miss the "cosmotheandric vision," to use the expression of Raimon Panikkar, that *Laudato Si'* alludes to: the mystical meaning of

---

[63] Donella H. Meadows, Dennis L. Meadows, Jørgen Randers, and William W. Behrens III, *The Limits to Growth: A Report for the Club of Rome's Project on the Predicament of Mankind* (New York: Universe Books, 1972), 23. Cf. Patxi Alvarez de los Mozos, *Serving the Poor: Promoting Justice* (Spain: Ulzama, S.L.—Huarte [Navarra], 2019), 303.

[64] As quoted in "Pope Francis and Respect for Diversity: A Mapping Employing a Green Theo-Ecoethical Lens," *New Blackfriars* 99, no. 1083 (2018): 603.

[65] See Benedict XVI, *The Environment* (Huntington, IN: Our Sunday Visitor, 2012).

[66] Pope Francis, *Laudato Si' (On Care for Our Common Home)* (2015), no. 3, 16, hereinafter *LS*.

consciousness—the dancing cosmos, divine and human (sacramentality). Francis writes:

> The universe unfolds in God, who fills it completely. Hence, there is a mystical meaning to be found in a leaf, in a mountain trail, in a dewdrop, in a poor person's face. The ideal is not only to pass from the exterior to the interior to discover the action of God in the soul, but also to discover God in all things. Saint Bonaventure teaches us that "contemplation deepens the more we feel the working of God's grace within our hearts, and the better we learn to encounter God in creatures [signs and symbols] outside ourselves.[67]

Thus, a creation-centered spirituality pushes us to be open to a sense of wonder for the creation, and to fight all that oppresses human dignity and journey toward a mystical perspective of the unity of all in God (*advaita*). The sense of interconnectedness and cosmic solidarity with nature brings forth the spirit of compassion (*karuna*) and of nonviolence (*ahimsa*). It invites us to appreciate God's wonderful creation and helps us reflect on ethics and how to be responsible environmental stewards. As Article 51(g) of the Indian Constitution states: "It shall be the duty of every citizen of India . . . to protect and improve the natural environment, including forests, lakes, rivers, and wildlife and to have compassion for living creatures."[68] Thus, there is a need to "till" and "keep" God's creation, our "common home."

Conclusion

The goal of Christian witness and mission is to bring life and all its relationships to the worshipful (liturgy) presence of God, and "to participate in the great truth of our salvation."[69] All things have been received as gifts; therefore, they are to be shared. The bread and wine are offered, blessed, and shared. The eucharistic bread and wine symbolize the Lord's blessings and human hard work, and they are to be respected and shared in an atmosphere of justice. Justice has to be exercised at all levels: from the farmer who produces the wheat/rice, to the science and technology

---

[67] *LS*, no. 233.
[68] *Constitution of India* (1950).
[69] David Vincent Meconi, ed., *On Earth as It Is in Heaven: Cultivating a Contemporary Theology of Creation* (Grand Rapids, MI: W.B. Eerdmans Publishing Company, 2016), 295–98.

involved in transporting the product, to the business people who buy it from the farmer in order to market it.

In today's world we need to develop a "creational spirituality" or "agrarian spirituality" that takes our commitment to ecology (earth) and the farming community across the world seriously. Such a spirituality calls for a radical participation in the mission of the Son of God, Jesus Christ—the Good Sower. Jesus deliberately took the side of the "people in pain," and today we need to take the side of the farmers. Only then will "a new heaven and a new earth"[70] become a tangible reality that reflects our eschatological commitment to the kingdom of truth and life, and to a world of justice, peace, and love. If we fail the farmers, we fail not just them but all those who are vulnerable and oppressed in the world; we fail not just democracy, but the Indian Constitution, the United Nations Declaration on Human Rights, Catholic social teaching, and the philosophy of peaceful protest (*satyagraha*) popularized by Mahatma Gandhi, Daniel Dolci, Lanza del Vasto, Martin Luther King Jr., Adolfo Pérez Esquivel, Archbishop Hélder Câmara, Nelson Mandela, Harsh Mander, and Medha Patkar; ultimately, we will fail our own conscience. Let us go and encounter Jesus the Farmer "Outside the Gates."

[*Note: A few weeks after the Mission Symposium, on November 19, 2021, Prime Minister Narendra Modi announced the repeal of the contentious laws, and on November 30, 2021, the Farm Laws Repeal Act was accepted.*]

Pudota Rayappa John, SJ, holds a doctorate in dogmatic theology from Leopold-Franzens University, Innsbruck, Austria. He was the director of Kala Darshini, an institute of evangelization and culture in Vijayawada, Andhra Pradesh, and is at present the principal of Vidyajyoti College of Theology, Delhi, India. His writings are expressions of his attempts at contextualizing theology.

---

[70] Rev 21:1.

PART THREE

NEW TRENDS IN MISSION

Introduction to Part Three

Bryan Lobo, SJ

As it is commonly known, healthy movement or change is life, while stagnation is death. Heraclitus may not have thought of change as life-giving, but he was the first to think of it as a fundamental law of the universe. As a fundamental law, it cannot be absent from human reality in any context whether religious, social, political, cultural, or even missionary. If mission is to give life, it has to be in movement—in constant transformation or constant *conversion,* a word used by Pope Francis when he invited all communities to "devote the necessary effort to advancing along the path of a pastoral and missionary *conversion* which cannot leave things as they presently are."[1]

Using the phrase *new trends in mission* is another way of verbalizing how mission is moving and life-giving. It challenges a static understanding of mission that is sometimes fanatically or fearfully held on to, even in changing circumstances. If Jesus had held on to the Mosaic law as the Pharisees did, he would perhaps not have been able to fulfill his salvific mission. The mission of the Law had to be fulfilled by the mission of the reign of God of love and mercy, culminating in Jesus's death, resurrection, and ascension, and continued by the Holy Spirit, in and through the church. Furthermore, the history of the church bears testimony to the fact that the understanding of mission has gone through various changes down the centuries, rooted always, however, in the Christ-event.

Merely because in a certain period there existed a certain paradigm or a way of doing mission, it cannot be slavishly followed in a later period. Periodic changes in human conceptualization, knowledge, worldview, interaction, and lifestyle lead to missional changes, thereby creating trends in mission and even paradigm shifts in the understanding and theology

---

[1] Pope Francis, apostolic exhortation *Evangelii Gaudium (The Joy of the Gospel)* (2013), no. 25, italics added.

of mission, as proposed by David Bosch.[2] Enlightened awareness of the current situation, or any situation for that matter, enthuses the missiologist not only to reflect on the contemporary missionary methods but also to recommend new ones for integral human and ecological salvation.

The topics in this section were selected in the hope of a pro-reflective-active contribution to create more awareness and commitment in mission, whether it is in interreligious dialogue, ecumenism, justice and peace, ecology, interculturality, media, healing, education, secularization, pastoral activity, laity, or the youth. These are no doubt common trends in mission, but they have evolved from past experiences and activities believed to be inspired by the Holy Spirit. It is the Spirit who is finally the "protagonist" of the process of mission in the church.

Mission evolves not only from the Christ-event but much before that from the symbolic event of the creative act of God. God created out of God's free will; nonetheless, "he wanted to make his creatures share in his being, wisdom, and goodness."[3] There was, therefore, an intention in creating the world, at least as understood by Christianity, and in that intention the missionary aspect becomes evident. Given the missionary mandate by the risen Lord to go and baptize people in the name of the Father, the Son, and the Holy Spirit, if the creative act of God is not seen as intrinsically related to mission, then that mandate is incomplete and unholistic because it must be inclusive of the intention behind the creative act of God in whom we are baptized. Moreover, in the divine intention of that one creative act, the various cultures, religions, communities, and peoples of all times are incorporated. The Christ-event concretely guarantees us the realization of that intention, which in common Christian parlance is called salvation, in the person and teaching of Jesus, whether acceptable or not to non-Christians at various levels: rational, social, political, and religious.

With all the differences between religions and communities, the need for love, justice, and peace is recognized as a common denominator across all human divides. That need may be acquired and expressed in different and even conflictual ways because of a particular conditioning of one's milieu. It is here that mission, in general, requires a global consensus in the ways of acquiring and expressing love, justice, and peace that are liberative and not oppressive in their consequences. If the missionary expression of one's love for God, or faith, or spirituality, or ideology unfolds into hatred

---

[2] See David Bosch, *Transforming Mission: Paradigm Shifts in Theology of Mission* (Maryknoll, NY: Orbis Books, 1991).

[3] Pope John Paul II, *Catechism of the Catholic Church* (1992), no. 295.

or killing or proselytizing or denouncing the other as diabolical, then that amounts to a grave missionary "sin" because it finally destroys the very love, justice, and peace that one aims to express and attain.

The platform for missionary reflection created by the present COVID-19 pandemic is phenomenal because even though all people, irrespective of their differences, have to come together to confront this situation for medical and material needs, each has to remain in isolation. *Isolational communities,* a contradiction in terms, has become a regular practice. Physical presence that once led to creating community, solidarity, friendship, education, and charity, has now changed to digital presence that cannot replace physical presence but still is the only way of human bonding and activity in most cases today. Digital presence facilitates participation not only at the local level but at the global level as well. In such a situation, can the church "go digital" with the sacraments with all the precautions well discussed and explained? This could perhaps be one trend in the missionary endeavor of the church in COVID-19 times—discerning the impulse of the Holy Spirit that may be inviting us to go digital for greater connectivity and impact. The church has gone all out to do charity in these circumstances, but can it press for justice in ways that are presumably different from the non–COVID-19 times for the poor who have been badly hit by this pandemic? These may be difficult questions to answer for the present, but it must be acknowledged that new trends in mission always begin with questions that are not easy to answer. However, over time one cannot avoid them but must respond to them through the guidance of the Holy Spirit. It is only then that a baptism in the Spirit can be expected, giving birth to new trends in mission with the hope that they will "renew the face of the earth."[4]

> **Bryan Lobo, SJ,** who was born in Mumbai, India, is dean of the Faculty of Missiology at Pontifical Gregorian University, Italy. His doctoral dissertation was titled "Trinitarian Theology as *Fides Docens Intellectum*: An Inference Drawn from the Trinitarian Theologies of Thomas Aquinas, Brahmabandhab Upadhyay, and Karl Rahner."

---

[4] Ps 104:30.

Secularization
Mission in a Secular Age

Daniel Patrick Huang, SJ

Although the words *secular, secularization,* and *secularism* are often used as though their meanings were identical, they are distinct concepts, and an initial clarification is necessary when using them. The term *secular* is a category used in various disciplines to describe a *realm* that is distinct from the religious. *Secularization,* on the other hand, refers to world-historical *processes* by which the secular and the religious are differentiated. Finally, *secularism* refers to a range of *worldviews*, professed explicitly or held unreflexively, that usually perceive the relationship between secular and religious in a normative way.[1] These initial distinctions are meant to help clarify the focus of this brief consideration on Christian mission in an age that, in many cultural contexts of the world, might be described as secular.

Secularization as a Departure from the Official Religions

Secularization, as mentioned above, might be broadly understood as the historical processes of differentiation between the religious and the secular spheres. However, the late nineteenth and early twentieth centuries saw the growth of a widespread consensus on what has been called secularization theory or the secularization thesis, which held that modernization—

---

[1] José Casanova, "The Secular, Secularizations, Secularisms," in *Rethinking Secularism*, ed. Craig Calhoun, Mark Juergensmeyer, and Jonathan VanAntwerpen (New York: Oxford University Press, 2011), 54–55. Precisely because there have been varied processes of differentiation between the secular and the religious with differing goals and results, and because there is also a broad range of conceptions of the relationship between the religious and the secular, it is also more accurate to speak of *secularizations* and *secularisms*, in the plural (see ibid., 60, 67).

technological, economic, and political progress—would lead *automatically* to the weakening and eventual withering away of religion. The eminent German sociologist Hans Joas, evaluating this secularization thesis, put it bluntly: "This assumption . . . is wrong"—or, at least, "most experts now consider it wrong."[2]

The secularization thesis is viewed today as an unwarranted universalization of the European experience of modernization and religious change that has not always taken place in other contexts in which modernizing processes have been at work. Religion, for example, has not disappeared in the prosperous and modern cultures of the United States and South Korea; the new prosperity of China has seen a concomitant revival of Buddhism and Christianity;[3] and modernization has not eradicated but rather seen the resurgence of Islam in the Middle East, Hinduism in India, and Buddhism in Sri Lanka. Joas warns: "It is crucial to liberate ourselves from the notion of religion as a relic and take seriously the contemporary creative power of religious motives."[4]

Within Christianity, the phenomenal growth of the Pentecostal churches, particularly in Latin America and Africa, from 58 million Pentecostals in 1970 to 656 million in 2021—26 percent of all Christians today, more than the Orthodox, the Anglicans, and Lutherans combined[5]—should call into question theories that posit a "law-like connection between modernization and secularization."[6]

Questioning the assumed *necessary* correlation between modernization and secularization does not mean, however, denying the *reality* of secularization, particularly in the sense of the *decline of religious belief, practice, and belonging* in many cultural contexts.[7] Without overlooking the centers of religious vitality in Europe, for example, it has become widely acceptable to describe Europe, or at least Western and Southern Europe, as post-Christian, a label that is actually experienced by those

---

[2] Hans Joas, *Faith as an Option: Possible Futures for Christianity* (Stanford, CA: Stanford University Press, 2014), 3.

[3] See Evan Osnos, *Age of Ambition: Chasing Fortune, Truth and Faith in the New China* (New York: Farrar, Straus and Giroux, 2014.)

[4] Joas, *Faith as an Option*, 17.

[5] Gina A. Zurlo, Todd M. Johnson, and Peter F. Crossing, "World Christianity and Mission 2021: Questions about the Future," *International Bulletin of Missionary Research* 45, no. 2 (2021): 18–19.

[6] Joas, *Faith as an Option*, 21.

[7] For the purposes of this essay, we focus on this aspect of secularization, mindful that, in his book *Public Religions in the Modern World,* José Casanova has famously identified two other "secularizations," namely, the differentiation of secular spheres (e.g., the state, science) from religious control and norms, and the privatization of religion in democratic politics.

who see empty churches, aging churchgoers, and the marginalization of the church in public affairs. Charles Taylor makes the nuanced conclusion that "there has been in Western society in general a certain kind of 'departure' from religion, . . . by which I mean a departure from official religions which have in the past played a key role in binding societies together."[8]

Moreover, José Casanova perceptively observes that, particularly in Western Europe, this departure is linked to what he calls a "historical stadial consciousness,"[9] an assumed attitude that to be modern and enlightened necessarily means leaving the myths of religion behind so as to be considered autonomous, mature, and rational. Thus, interestingly, Casanova notes that while Americans tend to overstate their religiosity in polls, Europeans tend to understate their religiosity, in order to conform to the assumed cultural metanarrative that does not regard being religious as a positive trait.[10]

Although the United States has often been held up as an example of modernization without European-style secularization (one recalls sociologist Peter Berger's oft-quoted quip that the United States is a "country of Indians governed by an elite of Swedes"),[11] recent research highlights the dramatic growth of religious disaffiliation in the last two decades. From 1937 to 1998, "church membership [in the United States] remained relatively constant, hovering at about 70 percent"; over the past twenty years, however, "that number has dropped to 50 percent, the sharpest recorded decline in American history."[12] Meanwhile, the number of Nones—those who identify themselves as not belonging to any religion—has increased to 26 percent of the population, almost 80 million people. The percentage of Nones among millennials—those born after 1990—is almost 40 percent. The Nones represent "the single biggest religious demographic figure in America, as well as the fastest-growing one."[13]

As Tara Isabella Burton, in her recent study of religiously nonaffiliated millennials, points out, the majority of the Nones were former Christians, and that "retention rates among Hindus, Buddhists, Muslims, and Jews all

---

[8] Charles Taylor, "Shapes of Faith Today," in *Renewing the Church in a Secular Age: Holistic Dialogue and Kenotic Vision*, ed. Charles Taylor, José Casanova, George F. McLean, and João J. Vila-Chã (Washington, DC: Council for Research in Values and Philosophy, 2016), 276.

[9] Casanova, "The Secular, Secularizations, Secularisms," 67.

[10] See ibid., 68.

[11] See Albert Mohler, "Rethinking Secularization: A Conversation with Peter Berger," October 11, 2010, www.albertmohler.com.

[12] Shadi Hamid, "America without God," *The Atlantic* (April 2021).

[13] Tara Isabella Burton, *Strange Rites: New Religions for a Godless World* (New York: Public Affairs, 2020), 16.

remain much higher than among Christians."[14] Stephen Bullivant, in his investigation of religious disaffiliation among Catholics in the United States and Britain, observes that recent data reveals that a third of US Catholics (34 percent) "no longer identify as Catholic," a proportion he rightly regards as "serious."[15] While studies like that of Burton or of Elizabeth Drescher[16] indicate that many Nones continue to regard themselves as spiritual and craft their own spirituality, the data confirms Taylor's earlier mentioned observation that there is a "departure from official religions"[17] in the United States. Sociologist Ryan P. Burge concludes from the data of disaffiliation that "the United States is seeing a wave of delayed secularization . . . and the United States will look more and more like Europe as time passes."[18]

While secularization as the decline of religious belief, practice, and belonging is most characteristic of North Atlantic contexts, it is by no means absent in others. A 2020 survey shows that 77.7 percent of Mexicans identify themselves as Catholics, the "lowest rate ever recorded" (down from 88 percent in 2000), while 8.1 percent (about 10 million people) now consider themselves as belonging to "no religion," a "significant increase" from the 4.7 percent in 2010.[19] Already two decades ago, the sociologist David Brown, in his important book on Pentecostalism, noted that in Chile, among Pentecostals, "43 percent ceased to be evangelicals in the second generation, of whom the great majority described themselves as 'nothing.'"[20] A 2018 report of the Pew Research Center shows that young adults are less likely to identify themselves as belonging to a religion in North America and Europe, but also in 14 countries of Latin America, not to mention South Korea, Japan, and Australia, in the Asia Pacific region—41 of the 106 countries surveyed.[21] Nor should one ignore

---

[14] Ibid., 52.

[15] Stephen Bullivant, *Mass Exodus: Catholic Disaffiliation in Britain and America since Vatican II* (New York: Oxford University Press, 2019), 28.

[16] Elizabeth Drescher, *Choosing Our Religion: The Spiritual Lives of America's Nones* (New York: Oxford University Press, 2016).

[17] Cf. Taylor, "Shapes of Faith Today."

[18] See Ryan P. Burge, *The Nones: Where They Came From, Who They Are, and Where They Are Going* (Minneapolis: Fortress Press, 2021), 42.

[19] Youna Rivallain, "Protestantism Is Beginning to Outpace Catholicism in Mexico," *La Croix*, February 11, 2021.

[20] David Martin, *Pentecostalism: The World Their Parish* (Malden, MA: Blackwell Publishers, 2002), 113.

[21] Pew Research Center, "Young Adults around the World Are Less Religious by Several Measures," June 13, 2018.

what Peter Berger observed two decades ago: there exists a globalized secularized elite, small in number but with great influence insofar as they "control the institutions that provide the 'official' definition of reality,"[22] such as academe and the media.

The Secular as a New Set of Cultural Conditions

The perception that secularization has led to the decline of religious belief, practice, and belonging in certain contexts has led to concern among religious leaders and believers alike, as well as to calls for renewed mission. Pope John Paul II popularized the idea of a "new evangelization" aimed at reaching "entire groups of the baptized [who] have lost a living sense of the faith, or even no longer consider themselves members of the Church."[23] In *Evangelii Gaudium* Pope Francis noted with concern the "breakdown in the way Catholics pass down the Christian faith to the young," and acknowledged as "undeniable" the fact that "many people feel disillusioned and no longer identify with the Catholic tradition."[24]

One problem, however, with focusing solely on secularization as a process that leads to a decline in religious belief, practice, and/or belonging is that it tends to mutate into a narrative of loss, in what Charles Taylor calls a "subtraction story": *Once upon a time, a culture or society was religious; now, it has largely abandoned religion.*[25] A culture is then deemed to be "secular" because it has given up on religion; and the "secular" is what remains after religion is gone, the "natural" state of humanity and culture shorn of religion. This is problematic for Taylor because, in fact, what makes a culture secular is not simply the absence of religion, but the presence of a new "social imaginary," a different cultural construct of reality, a new set of conditions of plausibility for belief that affect religious believer and unbeliever alike.[26] Unless one understands these new conditions that

---

[22] Peter Berger, ed., *The Desecularization of the World: Resurgent Religion and World Politics* (Grand Rapids, MI: Eerdmans, 1999), 10.

[23] Pope John Paul II, *Redemptoris Missio (On the Permanent Validity of the Church's Missionary Mandate)* (1990), no. 33.

[24] Pope Francis, apostolic exhortation *Evangelii Gaudium (The Joy of the Gospel)* (2013), no. 70, hereinafter *EG*.

[25] Charles Taylor, *A Secular Age* (Cambridge: Harvard University Press, 2007), 22.

[26] This point is highlighted in an illuminating way in James K. A. Smith's *How (Not) to Be Secular: Reading Charles Taylor* (Grand Rapids, MI: Eerdmans, 2014), a helpful introduction to Taylor's dense and complex *A Secular Age*.

constitute a culture as secular, one will not be able to respond adequately on mission. Put somewhat differently, if one's conception of secularization is solely linked to a narrative of loss, then mission will tend to be conceived of as a project of restoration, of recovering lost ground, and bringing back the "good old days." If, on the other hand, one conceives the secular as a new set of cultural conditions that renders belief challenging for those embedded in the culture, one might be in a better position to respond more creatively and more effectively on mission.

Three Features of Secular Cultures

Within the scope of this brief reflection, it will not be possible to present a comprehensive picture of the new social imaginary that characterizes secular cultures. For our purposes, we will highlight only three features.

Faith Becomes an Option

Hans Joas, José Casanova, and Charles Taylor all observe that, while modernization does not automatically lead to secularization, what it does "irremediably" is bring about the "pluralization of options, individual, communitarian, as well as collective, in all kinds of directions, religious and secular."[27] Modernity means living in a world marked by "the massive increase in individual action options,"[28] whether those options involve the choice of consumer goods, a life partner, a worldview, religion, or way of life.

Where religion is concerned, Charles Taylor further observes that this pluralization is compelling precisely because the available options are not simply abstract, theoretical options, but living, viable options. In modern societies people generally know "other people, equally if not more intelligent, or perceptive, who are living another option," and so the attitude that dismisses those who opt for other faiths or no faith as "morally deficient" or "catastrophically blind" becomes less and less tenable.[29] There is an "unbundling" of religion and society, so that

---

[27] José Casanova, "A Catholic Church in a Global Secular World," in Taylor et al., *Renewing the Church in a Secular Age*, 72.
[28] Joas, *Faith as an Option*, 73.
[29] Taylor, "Shapes of Faith Today," 269.

- religion is no longer simply a predetermined given of belonging to a particular culture, but more and more a personal choice;
- there emerges a multiplicity of available, viable options, alongside the disappearance of social stigmas for those who change or opt out of religion; and
- the dominant global consumer culture creates a *habitus* of personal choice and presents religion as a range of private lifestyle options.[30]

These developments all work together toward creating a unique modern context for spiritual or religious life, summarized well in the title of Hans Joas's book: *Faith as an Option*.

It will not be possible to develop this point further in these pages, but it is important to note that the optionality of religion in modern society does not necessarily lead to relativism or a weakening of commitment, as some would claim. As Joas wryly observes, "The mere awareness that there are billions of other women on the planet does not shatter my commitment to my wife."[31] Optionality does change, however, the context, the path to, and the mode of commitment and of engaging in religious mission. These are worth exploring at some other time.

An "Exclusive" Humanism

If "optionality" characterizes the exercise of religion in modern societies, the acceptability and the prevalence of a *secular* option is perhaps the most important factor in identifying a culture as secular. In his now canonical book *A Secular Age*, Charles Taylor asks: "Why was it virtually impossible not to believe in God, in, say, 1500 in our Western society, while in 2000, many of us find this not only easy, but even inescapable?"[32] His answer, its genealogy traced in the book's many pages, is the emergence of "exclusive humanism" as a viable option. *"For the first time in history, a purely self-sufficient humanism came to be a widely available option."*[33] Not only is it "legitimized as a possibility" to imagine a fulfilled human life completely lived in what Taylor calls a closed "immanent frame," without any reference

---

[30] Cf. Bryan S. Turner, "Post-Secular Society: Consumerism and the Democratization of Religion," in *The Post-secular in Question: Religion in Contemporary Society*, ed. Philip S. Gorski, David Kyuman Kim, John Torpey, and Jonathan VanAntwerpen (New York: New York University Press, 2012), 135–58.

[31] Joas, *Faith as an Option*, 85.

[32] Taylor, *A Secular Age*, 25.

[33] Ibid., 18, emphasis added.

to or need for the divine or the transcendent for meaning and flourishing, but in some contexts, this option has become "normalized"[34] to the point of actually becoming the default cultural position.

For some, such as many modern Europeans, an underlying cultural narrative that connects exclusive humanism to a "superior moral stage that supersedes and overcomes a prior more primitive or more traditional religious stage" legitimizes this option.[35] Here, one is dealing with a particular version of secularism, one that Casanova calls a "philosophical-historical" secularism that has become a "taken-for-granted assumption" of ordinary people.[36] In this connection Taylor has an interesting discussion on how modern "conversions" to unbelief often involve a narrative of growing up, of facing reality, of courage to give up a childish faith.[37] This sense of the moral and intellectual superiority of the secularist vision of human flourishing also merits missiological reflection.

Suspicion of Institutional Religion

In this new cultural sensibility, religious institutions and institutional forms of religious belonging and practice are relativized or problematized.

On the one hand, related to pluralization and optionality (along with many other developments in contemporary society) is what Taylor calls "the social imaginary of expressive individualism."[38] This holds that each person has his or her own way of realizing their humanity, and this path must be searched for rather than simply conforming to models imposed from the outside by religious institutions. Thus, the widespread preference for "spirituality" as opposed to more institutionally determined "religion."[39]

On the other hand, there exists a prevalent generalized mistrust of institutions, including or perhaps especially religious ones,[40] a mistrust profoundly deepened by the sexual-abuse scandal and other revelations of historical failures (for example, involvement in slavery, racism, and

---

[34] Hans Joas, "The Church in a World of Options," in Taylor et al., *Renewing the Church in a Secular Age,* 89.

[35] Casanova, "A Catholic Church in a Global Secular World," 76.

[36] Casanova, "The Secular, Secularizations, Secularisms," 67.

[37] See Taylor, *A Secular Age,* 365ff.

[38] Taylor, *A Secular Age,* 486.

[39] Tara Isabella Burton's fascinating book *Strange Rites* shows how consumer and internet culture have exponentially amplified the unbundling of religious identity and practice from religious institutions in favor of bespoke, uniquely personal religions and spiritualities (see esp. 20–26).

[40] See Burges, *The Nones,* 54–61.

colonialism) that have tainted institutional religions and compromised their credibility.[41]

Mission in a "Secular" Age

Understanding secular cultures, not simply as cultures without religion, but rather as contexts in which (1) there is a *pluralization of options*; (2) the option of *exclusive humanism* is normalized and valorized; and (3) *institutional religions* are regarded *as problematic*, how should the church respond in mission? We limit our reflection to three points, touching each of these aspects of secular culture.

Embracing Pluralism as a Value

It is important not simply to resign oneself to the pluralism of options of modern secular society as a given, but to embrace it *as a value for Christian mission*. This does not mean endorsing all worldviews, value systems, and ways of life as equally valid; indeed, a robust dialogue with other visions of the "good life"—at times appreciative, at other times critical, even sharply so—remains crucial. Nor is it to deny that, while some view the sheer multiplicity of possibilities and the optionality of modernity as liberating, others experience it as threatening, bewildering, and disorienting, and thus seek refuge from the maelstrom in religious groups that promise clear identity, stability, and security.[42]

The reality of pluralism and optionality means letting go of a hankering for the protection and privileges of "Christendom" and the mindset of dominance (the "temptation of hegemony")[43] that are associated with this particular institutional realization of Christianity—or of nostalgic idealizations of it. In the words of Julián Carrón: "We are called to live the faith without a context to protect us; not only without privileges, but sometimes even persecuted."[44] But the loss of the coercive pressures of state, society, and culture in favor of Christianity is not to be mourned, since it has allowed the rediscovery of the "nature of truth and of the

---

[41] For the effect of the sexual-abuse scandals on Catholic belonging and practice in the United States and Britain, see Bullivant, *Mass Exodus*, 223–53.

[42] See Gerard Arbuckle, *Fundamentalism at Home and Abroad: Analysis and Pastoral Responses* (Collegeville, MN: Liturgical Press, 2017).

[43] Julián Carrón, *Disarming Beauty: Essays on Faith, Truth, and Freedom* (Notre Dame, IN: University of Notre Dame Press, 2017), 29.

[44] Ibid., 54.

path to reach it": "the truth cannot be imposed from the outside; it must be embraced and appropriated by man in freedom."[45]

Carrón's articulation of the Christian missionary stance, so to speak, in a pluralistic culture, without the reactive anger of culture wars or fearful withdrawal into enclaves of the like minded, deserves to be quoted in full:

> We need to find a way of living the faith, within this social and pluralistic culture, such that others can perceive our presence not as something to defend themselves from, but as a contribution to the common good and their own personal good. We need a way of being present without a will to dominate or oppress, and at the same time, with a commitment to living the faith in reality, in order to show the human benefit of belonging to Christ.[46]

Human Flourishing and Spiritual Experience

Carrón's final phrase—showing the "human benefit of belonging to Christ"—points to an important second challenge to mission in a secular age. Exclusive humanism, as the ordinary vision and way of life in secular culture, means that many of our contemporaries live their life in all its different dimensions—professional, family, relationships, communications, culture, and entertainment—in ways that are so sufficiently meaningful and fulfilling that they do not need the "hypothesis of God" as explanation, problem solver, or source of meaning and joy. Furthermore, the global consumer culture, perhaps the most powerful formative system in our contemporary world, shapes human imagination and desire toward visions of human flourishing that are resolutely immanent and proposes continuing cycles of entertainment and distraction that silence or deaden sensitivity to deeper desires.[47] The "flatness" of the reductionist view of exclusive humanism of the human being gives rise among some to a search for the spiritual—but even spirituality can be experienced and lived within

---

[45] Ibid., 19, 32. Carrón is, of course, explaining and affirming the teaching of *Dignitatis Humanae*.

[46] Ibid., 54.

[47] See James K. A. Smith, *Desiring the Kingdom: Worship, Worldview, and Cultural Formation* (Grand Rapids, MI: Baker Academic, 2009); and Mark Clavier, *On Consumer Culture, Identity, the Church, and the Rhetorics of Delight* (New York: T & T Clark, 2019).

a completely immanent frame.⁴⁸ Often, in addition, this spiritual search is undertaken apart from historical Christianity, which post-Christian cultures dismiss as having been tried and found wanting.

The immense challenge then, both theological and pastoral, is *how to speak of God (and God's gift of salvation in Christ) to people who do not need God*. Put another way, the challenge is how to speak convincingly and intelligently of God and God's offer of salvation as *good news*, as an offer of full human flourishing, to people who do not, or no longer, regard such talk as good news, but as irrational, irrelevant, or oppressive.

Responding to this challenge is very much a work in progress. There is surely some truth in Clive Marsh's observation that Christian discourse on salvation is commonly perceived in secular cultures to focus excessively on what humans are saved from (sin) and on the otherworldly dimension of what they are saved for (heaven). There is little development of the positive aspects of salvation for this life.⁴⁹ This is perhaps why Pope Francis so emphasizes the "joy of the gospel," the transformed, full human existence that faith in the gospel makes possible even now. Miroslav Volf is surely correct when he insists that contemporary theology needs to address more deeply the question of what constitutes human flourishing, what makes human life truly human and worth living, and seek to articulate the beauty and depth of the religious and the specifically Christian visions of flourishing.⁵⁰ At the heart of that vision is friendship with the God of Jesus Christ—not the God who is simply the "'beyond' of human cognition," the hypothesis trotted out when explanations fail, but rather, as Dietrich Bonhoeffer provocatively suggested, the "God [who] is the beyond in the midst of our lives."⁵¹

---

⁴⁸ See Elizabeth Drescher's account of spirituality among the disaffiliated focused on family, friends, food, and Fido (pets) in *Choosing Our Religion*, 116–56. Taylor discusses how art and aesthetic experience took the place of religion during the Romantic period as the vehicle of "the spiritual, the higher" (see Taylor, *A Secular Age*, 352–56).

⁴⁹ Clive Marsh, *Si Salva Chi Non Può: Modi attuali di intendere la salvezza* (Bologna: EDB, 2020), 27–29. See also Clive Marsh, *A Cultural Theology of Salvation* (New York: Oxford University Press, 2018).

⁵⁰ See Mirsolav Volf, *Flourishing: Why We Need Religion in a Globalized World* (New Haven, CT: Yale University Press, 2015); and Miroslav Volf and Matthew Croasmun, *For the Life of the World: Theology that Makes a Difference* (Grand Rapids, MI: Brazos Press, 2019).

⁵¹ Dietrich Bonhoeffer, *Letters and Papers from Prison* (Minneapolis: Fortress Press, 2010), 367. I would like to thank my confrere, Fr. Antoine Kerhuel, SJ, Secretary of the Society of Jesus, for pointing me to this richly suggestive letter of Bonhoeffer to Eberhard Bethge, dated April 30, 1944.

This flourishing life in Christ is not, however, a mere set of ideas, but primarily *a spiritual experience*: As Pope Benedict XVI notes, "Being Christian is not the result of an ethical choice or a lofty idea, but the encounter with an event, a person, which gives life a new horizon and a decisive direction."[52] *Offering, facilitating, and deepening this "personal experience of the Christian event"*[53] *must be the priority of mission in a secular culture.* This will require presence and *closeness* (a favorite word of Pope Francis) to people, particularly in the moments when the closed immanent frame is unable to account for experiences of fullness (beauty, joy, life) or of limit (failure, loneliness, death.) This offer will only be accepted, however, if people in secular culture *encounter* people who, because of their faith in Christ, live a "different humanity,"[54] one that raises questions and perhaps awakens deeper desires, because of the quality of joy, compassion, and hope that characterizes their lives. As Julián Carrón writes: "There is no other way to communicate the truth except as embodied in our lives. This is called 'witness,' the category by which we understand our presence as Christians in society."[55]

Reforming the Church

Finally, in a secular age, in which institutional religion and religious institutions like the church are regarded as problematic at best, mission calls for the reform and the renewal of the church. On the one hand, this means honestly facing and taking responsibility for the serious historical failures of the past, what Stephen Bullivant, in his sociological study of Catholic disaffiliation in the light of the clergy sexual abuse, calls "CRUDs or 'Credibility Undermining Displays.'"[56] In 2019, philosopher Susan Neiman wrote an important book on German *vergangenheitsaufarbeitung* ("working off the past"), the long, painful, but ultimately fruitful, process by which Germans have confronted the nightmare of evil that was their Nazi history.[57] Reflecting on American reluctance to admit its racist past, she insightfully observes that owning up to one's evil is difficult for groups whose identity is tied up with aspirational narratives. This might help explain the unwillingness of some in the church to grapple with the

---

[52] Pope Benedict XVI, *Deus Caritas Est (God Is Love)* (2005), no. 1.
[53] Carrón, *Disarming Beauty*, 60.
[54] Ibid., 67.
[55] Ibid., 70.
[56] Bullivant, *Mass Exodus*, 227.
[57] Susan Neiman, *Learning from the Germans: Race and the Memory of Evil* (New York: Farrar, Straus and Giroux, 2019).

reality of the church's history of evil, given the idealistic and aspirational theological self-understanding of the church. Yet without the serious work of some form of ecclesial *vergangenheitsaufarbeitung*, the danger of repeating the harm done in the past remains, and the credibility of the church as a witness to the gospel will be compromised. It is good to recall that the holiness of the church is not that of a sinless body, but that of a graced community that seeks to respond continuously, by the power of the Spirit, to the Lord's gracious call to conversion.[58] That the church should be perceived as such a humble yet hopeful community would already bear testimony to the gospel.

On the other hand, the reform of the church must include what Pope Francis calls its "missionary transformation."[59] This means passing from a church that relied on "cultural Christianity" to do its work of evangelization to a church that recognizes that the gospel must now be transmitted "person to person."[60] The often-repeated phrase of Pope Francis, "*chiesa in uscita*," calls us to

- a church close to people, with shepherds "who share the smell of the sheep";
- a "welcoming Church";
- a church that shows mercy; and
- a church that promotes the "culture of encounter."[61]

All of these point to a way of living the life and mission of the church in a way that more closely reflects the Gospel.

Gerhard Lohfink has convincingly argued that the church is important in the plan of God because "there must be a place, visible, tangible, where the salvation of the world can begin," a community to which people can be drawn into the history of salvation, where "everyone . . . [has] the opportunity to come and see."[62] He observes however, that, for many contemporary Europeans, "the Church as the place of God's physical presence has become less and less recognizable."[63] Paradoxically, despite the most well-organized programs in religious education for children and adults in Germany, departures from the Church continue to increase, because "the

---

[58] See William T. Cavanaugh, "The Sinfulness and Visibility of the Church: A Christological Exploration," in *Migrations of the Holy* (Grand Rapids, MI: Eerdmans, 2011).

[59] Seee Chapter One of *Evangelii Gaudium,* which is entitled "The Church's Missionary Transformation."

[60] *EG,* no. 127. Cf. Roberto Repole, *Il Sogno di una Chiesa evangelica: L'ecclesiologia di Papa Francesco* (Vatican: Libreria Editrice Vaticana, 2017), 101.

[61] Most of these are explained in a single, dense paragraph in *EG,* no. 24.

[62] Gerhard Lohfink, *Does God Need the Church?: Toward a Theology of the People of God,* trans. Linda M. Maloney (Collegeville, MN: Michael Glazier, 1999), 27.

[63] Ibid., 319.

most conscientious lectures and presentations fall on deaf ears if there is no place where the great words . . . are really lived."[64] Without this concrete, convincing, corporate visibility of God and God's offer of transformed life in the community, belief in God fades: "the place has faded away, and therefore . . . God has vanished."[65] The renewal of the church cannot be regarded therefore, as of secondary importance.

Conclusion

Stephen Bevans describes Pope Francis's missiology as a "missiology of attraction," realized in a "message that attracts, a church that attracts, and a teaching that attracts."[66] One might ask, however: *attractive to whom?*

One wonders, for example, whether what Bevans presents as "attractive" would be primarily appealing to Christians already committed to a certain theological and pastoral orientation. *Would this message, form of community, and teaching be attractive to people living on the fringes of, or outside, the church in secular cultures?* One hopes that they might be. Perhaps, though, a more fully developed understanding of the social imaginary—the mindsets, the sensibilities, the yearnings, the imagination and experience of reality—of those living in a secular age is a necessary first step before one can respond adequately to this question.

What is clear is that understanding secular culture is crucial for the future of Christian mission, and not just only in the context of Europe and North America. Globalization and migration have made the walls between cultures more porous; global consumer, communication, and entertainment cultures have contributed to the "pluralization" of options, visions of life, and values that is one of the features of the secular social imaginary described above. For increasing numbers, because of this pluralization of options, religion is no longer simply a cultural given, but a decision based on a personal search—or unthinkingly put aside, in view of more attractive, more immediately satisfying possibilities.

There are, no doubt, significant differences among *secularizations, secularisms,* and the understanding and experience of the *secular* in the West and those in other, particularly non-Christian contexts. There is much to

---

[64] Ibid.
[65] Ibid.
[66] Stephen Bevans, "Pope Francis' Missiology of Attraction," *International Bulletin of Mission Research* 43, no. 1 (2019): 23.

explore and deepen.⁶⁷ However, even the resurgence of versions of religions that emphasize distinct identity, fundamentalism in its most extreme forms, is largely a reaction to the perceived threat or thinness of secular culture.⁶⁸ Moreover, although there is a need for more careful research,⁶⁹ many religious ministers, teachers, and parents in all cultures of the world share the experience of how the language and practice of faith simply make no sense to millions of young people in their care.

Jesuit Superior General Fr. Arturo Sosa asserts that "secularization, and the secular world that arises from it," is "one of the ways the Spirit is speaking to us and guiding us in this time."⁷⁰ If this is so, much more analysis, discernment, and creative rethinking are called for on the part of those who are concerned with mission.

Daniel Patrick Huang, SJ, a Jesuit from the Philippines, teaches at the Faculty of Missiology of the Pontifical Gregorian University. He received his doctorate in theology from the Catholic University of America. He served as general counselor of the Society of Jesus from 2008 to 2019.

---

⁶⁷ See, for example, Peter van der Veer, *The Modern Spirit of Asia: The Spiritual and the Secular in China and India* (Princeton, NJ: Princeton University Press, 2014); and Marian Burchardt, Monika Wohlrab-Sahr, and Matthias Middell, eds., *Multiple Secularities beyond the West* (Boston: De Gruyter, 2015).

⁶⁸ See Rabbi Jonathan Sacks, *Not in God's Name: Confronting Religious Violence* (New York: Schocken Books, 2015), 27–43. See, as well, John Allen's interesting discussion of what some perceive to be the return of "conservative" Catholicism, what he calls "evangelical Catholics" in his book *The Future Church: How Ten Trends Are Revolutionizing the Catholic Church* (New York: Doubleday, 2009), 54–94.

⁶⁹ For instance, the work done by the Springtide Research Institute, *The State of Religion and Young People 2020: Relational Authority.*

⁷⁰ Superior General Arturo Sosa Abascal, "Secularization Can Help Proclaim the Gospel, Superor General of Jesuits Says [at Youth Synod]," *Catholic News Service,* October 11, 2018.

Mission with Migrants

The Roots of "People on the Move"

Carmen Elisa Bandeo, SSpS

My name is Carmen Elisa Bandeo. I was born in Argentina-Misiones, a land well known for its Jesuit missions. My ancestors came as migrants from northern Italy and settled in the area of Argentine Chaco in the first half of the twentieth century.

Due to employment problems my family lived in different cities in Argentina, and ever since my childhood I have been well acquainted with what it means to leave one's familiar surroundings, country, and risk the unknown. I was born into a family with deep Catholic roots, and grew up in a parish environment where I learned that we are all missionaries by baptism—that the church is missionary by nature. In this context, God invited me to share God's life and mission in a closer way. I responded to this invitation by entering the Missionary Sisters Servants of the Holy Spirit, which sent me to different places in my own country and outside of it: to Taiwan, Italy, and now Greece.

I wished to start my presentation with this brief autobiography, because we are all real people, with a history that has shaped us and in which the dream of God for each of us and our own hopes, fears, and experiences have been woven together. To speak of mission and migration means to speak of my roots, of two essential elements in my life, which have contributed to the person I am today, and somehow strengthen my missionary service.

Father Arnoldo Janssen's Concept of Mission

Let me begin by sharing the concept of mission of the founder of our congregation, because the two congregations that he founded—Society of the Divine Word (SVD) and my own congregation—served the parish where I grew up in the faith. The inspiration that infused their tasks is at the root of my missionary vocation.

Father Arnoldo Janssen discovered his missionary vocation through belonging to the Apostleship of Prayer. One of the key ideas of this apostolate was to embrace the intentions of the heart of Jesus. Our relationship with Jesus gave rise to the wish to make the desires of his heart our own: for the glory of God, the salvation of souls, and the expansion of the kingdom of God.

At the beginning of his missionary work Father Arnoldo edited a magazine, describing his objective in these words: "That our Christian faith is increasingly the norm in the State, in the family, and in the life of the person." Justice undoubtedly forms an integral part of our faith; that is why, in the second edition of the magazine, he gave it the mission of being a "faithful defender of truth and justice."

The first two foundations established by Fr. Arnoldo Janssen have always captivated me: the Society of the Divine Word, with the aim to send the first priests to China, a land of "pagans" according to the concept of the time; and my congregation, SSpS, in which we were sent to Argentina among the Germans of the Volga to help those immigrants to keep the faith. In this I perceived a very inclusive and comprehensive concept of mission, of the kingdom of God, to which Jesus dedicated his life: that we, his followers, must likewise dedicate our lives. This mission becomes present in the world through Jesus and through us, and encompasses all the realities of the human being; it surpasses all confines.

At our 14th General Chapter we affirmed that "the Spirit—the protagonist of mission—impels us to convert toward deeper communion with God, with others, and with all of creation. In that light, justice, peace, and integrity of creation are not merely something we do; they are at the very heart of our religious missionary vocation toward communion."

The founder lived in great intimacy with God while at the same time having a clear vision of the reality that surrounded him, and he acted accordingly. Using the language of the Second Vatican Council, he knew "how to read the signs of the times." This is what the congregation has taught me, and it is the source of my personal concept of mission as well: *a call to share my experience of God and God's message.* To share my life with everyone, especially the presence of God and what God has done in me. In that interpersonal, intimate relationship with God, I can hear God's invitation to make God's wishes and dream for creation, mine. We are called to embrace each and every aspect of human life, walking toward the communion for which we have been created.

In this context, every service in favor of the dignity of the human person, the defense of his or her rights, and the integrity of creation are an inherent part. Nothing human is alien to God. And we see this in the incarnation: to tell us about the Father, the Son became one of us.

General Context of Migration

I will now share some statistics. This is not an exhaustive study but just a general picture of the actual migration trends.

In 1970, there were 84 million people living outside their country of birth, UN statistics show, but by the year 2000, that figure had jumped to 174 million;[1] in 2019, the figure was 271 million.[2]

While those who move from one country to another are considered economic migrants, many are fleeing poverty, war, political upheavals, or climate-induced catastrophes, known today as climate migration.

The UN estimates that there were 82.4 million forcibly displaced people around the world at the end of 2020, as a result of persecution, conflict, violence, human rights violations, and events seriously disturbing the public order.[3] They come from countries including Afghanistan, Syria, South Sudan, and Myanmar. This is a fraction of the world's total number of migrants—a figure that continues to grow.

Among them are nearly *26.4 million refugees, around half of whom are under the age of eighteen.* Children account for 30 percent of the world's population, but 42 percent of all forcibly displaced people.[4]

Contrary to some perceptions, most refugees remain in developing countries. Such nations account for hosting around 86 percent of the world's refugee population and 73 percent are hosted in neighboring countries.

In general terms, searching for asylum, 51,800 people arrived in Europe this year; 1,380 people were missing or lost at sea. This is in comparison with the previous year, when 95,000 people arrived in Europe, and 2015 when over one million came—so we see a clear reduction in the numbers during this period.[5]

---

[1] See International Organization for Mission, *IOM World Migration Report 2020* (2021), chap 2. "Migration and Migrants: A global Overview," 21.
[2] Ibid.
[3] The UN Refugee Agency (UNHCR), "Figures at a Glance," June 18, 2021.
[4] Ibid.
[5] UNHCR, "Europe Situations: Data and Trends—Arrivals and Displaced Populations" (July 2021).

Labor migration: In 2019, there were *169 million international migrant workers in the world,* and they constituted 4.9 percent of the global labor force in the destination countries.[6] These international migrant workers made up approximately 69 percent of the world's international migrant population of working age (aged fifteen and over) in 2019.[7] In 2020, 8.7 million non-EU citizens were employed in the EU labor market, corresponding to 4.6 percent of the total.[8]

Here we also need to mention the consequences of migration: the loss of human capital in some countries, the inhuman conditions of work, and human trafficking in its different forms: prostitution, forced labor, and the selling of organs. But we cannot fail to see that the remittance of foreign currency from migrants is important and irreplaceable for the well-being and upward social mobility of those who manage to succeed in this process.

Human Mobility in the Church

Migration has been a constant factor in human life since its origin. It has been part of the past, it is so in the present, and it will continue to be so in the future of humanity. This migratory phenomenon, as we have seen above, goes far beyond the simple movement of people from one place to another; it is related to the cultural, social, political, and religious transformation of peoples, and to the continuous reconfiguration of communities. Therefore, it represents a great challenge and a new opportunity for humanity. It raises important issues that are of great relevance to the global agenda, since the issue affects our planet, governments, religions in general, and the people of God on the way, in particular.

The Bible is deeply marked by the migration experience of the people of Israel. Jesus himself assumed our human condition and lived in exile, which provides a very rich source of inspiration. In its turn, theological reflection on human mobility has contributed (and continues to do so) to highlight its importance in the discourse about God, the church, and the daily life of faith of people and communities.

---

[6] ILO (International Labour Organization), 2021, www.ilo.org. The ILO is the UN specialized agency that seeks the promotion of social justice and internationally recognized human and labor rights.

[7] Ibid.

[8] European Commission: Statistics on Migration to Europe as of January 2020.

Migration, as an inherent dynamic of life, closely affects the pastoral dimension of the church who, as the people of God journeying on, perceives migration as a precious opportunity for creative synodality that opens up to communion in diversity thanks to specific people. From this point of view, pastoral care is not an apostolate "for" migrants, but "with" migrants: an experience in which we become a community shaped by the Spirit.

Today migrants and internally displaced people are a challenge to the church's evangelizing mission. Cornered in the peripheries of a self-referential and increasingly pragmatic and materialistic society, they are an invitation to put into action the gestures of the gospel we proclaim. Recall the four verbs that Pope Francis proposed to us in his "Message for the 106th World Day of Migrants and Refugees": "Welcome, protect, promote, and integrate," which constitute a comprehensive program of evangelization.

This entire migratory context is marked by a complex interweaving of social issues that affect the dignity of the human person, who in many cases is perceived as just another number. Here, the church could promote a deeper questioning of the policies of the countries and their capacity for reception, both in society and in local communities, by assuming its mission to advocate, lending its voice to advise and assist those in need rather than remaining merely a welfare charity.

General Situation in Greece

Greece saw more than a million people arrive (mostly by sea) in 2015, who then made their way to other more welcoming countries, of which Germany is foremost, followed by Sweden.

According to UNHCR data, in February of 2015, in Greece there were still more than 91,945 refugees and 80,784 asylum seekers. Many of these entered the country illegally; although the asylum application process has started (and is now faster), many have spent more than four years waiting for a response.

My time in Athens introduced me to a reality that I was unaware of—that of the urban refugee. The precarious conditions in rural areas drove many to the city, thus creating a housing problem that is a daily drama, which the government policies (or the absence of them) have exacerbated. The city has a large population of people who live on the streets: homeless vagabonds, drug addicts, asylum seekers, and even those who are recognized as refugees, with the right to international protection, cannot find housing.

During the time of the forced quarantine by COVID-19, as elsewhere the closure of practically all services and the restriction of movement was experienced in Greece, and many of the people we served had to be confined to the fields. They were living in tents or containers in settlements with very limited or nonexistent access to water, toilets, electricity, internet, and so on.

All the institutions and/or NGOs were obliged to close their doors and reinvent their presence and form of help for those most in need. Many succeeded, but others had to close their doors and wait, keeping open communication lines by telephone with the people.

The precarious situation, in which the refugees had lived before COVID-19, was made even worse! Today, with the promise of reopenings, there is an attempt to resume certain paths of normality, especially as the vaccine is finally widely available.

Our Experience—Our Challenges

Here in Athens we live in a community that my congregation calls *community in movement* because we constantly seek to respond to the new challenges posed by the migratory crisis, and we are always ready to move on when and to where it is needed. The religious provinces of the SSpS of Europe are cooperating by contributing personnel and finances, each according to its capabilities and for as long as possible. We also work in close cooperation with the Jesuit Refugee Service.

As a religious community we face many challenges here: community life, teamwork both internally and externally, poverty and the powerlessness of not being able to help sometimes because of the lack of proper means, and the sadness of listening to the accounts of the people we serve.

Here, many nationalities converge, giving us a privileged environment for the meeting of cultures, but the circumstances and difficulties encountered along the path that led them to Greece have stripped them of that daily routine with which human nature expresses itself. Fear and mistrust, which hinder dialogue, have taken root. At the social level the challenge is how to generate and build the true encounter that opens paths of integration.

Our life is in permanent tension but at the same time it is like a constant liturgy, where we place our lives, those of the refugees, our poverty, joy, and hope in the hands of God. Our good God, in prayer and the Eucharist, renews us and brings us together with them.

The projects and experiences in Greece have offered me the possibility of sharing the lives of these people on a daily basis. We often think that helping refugees/asylum seekers is like the heroic gestures we see on TV or in newspapers, big and important acts that make for good headlines! But we forget that life is full of small daily gestures that make one feel "human": a smile; patiently answering the same question a thousand times; dressing a wound, and then with a smile and the same attention attending to a tiny cut on a little girl's finger because on seeing the adult with a bandage, she wants one too; telling about the weather forecast in Germany or the people's customs, knowing that the next day they would try to enter that country illegally; accepting a little sweet from them; requiring them to be attentive in language classes and punctual for the lessons, correcting mistakes, and so on. Such proximity allows us to get to know and accept the refugees we serve, with all their imperfections and aspirations.

Many of them do not want to be called refugees because they are ultimately men and women, people with a concrete history and a dream to fulfill. Personally, I would love to somehow show this everyday life of the refugees, without exposing them to the media, so as to restore the human face of the crisis.

When I began my service as a volunteer at the Arrupe Center in Rome, I felt that every gesture counted and was important, that my presence helped to give them hope. In Athens, I understood that hope was and is present in their hearts; I simply accompany them on their path to help to sustain it. It is as if *their hopes are like a bonfire to which I add a piece of wood to keep it alight*.

Conclusion

Our faith and our daily lives share two intrinsic elements: *roots* and *movement*. Everything has an origin, and everything evolves, moves. The human being is by nature itinerant, but it is *the roots* that strengthen its identity. We, as the people of God, carry in our faith, in our relationship with God, that itinerancy that sprang from the communicative love of the Trinity. From there we are sent to set out together on the road to the kingdom.

The very history of mission is an itinerancy, it is to live in "tension," tending toward the definitive encounter with God. This journey, undertaken in the daily life of history, allowing people as the practical situations of life unfold to question themselves, means making the lights and shadows of humanity our own.

As a community of faith, we must challenge ourselves not only adapt to pastoral plans or be more assertive in offering humanitarian aid, but also to grow:
- Have I been able to unite my voice to the claim of these people?
- Have I realized that their culture and their distress challenge me?
- Has my silence been an accomplice of the injustices that marginalize them?
- Have I known how to strip myself of the power and security in which I live to understand their fragility, their fear, and their hope?

Today, migrants and refugees challenge us to remember our *roots*, to rediscover the *itinerant* dimension of our faith, and to act accordingly.

Carmen Elisa Bandeo, SSpS, originally from Argentina, has been serving as the coordinator of the Jesuit Refugee Service Education Project *Magistories* in Greece since November 2018. Sr. Carmen previously taught young people in Argentina, and she has also counseled undocumented migrant workers and victims of human trafficking in Taiwan. She is a member of the UISG International Migration Desk.

Mission among the Poor

"You Always Have the Poor with You" (Mk 14:7)

MARVI DELRIVO, SFP,
AND LICIA MAZZIA, SFP

Talking about mission among the poor, excluded, prisoners, invisible people, and all those who are on the margins of our societies also means talking about the daily service of very, very many of us and about the work of thousands of associations that are committed worldwide to social transformation and the promotion of fair, inclusive development models. The awareness of being many walking together in the pursuit of these goals encourages and motivates us, especially when the path is arduous. In recent years we have had a special companion on the journey, one who has confirmed our mission and given us renewed impetus by opening new paths. The Holy Spirit called Jorge Bergoglio to the papacy from the "ends of the earth," to serve the church and all humanity with the great heart of a pastor whose perspicacious vision focuses on the "periphery."

Pope Francis's Assist to the "Preferential Option for the Poor"

The preferential option for the poor was passionately relaunched by Pope Francis from the very first days of his pontificate. At the beginning of the globalized third millennium his dream of a "poor church for the poor"[1] has drawn attention to the geographical and existential margins, while his emphasis on mercy and compassion calls us to share in peoples' suffering, hopes, and prospects for change.

---

[1] "Pope Francis Wants 'Poor Church for the Poor," *BBC News*, March 16, 2013.

Francis's comparison of the church to a field hospital[2] refers to the urgent needs that are widespread in the world, to which we want to respond with new charitable initiatives. Thus, the gospel changes the world starting with the change of heart of each person; it guides our journey and monitors the shared response to the demands for healing, liberation, and the development of millions of brothers and sisters and of the poorest and most forgotten peoples on the planet.

The 2015 encyclical *Laudato Si' (On Care for Our Common Home)*, emphasizes the close relationship between the poor and the fragility of the planet. It is the weakest and most excluded people who are affected by the deterioration of the environment and of society.[3] The cry of the earth is the same as the cry of the poor, hence the need and the willingness to change our lifestyles as well as the models of production and consumption.[4] The encyclical also notes that because integral ecology is inseparable from the notion of the common good, in practice, committing ourselves to the common good means choosing to work for sustainable development and intergenerational solidarity, based on the preferential option for the poorest.[5]

In 2017, at the conclusion of the Jubilee of Mercy, Pope Francis instituted the First World Day of the Poor "so that throughout the world Christian communities can become an ever greater sign of Christ's charity for the least and those most in need." He continues, "This Day is meant, above all, to encourage believers to react against a culture of discard and waste, and to embrace the culture of encounter. At the same time, everyone, independent of religious affiliation, is invited to openness and sharing with the poor through concrete signs of solidarity and fraternity."[6]

Pope Francis lives the preferential option for the poor as solidarity with the poor. He seeks their closeness, appreciates their values and their way of living the faith, and listens to their legitimate aspirations. He becomes a pilgrim of mercy among the discarded people of society; on his apostolic journeys he celebrates the culture of encounter and favors the people of the suburbs; and he advocates for the rights of those who are without a voice. He opens the doors of the Vatican and provides facilities for the reception and care of the homeless.

---

[2] See Antonio Spadaro, SJ, "A Big Heart Open to God: An Interview with Pope Francis," *America,* September 30, 2013.

[3] Pope Francis, *Laudato Si' (On Care for Our Common Home)* (2015), no. 48, hereinafter *LS*.

[4] See *LS,* no. 59.

[5] *LS,* no. 159.

[6] Pope Francis, "Message for the First World Day of the Poor" (November 19, 2017), no. 6.

Pope Francis's exemplary lifestyle is the basis of the great themes treated in *Fratelli Tutti,* his 2020 encyclical on fraternity and social friendship, inspired by the inclusive vision of Francis of Assisi, who

> calls for a love that transcends the barriers of geography and distance . . . the essence of a fraternal openness that allows us to acknowledge, appreciate and love each person, regardless of physical proximity, regardless of where he or she was born or lives. . . . Francis felt himself a brother to the sun, the sea and the wind, yet he knew that he was even closer to those of his own flesh. Wherever he went, he sowed seeds of peace and walked alongside the poor, the abandoned, outcast, the least of his brothers and sisters.[7]

The social teaching documents and concrete gestures of Pope Francis have strengthened our commitment in such practical areas as the prison apostolate; welcoming the homeless; and caring not only for those who are victims of abuse, but also for those who have perpetrated the abuse. They have inspired new initiatives aimed at integrating excluded people into the social fabric in order to restore their dignity through work. In particular, they have given voice not only to women victims of trafficking, who have been abused and raped, but also to the entire female universe that has historically been penalized on all fronts. It should be remembered that poverty and exclusion in the world affect women first and foremost everywhere, starting with the innumerable girls who are deprived of the opportunity to study and to choose their career and future freely.

Our religious families continue to invest human and economic resources in all of these areas. They confront the dangers of war and political instability, facing bureaucratic or ideological obstacles, often despite their scant means, personnel, and skills. However, the feeling of powerlessness and failure we experience given the scope of our projects constitutes a valuable test in verifying our way of approaching our brothers and sisters in need.

From Mission from the Center to Mission from the Margins

We are living in a time of transition, in which a change of mentality and action is necessary. We need to change from a concept of mission that started at the center by those who considered themselves to be at the center—the privileged few who go on mission to those on the periphery,

---

[7] Pope Francis, *Fratelli Tutti (On Fraternity and Social Friendship)* (2020), nos. 1–2.

the marginalized of society—to a sense of mission that starts, instead, from the margins, from the poor, so that the poor can become the protagonists and agents of missioning.[8] The poor are able to understand the needs and concerns of those who are in the same condition, without the attitude of complacent paternalism that has often characterized "mission from the center."[9]

In this perspective of transition it is interesting to note the paradigm shift that took place at the Synod on the Amazon in October 2019: the periphery spoke from the center while standing in the center, aware that its experience was being heard as a prophetic voice for the whole church. In fact, the themes to be reviewed on the pastoral, cultural, ecological, and synodal levels, which were the outcome of the synodal process, now form the heart of the final document. Without such reappraisal, new paths cannot open up and there can be no real change. The post-synodal exhortation *Querida Amazonia* of February 2020 expressed the importance of listening to life, to people, their problems, and especially to discernment.[10] Whoever lives in a place, who suffers but who loves it passionately and is wise and experienced, can help to promote the rights and dignity of the poor. In mutual listening, intercultural relations can develop. Diversity does not represent a threat or justify a hierarchy of some categories of people to exercise power over others; rather, it allows for engagement in dialogue starting from different cultural points of view.

In our ministries we always feel we need to start by taking the situation into account, listening to those we meet. This is all the more important if we are "foreigners"—that is, if we were not born or raised in an environment, if we do not know its culture in depth, if that particular situation is unfamiliar. Dialogue, which starts from listening, is fertile ground for creativity and presents unexplored possibilities. The more we listen to, involve, and empower those who will subsequently take part in a project at the planning stage of our respective services, whether as collaborators or recipients, the more that project can become a shared space, as well as a good opportunity for growth and lasting change. We can learn a great deal by listening to the poor, our teachers of life. Through listening and

---

[8] Commission on World Mission and Evangelism, "Together towards Life: Mission and Evangelism in Changing Landscapes," *International Bulletin of Missionary Research* 38, no. 2 (April 2014): nos. 6, 38.

[9] See Dichiarazione della Commissione Missione Mondiale ed Evangelizzazione approvata dalla X Assemblea del Consiglio Ecumenico delle Chiese riunito a Busan, Corea del Sud, 2013.

[10] Pope Francis, apostolic exhortation *Querida Amazonia (Post-Synodal Exhortation to the People of God and to All Persons of Good Will)* (2020).

dialogue the poor can discover their potential and together we can look for appropriate and sustainable paths for development, equity, and inclusion. The poor can become agents of change.

Two religious communities of women have sent testimonies of transformation that resulted from listening. The names are fictitious:

> Eleonora, a young Albanian woman, arrived at the Sisters' Reception Center feeling exhausted, with her three-year-old daughter. Her family had recently moved to northern Italy due to her husband's ill health. He had undergone a liver transplant. The sisters tried to help Eleonora and her family. They were especially close to Eleonora, who bore the burden of her family's difficulties. They offered her work at their craft center, not only to offer her financial support, but also to give her the opportunity to encounter different people and situations. At the end of her experience, Eleonora told the sisters: "I am very happy with the wonderful experience I had at the center. I spent nine months learning to do many lovely things, to use many materials that I didn't even know existed, but above all I was able to share my life, my difficulties with others. I always met with understanding and practical help. I felt welcomed like a daughter. I now work in a different place, and I am helped by the memory of the family atmosphere I experienced at the center. I thank those who gave me the opportunity to come to know this reality. You helped me to mature and you gave me so much strength when I needed it. May God bless your mission."

> Willy works with the sisters at the Day Center for Street Children in a town in Negros Oriental, the Philippines. Near his home, he discovered a family consisting of a mother, grandmother and five children, who lived in a hut with a broken roof. The mother collects plastic from the dustbins and then sells it; that is their source of income. Willy told the sisters about them and they decided to go and visit this family, together with the social worker of the center. It was a cordial meeting; they talked to the mother and inquired about the children, none of whom was going to school. How could they find a better source of income? The mother would like to start a small farm with chickens and goats. So, the sisters then obtained the livestock for her, built a small enclosure, and the breeding began. Some kindhearted people donated some mattresses and clothes for the children, a table, and a few chairs for the hut. The sisters

contacted a school to take the children and Willy, with the help of a friend, built a toilet for the family. The mother feels appreciated, now that she can raise chickens and goats, and her children can go to school and receive an education. The collaboration among a group of people, wishing to embody the gospel charism of care, has created a wonderful opportunity for renewal.

These small projects, carried out on the margins of society, are capable of reviving hope. But what are they in the face of an ocean of poverty? Will we ever be able to overcome poverty, which, especially now due to the pandemic, has risen exponentially everywhere?

Put an End to All Forms of Poverty in the World by 2030

As a church, we cannot overcome poverty alone, even though we have a tradition of attention to the poor. For decades the United Nations and other international agencies have set ambitious goals for ameliorating global poverty. However, the results are not commensurate to the immense means put in place to achieve them.

One such initiative is the 2030 Agenda for Sustainable Development, an action program signed in September 2015 by the governments of the 193 UN member-states. It lists seventeen goals, of which the first is "End poverty in all its forms everywhere [by 2030]."[11]

Extreme poverty rates have fallen by more than half since 1990. Despite this, 836 million people worldwide still live in extreme poverty. In developing regions roughly one in five people lives on less than $1.25 per day.[12] The vast majority of these people live in South Asia and Sub-Saharan Africa.

For the first time, after decades of slow and steady reduction, extreme poverty is estimated to have increased for about 115 million people in 2020, to which another 23 million to 35 million will probably be added over the course of 2021.[13]

Furthermore, the rise in poverty risks jeopardizing the already uncertain achievement of the goal of ending extreme poverty by 2030, as envisaged

---

[11] United Nations, Department of Economic and Social Affairs, "The 17 Goals."

[12] United Nations, "We Can End Poverty: Millennium Development Goals and Beyond, 2015."

[13] World Bank, "COVID-19 to Add as Many as 150 Million Extreme Poor by 2021" (October 7, 2020).

by the 2030 UN Agenda for Sustainable Development. Moreover, if the pandemic represents the greatest threat in the short term, conflict and climate change are the major long-term obstacles to achieving the goal of ending extreme poverty. Without an appropriate global response, the cumulative effects of the pandemic and the resulting economic crises, armed conflicts, and the climate emergency will take a high human toll and lead to great economic costs in the future.[14]

The pandemic came suddenly and caught the whole world unprepared, leaving a great sense of disorientation and helplessness. After more than a year and a half, we feel poorer and weaker because we have experienced a sense of limitation and the loss of certainties. Humanity as a whole is at grips with the same storm, but do we feel we are on the same boat? This is a favorable time to recognize that we need one another, and that we have a common responsibility toward the world and the common good of the whole planet. But are we welcoming and living this opportunity?

Wherever we are, the ministry to the poor of our religious congregations has been seriously affected by the consequences of this planetary upheaval. We have had to adapt with the means we had at our disposal, often in conditions of extreme precariousness and risk—especially in the first wave of the virus, when we were without safety measures.

But we reacted, "reinventing" new opportunities wherever we could as we tried to find creative ways to meet the needs that were increasing around us. We know that poor people have paid the highest price of the pandemic. Small traders were unable to take home enough earnings for household expenses, and those living in cramped housing without access to drinking water or essential healthcare had no chance to prevent or defend themselves from the virus. Even now, access to the vaccines in many poor countries is extremely limited.

The pandemic has also created new poor people in various wealthy areas of the planet, where we see longer and longer queues at the soup kitchen as the numbers of unemployed and homeless people have increased. Fear of contagion has more than redoubled the marginalization of those who were already on the margins, as lockdowns and other restrictions have isolated the elderly and other vulnerable populations.

The fight against poverty is at an impasse, as we see more and more people lacking in basic needs such as food, clothing, shelter, medicine, and hygiene products. We see the effects of psychological isolation, the challenges of remote learning for children, and the loss of far too many jobs.

---

[14]World Bank, "Poverty: Overview," see most recent update.

This time of uncertainty and desperate need has only strengthened our motivation to be among poor people and to support their dignity and development. We have an insidious virus to fight, one of social injustice, unequal opportunity, marginalization and exclusion, and the lack of protection of the weakest. So let's continue to do our part; let us cooperate in synergy among ourselves and with all those who pursue these objectives.

"You Always Have the Poor with You" (Mk 14:7)

"You always have the poor with you": Jesus pronounced these words in Bethany, shortly before his death. A woman entered Simon's house with a jar full of precious perfume and poured it over Jesus's head, arousing the scandalized reaction of the people present: "Why was the ointment thus wasted? For this ointment might have been sold for more than three hundred denarii, and given to the poor."[15] There is something to be learned from this reaction. The common perception is that with almsgiving, funding, and development plans, the problems of poverty can be solved. And it is easier to give something to the poor than to give of yourselves, but the latter is exactly what we must do. "Break a path for the poor, forgetting about yourself," Don Lorenzo Milani wrote, thus summarizing what he had learned at the school of the marginalized.[16]

In Bethany and in all the gospel events, Jesus's gaze far surpasses the limited vision of those close to him. He welcomes the prophetic gesture of the woman who anointed him, foreshadowing his death.[17] We should have a profound empathy with the woman who recognized Jesus as the poorest of the poor. Jesus is all the poor, the marginalized, the lonely, the prisoners, the condemned to death, the renegades. Jesus dies for everyone, and in Jesus all of us who are poor find the hope of redemption and salvation. There is a lesson to be learned from the woman of Bethany: it is merciful love that enables one to empathize and recognize the face of Jesus in the poor, suffering, rejected, excluded, marginalized brother and sister. The woman of Bethany teaches us to recognize Jesus by recognizing our own poverty. The poor lead us to an authentic encounter with God, and thus the poor people evangelize us; this is their gift to us, certainly greater than anything we can offer them.

---

[15] Mk 14:4–6.

[16] Don Lorenzo Milani, *Letter to a Teacher* (Firenze: Scuola di Barbiana, 1967). Don Lorenzo Milani was an Italian Catholic priest, writer, professor, and teacher.

[17] Mk 14:8.

"You always have the poor with you." This sentence is a guarantee that Jesus is always with us, when we welcome him and allow ourselves to be welcomed "as one of the least of these my brothers."[18] We hope we may have eyes and hearts capable of recognizing and loving him in the brothers and sisters we meet on our daily mission.

Marvi Delrivo, SFP, holds a degree in psychology and served religious life and youth in Senegal. A member of the Franciscan Sisters of the Poor, she is currently a congregational councilor.

Licia Mazzia, SFP, holds a degree in law and a licentiate in theology of consecrated life, and has served young generations and women who are victims of human trafficking. She is at present the congregational minister of the Franciscan Sisters of the Poor.

---

[18] Mt 25:40.

Reconciliation

The New Face of Evangelization in Africa

Anne Béatrice Faye, CIC

Following the Synod of African Bishops, held in Rome in 2009, Pope Benedict XVI said that "evangelization today takes the name of reconciliation" in Africa.[1] The task we must outline is not an easy one, for reconciliation is situated between immediate engagement in politics and possible withdrawal or escape into theological and spiritual theories. As part of this reflection, we shall attempt to discern how reconciliation may be employed as an integrating element in the church's multifaceted mission in Africa and to show how this use clarifies the very notion of reconciliation. In view of the polysemous use of the concept of reconciliation, we propose to treat it in three steps.

First, it is important to *establish the perspective* from which we will approach reconciliation. The second step will lead us to encounter a reconciled figure through the testimony of Sr. Geneviève Uwamariya in order to illustrate *the importance of testimony in the process of reconciliation*. And, finally, to show that today reconciliation is being reappraised, not only with regard to the sacrament of penance, now called reconciliation, but even more as an expression that sums up the whole work of salvation.[2] The theological language of reconciliation will help us in the third step to rediscover the meaning of suffering and how Christianity can be an *experience of salvation and social liberation* with the kingdom of God as its horizon.[3]

---

[1] Pope Benedict XVI, post-synodal apostolic exhortation *Africae Munus: The Church in Africa in Service to Reconciliation, Justice, and Peace* (2011), no. 174: "You are the salt of the earth.... You are the light of the world" (Mt 5:13, 14).

[2] Bernard Sesboüé, *Jésus-Christ, l'unique médiateur: Problématique de la relecture doctrinale*, vol. 1 (Paris: Desclée, 1988), 110.

[3] 2 Cor 5:11—6:2; Rom 5:1–11.

Which Form of Reconciliation?

The reconciliation in question concerns individual situations and very frequently society as a whole, if not all of humanity. The particular angle from which we will consider reconciliation will therefore not be its sacramental dimension. We will not dwell on the individual and sinful character of what is to be reconciled—in fact, we will not even use the term *sin*. This does not mean that sin is dissociated from the context of reconciliation, but rather that reconciliation mostly refers to a final state of peace (or at least the absence of conflict) where the past no longer determines the present and the future. This is a good description of the goal of reconciliation, even though we know that, in practice, such reconciliation is rarely, if ever, achieved.

In theological terms it is the human being who responds to God's initiative through faith. The result is the reconstitution of the human community understood as a new creation. For Christians, therefore, the hope of reconciliation is strictly linked to faith in Christ's redemptive action among us.[4] However, these existential values are not always in vogue.[5] This definition immediately *situates the work of reconciliation within the framework of a relationship between God and God's people*.

The other essential element that this definition highlights is the centrality of the relationship. The work of restoration is at the heart of the reconciliation process, as shown by Sr. Geneviève Uwamariya's experience of reconciliation as a survivor of the genocide in Rwanda.

At the Crossroads of Reconciliation:
Cooperating to Rebuild over and beyond the Rupture

The poignant testimony of Sr. Geneviève Uwamariya, of the Sisters of Sainte-Marie-de-Namur in Rwanda, impressed not only those who were at the 2009 synod, but all who heard or read her story. God evidently enabled her to view her experience in the light of the word of God.

As she was led to the prison cell of an executioner by members of a group of Catholic mediators called the Ladies of Divine Mercy, Sr. Geneviève heard them say:

---

[4] David Hollenbach, SJ, "Réconciliation et justice. Conseils éthiques pour un monde brisé," *Promotio Iustitiae* 103 (2009): 74–78.

[5] Olivier Abel, ed., *Le pardon, briser la dette et l'oubli* (Paris: Éd. Autrement, 1991), 1.

If you have killed, pledge to ask the surviving victim for forgiveness, in this way you help him to free himself from the burden of revenge, hatred and resentment. If you are a victim, undertake to offer your forgiveness to the one who wronged you and thus help him to free himself from the burden of his crime and the evil that inhabits him.[6]

Sr. Geneviève met the executioner like a brother. He threw himself at her feet and cried: "Mercy, mercy!" Seized with compassion, she made the leap of faith. She raised the executioner up, embraced him, and said: "You are and remain my brother." Continuing her testimony, she stated: "I felt relieved of a great weight. I found inner peace and I said 'thank you' to the one I still held in my arms." For his part, the executioner exclaimed, "Justice can take its course and sentence me to death; now I am released!" Sr. Geneviève concluded her testimony with these words:

> From this experience, I deduced that reconciliation is not so much about bringing two people together or two groups in conflict. Rather, it is about re-establishing each one in love and allowing the inner healing to take its course and bring mutual liberation. And this is the importance of the Church in our countries since her mission is to offer the Word: a word that heals, frees and reconciles.[7]

As Benedict XVI writes:

> Listening to and meditating upon the Word of God means letting it penetrate and shape our life so as to reconcile us with God, allowing God to lead us toward reconciliation with our neighbor; a necessary path for building a community of individuals and peoples. On our faces and in our lives, may the Word of God truly take flesh![8]

To be effective, all forms of reconciliation must be accompanied by courageous and honest action. In the first place the ringleaders, those responsible for the conflicts, those who ordered the crimes, and those

---

[6] Testimony given on October 9, 2009 by Sr. Geneviève Uwamariya, woman religious of Sainte-Marie de Namur (Rwanda), listener at the Synod of African Bishops. See Paul Béré, "The Word of God as Transformative Power in Reconciling African Christians," in *Reconciliation, Justice, and Peace: The Second African Synod*, ed. A. E. Orobator (Maryknoll, NY: Orbis Books, 2011).

[7] Ibid.

[8] *Africae Munus*, no. 16.

involved in all kinds of trafficking, must be found and their responsibility must be proved. The victims have the right to the truth and to justice. It is important both now and for the future to purify and heal the memory of these events in order to build a better society in which such atrocities will not be repeated.

Since violence is a dehumanizing act, the forgiveness and reconciliation it requires are acts of hope and humanization. In reconciliation God creates a new heart in each person and reconciles each person to God and to others. By virtue of reconciliation, individuals or communities requesting or granting forgiveness have succeeded in healing their memory, and families once in conflict now live in harmony once more. On the paths of human history God is *present with us every day*. Reconciliation places this relational dimension at the center of our reflection.

What we can learn from this experience is that God is the author of all genuine reconciliation. God's main concern in the reconciliation process is the healing of the victims. Furthermore, in reconciliation, God makes both the victim and the offender a "new creation."[9] Hence, every Christian should give meaning to his or her suffering by viewing it as part of *the suffering, death, and resurrection of Christ*. This means that reconciliation will not be complete until "the whole universe" is united in Christ.[10]

Understanding Forgiveness and Reconciliation from a Biblical-Theological Perspective

Reconciliation transforms the parties concerned, or rather, makes the relationship evolve. In addition, to reconcile is to do things differently, to create surprise and novelty as the woman of Tekoa shows us.[11]

Social Reconciliation: The Woman of Tekoa

In the Old Testament one can find various accounts of reconciliation, such as that of Joseph and his brothers[12] or the beautiful passage between Jacob and Esau.[13] We have chosen the account of the wise woman of Tekoa for

---

[9] 2 Cor 5:17.
[10] Cf. Eph 1:10.
[11] We find seven citations in the Bible regarding Tekoa: 2 Sam 14:2; 1 Chr 2:24; 4:5; 2 Chr 11:6; 20:20; Jer 6:1; Am 1:1.
[12] Gen 50:15–21.
[13] Gen 33:1–17.

her sympathetic attitude. She shows us the meaning of the journey, the itinerary, and the crossover that are at the heart of reconciliation, and how "what *connects* (relays), *relates*."[14]

King David, confronted with the fratricidal struggle of his sons, banished Absalom, his eldest son. His commander-in-chief, Joab, felt the royal house was threatened. But despite his military victories, he felt powerless to turn the father's heart back toward his son. He then asks a woman for help. She comes to meet the king and tackles the problem by recounting a narrative in which she places herself in a situation similar to that of the king:

> Help, O king, I am a widow; my husband is dead. And your handmaid had two sons, and they quarrelled with one another in the field; there was no one to part them and, one struck the other and killed him. And now the whole family has risen against your handmaid, and they say, "Give up the man who struck his brother, that we may kill him for the life of his brother whom he slew," and so they would destroy the heir also. Thus they would quench my ember which is left, and leave to my husband neither name nor remnant upon the face of the earth.[15]

The woman of Tekoa is a symbol of so many women around the world who are in mourning as she was, and her story offers us an example of the power of relationships and reconciliation.

Fratricide is one of the situations we often experience in our world today, especially in Africa. The difficulty is how to rebuild relationships when brothers have introduced death into the family circle? The woman of Tekoa helped King David to look objectively at the situation that reflected his own. Her main argument in defense of the murderer was that life goes on through the inheritance of the "father's name." The empathy she aroused disposed the king's heart to mercy and reconciliation with his son. The testimony of this woman sent by Joab, the military commander, shows that although warlords fail to explore the true paths to peace, those of reconciliation and justice, they nevertheless know that a woman is the best mediator in reconciling hearts.

A wise woman can inspire and offer meaningful advice to our world today, where multiple conflicts indicate the difficulty of "coexistence" in countries tormented by politico-ethnic rivalry among political leaders

---

[14] Édouard Glissant, *Poétique de la Relation* (Paris: Gallimard, 1990), 187.
[15] 2 Sam 14:4–7.

and among religious denominations.[16] Women can help us rebuild more humanizing relationships for life. Reconciliation permits relations to be restored between peoples through the resolution of differences and contentious motives.

Reconciliation on the social plane contributes to peace following hostilities. It reestablishes the unity of hearts and life. Through reconciliation, nations long at war have found peace, and citizens ruined by civil war have rebuilt their unity. Reconciliation helps to overcome crisis, restore human dignity, and pave the way for development and lasting peace among peoples at all levels.

Mission Identifies with Reconciliation in Africa

Reconciliation reaches out to men and women of all ages and people of all cultures. It embraces the multiple relational dimensions of human life, whether in reconciliation among individuals; among ethnic, national, and religious groups; among nations; with oneself, with one's own history and God; or today, in the face of the ecological crisis, our reconciliation with nature.

To work for the promotion of reconciliation is to recognize and foster the divine dynamism that is present in human history and transforms it.[17] Reconciliation is therefore not an act of personal piety; it is part of a much larger sacramentality that concerns the entire community. The church in Africa shares the reconciling mission received from Christ with the universal church. The African bishops have repeatedly reminded Christian communities that the gospel is a message of reconciliation.[18] While recognizing Christ as the sole mediator and the church as a sign and instrument of salvation,[19] we think that the grace of forgiveness and reconciliation goes far beyond the ritual of the confessional to imbricate all human relations and creation.

When one revisits the theology of reconciliation, as the New Testament exegete Alain Gignac has,[20] one notes that in the Pauline passages,

---

[16] Cf. Kä Mana, *Théologie africaine pour le temps de crise. Christianisme et reconstruction de l'Afrique* (Paris: Karthala, 1993), 91.

[17] Pope John Paul II, post-synodal apostolic exhortation *Reconciliation and Penance* (1984), no. 12.

[18] Maurice Cheza, ed., *Le Synode africain. Histoire et textes* (Paris: Karthala, 1996), 130–31.

[19] Pope John Paul II, *Redemptor Hominis* (1979), no. 9.

[20] Alain Gignac, "La réconciliation chez Paul (2 Co 5:11—6,2; Rom 5:1–11): Perspective discursive et sociopolitique," *Thologies de la rconciliation in revue Thologiques* 23, no. 2 (2015): 103–31.

the reconciliation Christ brought about does not primarily concern the individual (or interpersonal), but the whole of creation. The reference to creation includes, from a Christian perspective, a reference to the Creator as well as to creatures. Reconciliation with creation opens a new perspective by integrating God and neighbor in a new salvific relationship with creation.

Conclusion

As shown above, the theme of reconciliation evokes a rich and varied picture. Thus, several initiatives for reconciliation have been started in countries long divided by conflict (such as South Africa and Rwanda).[21] On the ecclesial level, the Catholic Church since the Second Vatican Council has presented reconciliation as a sacrament. At the biblical level, there are various approaches—as noted above, St. Paul uses it as a symbol of salvation. In the general context of concern for the environment, the need for reconciliation "with creation" has become urgent and the reference to creation has introduced a "holistic" vision of mission. Thus, reconciliation is a fertile theological ground.

Only authentic reconciliation can generate lasting peace in society. Often, after a conflict, the reconciliation discreetly carried out and obtained in silence restores unity of hearts and peaceful coexistence. Thus, after long periods of war, nations find peace and societies deeply wounded by civil war or genocide can rebuild their unity. It is in giving and receiving forgiveness[22] that the wounded memory of individuals or communities is healed and families once at variance find harmony. Reconciliation overcomes crises, restores human dignity, and paves the way for the development of lasting peace among peoples at all levels.

What we learn from Sr. Geneviève's testimony is that she sought *the truth* by wishing to meet the executioner who murdered her father. She is *committed to condemning sin but saving the sinner*. Thus, both the torturer and the victim must be genuinely ready to turn over a new leaf. Sr. Geneviève *disposed her heart to compassion and mercy* by viewing the executioner as a "brother" and taking him in her arms, because she understood in her heart that he had only been a puppet manipulated by evil. This is also

---

[21] Laetitia Bucaille, "Vérité et réconciliation en Afrique du Sud. Une mutation politique et sociale," *Politique trangre* 2 (2007): 313–25.

[22] Cf. Pope John Paul II, *Message for the Celebration of World Peace Day 1997*, no. 1.

the experience of Jesus on the cross when he cries out: "Father, forgive them; for they know not what they do."[23]

From the woman of Tekoa we can learn that it is by forgiving that one disposes one's heart to receive forgiveness in order to heal it. The traumas in life leave wounds in our hearts that we must dare to look at and name, and patiently heal with the word of God, which heals, liberates, and reconciles. We must, like King David, understand that the cycle of hatred, revenge, and resentment sometimes constitutes lifelong imprisonment.

In short, reconciliation is part of the fabric of human existence.[24] It always involves action: the *redirection* and *review of the limited goals* that feed a larger process. The difficulty lies in the fact that we all approach the question of reconciliation from personal experience involving *our* own or the collective identity. Very often we focus too much on the hoped-for goal or outcome of reconciliation, forgetting that it is mostly achieved through a patient and deliberate process.

Africae Munus ends on a note of hope: "Once more I say: 'Get up, Church in Africa. . . . Set out on the path of the new evangelization with the courage that comes to you from the Holy Spirit.'" And this new evangelization takes the name of reconciliation, which is "an indispensable condition for installing in Africa justice among the men and women, and building a fair and lasting peace that respects each individual and all peoples; a peace that . . . is open to the contribution of all people of good will over and above their respective religious, ethnic, linguistic, cultural and social background."[25]

Reconciliation is an act of hope; through it, Christians look to the future, which reconciliation opens and renews with and in God for all human beings.[26]

Anne Béatrice Faye, CIC, is a Senegalese member of the Congregation of the Sisters of Our Lady of the Immaculate Conception of Castres (CIC). She holds a PhD and is currently professor at Al Mowafaqa in Rabat, Morocco, and a member of the Commission of Theologians for the next synod (2023).

---

[23] Lk 23:34.

[24] Charles Kasereka Pataya, "La dynamique du pardon et de la réconciliation dans le contexte des conflits en Afrique," *Revue Lumen Vitae* 68, no. 2 (2013): 167–76.

[25] *Africae Munus,* nos. 174, 158.

[26] Lytta Basset, *Le pouvoir de pardonner,* in *Coll. Spiritualités vivantes* (Paris/Genève: Albin Michel/Labor et Fides, 1999), 11.

Mission and Women

"Her-Story" of Mission

Mary T. Barron, OLA

In March 2018, prior to the World Council of Churches Mission Conference held in Arusha in Tanzania, I had the privilege of attending the Women's pre-conference, which had as one of its aims "to make visible her-stories of mission that weave the then and now through mentorship as transformative discipleship that build spiritual and leadership empowerment." This ecumenical gathering of approximately fifty women from different contexts reflected on the place of women in mission, particularly the mission movement of the mid- to late-nineteenth century. A central theme for consideration was the perceived invisibility of women in the stories of mission that have been recorded through the centuries. While acknowledging that "women have been prominently in mission spreading the gospel of Jesus's life, death and resurrection since the time of Jesus," the conference proceedings noted that "the mainline story of mission has often downplayed women's role in mission. The mission story has been (his) story not (her) story—failing to take seriously the centrality of women in mission."[1]

No book reflecting on emerging trends in mission would be complete without a reflection on women and mission. Within the confines of this brief article it is impossible to retell the entire story of mission through a feminine lens, thus adding a complementary *her-story of mission* to the his-story already documented.[2] Nor is it possible to delve into the myriad

---

[1] World Council of Churches, "Women's pre-conference," March 6–7, 2018, Arusha, Tanzania. The theme of the conference was "Women in Mission on the Move of the Spirit."

[2] For an overview of the contribution of Catholic women to mission that traces the evolution of that engagement in approach and prominence, see Susan Smith, "Catholic Woman in Mission 1910 to 2010," in *A Century of Catholic Mission: Roman Catholic Missiology 1910 to the Present*, ed. Stephen B. Bevans (Oxford: Regnum Books International, 2013).

and complex issues relating to this topic, not least of which relates to the experience of women within the Catholic Church. While acknowledging that the theme of *woman and mission* can only be considered within this wider church context, a context that generates passionate debate about the current position of women in the church, this article listens to the voices of several women in mission today, appreciating how they describe their personal experience of mission and how they live out their role and contribution in different mission contexts. Testimonies were invited from a small number of women missionaries in and from different contexts, lay and religious missionaries alike.[3] The reflections presented here are subsequently based on the lived experience of these women and while it may not be taken as comprehensive research on any facet of the broad topic under consideration, from their experiences emerge some key aspects of woman and mission for our modern day.

The topic *woman and mission* conjures up different scenarios, possibilities, contexts, and situations that are greatly influenced by one's own perspective. Perhaps one may be drawn to reflect primarily on the many women, both religious and lay, who devote their lives to the proclamation of the kingdom in a distinctly missionary key. Or one may be attracted to a consideration of the need to focus mission energies on women and those dependent on them, since systematically they suffer most from poverty, exclusion, and discrimination throughout our world. In such a global scenario any proclamation of the kingdom and any missionary effort would surely be first and foremost directed to those who are the poorest and who are suffering most from the injustices and discriminatory policies prevalent in our societies. One may consider what a feminine approach to mission might be or may simply consider some of the joys and challenges associated with this topic of woman and mission in our day. After

---

[3] Four missionary women shared their personal reflections on woman and mission with the author for this article: Veronica Rubi, a lay missionary from Argentina with experience in Argentina and Mozambique and who is currently working with the Ticuna Peoples in the Brazilian Amazon; Sr. Scholasticah Nganda, Religious Sisters of Mercy, from Kenya, who has experience in Kenya and Ireland and is currently working in the Solidarity with South Sudan Project; Sr. Veronica Onyeanisi, Sisters of Our Lady of Apostles, from Nigeria, who is working in Kaduna Nigeria with the Women's Interfaith Council, recipients of the 2021 International Aachen Peace Award; and Sr. Terezinha Esperança Merandi, MSC, a Missionary Sister of the Sacred Heart of Jesus (Cabrini Sisters), who is of dual citizenship—born and raised in the United States, naturalized and having lived most of her missionary life in Brazil and Latin America, along with twenty years of mission experience in Ethiopia and Uganda before being missioned to the Solidarity with South Sudan Project. The author is from Ireland with mission experience in Tanzania.

a brief consideration of the concept of complementarianism, which in its simplistic form sets the scene for complementarity and even reciprocity of gendered roles in mission, the remainder of this article will consider *woman and mission* by briefly addressing the broad areas mentioned above.

Setting the Context of Complementarianism

Catholic tradition speaks of complementarianism, which is a concept that attributes different roles and functions to men and women. In an ideal context these are roles that complement each other and work together in harmony for the greater common good. Although this is a deeply contested notion, it is suggested that the modern understanding of the concept in the Catholic Church reflects the church's intention not to create a hierarchy of gender, but to allow individuals to live most fully their unique vocations.[4]

Pope John Paul II spoke often and eloquently of the "feminine genius,"[5] thus bringing to the fore and naming a concept that was already promulgated by Pope Pius XII as far back as 1957 and developed by subsequent pontificates. Women have a distinct contribution to offer in every walk of life by nature of the distinct attributes they possess, the approaches they adopt, and the creativities they engage in to address the challenges they face. Is there a distinctly feminine approach to mission? How is the "feminine genius" incarnated by women in mission? Pope Francis also frequently lauds the contribution of women engaged in mission and alludes to the "feminine genius," suggesting that women have a specific and unique perspective of mission. In his message for World Mission Day in 2016 he stated:

> Together with the evangelizing and sacramental work of missionaries, women and families often more adequately understand people's problems and know how to deal with them in an appropriate and, at times, fresh way: in caring for life, with a strong focus on people rather than structures, and by allocating human and spiritual resources towards the building of good relations, harmony, peace, solidarity,

---

[4] Amanda Schar, *Feminism and Faith: How Women Find Empowerment in the Roman Catholic Church* (Rock Island, IL: Celebration of Learning, 2019).

[5] For example, see Pope John Paul II, *Mulieris Dignitatem (On the Dignity and Vocation of Women)* (1988).

dialogue, cooperation and fraternity, both among individuals and in social and cultural life, in particular through care for the poor.[6]

From this brief quotation emerge some of the dimensions of the "feminine genius" that are re-echoed in the lived experience of the women missionaries contributing to this article: the importance afforded to *nurturing* (of relationships and of a dignified life for all); a deeper *sensitivity* to the real issues at play in the challenges that people face, with a particular sensitivity to the poorest peoples; and *creativity* in the responses provided. Perhaps these dimensions are not unique to the "feminine genius," but they are strongly experienced and lived out by women in mission.

Women and Mission—A Necessary Partnership

Sr. Terezinha, with more than forty years of experience in mission in different contexts in the Americas and Africa, suggests that women and mission go together, hand in hand, part and parcel of each other because both are life-giving. The missionary impulse that led to the foundation of so many female missionary congregations in the latter half of the nineteenth and early twentieth centuries attests to the necessity and centrality of women to the fruitfulness of mission and to bringing life to mission endeavors. A brief review of the foundation of the Sisters of Our Lady of Apostles, the missionary congregation to which I belong, attests to the veracity of this statement. Our congregation was founded in 1876 by Fr. Augustine Planque, SMA, twenty years after the foundation of the Society of African Missions (SMA), of which he was one of the founding members. From the outset there was a great awareness among the early SMA missionaries that to make any lasting progress in the formation of Christian families, attention needed to be focused on women, as their role within the family ensured the faith would be passed on to their children. And for this to happen women missionaries were needed, women who could communicate and journey with the local women in the various mission contexts, thus sowing the seeds for Christian families to grow and flourish. Different variations of this story have been replicated across the world, creating the possibility for women, in spite of contextual restrictions, to be and become central protagonists in the evolving story of mission.

---

[6] Pope Francis, "Message of Pope Francis for World Mission Day 2016: Missionary Church, Witness of Mercy" (2016).

Women in the Peripheries—Focusing the Energies of Mission

This is not the place for an exploration of the feminization of poverty or a discussion of the global reality that women are less likely than men to be involved in decision making, to own land or property, or to have access to education and employment. However, it is impossible to ignore statistics showing that violence against women is one of the most widespread abuses of human rights, that development outcomes are consistently worse for women than for men, and that women and children account for around 80 percent of all refugees worldwide.[7] Women missionaries are particularly sensitive to this reality and to the injustices that perpetuate disproportionate suffering for women in their different contexts. From South Sudan, Sr. Scholasticah notes:

> Arguably, women and those depending on them persistently remain the largest social group mired in poverty world over. This reality is not an accident; it is the direct outcome of the effect of social roles and social expectations placed upon women and of discrimination. Unfortunately, women and girls in South Sudan have suffered most as victims of sexual abuse and rape in all the wars that have rocked South Sudan.

Similarly, from Nigeria, Sr. Veronica Onyeanisi notes that "gender inequality is still deeply rooted in Nigeria with more women at risk of poverty, illiteracy, and insecurity because of the systematic discrimination they face in education, healthcare, employment, leadership positions, and control of assets."

The world over, although women are often the most disadvantaged, their presence and their commitment to family, community, and the development of society mean that their role as protagonists in mission is central to any fruitful mission encounter. From the reflection of Sr. Veronica Rubi we sense the key role women can play in mission and in spreading the gospel, in spite of the suffering and discrimination they may endure. Reflecting on the traditional liminal rite of passage from girl-child to adulthood among the Ticuna people in the Latin American context, Veronica offers some insights into the esteem in which women were and are held by that traditional culture, albeit in modern day-to-day life this esteem is not so easily recognized.

---

[7] Mark Chamberlain, "CAFOD's Work with Women Explained" (March 7, 2019).

Ticuna female adolescents are prepared from puberty to assume the roles that are appropriate to the adult woman in their tradition. That preparation begins with first menstruation: At that moment the girl's social life is interrupted. She is kept in her room—sometimes for months—while the family prepares everything necessary to perform the Fiesta de la Nueva Joven (feast of the new young woman), the rite that paves the way to adulthood for the woman and after which traditionally she is ready for marriage. Various rites are performed during the three-day festival, including the central rite, which is to shave the girl's head, symbolizing that with the endurance of this pain, she is now prepared to face life's difficulties. Male adolescents have no such rite of maturity to endure as a rite of passage to adult life. Having journeyed with the Ticuna people for more than seven years, as one of the first missionaries among these people, Sr. Veronica Rubi sees in this ritual the recognition by the Ticuna people of the importance of the life of the woman for their culture, for the knowledge that she possesses and transmits to new generations.

Perhaps this experience also reflects the story of women within the Catholic Church—innately and intuitively the entire church is aware that women are undoubtedly important to society and to the mission of God especially within the church, and there is an awareness and appreciation of their role and commitment. This is evident in the following quotation from Pope Francis:

> In the Amazon region, there are communities that have long preserved and handed on the faith even though no priest has come their way, even for decades. This could happen because of the presence of strong and generous women who, undoubtedly called and prompted by the Holy Spirit, baptized, catechized, prayed and acted as missionaries. For centuries, women have kept the church alive in those places through their remarkable devotion and deep faith. Some of them, speaking at the Synod, moved us profoundly by their testimony.[8]

But unfortunately, in the daily reality of church life this awareness and appreciation is not always experienced.

A Feminine Approach?

Mary Jo Anderson highlights four dimensions of the feminine genius that are essential to life in the church and which I suggest also emerge from

---

[8] Pope Francis, post-synodal exhortation *Querida Amazonia* (2020), no. 99.

the reflections of women in mission today, namely, "receptivity, sensitivity, generosity, and maternity."[9] A common reflection shared by these women missionaries is the place of encounter and openness to the other as an integral part of mission. Regardless of the original motivation for the missionary presence, inevitably the interpersonal relationships become the keystone of mission. The missionary relationship may begin as a response to a need, as the provision of services and supports, but ultimately mission is experienced and bears fruit as encounter. An encounter is born out of receptivity to others and sensitivity to their needs and to their capacity to journey together in solidarity. Sr. Veronica Rubi eloquently expresses her experience:

> When that encounter is experienced, the same Jesus, the kingdom and the good news of the gospel are present. That's the miracle of the mission. That's where the Spirit works by making all things new. Bonds, relationships based on the love of Jesus save us. Love heals, love convokes, love keeps us united. This is my mission experience, not so much because of what I brought in my heart, but because of what I learned from this indigenous Ticuna people, who live with a strong sense of community, where the seeds of the word are since the beginning of time.

In a similar vein, Sr. Scholasticah speaks of incarnating love in the daily encounter with others as the core of mission. Referring to a missiology lecture she attended, she says:

> I managed to pick up something that spoke to me loudly. In his presentation, the professor had stressed that "the church is servant, and the mission is God's." . . . The church's mandate is to conform to God's purposes by serving through loving. The word *loving* in the context of mission has stayed with me since. And as I reflect further on this phrase, I hear an invitation to encounter the world around me with kindness, understanding, compassion and justice. This indeed is an awesome responsibility of being in solidarity with others, of gracefully encountering others through love, and seeing the world through the same lens.

Following receptivity and sensitivity, the next dimensions of the "feminine genius" reflect the generosity and creativity of a community's

---

[9] Mary Jo Anderson, "Feminine Genius," *Catholic Answers* (July/August 2005), 18–21.

response, a calling to the birth of life-giving and life-changing mission initiatives. From Sr. Veronica Rubi's mission story, the simple response among the Ticuna Youth is life saving:

> Mission began among this particular Ticuna people through the sensitivity and commitment of one woman, a leader-catechist in the community called Lucinei, an attentive and sensitive woman, concerned about the youth of her people. Witnessing the high rates of suicide among young people there, Lucinei appealed to missionaries to help and a small group accepted the challenge. The mission began humbly, meeting every Saturday performing recreational, playful and reflecting activities with young people, with the aim of motivating within them the desire to live, to strengthen their identity, to highlight the values of their culture, deepen the rites of their people and help them recognize that the love of Jesus gives meaning to our entire existence.

From there, because of the bonds of fraternity that were developing, both for the young people and for Veronica, life and mission became different.

In Northern Nigeria the engagement of women of different faiths in peacebuilding initiatives is also bearing life-giving fruit. Sr. Veronica Onyeanisi shares her experience:

> In the past women were not involved in peace building processes, but today through women-led organizations women are trained in mediation and peace building processes. They have assumed new roles in peace building and are no longer only victims. They now play vital roles as mothers of peace.... Their involvement in the process of mediation and developing strategies for securing and maintaining peace through nonviolent means has so far yielded much fruit in the communities as well as building peaceful coexistence among different religions.

These are simple yet profound examples of the ongoing commitment of women in mission. Through their receptivity and sensitivity and their generous gift of self to journey in solidarity with communities, they generate life-giving, life-protecting, and life-enhancing mission initiatives, thus incarnating the gospel and witnessing to God's reign of love, peace, and justice.

Conclusion

To conclude this brief reflection, a final common thread that arose from the contributors is the need to continually awaken to, challenge, and resist the injustices in our world. As we currently witness the evolving situation in Afghanistan and the particular concern for the situation of women in that country, it is fitting to challenge ourselves to do more as missionaries to challenge all situations of injustice, discrimination, and poverty. Sr. Terezinha's reflection on the awakening of consciousness to injustice offers appropriate concluding words that challenge all missionaries to perhaps pay more attention to this advocacy dimension of mission:

> There is a greater attentive consciousness to social and political dilemmas, which make the fulfillment of their [women in Africa and Latina America] daily tasks all the more burdensome and unjust. These injustices exist in both realities, but women are waking up gradually to making their voices heard, their legitimate rights seen, and their presence to be felt on an equal footing with the dominant powers at hand. Women religious are those who have stood and stand with their sisters in life, in communities, favelas, homesteads, barrios, tribes, and clans, on the margins, in the camps, migrating and always on the move. They, like Mary of Nazareth, are seeking something better, deeper, having tasted for themselves in Jesus and wanting to nourish future generations so as to have and promote "life and life in abundance" (Jn 10:10). This revolutionary and feminine liberating spirit of the gospel is life-changing, life-enhancing for women and the whole of creation which their lives touch. It is with and from these women, with whom I have traveled roads, experienced, known, lived with, learned from, shared struggles, dangers and joys, that the gospel has become real and incarnated. Jesus walks among us, teaches us, guides us, showing the way and leading forward in building the family, the community, the kingdom here and now.

> **Mary T. Barron, OLA,** from Ireland, is currently superior general of the Sisters of Our Lady of Apostles. She has served as a missionary in Tanzania, on the Mission Alive Project in Ireland, and in leadership both at the provincial and congregational level. A speech and language therapist, she holds an MA in international development studies and in healthcare management.

Peacebuilding

Peace Promotion as Integral to Evangelization

James H. Kroeger, MM

Many English-speaking Catholics are familiar with some songs about peace that are used in the liturgy or in prayer groups. For instance, a 1969 song by Sy and Jill Miller has this opening line: "Let there be peace on earth and let it begin with me." One recalls that in 1967 Sebastian Temple produced the song "Make Me a Channel of Your Peace." In addition, Carey Landry is known for the song "Peace Is Flowing like a River." As we repeatedly sing our favorite melodies, the meaning and importance of the lyrics seep deeply into our consciousness.

The popularity of such peace songs reminds all that the promotion of peace, along with justice, love, and harmony, is intimately linked to the very foundations of Christianity. Peace promotion has deep roots in the Christian faith; it is integral to the Christian vocation; and it becomes an authentic manifestation of living faith. This brief piece seeks to capture the core elements of the vision of peace promotion in the church, and how it is undeniably linked to the Catholic faith, in five interrelated sections. A final conclusion seeks to integrate these various aspects and insights.

Church Teaching on Peace Promotion

Although peace initiatives in the church have a long history, one notices that in the Vatican II era a renewed emphasis emerged. One might associate this with the last encyclical of Pope Saint John XXIII, *Pacem in Terris*, published in 1963, only weeks before his death. Several authors and film producers have given him the title "Pope of Peace" and have noted how he carefully discerned the "signs of the times."

John XXIII brought to the forefront the importance of peace in an era following the devastating Second World War; it was also a time of nuclear proliferation, tension between the Soviet and American power blocs, and the Cuban missile crisis. *Pacem in Terris* can be said to be an encyclical of peace and human dignity as it emphasizes the common task to establish truth, justice, love, freedom, and solid relationships within human society. It calls upon the world community and its leaders to address and solve problems of an economic, social, political, or cultural nature so as to serve the common good. Notably, this is the first time that a church document is addressed to "all people of good will."

Vatican II's *Gaudium et Spes (Pastoral Constitution on the Church in the Modern World)* (1964) presents the face of a church in intimate union with the entire human family, making "the joy and the hope, the grief, and anguish of the people of our time" (*GS,* no. 1) her deep concern. The entire fifth chapter of this document is devoted to "Fostering of Peace and Establishment of a Community of Nations." For example, one reads that: "Accordingly, the Council proposes to outline the true and noble nature of peace . . . and earnestly to exhort Christians to cooperate with all in securing a peace based on justice and charity and in promoting the means necessary to attain it, under the help of Christ, author of peace" (*GS,* no. 77).

Saint Pope Paul VI has given the church many profound insights on peace. Perhaps his most frequently repeated quote is: "Development is the new name for peace." This appears as the title of one section (nos. 76–77) of his 1967 encyclical *Populorum Progressio.* The pope sees that authentic development should benefit everyone and respond to the many demands of justice—all in the service of worldwide peace. A significant contribution of Paul VI was the establishment of the Pontifical Council *Iustitia et Pax* in 1967; this fulfilled the wishes of Vatican II that "an organization of the universal Church be set up in order that both the justice and love of Christ toward the poor might be developed everywhere" (*GS,* no. 90).

Due to the initiative of Paul VI, beginning in 1968 the church celebrates the World Day of Peace every January 1. The pope explained his purpose in his very first World Day of Peace Message: "It is our desire that then, every year, this commemoration be repeated as a hope and as a promise, at the beginning of the calendar which measures and outlines the path of human life in time, that Peace with its just and beneficent equilibrium may dominate the development of events to come." It is significant that 2021 marked the fifty-fourth continuous year of the World Day of Peace, as these annual papal messages provide a rich library of insights on the church's mission of peace promotion; they expand and enrich the corpus of the social teaching of the church.

Undoubtedly, the church's treasure trove of reflection on her mission of promoting peace is vast, profound, and enriching; only a few pivotal highlights have been presented here. It is to be hoped that this brief section has alerted readers to explore further the church's reflective insights on the vast topic contained in the simple word *peace*.

Scriptural Insights on Peace

Sacred Scripture is replete with profound insights on God's gift of peace; a long list of quotations could be presented. However, this author chooses to focus on one passage in particular, integrating other items within this basic perspective. In the Beatitudes in Matthew's Gospel, Jesus declares: "Blessed are the peacemakers, for they shall be called children of God" (5:9).

It is noteworthy that Jesus says that the blessing is on "peacemakers," namely, peacebuilders, not necessarily on peace lovers or peacekeepers. This clearly implies taking action or engaging in initiatives to foster peace. A peacemaker is someone who gets involved in a situation with the intention of building bridges between two parties that may be at odds with each other; that person risks involvement in order to bring reconciliation and harmony. Such an individual is fulfilling the command found in Hebrews 12:14, variously translated as, "Make every effort to live in peace" or "Pursue peace with everyone." Again, such a person must "seek peace and pursue it" (1 Pet 3:11).

A genuine peacemaker is someone who emulates Jesus, the Prince of Peace (Isa 9:6), by working to reconcile people with God and with one another. The apostle Paul asserts: "It was God who reconciled us to himself through Christ and gave us the work of handing on this reconciliation. . . . So, we are ambassadors for Christ . . . and the appeal that we make in Christ's name is: be reconciled to God" (2 Cor 5:18–20). Undoubtedly, the peacemaker's initiatives as an "ambassador of peace" emerge from one's own direct experience of being at peace with oneself, with God, and with neighbor.

Christians are very familiar with many of Christ's words about peace, particularly those spoken at the last supper: "Peace I leave with you; my peace I give you, a peace the world cannot give; this is my gift to you" (Jn 14:27). Jesus tells his disciples about his Father, "so that in me you may have peace" (Jn 16:33). After the resurrection, Jesus comes to his disciples on various occasions; his words of greeting are always, "Peace be with you" (see Jn 20:19, 21, 26). The apostle Paul echoes Jesus's words when he writes to the Romans: "May the God of peace be with you all" (Rom 15:33).

A deeper understanding of Jesus's call to be peacemakers can result from an appreciation of the word *peace*. In Greek the word is *eirene*; in Hebrew it is *shalom*; and in the Near East it is *salaam*. Its meaning is rich, exceeding a simple "absence of trouble." In Hebrew, *peace* means everything that contributes to a person's highest good, the possession and enjoyment of all good things. In addition, Jewish rabbis held that the most honorable task one can perform is to establish right relations between people and with God. This is what Jesus means when he invites his followers to be peacemakers, doing a Godlike work, indeed, a lofty goal and a source of blessedness and beatitude! What a privilege to be called "children of God" due to our efforts to be peacemakers!

Saints of Peace

As Christian peacemakers we draw inspiration and insight from the church's teaching and from Sacred Scripture. Yet, another valuable source to guide our endeavors is to look to several saints whose lives are identified with the promotion of peace. The insights of five canonized saints who advocated peace are briefly presented for our emulation.

Mother Teresa of Calcutta promoted peace, not only with her words, but also with her deeds; she won the Nobel Peace Prize for her dedication to the poor and the sick. Her pithy statements contain profound insights:
- "Peace begins with a smile."
- "All works of love are works of peace."
- "If we have no peace, it is because we have forgotten that we belong to each other."
- "Let us more and more insist on raising funds of love, of kindness, of understanding, of peace. The rest will be given."
- "What can you do to promote world peace? Go home and love your family."

Francis of Assisi, son of a wealthy cloth merchant, experienced a profound conversion when he was captured and spent a year in prison in Perugia; upon his return to Assisi, the rich boy began to serve the poor and sick. His thoughts enhance our peace efforts:
- "While you are proclaiming peace with your lips, be careful to have it even more fully in your heart."

- "It is in pardoning that we are pardoned."
- "It is no use walking anywhere to preach unless our walking is our preaching."
- "It is in giving that we receive."
- "Start by doing what's necessary; then do what's possible; and suddenly you are doing the impossible."
- "Lord, make me an instrument of your peace."

Pope John XXIII served in several roles in the church: he actively worked to save Jewish people during World War II; he convoked the Second Vatican Council; he authored the encyclical *Pacem in Terris*; and he became known as "Good Pope John" during his short pontificate (1958–63). We listen to his insights, assisting the promotion of peace:

- "See everything, overlook a great deal, correct a little."
- "Consult not your fears, but your hopes and your dreams. Think not about your frustrations, but about your unfulfilled potential. Concern yourself not with what you have tried and failed in, but what it is still possible for you to do."
- "If God created shadows, it was to better emphasize the light."
- "O Lord, do not let us turn into 'broken cisterns' that can hold no water."

Saint Óscar Romero served as Archbishop of San Salvador, guiding the church in an extremely difficult period; he was assassinated in 1980 while celebrating the Eucharist. His life and words provide much inspiration:

- "Each of you has to be God's microphone. . . . Let us not hide the talent that God gave us on the day of our baptism."
- "Peace is not the product of terror or fear. Peace is not the silence of cemeteries. Peace is not the silent result of violent repression. Peace is the generous, tranquil contribution of all to the good of all. Peace is dynamism. Peace is generosity. It is a right and a duty."
- "Peace is the product of justice and love."
- "We are workers, not master builders; ministers, not messiahs. We are prophets of a future not our own."

Pope Saint John Paul II led the church as pope from 1978 to 2005; he was the first non-Italian pope in over four hundred years, and he played a significant role in helping to end Communist rule in his native Poland and eventually in all of Europe. We appreciate his wisdom:

- "Opting for peace does not mean a passive acquiescence to evil or compromise of principle. It demands an active struggle against hatred, oppression, and disunity, but not by using methods of violence. Building peace requires creative and courageous action."

- "If you want peace, work for justice. If you want justice, defend life. If you want life, embrace truth."
- "Peace is not just the absence of war. Like a cathedral, peace must be constructed patiently and with unshakable faith."

The multifaceted engagement of Jesus's followers in the active promotion of peace necessarily addresses two additional areas: the *principles* guiding the process and the concrete *practice* of implementation. Both *theory-vision* and *practical initiatives* contribute to effective and lasting results within the church's mission of integral evangelization. This presentation now identifies *four guiding principles*; these will be followed by a separate section highlighting a wide variety of possible, *concrete, "do-able" actions*.

Four Principles of Peace Promotion

A basic premise that Christians follow in their peace work is that a vision of peace is rooted in *a relationship with God*; it is not simply a human endeavor. God is ruler of all creation, the world, and all peoples who are striving for right relationships. Peace is ultimately a gift from God and reflects the inner life of the Trinity. In addition, genuine peace is built upon the reconciling work of Jesus's life, death, and resurrection. It is at the heart of the good news proclaimed by Jesus; the Holy Spirit is always guiding peace initiatives. Thus, all peace efforts need the "faith attitude" of listening and a profound openness to God.

The promotion of peace and harmony is integral to the *mission of God's people, the church*. Doing justice, loving authentically, and living harmoniously are integral to the Christian vocation. One is reminded of the words of the prophet Micah (6:8): "What does the Lord require of you but to do justice, and to love kindness, and to walk humbly with your God?" Such an approach proclaims the presence of God's kingdom in people's lives, guiding the church's thinking and action.

Authentic peace initiatives necessarily incorporate *social and political engagement*. Genuine peace cannot be separated from God's righteousness, justice, and compassion. Thus, working for peace, which is concerned with establishing right relations with people, societies, and nations, necessarily includes all areas of public life. It is nurtured by charity and seeks a "just peace" that hopes to overcome oppression, enmity, and discrimination. It reflects our belief that all persons are uniquely created in the image of God; respect for human dignity is foundational.

Peacemaking demands a *holistic vision of peace*. It means seeking a dynamic state of well-being and harmony from which nothing and no one is excluded, including all nations, cultures, and peoples, the entire earth and the cosmos. Difficult historical and social factors, as well as programs for sustainable economic and social development, must be addressed—all based on the desire for the resolution of conflicts in order to ensure lasting peace.

Readers may feel overwhelmed as they reflect on these fundamental principles guiding Christian efforts to foster peace. Undoubtedly, they are comprehensive and extremely demanding. Everyone cannot achieve everything. However, this cannot be an excuse for not taking various initiatives. We have our Christian faith and our church communities to support us. Thus, we now turn to mentioning some possible strategies and programs for implementing Christ's farewell gift of peace.

Strategies and Programs of Peacebuilding

A brief presentation such as this obviously cannot cover in depth the many dimensions of the church's commitment to peace, yet a vision is set forth and various possibilities are explored. We enumerate some possible concrete responses that may encourage a committed Christian to become engaged in this vital aspect of the church's mission. The items mentioned are randomly presented; may they serve as a simple "spark" to ignite the passion or "fire" for peacemaking so as to merit the blessed title "children of God" (Mt 5:9).

- Be committed to treat all people with kindness, regardless of race, gender, religion or nationality, recalling that each human person is made in the image of God.
- Volunteer at a local charity that serves the needy in your neighborhood.
- Teach and show children how to be kind to animals; advocate animal rights.
- If you see someone in trouble, stop your activity and provide assistance; engage in random acts of kindness on a regular basis.
- Have the courage to admonish people when you see them acting in an inappropriate way; speak out against prejudice and discrimination when you see it.
- Research influential peace promoters in history, like Martin Luther King Jr., Dorothy Day, the Berrigan brothers, and Thomas Merton.

- Read books about peace; recommend and share them with others.
- Help the homeless; volunteer at a shelter for the needy or victims of violence.
- Regard anyone who hurts your feelings as a personal teacher helping you to mature and maintain a peaceful nature.
- Volunteer to take training as a mental health counselor to assist those (especially the youth) who may be emotionally unstable.
- Study the social teachings of the church, so as to appreciate better how they can positively influence difficult concrete situations that may lead to conflict and violence.
- Consider joining a religious peace initiative (for example, Plowshares Movement, Catholic Worker, *Pax Christi* International, etc.).
- If you are a member of a religious community, seek ways to be more involved in promoting peace through its programs and ministries.
- Take time to meditate and pray, examining your own "peace quotient" and how it can be enhanced.
- Adopt a positive attitude toward life, recognizing that there is still an abundance of good in this world.
- Beg the Lord Jesus to grant you personal peace and to become his instrument as an authentic peace-maker.

Conclusion

This modest piece is no more than a brief overview of some key elements that show how a commitment to peace promotion is an integral part of the mission of the church. A vision has been presented; challenges have been identified; simple guidelines have been outlined; possible action has been noted. Yet, "the doing remains"! Our humble daily prayer is fervent and sincere:

> Lord, make me an instrument of your peace!
> Jesus, pour your love and peace into my heart!

James H. Kroeger, MM, has served on missions in the Philippines and Bangladesh since 1970. Currently he teaches Christology, ecclesiology, missiology, and Asian theology at Loyola School of Theology, East Asian Pastoral Institute, and Mother of Life Catechetical Center in Metro Manila. His recent books include *Go, Teach, Make Disciples*; *Exploring the Priesthood with Pope Francis*; and *The Gift of Mission*.

Interreligious Dialogue

Interreligious Dialogue in the Context of Mission

Maria De Giorgi, MMX

On May 19, 2021, the Pontifical Council for Interreligious Dialogue organized an international webinar[1] on the occasion of the thirtieth anniversary of the publication of *Dialogue and Proclamation: Reflection and Orientations on Interreligious Dialogue and the Proclamation of the Gospel of Jesus Christ*. Speakers included Cardinal Michael Louis Fitzgerald, MAfr, former secretary (1987–2002) and then president (2002–2006) of the Pontifical Council for Interreligious Dialogue, and Cardinal Luis Antonio Tagle, current prefect of the Congregation for the Evangelization of Peoples. Their presence sought to underline how, from the very beginning, the document was conceived in profound synergy by the two dicasteries in the certainty that "proclamation and dialogue are thus both viewed, each in its own place, as component elements and authentic forms of the one evangelizing mission of the Church. They are both oriented towards the communication of salvific truth."[2]

As an "attitude" that the church must assume in fidelity to the duty it has to proclaim the gospel to the world, the term *dialogue* (Latin: *colloquium*) officially entered the documents of the church with Pope Paul VI's encyclical *Ecclesiam Suam*,[3] and gradually became current during the pontificates of John Paul II, Benedict XVI, and Francis. Here I limit myself

---

[1] Pontifical Council for Interreligious Dialogue, "Dialogue and Proclamation: 30th Anniversary (1991–2021)," Rome, May 19, 2021, in *Pro Dialogo* 167 (LVI) 2021/1.

[2] *Dialogue and Proclamation: Reflection and Orientations on Interreligious Dialogue and the Proclamation of the Gospel of Jesus Christ* (Rome: Pontifical Council for Interreligious Dialogue and the Congregation for the Evangelization of Peoples, May 19, 1991), no. 2.

[3] Pope Paul VI, *Ecclesiam Suam* (1964), hereinafter *ES*.

to underlining how *dialogue and mission*⁴ and *dialogue and proclamation* have gradually become inseparable terms.

In *Ecclesiam Suam*, not surprisingly called the Magna Carta of dialogue, Paul VI writes:

> If, as we said, the Church realizes what is God's will in its regard, it will gain for itself a great store of energy.... It will have a clear awareness of a mission received from God, of a message to be spread far and wide. Here lies the source of our evangelical duty, our mandate to teach all nations, and our apostolic endeavor.... The very nature of the gifts which Christ has given the Church demands that they be extended to others and shared with others. This must be obvious from the words: "Go therefore, teach ye all nations," Christ's final command to His Apostles.... To this internal drive of charity which seeks expression in the external gift of charity, we will apply the word "dialogue."⁵

And then again: "The Church must enter into dialogue with the world in which it lives. It has something to say, a message to give, a communication to make."⁶

Since then, the term and the spirit of dialogue entered the conciliar documents, determining their tenor and content. We know, in fact, that *Ecclesiam Suam*, published on August 6, 1964, had a strong impact on the ongoing Second Vatican Council—especially on fundamental documents such as *Lumen Gentium*, *Nostra Aetate*, and *Ad Gentes*—and how the deep relationship between mission and dialogue found its authoritative recognition.⁷

Not surprisingly, as the great master of dialogue, Msgr. Pietro Rossano, for many years undersecretary (1967–73) and secretary (1973–83) of the Secretariat for Non-Christians, noted:

---

⁴The document of the Secretariat for Non-Christians, *The Attitude of the Catholic Church towards the Followers of Other Religious Traditions: Reflections on Dialogue and Mission*, was dedicated to the dialogue/mission relationship; *AAS* 75 (1984): 816–28; see also *Bulletin of the Secretariat for Non-Christians* 56 (1984/2), no. 13.

⁵*ES*, no. 64.

⁶*ES*, no. 65.

⁷Although in *Ecclesiam Suam* Paul VI speaks of four levels of dialogue (dialogue with the world; dialogue with believers in God such as Jews, Muslims, and followers of the great Afro-Asian religions; dialogue with separated brothers; and dialogue within the church), it was his references to "dialogue with believers," or more specifically, dialogue with members of non-Christian religions, that became more widely known.

Ad Gentes, dedicated to evangelization and mission, continually insists on the need for dialogue (AG 2; 12; 16; 34; 41); while the Declaration *Nostra Aetate*, dedicated to the relationship between the church and non-Christian religions, therefore to dialogue, resolutely affirms the necessity and urgency of mission: *"Ecclesia annuntiat et annuntiare tenetur Christum in quo est via, veritas et vita, in quo homines plenitudinem vitae religiosae inveniunt"* (*NA* 2). This means that the church intends to inseparably link mission to dialogue; that in fulfilling the mandate of evangelization and mission the church wants to adopt the method and spirit of dialogue.[8]

St. John Paul II, in his missionary encyclical *Redemptoris Missio*,[9] in line with these premises consistently repeated: "Inter-religious dialogue is a part of the Church's evangelizing mission. Understood as a method and means of mutual knowledge and enrichment, dialogue is not in opposition to the mission *ad gentes*; indeed, it has special links with that mission and is one of its expressions."[10]

For his part, Benedict XVI, in one of his numerous interventions on dialogue, said:

> The Church considers an essential part of the proclamation of the Word to consist in encounter, dialogue, and cooperation with all people of good will, particularly with the followers of the different religious traditions of humanity. This is to take place without forms of syncretism and relativism, but along the lines indicated by the Second Vatican Council's Declaration *Nostra Aetate* and subsequently developed by the Magisterium of the Popes.[11]

Lastly, Pope Francis too, in his apostolic exhortation *Evangelii Gaudium,* affirms:

> In this dialogue, ever friendly and sincere, attention must always be paid to the essential bond between dialogue and proclamation, which leads the Church to maintain and intensify her relationship with non-Christians. A facile syncretism would ultimately be a totalitarian

---

[8] P. Rossano, *Dialogo e annuncio cristiano. L'incontro con le grandi religioni* (Cinisello Balsamo: Edizioni Paoline, 1993), 21.

[9] Pope John Paul II, *Redemptoris Missio (On the Permanent Validity of the Church's Missionary Mandate)* (1990), hereinafter *RM*.

[10] *RM,* no. 55.

[11] Pope Benedict XVI, post-synodal apostolic exhortation *Verbum Domini* (2010), no. 117.

gesture on the part of those who would ignore greater values of which they are not the masters. True openness involves remaining steadfast in one's deepest convictions, clear and joyful in one's own identity, while at the same time being "open to understanding those of the other party" and "knowing that dialogue can enrich each side." . . . Evangelization and interreligious dialogue, far from being opposed, mutually support, and nourish one another.[12]

The insistence with which the post-conciliar papal magisterium reaffirmed the essential bond among mission, dialogue, and proclamation was not accidental. Rather, it stems from the renewed awareness that the mission of the church—as Vatican II teaches—is essentially participation in the *missio Dei* and, as such, has an intrinsic trinitarian connotation that reverberates in history: "The pilgrim Church is missionary by her very nature, since it is from the mission of the Son and the mission of the Holy Spirit that she draws her origin, in accordance with the decree of God the Father."[13]

The Mission of the Church: Participation in the Mission of the Son and of the Holy Spirit

"Divinely sent to the nations of the world,"[14] the church is called to cooperate in the mission of the Son and the mission of the Holy Spirit. Indeed, *Ad Gentes* reminds us, "It is from the mission of the Son and the mission of the Holy Spirit that she draws her origin, in accordance with the decree of God the Father."[15]

In this trinitarian interdependence, the mission of the Son is configured as a movement of descent from the world of God to the human world; as the sharing and assumption of all that—except sin—is proper to the human condition[16] to elevate it, redeem it, and make human beings partakers of the divine nature.[17] On the other hand, the mission of the Spirit

---

[12] Pope Francis, Apostolic Exhortation *Evangelii Gaudium* (November 24, 2013), no. 251, hereinafter *EG*.

[13] Second Vatican Council, *Ad Gentes (Decree on the Church's Missionary Activity)* (1965), no. 2, hereinafter *AG*.

[14] *AG*, no. 1.

[15] *AG*, no. 2.

[16] Cf. Phil 2:6–11.

[17] Cf. 2 Pet 1:4.

is configured as a raising agent that "from within the plan of salvation"[18] progressively moves and pushes humanity toward the fullness of encounter and communion with God in Christ: anticipating, accompanying, and directing the apostolic action itself. At the same time, the Spirit encourages the church to spread to the ends of the earth and to the end of time.

Participating in this dynamism, the church shares in the mission of the Son: proclaiming his coming in the flesh to the world; bearing witness to his death and resurrection; leading all peoples to the faith, the freedom, and the peace of Christ through preaching, through the sacraments, and through other means of grace.[19] She also shares in the mission of the Spirit, "to foster and take to herself"[20] everything good and holy God worked in the world "even before Christ was glorified";[21] purifying and elevating the elements of "truth and grace"[22] present among the peoples; and recognizing the "seeds of the word" God sowed in "cultures already prior to the preaching of the Gospel."[23]

This multiplicity of tasks is clearly defined in *Ad Gentes* (no. 6), where the uniqueness of the mission is reaffirmed. In fidelity to the "ways of a true incarnation,"[24] it is indeed recognized that in the long pilgrimage through history, missionary activity can and must take different forms and modalities according to the historical and sociocultural situation of the peoples to whom it is addressed. The prevalence of a model in a given context, or in a particular historical phase, does not nullify the validity of other models that are more suited to other contexts and other historical moments. Therefore, the church's unique mission can be simultaneously expressed as witness of life and dialogue,[25] presence of charity,[26] evangelization and conversion,[27] foundation and formation of the Christian community,[28] and promotion of religious life.[29]

On her journey the church also gradually discovers the variety of services she is called to carry out in history to bring God's plan to fulfillment. *Ad Gentes*, besides declaring the missionary task of the church to be one and

---

[18] *AG*, no. 4.
[19] *AG*, no. 5.
[20] *Lumen Gentium*, no. 13.
[21] *AG*, no. 4.
[22] *AG*, no. 9.
[23] *AG*, no. 18.
[24] *AG*, no. 3.
[25] *AG*, no. 11.
[26] *AG*, no. 12.
[27] *AG*, no. 13.
[28] *AG*, no. 15.
[29] *AG*, no. 18.

immutable, recognizes that its implementation may vary according to the times, situations, and circumstances of the peoples to whom she is sent.[30]

The Mission of the Church Today

As the *Pastoral Constitution on the Church in the Modern World (Gaudium et Spes)* reminds us:

> To carry out such a task, the Church has always had the duty of scrutinizing the signs of the times and of interpreting them in the light of the Gospel. Thus, in language intelligible to each generation, she can respond to the perennial questions which men ask about this present life and the life to come, and about the relationship of the one to the other.[31]

Undoubtedly, the anthropological, sociological, and theological implications of this statement in *Gaudium et Spes* also challenge the mission of the church today, especially due to the frenetic pace of the modern world, now also dramatically marked by the current pandemic. The profound changes that have taken place in recent decades are there for all to see. The massive migratory flows, both to Europe and to other continents, have affected the social, cultural, and religious geography of many countries where peaceful coexistence and mutual integration cannot be predicted or taken for granted. World peace seems to be increasingly compromised by the reemergence of systems such as neo-imperialism of states, financial interests of the great centers of power, and fundamentalism. The problem of pollution and climate change, also linked to the "throwaway culture," now afflicts the whole planet and demands shared solutions. The virtual world, with its undeniable opportunities, is also drastically changing the style and modalities of interpersonal relations.

Last but not least, the challenge of growing secularism not only marginalizes religions and denies them a social role but favors ethical relativism and the emergence of ideologies that actually deny natural law and compromise peace in the world. It is precisely in this context that the church's commitment to dialogue, both intercultural and interreligious,

---

[30] *AG*, no. 6. Cf. M. De Giorgi, "Fondamento teologico della missione e suoi modelli costitutivi," in *Credere Oggi. Teologia della missione* (Padova: Edizioni Messaggero, 2010), 20–29.

[31] Second Vatican Council, *Gaudium et Spes (Pastoral Constitution on the Church in the Modern World)* (1965), no. 4.

becomes a clear response to the "signs of the times": a historical imperative that cannot be ignored.

Reacting to these challenges, right from the beginning of his pontificate, Pope Francis assumed a clear position in this regard, indicating to the church the "path of dialogue" as inscribed in her own mission. In *Evangelii Gaudium* Francis stresses: "Interreligious dialogue is a necessary condition for peace in the world, and so it is a duty for Christians as well as other religious communities,"[32] and, "In this dialogue, ever friendly and sincere, attention must always be paid to the essential bond between dialogue and proclamation, which leads the Church to maintain and intensify her relationship with non-Christians."[33] And in the encyclical *Laudato Si'*, Francis addressed an emphatic appeal to all: "I urgently appeal, then, for a new dialogue about how we are shaping the future of our planet. We need a conversation which includes everyone, since the environmental challenge we are undergoing, and its human roots, concern and affect us all," while also openly affirming: "The majority of people living on our planet profess to be believers. This should spur religions to dialogue among themselves for the sake of protecting nature, defending the poor, and building networks of respect and fraternity."[34]

Similarly, in the encyclical *Fratelli Tutti*, Pope Francis reiterates:

> One fundamental human right must not be forgotten in the journey towards fraternity and peace: it is religious freedom for believers of all religions. That freedom proclaims that we can find "a good understanding between different cultures and religions; it testifies to the fact that the things we have in common are so many and important that it is possible to find a means of serene, ordered and peaceful coexistence, accepting our differences and rejoicing that, as children of the one God, we are all brothers and sisters."[35]

Again—explicitly recalling the *Document on Human Fraternity for World Peace and Living Together*, signed in Abu Dhabi on February 4, 2019, with the Grand Imam of Al-Azhar, Ahmad Al-Tayyeb—Pope Francis strongly reaffirms: "In the name of God and of everything stated thus far, [we] declare the adoption of a culture of dialogue as the path; mutual coop-

---

[32] *EG*, no. 250.
[33] *EG*, no. 251.
[34] Pope Francis, *Laudato Si' (On Care for our Common Home)* (2015), nos. 14, 201.
[35] Pope Francis, *Fratelli Tutti (On Fraternity and Social Friendship)* (2020), no. 279, hereinafter *FT*.

eration as the code of conduct; reciprocal understanding as the method and standard."[36]

Conclusion

In the encyclical *Redemptoris Missio*, John Paul II not only declared that "dialogue is a path toward the kingdom and will certainly bear fruit, even if the times and seasons are known only to the Father,"[37] but he recalled that "each member of the faithful and all Christian communities are called to practice dialogue, although not always to the same degree or in the same way."[38]

A crucial statement that, on the one hand, emphasizes the universality of the call to practice dialogue ("all the faithful and all Christian communities"), on the other, repeats the intrinsic need to coordinate tasks and responsibilities ("even if not to the same degree or in the same way") aimed at carrying out this important service to the evangelizing mission of the church. These tasks and responsibilities presuppose an appropriate preparation and formation, both of those responsible for the life of the church in the various countries, and of the individual faithful and their respective communities.

To this end, in recent decades important initiatives have not been lacking, especially at the institutional level. In many Catholic universities—not least the pontifical universities—centers and departments for the study of religions and interreligious dialogue have been created; commissions for interreligious dialogue have been established within many episcopal conferences; and diocesan offices for interreligious dialogue have been set up in numerous dioceses, alongside the diocesan missionary offices.

However, all these commendable initiatives are waiting to be further strengthened, especially in the light of a renewed theological reflection on religions and on interreligious dialogue. Such renewed theological reflection—taking into due account the church's orientation and experience matured in recent decades in different cultural and religious contexts—must guide the praxis and the pastoral care of dialogue. To this end the contribution of missionary and religious institutes, which have inaugurated important paths of dialogue in different contexts, can be decisive. The future of the mission and of interreligious dialogue largely

---

[36] *FT*, no. 285.
[37] Cf. Acts 1:7.
[38] *RM*, no. 57.

depends on the appropriate formation of the Christian communities in all its aspects, as Pope Benedict XVI reminded the participants at the Tenth Plenary Assembly of the Pontifical Council for Interreligious Dialogue: "It is important to emphasize the need for formation for those who promote interreligious dialogue. If it is to be authentic, this dialogue must be a journey of faith. How necessary it is for its promoters to be well formed in their own beliefs and well informed about those of others!"[39]

The awareness of being at the beginning of a journey, in some respects still unprecedented, must make us both humble and confident, animated by evangelical *parresia*[40] in the certainty that "God desires all human beings to be saved and to come to the knowledge of the truth."[41]

> **Maria A. De Giorgi** is an Xaverian missionary in Japan. Beginning in 1987 she served at Shinmeizan Interreligious Center (Kumamoto Prefecture), and from 2005 to 2019 she was associate professor at the Pontifical Gregorian University in Rome. Currently she is a consultor to the Pontifical Council for Interreligious Dialogue and to the Sub-Committee for Interreligious Dialogue of the Bishops' Conference of Japan.

---

[39] Pope Benedict XVI, *Address to the Participants in the Tenth Plenary Assembly of the Pontifical Council for Interreligious Dialogue*, June 7, 2008.
[40] 2 Cor 3:12.
[41] 1 Tim 2:4.

Islam

A Mission of Mercy

John Mallare, CICM

In this short essay I focus on the theme of mercy in relation to doing mission, particularly in an Islamic context. Inevitably, this means presenting interreligious dialogue as an indispensable component of mission. This involves putting emphasis on the concept of the God of mercy as a unifying motivation for dialogue.

I have decided to present this theme in four parts. The first part is the notion of mercy in Christianity, based especially on the Bible. The second part is the notion of mercy in Islam. In the third part I identify the points of convergence of both notions of mercy. And in the last part I focus on interreligious dialogue as a mission of mercy. The aim of this essay is to provide a clearer view of the way Christianity and Islam look at mercy and to explore how comparing both views will lead a to a more realistic approach of mission in the Islamic milieu, and could prove to be a very valid approach for the whole of interreligious dialogue.

The Notion of Mercy in Christianity

In his *Bull of Indiction* of the Extraordinary Jubilee of Mercy, Pope Francis suggested that "the season of Lent in this Jubilee Year be lived more intensely as a privileged moment to celebrate and experience God's mercy."[1] In this document he called for an attentive and prayerful listening to God's prophetic word. The pope strongly believes that the mercy of God is a proclamation made to the world that has to be experienced firsthand by

---

[1] Pope Francis, *Message for Lent 2016*, no. 1.

a Christian, like in the case of a loving mother and a faithful father, as he explains in the following extract:

> Mercy, seen in feminine terms, is the tender love of a mother who, touched by the frailty of her newborn baby, takes the child into her arms and provides everything it needs to live and grow (*rahamim*). In masculine terms, mercy is the steadfast fidelity of a father who constantly supports, forgives and encourages his children to grow. Mercy is the fruit of a covenant; that is why God is said to remember his covenant of mercy (*hesed*).[2]

In the New Testament one can be reminded of the event of the annunciation, wherein the Blessed Virgin Mary rejoices in God's mercy for having chosen her:

> After receiving the Good News told to her by the Archangel Gabriel, Mary, in her Magnificat, *prophetically sings of the mercy* whereby God chose her. The Virgin of Nazareth, betrothed to Joseph, thus becomes the perfect icon of the Church which evangelizes. This is because Mary was, and continues to be, evangelized by the Holy Spirit, who made her virginal womb fruitful.[3]

Likewise, we see two parables in the Gospel of Luke that clearly show the relationship between God's mercy and our own. These are the parables of the Prodigal Son[4] and of the Good Samaritan.[5] In these parables Jesus shows how mercy should pass from God to us. Our experience of God's mercy invites us to practice it toward our brothers and sisters. Our mercy is based on that of God, who exhorts us to *"be merciful, just as your heavenly father is merciful."*[6] Mercy is not a fleeting emotion that simply "stirs" the heart and stops there, but a concrete, tangible, and creative commitment that mobilizes the whole human person.

In the parable of the Prodigal Son, Jesus reveals God's unlimited mercy toward sinners. The father did not stop at the emotions. His heart was moved, but he also runs toward his son, kisses him, and prepares a great

---

[2] Pope Francis, *Retreat for Priests 2016, Introduction and First Meditation*, Basilica of Saint John Lateran, June 2, 2016.
[3] Pope Francis, *Message for Lent*, no. 1. Emphasis mine.
[4] Lk 15:11–32.
[5] Lk 10:25–37.
[6] Lk 6:36.

feast for him. He gives him the best of his blessings by restoring to him his original dignity.

In the parable of the Good Samaritan, it is remarkable that Jesus chose a figure from Samaria to rescue the wounded Jew, despite the centuries-old hostility between Samaritans and Jews. What Jesus wanted to show by this gesture is that mercy transcends all borders and breaks down all walls. It is mercy showed toward the human being as such, regardless of race, religion, faith, color, language or ethnicity. The Good Samaritan, after having felt compassion, takes concrete initiatives toward the wounded Jew, one after the other: He heals his wounds, carries him on his animal, brings him to the inn, and foots the bill. Jesus concludes the parable by saying: "Go, and do you likewise."[7]

As the mercy of God knows no borders, so should the mercy of man be toward his neighbor and especially toward the weak, the oppressed, the migrants, the displaced, and those who live in the margin of society. This reminds us of the duty of the church to go to the peripheries as expressed by Pope Francis:

> The word of God constantly shows us how God challenges those who believe in him "to go forth." Each Christian and every community must discern the path that the Lord points out, but all of us are asked to obey his call to go forth from our own comfort zone in order to reach all the "peripheries" in need of the light of the Gospel.[8]

Divine mercy holds a central and fundamental place in Christianity. It is "the beauty of the saving love of God made manifest in Jesus Christ who died and rose from the dead."[9] Pope Francis summarizes the notion of mercy: Jesus is the primary face of God's mercy, which allows us to see into the eyes of our brothers and sisters and to continue loving them despite their faults:

> Jesus Christ is the face of the Father's mercy. . . . We need constantly to contemplate the mystery of mercy. It is a wellspring of joy, serenity, and peace. Our salvation depends on it. Mercy: the word reveals the very mystery of the Most Holy Trinity. Mercy: the

---

[7] Lk 10:37.

[8] Pope Francis, *Evangelii Gaudium (On the Proclamation of the Gospel in Today's World)* (November 24, 2013), no. 20.

[9] Ibid., no. 36.

ultimate and supreme act by which God comes to meet us. Mercy: the fundamental law that dwells in the heart of every person who looks sincerely into the eyes of his brothers and sisters on the path of life. Mercy: the bridge that connects God and man, opening our hearts to the hope of being loved forever despite our sinfulness.[10]

There are many things that can still be said regarding the notion of mercy in Christianity, but we will limit ourselves to the above discussion, which, I think, has allowed us to have some idea regarding this topic. After giving a brief overview of the notion of mercy in Christianity, I shall now proceed to give an overview of the notion of mercy in Islam.

The Islamic Notion of Mercy

An ordinary definition sometimes used to describe mercy is *grace or forgiveness given to those who may be punished*. However, it must be said that Islam has given mercy an even deeper meaning, making it an essential aspect of Muslim life, through which God[11] recompenses the repentant sinner. Mercy is among the qualities of God that befits God's majesty. Mercy is a quality of perfection in creatures because with mercy, creatures feel tenderness toward one another. For example, he who is strong has pity on him who is weak. The stronger one helps him and protects him against evil.

Mercy is found in human nature created by God, but this human nature can be erased because of sins. For this reason mercy disappears and makes the hardened heart no longer feel any mercy. Mercy is part of human nature and is a great quality that God has created in God's servant. Moreover, Islam commands Muslims to be merciful because Islam is a religion of mercy. The mercy of God, which God bestows on all God's creatures, is manifest in everything around us: in the sun that gives light and heat, as well as in the air and water that are essential to life. The Prophet Muhammad also promised God's reward for acts of kindness and compassion.

A large number of traditions,[12] moreover, underline the reciprocal love that exists between the true believer, humble and poor before his God, and Godself who considers him as a friend (*walī*). Muslims love to find

---

[10] Pope Francis, *Misericordiae Vultus* (2015), nos. 1 and 2.

[11] I have chosen to use "God" instead of "Allah" for the purpose of consistency, except in direct quotes and whenever the circumstance obliges.

[12] "Traditions" in Islam: These are words and deeds of the Prophet Muhammad as compiled in the "Hadiths."

this intimacy between God and Muhammad, whom the Qur'an says is sent as a *raḥma*, or mercy, from God: "And We sent you only in mercy for the universe."[13] This demonstrates that Islam is based on mercy and that God sent the Prophet Muhammad as mercy to all creatures without exception. God also says in the Qur'an: "There certainly has come to you a messenger from among yourselves. He is concerned by your suffering, anxious for your well-being, and gracious and merciful to the believers."[14]

The manners and behavior of the Prophet at every moment confirmed these verses, for he suffered many trials during his mission. It was with great gentleness that the Prophet invited people to Islam, and even if they wronged him, he asked God to forgive them for their ignorance and cruelty.

The Two Most Often Mentioned Names of God: Al-Rahmān and Al-Rahīm

At this point I would like to do a brief discussion of the two most often mentioned names of God in Islam: *al-Rahmān* and *al-Rahīm*.

Al-Rahmān describes the nature of God to be All-Merciful, while *al-Rahīm* describes God's acts of mercy toward God's creation. As one can observe, there is a subtle difference; that is, the first one refers to Godself and the second is God's attitude toward God's creatures. Nevertheless, this does not seem to create any major problem as creatures can call upon God by any of God's names, as expressed in the following verse: "Say (to the people): 'Call upon God or call upon the Merciful; whatever, name you call Him by, He has the most beautiful names.'"[15]

The term *raḥma* occurs more than one hundred times in the Qur'an.[16] This term characterizes something that is more than love (translated in Arabic as *ḥubb, wudd,* and their derivatives). It refers rather to the relationship between the Creator and the world. While the concept of ordinary

---

[13] Q 21:107. For most of this essay, I preferred to use the English translation of the Qur'an by Mustafa Khattab entitled *The Clear Quran*, accessible online.

[14] Q 9:128.

[15] Q 17:110.

[16] A total of 117 times, according to E. M. Badawi and M. Abdel Haleem, *Dictionary of Qur'anic Usage*, www.brillonline.com; or 114 times, according to D. Gimaret, "Raḥma," *Encyclopaedia of Islam*, 2nd ed., ed. P. Bearman, Th. Bianquis, C. E. Bosworth, E. van Donzel, and W. P. Heinrichs. These two are among the most frequently used names of God in the Qur'an: *Al-Rahmān* is mentioned 57 times, while *al-Rahīm* appears twice as frequently (114 times). In fact, an entire sūra of the Qur'an (Q 55) is called *Al-Rahmān*, that is, The Most Merciful. For more information, see Ida Zilio-Grandi, "Réflexions sur la Rahma dans la tradition religieuse Islamique," *Islamochristiana* 41 (2015).

love presupposes the inferiority of its object, *raḥma* is based on a relationship of reciprocity. The divine names of *al-Rahmān* and *al-Rahīm*, which occupy the second and third places after the name Allah in the lists of traditional "Most Beautiful Names," carry considerable weight in Islamic prayer, since they appear in the invocation formula known as *basmala*[17] or *tasmiya*.[18]

William Chittick provides us with an illustrative definition of these two terms: "'All-merciful' *(rahmān)* and 'Ever-merciful' *(rahīm)* are derived from the word *rahma*, which is variously translated as mercy, compassion, and benevolence. *Rahma* is an abstract noun derived from the concrete noun *rahim*, 'womb.' Mercy is the mother's attitude toward the fruit of her womb."[19] And:

> The close connection between mercy and motherhood is obvious in many sayings of the Prophet. For example, he said that when God created mercy, he created it in one hundred parts. He kept ninety-nine parts with himself and sent one part into the world. Mothers are devoted to their children and wild animals nurture their young because of this one part. On the day of resurrection, the Prophet added, God will rejoin this one part with the ninety-nine parts—all for the benefit of those who dwell in the posthumous realms, whether paradise or hell. Among the several points embedded in this saying is the typical stress on *tawhīd*, the assertion of the uniqueness of the divine reality that is the foundation of Islamic thought: What we experience as mercy, compassion, and love can only be a pale reflection of a tiny fraction of the real thing.[20]

According to the Hadith, the pronunciation of the divine names of *Al-Rahmān* and *al-Rahīm* elicit a divine response: "When the servant says: Praise be to Allah, the Lord of the universe, Allah the Most High says: My servant has praised Me. And when he (the servant) says: The Most Compassionate, the Merciful, Allah the Most High says: My servant has lauded Me."[21]

---

[17] The *Sūra al-Fatiha*, the prayer that Muslims recite at least 17 times a day, starts with the *Bismillah*: "In the Name of God, the Most Gracious, the most Merciful." This prayer is a constant reminder of the infinite mercy of God and his many blessings. Except for one chapter, all the chapters of the Qur'an begin with this phrase.

[18] Zilio-Grandi, "Réflexions sur la Rahma," 129–30.

[19] William Chittick, "The Islamic Notion of Mercy," *HuffPost* (December 14, 2010), transliterations mine.

[20] Ibid.

[21] "The Book of Prayers," *Sahih Muslim* 395a. https://sunnah.com/muslim:395a.

Moreover, God assures us that anyone who commits a sin will be forgiven if he sincerely repents and stops committing the same sin: "Your Lord has taken upon Himself to be Merciful. Whoever among you commits evil ignorantly or recklessly, then repents afterward and mends their ways, then Allah is truly All-Forgiving, Most Merciful."[22]

These names are a constant reminder to the Muslim that he is surrounded by divine mercy. Before eating, drinking, writing a letter, or doing anything important, Muslims say or write "In the name of God" in order to express their total dependence on God, to remember God's graces, and to show how they love God. This invocation of divine blessing, recited at the beginning of every mundane daily act, gives it importance, and purifies it. It is in this way that the Muslim believer's spirituality flourishes in everyday life.

Points of Convergence

Before proceeding to give my reflection on mission and interreligious dialogue, I would like to identify the points of convergence between the Christian and Islamic notions of mercy, based on what we already discussed.

I would say that both Christianity and Islam present to us the image of a merciful God, a Father who is ready to forgive, although the concept of a God of retribution and vengeance may be a bit stronger in Islam. Moreover, both notions promote the idea of justice. In the end time God will reward those who have been obedient to him and punish those who were not respectful of him.

It is also clear that God's mercy in both notions inspires the desire to embrace the whole of humanity. In other words, there is a universal aspect wherein discrimination does not exist. God looks at the heart and not at the color, race, ethnic group, economic, or the social status of people. Jesus's missionary work clearly paints the image of a God who is near to those who call upon God, especially the poor, the needy, the suffering, and the forgotten.

The notion of mercy in both religions also presents a God who respects the freedom of each human being. Nevertheless, God guides them and leads them to the straight path. Though God is more of a transcendent God in Islam, God still watches over God's creatures and does not abandon them. God treats them with justice and equality.

---

[22] Q 6:54.

Jean-Marie Gaudeul warns us, though, regarding the danger of creating the notions of the God of Love in Christianity and the God-Judge of Islam. He says that there is a need

> to avoid the schematism of an approach that would oppose the God of love of Christians and the God-Judge of Islam. Our God to all is a living God who constantly acts in the hearts of each other to tell them of his Father's love. His compassion crosses all the barriers that our dogmas and especially our classifications would raise between his mercy and our need to be loved by him.[23]

These points of convergence are just a few of the things we have seen in our short survey of both religions' notion of mercy. Nevertheless, they can already help us make a reflection on the mission of mercy in the context of interreligious dialogue.

Interreligious Dialogue and the Mission of Mercy

It was in 1970 that the Secretariat for Non-Muslims (now the Pontifical Council for Interreligious Dialogue) published a series of booklets that gave theoretical and practical indications regarding encounters with other religions in accordance with the demands of Vatican II. Among these was the booklet entitled *Guidelines for Dialogue between Christians and Muslims*.[24] After ten years (1980) a new edition was released; its publication was entrusted to Fr. Maurice Borrmans, a former professor at the Pontifical Institute for Arabic and Islamic Studies in Rome. This booklet contains many valuable points that are extremely useful, even today, especially for those who engage in dialogue with Muslims. I would like to enumerate some of them:

1. God invites the followers of Islam and Jesus "to draw lessons from their history which will help them realize that by following the path of

---

[23] Jean-Marie Gaudeul, "Le Dieu miséricordieux dans l'islam" (April 13, 2021), *Frontieresblog,* my translation.

[24] Pontifical Council for Interreligious Dialogue, *Interreligious Documents I: Guidelines for Dialogue between Christians and Muslims*, ed. Maurice Borrmans, trans. R. Marston Speight (New York: Paulist Press, 1981).

dialogue, they will be able to give a better witness to cooperate peacefully in service to God and humanity."[25]

2. Vatican II asked Catholics "to rediscover the apostolic requirements of an open dialogue in which the participants fully accept each other and share together both the content of their faith and the values of their tradition,"[26] since Christians and Muslims today find themselves interacting with each other "in a great variety of historical situations and personal circumstances."[27]

3. It has been a common experience that "many people talk about dialogue without a good understanding of its requirements and its methods. It has nothing to do with the extremes, either of a *facile syncretism* that would make all religions alike, or an *uncompromising polemic* that would deny that different religions can ever meet each other."[28]

4. Dialogue in the context of faith encounter, is "rather, *a daring adventure* engaged in by people desiring mutual enrichment from their different ways, fellowship in sharing common values and openness to whatever way the Lord might speak to them in the intimacy of their conscience."[29]

5. Christians are invited to "develop a spirit of dialogue marked with respect and love as well as with intelligence and understanding."[30] This is because "Christians who want to be faithful to the Gospel cannot be indifferent to a true encounter with those who, although they do not have the same faith, are nevertheless seeking to honor God as they proceed on their particular way toward him."[31]

6. When engaging in dialogue, *one must avoid doctrinal rigidity or a polemical spirit*. Christians "must explore, under the Spirit's guidance, any possible ways of convergence between them and Muslims."[32] It is important, before

---

[25] Ibid., 9. In fact, in history, Christians and Muslims were very close to each other, even during the life of the Prophet. This is what I insist on when I share about interreligious dialogue. It is worth noting that it was a Christian, Waraqa ibn Nawfal, who was among the first to say that it was indeed the angel of God who revealed the verses of the Qur'an to the Prophet. A Nestorian monk, Bahira, recognized that Muhammad was really the Prophet sent by God after he saw a sign between his shoulders. Muhammad also had a Christian wife, Mary the Copt, with whom he had a son, Ibrahim, who died at only eight months. It was said that Muhammad loved Mary very much.

[26] Ibid., 10.
[27] Ibid.
[28] Ibid., emphasis added.
[29] Ibid., emphasis added.
[30] Ibid.
[31] Ibid.
[32] Ibid.

engaging in dialogue, to make the gospel our rule and ideal. There is a need to constantly emphasize the common values that unite Christians and Muslims at all levels, both of their experience of God and of their service to humanity.

7. It is the purpose of dialogue to essentially seek "a better understanding of one another, a deepening of one's faith and religious awareness, a more zealous and single-minded quest for the will of God and conversion to the Lord, the One who calls us all into question, who pardons and who transforms."[33] Dialogue, therefore, "*cannot have as its purpose the will to 'convert' the other person to one's own religion at any price or to try to make them doubt the faith in which they were raised.*"[34] Rather, those who believe in dialogue "compete" with one another in doing good works, as expressed in the Qur'an: "So, compete with one another in doing good. To Allah you will all return, then He will inform you of the truth regarding your differences."[35]

Dialogue is vast and diverse. In order to provide a direction in our interfaith encounters, the church has identified four forms of dialogue: (1) dialogue of life; (2) dialogue of action; (3) dialogue of theological exchange; and (4) dialogue of religious experience.[36] Knowing these gives us the assurance that dialogue can be carried out in many forms according to one's own charism, situation, ability, and context. It is also important to recall the words Pope Emeritus Benedict XVI spoke at a meeting with organizations for interfaith dialogue in Jerusalem in 2009:

> But we know that our differences need never be misrepresented as an inevitable source of friction or tension either between ourselves or in society at large. Rather, they provide a wonderful opportunity for people of different religions to live together in profound respect, esteem and appreciation, encouraging one another in the ways of God.[37]

Being open to dialogue means being absolutely consistent with one's own religious tradition. Openness to others should never be separated

---

[33] Ibid.

[34] Ibid., 11, emphasis added.

[35] Q 5:48.

[36] See Pontifical Council for Interreligious Dialogue, *Dialogue and Proclamation: Reflection and Orientations on Interreligious Dialogue and the Proclamation of the Gospel of Jesus Christ* (1991).

[37] Pope Benedict XVI, *Address during the Meeting with Organizations for Interreligious Dialogue,* Jerusalem, May 11, 2009.

from fidelity to Christ and the gospel. This unconditional adherence to Christ does not prevent Christians in dialogue from conversing with the exponents of other religions.

Going back to the theme of this essay, I realized that the best way to present interreligious dialogue is as *a mission of mercy*: presenting God as a merciful God, removing fear, biases, and prejudices against the other religions, and being open, that is, having the desire to know more about them. We have to counter the ignorance that breeds all this negativity. It is through this mission of mercy that we can begin to dialogue with them. Yet, this process is not only applicable when it comes to dialogue with other religions. Respect, tolerance, openness, humility, patience, and love are just some of the many virtues that we nurture even in our own families, work places, religious communities, and all areas of encounter.

Jesus's way of imparting mercy in his mission was not to insist on his superiority, as when he humbly encountered the Samaritan woman. Indeed, it is normal for us to speak of Christianity as the best religion, which should certainly be the case or else we would have chosen to affiliate ourselves with another religion or convert to it. However, insisting that our religion is superior, and that others are inferior, might not be a good approach. This is because interreligious dialogue believes that each religion offers its own path to salvation to its adherents.

Conclusion

In dialogue, we need to start from the things that are similar and familiar to both parties, rather than from our differences. This encounter demands creating an attitude of respect and love, considering that God loves all human beings, regardless of culture, race, or religion. The model of interreligious dialogue for all of us Christians is Jesus himself, who, in many instances in the Gospels, reached out to the non-Jews, the Gentiles, and the marginalized. This is because he carried out with mercy and compassion the mission entrusted to him by God the Father. Everywhere he went, he was a model of humility and respect.

I have a favorite Quranic verse that expresses concretely the way Muslims look at Christians, especially their religious leaders. This remains as one of the most touching Islamic texts that I have ever read throughout my journey of Islamic studies so far:

Certainly, you will find the most violent of people in enmity for those who believe (to be) the Jews and those who are polytheists, and you will certainly find the nearest in friendship to those who believe (to be) those who say: We are Christians; this is because there are priests and monks among them and because they do not behave proudly.[38]

When a missionary engages in interreligious dialogue, part of the mission of mercy is to appreciate the value of each person, just as he or she is, and to recognize the presence of God in him or her. Authentic dialogue gives one the skill to understand the other religion from the point of view of its adherents. Once they feel that their beliefs and practices are respected, a positive atmosphere for dialogue is created.

Interreligious dialogue, as an aspect of mission, is not at all contrary to evangelization. It is part and parcel of it, as it bases itself on a solid witnessing of one's faith, although it is clear that there could be obstacles and setbacks along the path. Indeed, the primary prerequisite before engaging in dialogue is a solid faith in God and knowledge of one's own religious beliefs and convictions, which can, in fact, be further enhanced as one engages deeper into dialogue. It is only then that one can be able to say that the person has entered into a more authentic dialogue with his or her brothers and sisters of other faiths.

> **John Mallare, CICM**, is a missionary priest of the Congregation of the Immaculate Heart of Mary, currently assigned as parochial vicar in Dakar, Senegal, and is guest professor at CICM–Maryhill School of Theology in Manila. He earned a doctorate degree in Arabic and Islamic Studies from the Pontifical Institute for Arabic and Islamic Studies in Rome, Italy.

---

[38] Q 5:82. Qur'an translation by Shakir, https://corpus.quran.com/.

Eastern Religions
Trusting Christianity's "Incarnational" Thrust

Gerard Hall, SM

In most conceptions of the world religious map, Judaism, Christianity, and Islam—the three religious traditions founded on Abraham—are themselves Eastern religions, emerging from Palestine and the Middle East. Although in time Christianity became primarily a "Western religion," associated with the Roman Empire and Greek thought, today it is called to deep dialogue with the Eastern traditions.[1] This is challenging from a multitude of viewpoints.

First, there is the reality of European colonization, which too often went hand in hand with Christian evangelization and, despite some notable exceptions, showed little interest in dialogue with Eastern religious thought and practice. Second, there is a naive understanding of the Abrahamic traditions as monotheism—believers in the Oneness of God—versus the Asian predilection for polytheism—believers in multiple divinities. And third, there is the sometimes called postmodern realization that religions express incommensurable, mutually exclusive, respectively contradictory, and finally unbridgeable values and beliefs that no dialogue can resolve or overarching theory illuminate.

Moreover, we need to make clear from the start that just as there is no overarching Christianity—but multiple Christian churches, doctrines, denominations, and cultural expressions—Eastern religious traditions are even more profoundly expressive of the multitude of spiritualities in the myriad Asian and other cultures dotting our planet. Furthermore, there is the never-ending discussion of what constitutes religion as distinct from philosophies and spiritualities that may not explicitly articulate belief in a

---

[1] For the purposes of this essay, Eastern religions will be restricted to the non-Abrahamic religions of East Asia.

sacred, transcendent power. After all, the word *religion* itself is a relatively modern Western construct that does not necessarily correlate well with Eastern spiritual traditions. However, rather than seeking to resolve these somewhat academic questions, our approach will be simply to trace some significant examples of mainly Roman Catholic practitioners of interreligious dialogue with selected Eastern traditions.

Christianity's "Incarnational" Thrust

My fundamental conviction is that Christianity's "incarnational" thrust—even in times of an exaggerated sense of Christian superiority according to an exclusive reading of *extra ecclesiam nulla salus*[2]—kept the embers at least partly alight for genuine encounter and the call to dialogue with other religions. After all, it has long been recognized that the success of the early Christian movement was due to its ability to inculturate in, learn from, and dialogue with the ancient Greco-Roman world. As we shall see, even at the high point of post-Reformation, Catholic-Christian missionary activity (from the sixteenth century onward) where the main model followed the *tabula rasa* approach—that is, the wholesale replacing of local, cultural, and religious beliefs and practices with European-Christian ones—there were nevertheless notable exceptions that sought to accommodate the Christian gospel to the ordinary lives and beliefs of the people. This entailed learning the languages of the local peoples and, in the Asian situation, learning from the deep experiences of the Confucian, Buddhist, Taoist, Shinto, Hindu, Jain, and other spiritual-religious traditions.

I need to acknowledge that my own interest in interreligious dialogue with Eastern religions arose from my introduction to the life and writings of Raimon Panikkar (1918–2010)—sometimes called the Apostle of Interreligious Dialogue.[3] Born in Barcelona, Panikkar was the child of an Indian Hindu father and a Catalan Catholic mother. Although educated in Western philosophy and theology and ordained a Roman Catholic priest, in his mid-thirties he made his way to India. Among his most important experiences were his encounters with the three most significant figures associated with depth Hindu-Christian dialogue: Jules Monchanin

---

[2] The term *extra ecclesiam nulla salus* (outside the church no salvation) is attributed to St. Cyprian in the third century and was explicitly taught by the Fourth Lateran Council (1215) and the Council of Florence (1442).

[3] See Joseph Prabhu, "Raimon Panikkar: 'Apostle of Interfaith Dialogue,'" *National Catholic Reporter* (August 31, 2010).

(1895–1957), Henri Le Saux (Abhishiktananda) (1910–73), and Dom Bede Griffiths (1906–93). Albeit in diverse ways, these Benedictine pioneers of interreligious dialogue, who cofounded Shantivanam Ashram in Tamil Nadu, were attempting to blend Hindu and Christian mystical experience in a manner they hoped would transform both religions. Learning from them, we will further examine below Panikkar's approach to interreligious dialogue, especially with Hinduism and Buddhism.

The "Accommodational Approach" to Mission

We need to acknowledge earlier examples of Christian encounters with Eastern traditions.[4] Perhaps the best known is Matteo Ricci (1552–1610) and his Jesuit companions, who sought to express the Christian-Catholic faith with the aid of Confucian symbols, rituals, and insights. Ricci did not actually interpret Confucianism as a religion, which enabled him to "inculturate" and "accommodate" Christian belief and practice in an enticing way for scholarly Chinese Confucians. Another Italian Jesuit, Robert de Nobili (1577–1656), made similar accommodations in India to Hindu customs, even to the point of accepting the ancient caste system. The French Jesuit Alexander de Rhodes (1591–1660) moved in a similar direction with Buddhism in Vietnam to the extent of writing Vietnamese in an adapted Roman alphabet that remains the national script today. In various ways, Ricci, de Nobili, and de Rhodes are precursors of what came to be called the Catholic inculturation paradigm, whereby the missionary is guru, scholar, and dialogue partner.[5] Of course these dialogue precursors remained people of their time with their strengths and shortsightedness. Ricci, for example, had no time for either Buddhism or Taoism. It should also be noted that he and de Nobili were mainly involved in dialogue with the intelligentsia rather than the common people, whereas de Rhodes dialogued much more with the common folk. Yet they were all committed to a Christianity that could be much more radically inculturated in Asian traditions.

For a variety of reasons these early attempts to dialogue with Asian cultures, traditions, and religions—the "gentle way" or "accommodational

---

[4] See Stephen Bevans and Roger Schroeder, *Constants in Context* (Maryknoll, NY: Orbis Books, 2004), 183–95. Also note Ambrose Mong, *Accommodation and Acceptance* (Cambridge: James Clark and Co., 2015), 7–30; Peter Phan, *Mission and Catechesis* (Maryknoll, NY: Orbis Books, 1998).

[5] Bevans and Schroeder, *Constants in Context*, 195.

approach" to mission—came to a relatively abrupt end due to disputes among and within the religious missionary orders and the infamous Rites Controversy of the late seventeenth and early eighteenth centuries.[6] At base was the question of just how "European" Christianity needed to be. The accommodation approach was seen as "selling out" and compromising Christian faith; yet, for the accommodationists, the *tabula rasa* approach clearly denigrated non-Western cultures. Questions were particularly directed to missionaries in China and India in relation to the use of the word *God*, ancestor veneration (China) and caste system (India), and the extent to which the Christian sacraments could be adapted to local cultures. Eventually, the accommodational approach was condemned by Pope Clement XI, leading to Emperor Kangxi's expulsion of Christian missionaries from China. It was not an uncommon scenario throughout history, once dialogue had broken down not only between the gospel and cultures, or Rome and Asia, but also among the Roman Catholic missionaries themselves.

The Dialogue of Spiritual and Religious Encounter

If we fast forward to the twentieth century, profound historical changes—two World Wars, economic depression, rise (and fall) of communist and fascist regimes, and postcolonial independence movements, to name a few—presented new and diverse challenges to all religions and cultures, East and West. The Catholic desire to reassess its life and mission in this fast-changing world was expressed in Pope John XXIII's calling of the Second Vatican Council (1962–65). The council's shortest document, but among the most ground-breaking, is *Nostra Aetate*, which totally recharts a Christian approach to other religions in a positive way, noting that "the Catholic Church rejects nothing of what is true and holy in these religions."[7] Although only four religions are specifically named, these include the two major Eastern traditions of Hinduism and Buddhism. Moreover, Christians are encouraged to "enter into dialogue and collaboration" with representatives of these various religions. This was a watershed moment in official Catholic teaching, which developed further into the call to "interreligious dialogue" in the years since the council.[8]

---

[6] Ibid., 192–95.

[7] Vatican II, *Nostra Aetate (Declaration on the Relation of the Church to Non-Christian Religions)* (1965), no. 2.

[8] See, for example, Gerard Hall, "Catholic Church Teaching on the Relationship to Other Religions since Vatican II," *Australian eJournal of Theology* 1 (2003); and idem, "The Role of Interfaith Dialogue in Recent Catholic Theology" (2008).

While there are many examples of later-twentieth-century East-West religious dialogue, we shall begin with Raimon Panikkar who, in the footsteps of his Benedictine forebears in India, focuses on the dialogue of spiritual and religious encounter—or what the Catholic Church would later call the dialogue of religious experience in contrast to the dialogues of life, action, and theological exchange.[9] In his writings from the late 1960s onward, Panikkar articulated his "multireligious experience" in his now-famous words: "I 'left' (Europe) as a Christian; I 'found' myself a Hindu; and I 'return' as a Buddhist, without having ceased to be a Christian."[10] Increasingly, Panikkar became less concerned with providing an intellectual basis for what came to be called religious pluralism, suggesting instead that the meeting of the world's traditions is "mythic" in view of the emerging reality of the urgent call to global solidarity, all the while acknowledging radical differences.

Panikkar's *The Unknown Christ of Hinduism* outlined a "functional similarity" between Ishvara in Hinduism and Christ in Christianity.[11] While the identification of Christ with the historical Jesus is at the heart of Christian faith, Panikkar also insists that Christ, as the Alpha and Omega, speaks not only through Israel's prophets but also through the non-Abrahamic religions, including the Hindu sages. Christians and Hindus are also "functionally similar" in seeking to be united with the Absolute—albeit diversely interpreted as the personal God or an impersonal Brahman. In spite of the very real differences in Christian and Hindu belief, for Panikkar this does not preclude the more profound religious encounter in the presence of the Spirit of God. For Panikkar, such a meeting or encounter is itself a religious act performed in faith, hope, and love. He calls this "*intra*-religious dialogue,"[12] in which the focus is not on the conversion of the other, but of oneself, through the awakening of shared if divergent religious experience.[13]

---

[9] See Pontifical Council for Interreligious Dialogue and Pontifical Congregation for Evangelization, *Dialogue and Proclamation* (1991).

[10] R. Panikkar, "Faith and Belief: A Multireligious Experience," *Anglican Theological Review* 52, no. 4 (October 1971): 220.

[11] R. Panikkar, *The Unknown Christ of Hinduism* (London: Darton, Longman & Todd, 1964); rev. ed. *The Unknown Christ of Hinduism: Towards an Ecumenical Christophany* (Maryknoll, NY: Orbis Books, 1981).

[12] R. Panikkar, *The Intra-Religious Dialogue* (New York: Paulist Press, 1978; rev. 1999).

[13] For other approaches to Christian-Hindu theological dialogue see, for example, Bede Griffiths, *Christ in India: Essays Towards a Hindu-Christian Dialogue* (Springfield, IL: Templegate, 1983); Francis Clooney, *Hindu God, Christian God: How Reason Helps Break Down the Boundaries between Religions* (Oxford, UK: Oxford University Press, 2001).

God as Beyond Both Being and Non-Being

Panikkar was always suspicious of Western theology's overenthusiasm for equating God with Being. He offset this with reference to the mystical-apophatic[14] dimension of religious experience, which recognizes God as beyond both Being and Non-Being. Reflecting on the trinitarian God of Christian faith, Panikkar presents three distinct spiritualities in relation to the Persons of the Trinity.[15]

1. The apophatic spirituality of the Father, represented by the Father's silence—"everything the Father is he transmits to the Son"[16]—expressed powerfully in Buddhist emphasis on *nirvana* (liberation from desire) and *sunyata* (emptiness) as well as the Buddha's "noble silence" regarding God.[17]
2. Christianity and the other Abrahamic religions are said to stress the personalist spiritualities of the Son who mediates God's Word.[18]
3. The spirituality of the Spirit, understood as the revelation of the immanent God evident in the world's cosmic traditions, is most advanced in the Hindu *advaitic* (non-dual) approach to the divine mystery.

In a different language, Panikkar speaks of the "cosmotheandric experience" in which the divine, human, and cosmic realities are interrelated, disclosing infinite possibilities for new life and freedom.[19] This is also most profoundly expressed in the Buddhist notion of the interrelatedness or "radical relativity" (*pratítyasmutpáda*) of all and every reality—cosmic, human, and divine.

In some ways dialogue with Buddhism needs to take precedence in East Asia in view of its spread from Indian soil to become such a significant

---

[14] Negative or apophatic theology stresses that God transcends all human concepts. Key spokesperson for this tradition is fifth/sixth-century Syrian monk Pseudo-Dionysius, who writes of the profound unknowability of God.

[15] R. Panikkar, *The Trinity and the Religious Experience of Man* (London: Darton, Longman & Todd, 1973). Rowan Williams describes this work as "one of the best and least read meditations on the Trinity in (the twentieth) century"; see his *On Christian Theology* (Maiden, MA: Blackwell, 2000), 167.

[16] Panikkar, *The Trinity and the Religious Experience,* 46.

[17] R. Panikkar, *The Silence of God: The Answer of the Buddha* (Maryknoll, NY: Orbis Books, 1989).

[18] There is also an apophatic aspect of the personalist spirituality of the Son evident in Jesus's words of felt abandonment on the cross—"My God, my God why have you forsaken me?" (Mk 15:34)—which is then transformed into Jesus's cry of love: "Into your hands I commend my spirit" (Lk 23:46).

[19] R. Panikkar, *The Cosmotheandric Experience: Emerging Religious Consciousness* (Maryknoll, NY: Orbis Books, 1993).

presence throughout China, Japan, Tibet, Korea, Mongolia, Myanmar, Thailand, Cambodia, Laos, Vietnam, Sri Lanka, Taiwan, and Singapore. In this sense Buddhism in its multiple forms—Mahayana, Theravada, Vajrayana, and so on—is rightly acclaimed as "the most Asian among world religions."[20] It should also be noted that adherence to Buddhism does not preclude adherence to other religious or spiritual approaches such as Confucianism in China, Taoism in Korea, or Shintoism in Japan, whereas the Western mind, with its emphasis on belief and doctrine, tends to be suspicious of mixing religious traditions (syncretism). Perhaps, this is less of an issue with the Eastern emphasis on ritual, harmony, and right practice. It is also less of a problem for Westerners who focus on faith and religious experience.[21] However, as noted, we are also faced with the reality of the Buddha's silence in naming the Ultimate Reality, which makes Buddhism a nontheistic faith without, however, falling into crude atheism. The Sri Lankan Jesuit Aloysius Pieris opened up the possibilities—he would add "necessity"—of (Theravada) Buddhist-Christian dialogue by identifying diverse but complementary insights of each tradition while also focusing on the concrete reality of people's lives in Asia, characterized by "profound religiousness and an overwhelming poverty."[22]

A "Threefold Dialogue" with Asia

Moving beyond Panikkar's "cosmic trust" or "cosmotheandric confidence" in the encounter of Christianity with Asian traditions, Pieris focuses on the practical import of improving people's lives. This is also recognized by the Federation of Asian Bishops' Conferences (FABC) and Asian theologians who speak of the need for a "threefold dialogue" with Asia's poor and their cultures and religions—that is, liberation, inculturation, and interreligious dialogue belong together.[23] Pieris specifically developed what he calls "An Asian Theology of Liberation" which focuses on the suffering and struggle of Asia's poor.[24] Whether in dialogue with Buddhism or other Asian religions, Pieris emphasizes Christianity's need to adopt—or to inculturate—an Eastern spirituality evident, for example, in ascetical

---

[20] Mong, *Accommodation and Acceptance*, 82.
[21] See, for example, Paul Knitter, *Without the Buddha, I Could Not Be a Christian* (Oxford, UK: Oneworld Publications, 2009).
[22] Aloysius Pieris, *Love Meets Wisdom* (Maryknoll, NY: Orbis Books, 1990), 35.
[23] See, for example, Peter Phan, *In Our Own Tongues* (Maryknoll, NY: Orbis Books, 2003), 13–31.
[24] Aloysius Pieris, *An Asian Theology of Liberation* (Edinburgh: T & T Clark, 1988).

and contemplative practices and monastic forms. Such a spirituality, he believes, decenters the ego's thirst for power and greed for earthly possessions. This liberationist approach enables the church to realize it cannot fulfill its evangelizing mission unless it becomes a church *of* and *with* the poor on Asian soil—and a church that is called to be a "community" and "sacrament" of interreligious dialogue.

The complexity of Asian religiousness is increasingly evident if we turn our attention to Japan, where multiple forms of Mahayana Buddhism (noting such diverse schools as Zen and Pure Land) are practiced alongside or in conjunction with ancient Shintoism. Even more complicated is the fact that Zen Buddhism is an adaptation of China's Chan Buddhism, which adopted Taoist and Confucian rituals and ideas. In this sense, well before the Christians were involved, we can recognize the profound interaction of religious traditions throughout East Asia. Following Japan's defeat in World War II, the important dialogue with the West was one that promoted reconciliation. While many Western missionaries moved to Japan with the idea of promoting reconciliation in the context of Christian mission, they soon found themselves involved in dialogue with the religious profundity of Japanese culture. This led to deepening their interest in—and eventually depth encounter with—Zen Buddhism in East Asia. In brief, Zen represents the more mystical, nondual path of Buddhism in a manner similar to Christian mysticism, Sufi Islam, and Advaita Hinduism.

The many twentieth-century practitioners of Zen-Christian dialogue of religious experience include Jesuits Enomiya-Lassalle, Heinrich Dumoulin, William Johnston, and Kakichi Kadowaki, as well as Cistercians Thomas Merton and Thomas Keating. Keating, for example, developed a Christian approach to what he termed "centering prayer,"[25] based on zazen, by promoting the Zen-Buddhist lotus position for meditation. Less well known are two Japanese, Shigeto Oshida and Ichiro Okumura. They were educated as Zen Buddhists pre–World War II and converted to the Christian-Catholic faith (the former a Dominican, the latter a Carmelite) and, in time, became Japanese forerunners of Christian-Zen mystical meditation practices.[26] The more academic approach to interreligious dialogue, including Zen-Christian dialogue, which focuses on theological exchange, is especially promoted by the Nanzan Institute for

---

[25] Thomas Keating, *The Foundations for Centering Prayer and the Christian Contemplative Life* (London: Bloomsbury Academic Press, 2002).

[26] Information given to the author by Michael Jacques, SM, Sophia University, Tokyo, July 3, 2021.

Religion and Culture (Nanzan University of SVD, Nagoya), the Oriens Institute for Religious Research (Scheut-CICM, Tokyo), and the Institute for Christian Culture (Sophia University, Tokyo). In this context we should also acknowledge the Catholic Church's 2020 message "Christian and Shinto Followers Together: Protecting All Life."[27]

While this chapter has concentrated on the dialogue of spiritual experience with some attention to the dialogue of theological exchange, we need to realize it is primarily the dialogues of life and action that are catalysts for these other forms of dialogue. We hope we have also gained some insight into the fact that accommodation, acceptance, or integration of ideas and practices from other "religions" has been the norm rather than the exception of Asian religious life. Christianity's mostly later-day arrival on Asian soil has seen a mixture of success and failure in attempted dialogue with Asia's established spiritual traditions. We have not had the space to examine the very real differences and disputes that Catholic and other theologians express in terms of the challenges—and what some still see as dangers—of interreligious dialogue.[28] Nor have we examined the approaches of the Eastern traditions themselves, noting the enthusiasm of some—such as His Holiness the Dalai Lama and Thich Nhat Hanh—while many still remain suspicious of dialogue with (Western) Christianity. Given these and other issues, what we can say is that Catholic Christianity is undergoing a profound shift in its approach to mission, which it now understands to include inculturation, liberation, and interreligious dialogue. This raises the further question of how Christianity will emerge as a result of its ongoing dialogue with Eastern religions.[29]

Conclusion: The Jordan, the Tiber, and the Ganges

If we take Panikkar's answer to the above question, he will remind us that the history of Christian faith in its relationship to other religions is symbolically expressed by the three sacred rivers: the Jordan, the Tiber,

---

[27] Pontifical Council for Interreligious Dialogue, "Christian and Shinto Followers Together: Protecting All Life" (2020).

[28] Peter Phan deals with this in terms of different approaches to doing theology in *The Joy of Religious Pluralism* (Maryknoll, NY: Orbis Books, 2017).

[29] Note especially Peter Phan, *Christianity with an Asian Face* (Maryknoll, NY: Orbis Books, 2003); idem, *Being Religious Interreligiously* (Maryknoll, NY: Orbis Books, 2004). Also see "What Christians Can Learn" [Part III], in *Interfaith Dialogue: Global Perspectives*, ed. Edmund Chia (New York: Palgrave Macmillan, 2016), 117–79; and Raimon Panikkar, *The Experience of God: Icons of the Mystery* (Minneapolis: Fortress Press, 2006).

and the Ganges.[30] Jesus himself, his disciples, and the first converts were all Jews, metaphorically if not literally baptized in the River Jordan. Christianity was a Jewish sect; one had to be a Jew or adopt Jewishness to be authentically Christian. However, Christians were soon challenged to cross the River Jordan if they were to communicate the Christian faith in non-Jewish cultures. This is represented by the River Tiber, the historical and political river of Rome and the West, which increasingly identified the church with the empire, transforming "Christianity" into "Christendom." Now, the invitation is for Christianity to cross from the River Tiber to the River Ganges, a symbol especially of the world's Eastern traditions, where one learns to be authentically Christian in dialogue with, respect for, and appreciation of the sacred *christic* mystery throughout creation and all the world's traditions. This is the attitude of "Christianness," which, while not resolving all the intellectual challenges associated with interreligious dialogue, appreciates that depth encounter with the religious "other" is no longer a luxury, but a necessity, for our increasingly globalized world.

Gerard Hall, SM, is an Australian Marist Father and former head of theology and associate professor at Australian Catholic University, Brisbane, Australia. He is a student of Raimon Panikkar (the Apostle of Interreligious Dialogue), member of the International Academy of Practical Theology, and a founding member and former president of the Association of Practical Theology in Oceania.

---

[30] Raimon Panikkar, "The Jordan, the Tiber, and the Ganges: Three Kairological Moments of Christic Self-Consciousness," in *The Myth of Christian Uniqueness*, ed. John Hick and Paul Knitter (London: SCM Press, 1987), 89–116.

Indigenous Religions
Religious Congregations and Indigenous Australians

ROBYN REYNOLDS, OLSH

As religious congregations and members of religious institutes, being engaged with Aboriginal Christians today means being respectfully present in solidarity, leaning more toward receiving and learning rather than initiating, implementing, or even "empowering," not to mention "converting."

This article attempts to pay careful attention—*akangkweirreme*[1]—to aspects of the engagement between religious congregations in Australia and the nation's First Peoples, namely, the Indigenous Australians.

Pope John Paul II's memorable words invite such attention: "The Church in Australia will not be fully the Church Jesus wants her to be until you have made your contribution to her life and until that contribution has been joyfully received by others."[2] These words deserve to be seriously heard by the nation, as well as by the church. Religious congregations also might accept the challenge in considering to what extent they may have heard and welcomed the contribution and the voice of Indigenous people. Catholic missionaries were part of a history that Australians generally still struggle to acknowledge. Australia is the oldest living culture in the world, and while it has become a multicultural, multireligious nation, its relationship with the First Nations Peoples remains uneasy.

Stories of dialogue—of life, experience, theology, and action—are, and continue to be, complex and potentially dangerous, as well as liberating. It is important to acknowledge that some dialogues have *not* caused life to flourish. On the contrary, some encounters and significant engagements between religious and First Nations Peoples have stifled life: the stolen-generations stories, for example, and stories of grave abuse. There is a

---

[1] The word comes from the Central Australian language, Arrernte.
[2] Pope John Paul II, "Address to the Aboriginal People," in *The Pope in Australia* (Homebush, NSW: St. Paul Publications, 1986), 166–72 at 172, no. 13.

need to recognize and remember where little regard was shown for the dignity of others, where there occurred denial or denigration of religion, culture, and language. Religious congregations and members of religious institutes know these stories too well.

In recent years religious congregations have made public apologies and have engaged in practices of repentance, reconciliation, and justice. The NATSICC (National Aboriginal and Torres Strait Island Catholic Council) has welcomed these efforts and worked in solidarity with the churches and with religious groups and congregations to advance better communication and dialogue. Aboriginal and Torres Strait Islander Australians, in their famous 2017 Uluru Statement,[3] called for a *Makaratta* (peace-restoring) treaty and for dialogue.

An article of this size, of course, does not attempt any historical or current overview, or any summary of the very significant encounters between First Nations Peoples and religious congregations. Furthermore, to select just a few congregations is a dangerous exercise, carrying the risk of offending those overlooked or of avoiding the wider or deeper stories. Some congregations not mentioned may have had a longer engagement, or one that was more influential, more damaging, or more positive. Who is to tell? The historian? The Indigenous person or community? The religious congregation? This article, from the perspective of a non-Indigenous female religious missionary and writer, is but one glimpse into the big story. Reflections here relate to aspects of the engagements and to what could be some future trends.

Dialogues of Life

Benedictine John Bede Polding was appointed as the first archbishop of Sydney in 1842. In 1849 he proclaimed that "the wretched unfortunate Aborigines of the country—the first occupants of the lands over which your flocks and herds now roam—have a very strong claim upon you. Nor will the Lord hold you innocent if you have not used your best endeavours to promote their temporal and eternal well-being." His brave, dangerous statement at Australia's first plenary council largely fell on deaf ears. Eugene Stockton has concluded that at the time, Catholics generally reflected the attitudes of the wider community—apathy, racism, pre-occupation with

---

[3]The Uluru Statement was formulated and presented at the First Nations National Constitutional Convention in Alice Springs, Australia, on May 26, 2017.

their own internal or more immediate interests.[4] In his often-quoted paper, "Maverick Missionaries," however, Stockton does pay careful attention to the involvement of religious congregations and their members, living and working alongside Aboriginal people since 1843.[5]

Fortunately, many religious congregations and their members in Australia's early colonial history, despite wrongs that would ensue, did not need a later Vatican reminder of a truth which recognized that "consecrated life is at the very heart of the church as a decisive element for her mission."[6]

The arrival and engagement of women's congregations are often not included in the early written records. The foundations of missions certainly were generally the work of male religious, although often the presence and influence of religious sisters were simultaneous. But such was not always the case. The charisms, as well as the particular personal skills and contexts of religious women, often led them to respond to the needs of people in particular circumstances. The St. John of God Sisters, for example, and the Daughters of Our Lady of the Sacred Heart, set up leprosariums to serve and to walk alongside Aboriginal people suffering with Hansen's Disease.[7] Dialogues of life!

Pope Francis continues to challenge consecrated religious to receive and learn from the gifts and the wisdom of those who are poor, vulnerable, or struggling. And the tables are often turned as the religious realize it is they themselves who are being ministered to or invited to be transformed.

Margaret Tucker records a historic celebration in 1983—a coming together of East and West Catholic Aboriginal peoples in the Kimberleys. Sixteen religious orders are named in the story. She concludes her description honoring "the Aboriginal people who accepted the strangers and their new message, who adjusted to domination, assimilation, integration, and who finally, took back responsibility for their own lives and their own faith and became real partners with their companions in the

---

[4] Eugene Stockton, "Maverick Missionaries," in *Aboriginal Australians and Christian Missions*, ed. Tony Swain and Deborah Rose Bird (Bedford Park, SA: Australian Association for the Study of Religions, 1988), 202–3.

[5] Ibid., 201–10. These congregations included Passionists in Minjerriba, North Stradbroke Island, Qld (1843); Benedictines in New Norcia, WA (1847); Jesuits in Australia's Northern Territory (1882); and Daughters of Our Lady of the Sacred Heart, Thursday Island, Qld (1886).

[6] Pope John Paul II, apostolic exhortation *Vita Consecrata* (1996), no. 3.

[7] Stockton, "Maverick Missionaries," 201–10: Fantome Island on Palm Isl. Qld (1928) and Channel Island, Qld (1931); Daughters of Our Lady of the Sacred Heart; Derby (Bungarun), WA (1936); St. John of God Sisters; East Arm, NT (1955–1982); Daughters of Our Lady of the Sacred Heart.

Christian journey."[8] In her important research, and in the publication of her book, Tucker has given careful attention to the gains and losses in the dialogues of life.

In earlier days in the Kimberleys, an Indigenous women's religious congregation, Daughters of Mary, Queen of Apostles, had been formed in Beagle Bay and for some years (1938–50) was an active presence in the Kimberley region. "They lived the spirit of the gospel, but away from their home 'country,' they found it difficult to live the traditional monastic lifestyle, which was totally alien to the aboriginal culture and way of life."[9] What was the nature of the dialogue in this engagement, one wonders? Possibly the dialogue of life and of action was happening, but not the dialogue of a genuine, culturally appropriate religious experience, or of any real sharing of interreligious understandings and beliefs. When there is an integrity, a harmony, and interaction between the dialogues, there is, surely, more likelihood of human flourishing.

Dialogues of Experience

Since the late nineteenth century there have been members of religious congregations living in Aboriginal communities who have supported Indigenous leaders in the area of interreligious engagement and in the "dialogue of experience." Indigenous Catholics perform Kolumbaru healing rituals,[10] Tiwi funeral ceremonies, Wadeye baptism rites, smoking rituals from Yarrabah to Melbourne, and countless other sacred ceremonies across all states and territories throughout the country.[11] In some communities however, ceremonies were lost, hidden, or banned.[12] The words of Pope Francis came too late for some: "Let us not be quick

---

[8] Margaret Tucker, *From Patrons to Partners: A History of the Catholic Church in the Kimberleys* (Notre Dame, IN: University of Notre Dame, 1994), 201.

[9] Tucker writes: "Altogether about thirty-eight Aboriginal women entered the society and worked in all areas of the missions. Some of them stayed only a short time. Others stayed for years" (ibid., 115).

[10] The gathering, recorded in the film *Desert Healing*, describes engagement between the church and religious congregations (at the time the Jesuits, Mercy Sisters, and lay missionaries); it is a story of healing and reconciliation.

[11] Since 1911, missionary congregations such as the Missionaries of the Sacred Heart and the Daughters of Our Lady of the Sacred Heart have remained until today in Australia's Northern Territory.

[12] Stockton, "Maverick Missionaries," 201–10; John Harris, *One Blood: 200 Years of Aboriginal Encounter with Christianity: A Story of Hope* (Sutherland, NSW: Albatross Books 1990).

to describe as superstition or paganism, certain religious practices that arise spontaneously."[13]

A fine example of dialogues of experience can be seen at a national level, where, throughout Australia, Aboriginal Catholic Ministry (ACM) groups, along with NATSICC, continue to be supported by religious priests, sisters, and brothers. From communities as far apart as Tasmania and the Torres Strait, religious congregations are engaging with local Indigenous leaders in dialogue and practices around religious experience. The encounters take a very different shape from that of pre–Vatican II days, when they were often—on the part of many well-intentioned religious—patronizing and controlling.

Reflecting on the years following *Perfectae Caritatis*,[14] Brian Terry speaks of "religious as dialogue."[15] His insights sit very well with the wisdom and the hopes expressed in Indigenous Australians' Uluru Statement, which calls for their voice to be heard, and for truth telling. Terry's argument is that "to dialogue about God with the world, we must first see and name ourselves."[16] Genuine dialogue is more about who we are rather than what we do—or even what we may say. Terry goes even further than suggesting such dialogue will bring about change for those involved, but that in fact we ourselves must actually "be a dialogue because it is who we are, persons in radical faithfulness to the Other and to one another."[17] This personal integrity and honest truth telling is foundational for any genuine engagements in the Australian religious context.

Dialogue of Theology

Nungalinya[18] is an ecumenical training college for Aboriginal Australians in Darwin, Northern Territory. Over the years many religious congregations

---

[13] Pope Francis, post-synodal apostolic exhortation *Querida Amazonia* (2020), no. 78. John Fallon, MSC, wrote of his arrogance and ignorance, and of his strong objection to Tiwi cultural practices and objects; he acknowledged how, in his anger, at one time he destroyed some sacred *Pukanami* burial poles (John Fallon, MSC, "The Good Old Days," *Nelen Yubu* 48 [1991]: 12–16).

[14] Vatican II, *Perfectae Caritatis (Decree on the Adaptation and Renewal of Religious Life)* (1965).

[15] Brian Terry, SA, "Half Way Home: A Reflection from a Mendicant on Religious as Dialogue in Honour of Fifty Years of *Perfectae Caritatis*," in *A Future Built on Faith: Religious Life and the Legacy of Vatican II*, ed. Gemma Simmonds, CJ (Dublin, Ireland: The Columba Press, 2014), 115–26.

[16] Ibid., 117.

[17] Ibid., 121.

[18] NATSICC is on its governing body, and many religious throughout Australia are actively involved, for example, as tutors in remote home communities.

and individual religious have actively supported Aboriginal and Torres Strait Islander Catholic leaders to engage in linguistic, cultural, biblical, and theological studies. This is a place that actually combines—and reveals—the four dialogues of life, experience, theology, and action.

From distant, remote home communities, many religious sisters and brothers engage with Catholic Nungalinya students as mentors or tutors. In keeping with the mission of Nungalinya, which is to further the aspirations of Aboriginal Christians, religious offer support as conversation partners seeking to respectfully listen, learn, and share religious understandings and expressions.

Current trends of religious being together in a dialogue of theology are also reflected in programs and projects, mainly initiated by Indigenous persons or groups. Retreats on dialogues of theology to Uluru and to Lake Mungo are such examples, where Pneumatology and eco-theologies are exciting and promising signs of mutual enrichment as well as of reconciliation.[19]

Dialogue of Action

Australia's first canonized saint, Sister of St. Joseph Mary MacKillop, reached out to Aboriginal people in 1886. The Josephite Sisters, as have many religious women and men, have continued to work alongside Aboriginal people through the years. There has been and continues to be service, partnership, and engagement in communities, hospitals, schools, prisons, church and home communities, as well as in the law courts, in media, in artistic endeavors, in suburban and remote areas, "out bush," and by the sea, in cities, and in desert regions.

Many religious, especially those working in solidarity with Aboriginal Catholic ministries throughout the land, continue in voluntary and supportive roles. Many congregational schools and parishes employ Indigenous staff; others provide physical resources, financial support for educational initiatives, or scholarships for tertiary Indigenous students. Some congregations, in cooperation with Aboriginal and Torres Strait Islander people, have made records (photos, letters, documents, and so forth) freely available to individuals and communities still trying to access family and cultural histories.

---

[19] Examples in recent years have been national workshops and seminars in Central Australia and elsewhere, as well as retreat experiences at Uluru and regular visits to Lake Mungo, NSW.

How effective are these continuing dialogues? What could change for the better? Perhaps even the very physical shape itself—not sitting opposites at tables, or in meeting rooms, but sharing leaderships, insights, and struggles often from a softer, friendlier space, such as a circle. And perhaps "spreading the tent" to enable wider participation. Religious congregations *are* striving to engage in closer, more respectful partnership with "lay associates," "partners in mission," and "companions on the journey." Indigenous Catholics often model more inclusive ways of engaging and being comfortable with other Christians or non-Christians in the dialogues, including marginalized groups such as the elderly, children, and addicts.

Conclusion

Post–Vatican II religious women and men in Australia began to move aside from some of the more traditional roles in their ministry among First Nations Peoples. And today there is invitation to a more silent, humble place that may be nonetheless demanding, enlivening, and transforming. It is a place where congregations are voicing formal apologies, where members of religious institutes are in a place of genuine service, of waiting, accepting, listening, and receptivity, a place of *akangkweirreme*, a place of paying careful attention.

Indigenous Catholic leader Margaret Mary Kemarre Turner, OA, who has worked for many years alongside other members of the Catholic community, including religious priests, sisters, and brothers in Central Australia, writes:

> We can't have blaming business today, now. We can't do that, because we're living together. We're eating the same food, we're drinking the same water, we breathe the same air. . . . I'm saying here that I'm strong in my Catholicism and I'm strong in my own culture. . . . Two cultures can hold each other. It's a really good relationship, and it's in a really respectful way. . . . The people that I work with, I always recognize and acknowledge them. . . . And the feeling goes directly from me to those people, and it also comes back straight, and to me . . . and we're in a good learning relationship.[20]

---

[20] Margaret Mary Kemarre Turner, *Iwenhe Tyerrtye: What It Means to Be an Aboriginal Person* (Alice Springs, NT: IAD Press, 2010), 219–21.

Each one, Indigenous or not, in this mission of *missio Dei* strives to share and spread the good news of the gospel where genuine and ever-deepening dialogues occur. For all held in the embrace of the trinitarian God, it is about finding, longing for, and creating a new heaven and a new earth, and in Australia, Land of the Holy Spirit,[21] some new bright realization of the Divine Dream that all may be One.

Robyn Reynolds, OLSH, is a senior lecturer at Yarra Theological Union (University of Divinity, Melbourne). Robyn's doctoral thesis explored religious ceremony in the Catholic and Indigenous Australian encounter. Robyn previously spent ten years as dean at Nungalinya College in Darwin, following many years living and working in remote Aboriginal communities in northern and central Australia.

---

[21] In 1606, Spanish explorer Pedro Fernandez de Quiros named the country *La Australia del Espiritu Santo* (Ron Ross, "Person of Faith: Pedro Ferdinand De Quiros," Press Service International, *Christian Today*.

African Traditional Religion
Working Together to Promote the Culture of Life

BEDE UKWUIJE, CSSP

African Traditional Religion is part of the culture and environment in which most Africans were born and bred. Before the coming of the universalistic religions Islam and Christianity, African Traditional Religion englobed the cultural and political life of people. Unfortunately, African Traditional Religion has been misrepresented too often for different reasons, either for the sake of apologetics or in order to gain converts—or even to prevent syncretism. Christian evangelizers, informed by the evolutionist vision of history, dreamed of a time when it would even disappear in favor of a new Christendom. However, African Traditional Religion continues to determine the existential choices of many Africans. This makes dialogue between Christianity and African Traditional Religion more relevant than ever.

A Necessary Dialogue

The reasons for dialogue between Christianity and African Traditional Religion could be viewed from both religions.

First, dialogue is inherent in the Christian understanding of the unity of the human family. The Second Vatican Council's *Declaration on the Relation of the Church to Non-Christian Religions (Nostra Aetate)* states clearly that all men and women have a common origin, God the Father, that "all share a common destiny," and that different religions are ways in which human beings and cultures try to solve the enigma of the human condition.[1] Thus, Vatican II declares that "the Catholic Church rejects nothing of what is true

---

[1] Vatican II, *Declaration on the Relation of the Church to Non-Christian Religions (Nostra Aetate)* (1965), no. 1, hereinafter *NA*.

and holy in these religions. She regards with sincere reverence those ways of conduct and of life, those precepts and teachings which, though differing in many aspects from the ones she holds and sets forth, nonetheless often reflect a ray of that Truth which enlightens all men."² Dialogue, therefore, is a recognition that what unites us is greater than what separates us.

Second, African Traditional Religion is "the religion that has been handed down from generation to generation by the forebears of the present generation of Africans . . . a religion that Africans today have made theirs by living it and practicing it."³ Many African Christians, while practicing Christianity, feel obliged to resort to some practices of their traditional religion. This syncretism makes dialogue between Christianity and African Traditional Religion more necessary than ever.

Third, dialogue is necessary for healthy coexistence. It is "a meeting of different religions, in an atmosphere of freedom and openness, in order to listen to the other, to try to understand the other person's religion, and hopefully to seek possible cooperation."⁴ In that sense, dialogue is not geared toward converting the other to one's religion, but to learning to think from the point of view of the other. Through dialogue, different religious traditions can overcome the temptation to resort to violence in order to search for the truth together. Truth is not what justifies our position or what proves us right. Rather, truth is what judges us; it is the measure of our actions and words. When the Second Vatican Council, in the light of the Gospel (Jn 14:6), declares that "Christ is the way, the truth and the life, in whom men may find the fullness of religious life, in whom God has reconciled all things to Himself,"⁵ it means concretely that Jesus's life and teaching is the measure of our way of relating to each other and to other believers.

Belief System of African Traditional Religion

African Traditional Religion believes that the universe is harmonious.⁶ To live is to strive to maintain harmony in order to contribute to abundant

---

² *NA*, no. 2.

³ Omosade Awolalu and Adelumo Dopamu, *West African Traditional Religion* (Ibadan: Onibonoje Press, 1979), 26.

⁴ Francis Arinze, *Meeting Other Believers: The Risks and Rewards of Interreligious Dialogue* (Huntington, IN: Gracewing, Fowler Wright Book, 1979), 16.

⁵ *NA*, no. 2.

⁶ See Paulinus Odozor, "The Essence of African Traditional Religion," *Church Life Journal* (February 21, 2019).

life for self and others. The universe is a hierarchically organized unity of beings, ranging from God to lesser beings, divinities, spirits, ancestors, human beings, animals, plants, and inanimate things.

God and Spirits

The Ultimate Principle in the harmonious universe is God, the Creator and sustainer of the universe. God is said to dwell in the skies/heavens. There is a debate as to whether African Traditional Religion is monotheistic or polytheistic. The earliest experts in African Traditional Religion, like Bolaji Idowu[7] and John Mbiti[8] posited the thesis of African monotheism, the belief in God as the Supreme Being. However, the notion of God as a Supreme Being, though general, is not equally emphasized in all traditions. Central African traditions and cultures seem to affirm more strongly the centrality of the Supreme Being than some of the West African countries. Some other experts (such as Donatus Nwoga, Raymond Arazu, and Wole Soyinka) argue that African Traditional Religion is polytheistic and that the idea of monotheism is an imposition of Western philosophy through Christian apologetics.[9]

However, God in the heavens does not govern alone. Africans believe in the existence of mystical powers that are invisible. They are spirits or divinities who mediate God's powers. Idowu emphasizes that the divinities are "spiritual beings"[10] and personifications of God's activities and manifestations. They permeate different dimensions of the universe. The first among them is the earth goddess, Mother Earth. Several divinities manifest themselves through natural phenomena, the sun, rain, lightning, and so on. They can be approached through divination and the libation ritual for health, more abundant life, and protection.

---

[7] Bolaji Idowu, *Olodumare: God in Yoruba Belief* (New York: Plainview, 1960; 2nd ed., Nigeria, Longman, 1994), 29, 219.

[8] John Mbiti, *Concepts of God in Africa* (London: SPCK, 1970), xii; *African Religions and Philosophy* (London/Nairobi: Heinemann Educational Books, 1969), 30.

[9] Donatus Nwoga, *The Supreme Being as a Stranger in Igbo Religious Thought* (Ahiazu Mbaise: Hawk Press, 1984). See also Chinua Achebe, "Chi in Igbo Cosmology," in *Morning Yet on Creation Day* (New York: Anchor Books, 1976), 131–45; Raymond Arazu, "Chukwu and Yahweh: The Problem of Naming God in Igbo Language," in *God, Bible, and African Traditional Religion*, ed. Bede Ukwuije (Enugu: SNAAP Press, 2010), 6–30.

[10] Idowu, *Olodumare, God in Yoruba Belief*, 75.

Ancestors, the Living Dead

Eminent among God's associates are the ancestors, whom Africans venerate. They participate in the reproduction and perpetuation of life. An ancestor or "brother ancestor," as Charles Nyamiti states, is one who is a mediator to God, one who through death has acquired a supernatural status and by that fact is entitled to veneration.[11] Ancestors also possess the power of omnipresence; they can visit their descendants everywhere and in many ways, in the form of animals, trees, and so on. Ancestors are feared by the living, because negligence on the part of the living can attract the anger of the ancestors against them. This reason justifies the rituals of appeasement.

On the eschatological level, ancestors are role models, symbols of the fulfillment of the deepest aspirations of the African, namely, to live in a community where the living and the dead live in harmony, as stated by Bénézet Bujo.[12] In this sense, ancestors are those who have lived in a good relationship with God (God-fearing ancestors) and who exert a good influence on their descendants by showing how the power of life can be used according to God's will.[13] Because happiness can only be achieved through the solidarity of human beings with one another, ancestors perpetuate this solidarity beyond death.

The Human Person

In African traditions the human person is understood as a microcosm of the universe. In the human being is crystallized the principle of duality, which is at the heart of the African worldview. Africans conceive the person as relatedness,[14] a network of relations. This vision is embodied in the Igbo proverb, *Ife kwulu, ife akwudebe ya* (Something stands and something else stands beside it).[15] East and South Africans call it *Ubuntu*—our existence is bound together. They say, *Umuntu ngumuntu ngabantu*—"A person is

---

[11] Charles Nyamiti, *Christ Our Ancestor: Christology from an African Perspective* (Gweru: Zimbabwe, Mmabo Press, 1984), 35.

[12] Bénézet Bujo, "Nos ancêtres, ces saints inconnus," *Bulletin de théologie africaine* 1, no. 2 (July-December 1979): 166.

[13] See Bénézet Bujo, *African Theology in Its Social Context* (Nairobi: Paulines Publications Africa, 1992), 73.

[14] See Elochukwu Uzukwu, *A Listening Church: Autonomy and Communion in African Churches* (Maryknoll, NY: Orbis Books, 1996), 35–38; John Mbiti, *African Religion and Philosophy* (London: Heinemann, 1969), 224.

[15] See Elochukwu Uzukwu, *God, Spirit, and Wholeness* (Oregon: Pickwick Publications, 2012), 5–39.

a person because of others." This principle pervades the conception of all reality, the human person, the deities, society, and the entire cosmos.

It is said among the Igbo in Nigeria that before a child is born, it is already alive in the land of the spirits, and its coming into the world is the visit of an ancestor. This visit is called reincarnation or metempsychosis, though such concepts do not exactly represent what the visit means. Each person incarnates into the human world through the creative act of a protective (dynamic) spirit assigned to the person by God. This spirit is known in the Igbo tradition as *chi*. In some other traditions, it is known as *ori* (Yoruba), *kra* or *okra* (Eve, Asante), or *ka* (Ancient Egypt).[16] One's daily life is in constant negotiation with this spirit with whom one shares success and the blame for failure.[17]

As a connection between the visible and the invisible, the human being is sacred and consequently should be approached with reverence and deep respect. The sense of sacredness helps to structure the moral order in society. This order is encapsulated in the variety of taboos, customs, proverbs, and songs that guide the use of speech, food, dress, relationship with others, birth, work, marriage, funerals, and so forth. Profanation of the sacred is considered an abomination and can lead to excommunication. An abominable act can, however, be repaired through purification rituals meant to appease the earth goddess or the offended deity or ancestor.

Stepping Stones for Dialogue

Since African Traditional Religion is a way of life for the majority of Africans, dialogue takes place in the context of daily life. This dialogue assumes a significant dimension in the context of childbirth, naming ceremonies, initiation of adolescents into manhood or age grades, healing and reconciliation rituals, and marriage and funeral rites. From my childhood I learned to respect the traditions of my people. My father was a catechist. It was up to him, as a respected man in our clan, to conduct many delicate negotiations between the Christian community and different villages or families. As I was his first son, he often took me with him. Sometimes he would ask me to write the meeting reports or to copy the ones he wrote himself. I came to understand that African spiritual traditions are not evil in themselves. In certain cases traditional practices surrounding

---

[16] See Uzukwu, *A Listening Church*, 36.
[17] See Achebe, "Chi in Igbo Cosmology," in *Morning Yet on Creation Day* (New York: Anchor Books, 1976), 137.

marriage and funeral rites, especially the treatment reserved for widows, appear to be unjust to Christians and many well-meaning people. In this case the Christian community presents objections and insists on justice and fairness. However, many negotiations are conducted with tact and great openness. With time, this dialogue has helped Christians to affirm their freedom as children of God in their cultural context while reclaiming their rights and obligations in their traditions.

Culture of Life

African Traditional Religion, as we have seen, promotes life. Christianity, too, proclaims the gospel of abundant life as grace given to men and women in Jesus Christ (Jn 3:16). Therefore, Christians and African traditional religionists can work together to promote the culture of life. One way to do this is through a concerted effort to save the noble dimension of culture by fighting against the cultural perversion that is spreading through globalization.

The Second Vatican Council affirms that culture fosters the humanization of human beings and of society.[18] Before the council, Alioune Diop had defined culture as "the vital effort by which each people, each man, by his experience and his aspirations, his work and his reflection, rebuilds a world filled with life, thought and passion, appears more thirsty than ever for justice, love and peace. . . . Culture is the intimate song of our personality."[19] Because culture serves to humanize social life, it helps to overcome the anarchy of human instincts and violence. Therefore, African Traditional Religion fights the culture of death. Hence the suspicion in African cultures of occult practices, such as the practice of witchcraft.[20] Elochukwu Uzukwu explains that the practice of witchcraft is the "aggregate of oppressive forces or evil (political, economic, and spiritual) in society."[21] At the heart of the symbolism of witchcraft is the language of manducation or even cannibalism—it is said that one eats up the life or the vital force of the other. People mobilize diabolic and occult forces either for their own protection, or to gain power to dominate others, or

---

[18] Vatican II, *Pastoral Constitution on the Church in the Modern World (Gaudium et Spes)* (1964), no. 53, hereinafter *GS*.

[19] Philippe Verdin, *Alioune Diop, le Socrate noir* (Paris: Lethielleux, 2010), 57.

[20] Cf. Pope Benedict XVI, post-synodal apostolic exhortation, *Africae Munus* (2011), no. 96.

[21] Elochukwu Uzukwu, "From Nobody to Somebody: The Pertinence of African Liberation Theology," in *Movement or Moment? Assessing Liberation Theology Forty Years after Medellín*, ed. Patrick Claffey and Joe Egan (Oxford: Peter Lang, 2009), 102.

even to destroy others, their enemies or rivals. In most modern cases of accusation or practice of witchcraft, it is no longer a question of African Traditional Religion but a perversion, a manipulation of religion for personal, economic, and political reasons.

Cultural perversion is also manifest in the present context of jungle justice, rampant killings by military and police, and kidnapping and human trafficking. This includes the loss of the sense of the sacredness of the human person, as seen in hate speech and fake news. These acts wound and distort humanity. Christians and African traditional religionists can work together to promote the culture of life.

Integral Ecology

Belief in the sacredness of life in a harmonious universe, posited by African Traditional Religion, can be another point of dialogue with Christianity. During a 2010 symposium titled "Faith, Culture, and Development," co-organized by the Symposium of Episcopal Conferences of Africa and Madagascar (SECAM) and the Pontifical Council for Culture and the Congregation for the Evangelization of Peoples, in Abidjan, Ivory Coast, Archbishop Anthony Obinna of Owerri launched a challenge to rectify certain distortions of African cultures now undergoing a cultural and anthropological crisis. He clearly stated that the eruption of violence and discrimination against human beings as well as the enduring environmental crisis were due to the erosion of the sense of the sacred. He called for a rediscovery of the meaning of the event of the redemption of humanity in Jesus Christ, which is the revelation of both our filiation in God (*theofiliation*) and our kinship with the environment.[22]

This resonates with Pope Francis's radiant theologico-ecological project. In his encyclical letter *Laudato Si'*, Francis clearly states that the current environmental crisis stems from the fact that human beings no longer understand nature as a gift of God, as a place for the expression of his beauty and glory. Nature has become an object to be exploited for greater profit.[23] Francis calls us to take care of "our common home" by rediscovering respect for nature and the environment, not only as a gift of God, but also as an expression of the Creator. In his apostolic exhortation *Querida Amazonia*, the pope insists that our life depends on the environment, and writes: "The forest is not a resource to be exploited; it

---

[22] Anthony Obinna, "African Cultures and Development: The Rectifying Challenge," *Cultures and Faith* 18, no. 4 (Rome: Libreria Editrice Vaticana, 2010), 321–33.

[23] Pope Francis, *Laudato Si': On Care for Our Common Home* (2015), no. 2.

is a being, or various beings, with which we have to relate.... To abuse nature is to abuse our ancestors, brothers and sisters, creation and the Creator, by mortgaging the future."[24]

Connectedness of the Human Family

The African understanding of the human person, expressed as relation and connectedness, concurs with the Christian understanding of the human person as communion. The realization of one's life follows the logic of a harmonious vision that encompasses the individual, the community, and the cosmos. The Congolese theologian Bénézet Bujo equates this harmony with the concept of collective conscience. In his critical appreciation of the Catholic Church's definition of conscience in connection with a natural law deposited by God in the human being,[25] Bujo argues that from an African perspective, the idea of conscience as a natural law inscribed on the heart of the individual could lead to opposition between the individual and the community.[26] He notes that in Africa, contrary to the West, conscience is collective and not individual. Conscience is a shared gift, a participation in the word (*la parole*) received from the ancestors and reinterpreted in the community. In that sense, "words and experiences which contribute to reinforcing or correcting the intentions hidden in the heart are, as it were, a living anamnestic (*memoria*) conscience which recreates itself. This act of self-recreation is never individual, rather each community participates in it."[27] Bujo is of the opinion that this act of sharing in the anamnestic conscience is what is implied in the principle of *palaver* (*la palabre*), where people give birth to each other by "pronouncing only edifying and life-giving words."[28] Therefore, one cannot talk of a good conscience in the African perspective except in the sense that each person strives to give birth/give life to the other.

Bujo's proposal can be connected with Pope Francis's call to awaken the consciousness of our common humanity. In his encyclical letter *Fratelli Tutti*, informed by the experience of the global management of the COVID-19 pandemic, Pope Francis writes, "Unless we recover the

---

[24] Pope Francis, post-synodal apostolic exhortation *Querida Amazonia* (2020), no. 42.
[25] See *GS*, no. 16.
[26] Bénézet Bujo, *La vision africaine du monde. Pour un enseignement social de l'Eglise sans loi naturelle* (Fribourg: St. Augustin, 2018), 34.
[27] Ibid., 37.
[28] Ibid.

shared passion to create a community of belonging and solidarity worthy of our time, our energy and our resources, the global illusion that misled us will collapse and leave many in the grip of anguish and emptiness."[29]

God Is Not Available for War

African Traditional Religion is devoid of proselytism and refuses to use God for violence. God is left out of the hostilities that often occur between kindred, clans, or ethnic groups. The reason goes back to the belief in cosmic harmony and the principle of duality.

First, God cannot destroy the harmony God created and sustains. Furthermore, the African vision of the universe, duality, deeply abhors absolutism. The gods are not absolute. Even the Supreme Being negotiates its powers with the human being and society. In the Igbo tradition, for example, the name *Chukwu* (*Chi-ukwu*, the great *chi*) suggests that *Chukwu* has to merge with *chi* (the other of the human person). The name *Chineke* (*chi-na-eke*) suggests that this deity is a combination of a male deity, *chi* and a female deity, *eke* (destiny). Creation myths in West African traditions affirm this principle of duality. Among the Dogon (Mali) the primordial deities (Nomono, Anagono) were created in pairs, male and female. The primordial ancestors (Anagono Bile) were also created male and female. This duality also pervades the political reality in society. The Asante King (Ghana) receives power or authority through the Queen Mother. Also in Uganda, the Grand King receives authority through the Queen Mother. Through all these traditions, the relational tension mediates being-in-the-world. It is essential to the social health or wholeness of the community.

This can resonate with the Christian trinitarian concept of God. God is Trinity, the unity of three Persons: the Father, the Son and the Holy Spirit. God's life is love and communion, a life of self-donation, a communion in which no one tries to preserve self but instead lives for others. In the current context of growing religious violence, racial, and cultural discrimination, Christians and African religionists can offer the possibility of an alternative society. They can promote a lifestyle that does not seek self-preservation, but seeks to create communion among different people, cultures, and nations. Together they can fight the manipulation of the name of God for violence and domination.

---

[29] Pope Francis, *Fratelli Tutti* (2020), no. 36.

Conclusion

The fact that African Traditional Religion is the natural environment and culture of every African is a favorable ground for dialogue. Its core values like the belief in the harmony of the universe, the sacredness of life, the relatedness of the human person, and the refusal to use God for war offer stepping stones for genuine dialogue. African Traditional Religion can resonate with the Christian understanding of the unity of all humanity in God and the focus on integral ecology, the construction of our common home informed by the trinitarian faith. Dialogue between both religions can be facilitated by their mutual respect focused on a common project, namely, the protection of life.

Bede Ukwuije, CSSp, is the first assistant to the superior general of the Spiritans in Rome. He belongs to the Province of Nigeria South-East. He holds a doctorate in theology (ThD) from the Institut Catholique de Paris and a PhD in theology and religious studies from the Catholic University of Leuven, Belgium.

Ecumenism

Mission and the Search for Unity

Marie-Hélène Robert, OLA

In a secularized and pluralist context, the proclamation *ad extra* as well as the transmission of faith *ad intra* no longer follow the same rules, either in the public sphere or in the family or community context. When the transmission no longer takes place, this leads to at least two consequences for Christians: either moving on to other things and losing the wish to transmit the faith (for example, resignation due to a focus on the "illegitimacy" of the church to preach the good news because of its history or contemporary scandals), or vigorously taking up what constituted the strength of Christianity (the missionary and catechetical methods of the nineteenth century). If, on the other hand, one considers that the transmission continues to take place, but in a different way, two other possibilities appear: either exploring effective short-term formulas aimed at the growth of a single ecclesial group (at the risk of proselytism), or cooperating in working out a new successful formula (such as the common witness of the churches, where each one retains its ecclesial identity, in the medium and long terms).

I would like to explore these last two aspects in this essay. Is it desirable to promote and live a common mission in the twenty-first century? If so, under what conditions?

This reflection is based on the ecumenical research and practical mission I carried out for fifteen years at the national and international levels.[1] Although an intrinsic link exists between ecumenism and mission, mission

---

[1] In addition to missionary commitments in different contexts, I have been involved since 2006 in AFOM (Francophone Ecumenical Association of missiology); since 2010 in IAMS (International Association of Mission Studies); and since 2012 in the Pontifical Council for Promoting Christian Unity, in two dialogues, the first one on baptism with Mennonites and Lutherans, and the second one on church mission with Baptists.

may set the protagonists in opposition, make it possible for them to interrogate each other, or even gather the Christian communities around a common call, in keeping with Pope Francis's words in *Evangelii Gaudium*: "We must never forget that we are pilgrims journeying alongside one another. This means that we must have sincere trust in our fellow pilgrims, putting aside all suspicion or mistrust, and turn our gaze to what we are all seeking: the radiant peace of God's face."[2]

Is the Call to Mission, to Unity, Consistent?

Ecumenical events are usually regarded as events in which the baptized of different churches or Christian communities join, whether the event is a celebration, a meeting for reflection, a meal, or other activity. Such events show that it is possible to cooperate and do something important together; this is the outcome of decades of work since the mid-twentieth century, following the Second Vatican Council.

Just as the mission is viewed in different ways, which at times clash instead of completing each other, ecumenism may arouse various reactions:

- *Distrust:* ecumenism will only end in compromising the church's identity and truth; it will weaken our missionary power, or we will lose our social impact or even our own commitment; or
- *Indifference:* each church has its own calling; since the Second Vatican Council we have tried hard enough to move closer to the other/s, so let's lose no more time and energy on the matter; or
- *Convinced commitment:* ecumenism means journeying together toward the One; it is a gift of God but also a mission; ecumenism primarily requires that all peoples earnestly seek what we call unity.

From a Catholic point of view, ecumenism is not to be confused with a respectful juxtaposition of people, methods, and perspectives. It is a common search for the unity willed by Christ. It is the purpose and aim of the mission, "so that the world may believe."[3] As Francis asserts, "The credibility of the Christian message would be much greater if Christians could overcome their divisions."[4]

---

[2] Pope Francis, apostolic exhortation *Evangelii Gaudium (The Joy of the Gospel)* (2013), no. 244, hereinafter *EG*.
[3] Jn 17:21.
[4] *EG*, no. 244.

An ecumenical theology of mission helps us to understand how and why mission and the unity of the church are related in scripture.[5] God wants to bring all of his children together: "Ecumenism can be seen as a contribution to the unity of the human family."[6]

Pope Paul VI affirmed this strongly as early as 1975 in *Evangelii Nuntiandi*:

> The unity among His followers is not only the proof that we are His, but also the proof that He is sent by the Father. It is the test of the credibility of Christians and of Christ Himself. As evangelizers, we must offer Christ's faithful not the image of people divided and separated by unedifying quarrels, but the image of people who are mature in faith, and capable of finding a meeting-point beyond the real tensions, thanks to a shared, sincere and disinterested search for truth. Yes, the destiny of evangelization is certainly bound up with the witness of unity given by the church. This is a source of responsibility and also of comfort.[7]

Mission and the search for unity, according to Paul VI, invoke each other. An ecumenical missiology contributes to unity, as the horizon of mission, taking into account the theological differences, not to endorse them as such, but to consider how they could be included in the mission of the church. This means knowing and respecting the distinctive aspects, reworking them together, for a joint approach to mission. It is therefore not a question of confirming a simple coexistence along missiological lines, but of seeking to understand what is hindering combined mission work. Ecumenism is therefore an interfaith process, which integrates multi-faith experiences and a desire for conversion.

Unity is the condition of mission—it is unity in the sense of reciprocal coexistence, of a spiritual order. The mission's impact depends on unity, as we shall see. However, not all the churches and communities understand and seek unity in the same way. The differences imply a fundamental and contextual reflection on mission, even within the same church, when planting the church, proclaiming the gospel, silent presence, social commitment, and interreligious dialogue, are seen as oppositional rather than as complementary. All these forms of mission are necessary, and the respective churches will favor this or that approach,

---

[5] See Jn 13:35 or 17:17–23.
[6] *EG*, no. 245.
[7] Pope Paul VI, *Evangelii Nuntiandi* (1975), no. 77, hereinafter *EN*.

on the condition that other approaches are not belittled and that any form of proselytism is rejected. We will come back to this point later in this article.

The fact that all these forms of mission exist, but are not necessarily experienced by all, speaks to the different aspects of the one and universal mission of the church. Paul VI expressed his preoccupation with this when he said, "Unity is the test of the credibility of Christians and of Christ Himself."[8] He knew that this aim of unity had not been achieved in 1975. Has it now, almost fifty years later?

The Mission Arouses Opposition: Competition between Churches and the Weight of History and Theology

In the history of the church, mission often developed at the expense of Christian unity. The writings from the sixteenth to the nineteenth century show reciprocal deprecation between Catholics and Protestants.[9] The work of the other churches or Christian communities has overall been experienced more as competition than as emulation, including in the territories influenced by the Orthodox Churches.[10]

In the Protestant sphere, the first international conference to call itself ecumenical—the New York Ecumenical Missionary Conference—was held in New York in 1900. It brought together seven-hundred missionaries and two-thousand delegates representing 250 Protestant missionary societies. The adjective *ecumenical* was understood in the theological sense of a universal orientation of concerns and in the ecclesiological sense of a federative meeting. The Edinburgh Conference in 1910 followed up this intuition by establishing an ongoing committee (which became the International Missionary Council, or IMC, in 1921).[11] The committee was charged with the responsibility of organizing subsequent conferences, and in 1912 it established the *International Review of Missions*. In 1961, after

---

[8] *EN*, no. 77.

[9] Claude Prudhomme, "La querelle des universels," *Chrétiens et sociétés* 8 (2001): 73–98.

[10] For instance, Uniatism (Eastern Catholic Churches having left the Orthodox Church) left a regrettable record. Comité mixte catholique-orthodoxe en France, *Catholiques et orthodoxes: Les enjeux de l'uniatisme. Dans le sillage de Ballamand*, "Documents des Églises" (Paris: Le Cerf, 2004).

[11] At the Edinburgh Conference, the divisions, competition, and contempt of some missionaries for the people were denounced as a scandal; the rivalry between Protestant Christian communities was declared detrimental to their growth, their missionary impact, and their right relationship to the gospel. The reports of the conference are available online.

the Achimota Conference in Ghana held in 1958, the IMC merged with the WCC as the Standing Commission on Mission and Evangelization.

In the Catholic sphere it was not until the Second Vatican Council that the search for unity became understood as the promise of an "exchange of gifts."[12] This dynamic of exchange would meet with great success until the twenty-first century.[13]

The common commitment to mission and unity depends on the churches—Pentecostal, Orthodox, Lutheran Reformed, Evangelical—who have a specific understanding of mission. In practice, the relationship among the churches ranges from hostility to partnership, which has either a negative or positive impact on mission. Good relations are necessary. But are they sufficient? Should the criterion of ecumenism be missionary impact, or doctrinal agreement? In other words, do we have to wait until agreement is reached on all the points of doctrine in order to evangelize together without getting lost?

According to Pope Francis in *Evangelii Gaudium*:

> If we concentrate on the convictions we share, and if we keep in mind the principle of the hierarchy of truths, we will be able to progress decidedly towards common expressions of proclamation, service and witness. . . . How many important things unite us! They are so numerous and so precious, the realities that unite us! If we really believe in the abundant free working of the Holy Spirit, we can learn so much from one another![14]

Painful Experiences

However, the call to conversion and the explicit proclamation of the faith have often given rise to tension in the exercise of the mission, especially as emerging groups tend to assert themselves by opposing other groups as their identity is being formed. Such hostility is especially felt when the mission takes place through proselytism,[15] which tends to belittle other

---

[12] Expressed in *Lumen Gentium*, no. 13; then taken up in 1995 by Pope John Paul II in *Ut Unum Sint*, nos. 28, 57; and then in 2013 by Pope Francis in *EG*, no. 246.

[13] Michel Mallèvre, "L'œcuménisme comme 'échange de dons' selon Jean-Paul II," *Istina* 53 (2008): 47–75.

[14] *EG*, no. 246.

[15] Marie-Hélène Robert, "Proselytism in Christian Churches: Insights from the European Scene," in *The Oxford Handbook of Mission Studies*, ed. Kirsteen Kim, Knud Jørgensen, and Alison Fitchett-Climenhaga (Oxford: Oxford University Press, 2022).

communities and their methods by a "theft of sheep," by psychological or economic pressure, or by "the re-baptism" practiced by some churches,[16] despite the clear recommendations of the churches.

Proselytism leads to counter-testimony and to division, including in families. It is not a healthy competition in which by emulation and inspiration the different communities are prompted to rekindle their missionary zeal.[17] But to speak openly about one's faith is a Christian's duty, and even a right recognized both by the churches and by the law in Europe. As the European Convention for the Protection of Human Rights states, "Everyone has the right to freedom of thought, conscience and religion; to manifest his religion or belief, in worship, teaching, practice and observance . . . either alone or in community with others and in public or in private."[18]

But the boundary between proselytism and evangelization is not always easy to define. Indeed, accompanying a vulnerable person in his or her search for life, light, and truth calls for the witness of faith, so one must be careful. Discernment and respect for each person, who is in the image of God, are therefore essential tools of the missionary, who is preferably sent to vulnerable people. The missionary knows that God works in depth *through them* to save, heal, and comfort; it is not the missionary or the aids he or she put in place. As such, the mission lived jointly by Christians from different churches can be the test of a mission that brings people together, that unifies, because it is exercised with the common knowledge that the first and last action is God's. "My Father is still working, and I am working."[19] How can we better join together in God's work?

Mission Brings People Together: Common Research and Practice

The question of common witness is at the heart of the reflections the World Council of Churches has carried out since 1954. These lines from the 1997 reference text "Towards Common Witness" remain particularly relevant: "Common witness is constructive: it enriches, challenges,

---

[16] François-Xavier Amherdt and Mariano Delgado, eds., *Mission et œcuménisme. De la concurrence à la collaboration?* Actes du 9e "Forum Fribourg Église dans le monde," 12–13 Octobre 2017, Coll. Théologie pratique en dialogue 54 (Basel: Schwabe Verlag, 2020).

[17] Valérie Aubourg, *Réveil catholique. Emprunts évangéliques au sein du catholicisme* (Geneva: Labor et Fides, 2020).

[18] European Convention for the Protection of Human Rights, Art. 9.1.

[19] Jn 5:17.

strengthens and builds up solid Christian relationships and fellowship. Through word and deed, it makes the Gospel relevant to the contemporary world. Proselytism is a perversion of authentic Christian witness, and therefore a counter-witness."[20]

Common initiatives fostering further reflection on the unifying dimension of the mission in a pluralist context include: bilateral or multilateral ecumenical dialogues on mission and theological and pastoral formation; Miracle and Healing evenings; Alpha Courses; ecumenically oriented communities (Chemin Neuf); or joint action in the political and social spheres. Ecumenism may also be found in charitable work, in prayer (Abbé Couturier, charismatic groups, communities like Taizé), in theological thought (Faith and Constitution, Groupe des Dombes, international dialogues), and in proclamation (proclamation, testimony, Alpha Course).

One example of the result of such unified reflection is when, in highly secularized contexts, the churches, or a wing of these churches, form a "united front" to contest bioethical laws that do not respect life, governments that seek to limit the freedom to believe and live one's faith, or the rise in secularization itself.

These considerations are not exclusive to secular contexts. The International Missionary Council and the World Council of Churches' Commission on Mission and Evangelism held the World Conference on Mission and Evangelism in Arusha, Tanzania, in March 2018. It was attended by over one thousand representatives of contemporary Christianity. The theme of the meeting, "Moving in the Spirit: Called to Transforming Discipleship," led the participants to assert: "We are transformed personally and collectively and are agents of God's transforming love in a broken world. We hear this call, which unites us in our hopes and our prayers."[21]

Receptive ecumenism[22] encourages each one to receive the other, to learn from each other. And this leads to a conversion of self to otherness, to respect for the other, and to welcoming the work of God in the way God wants. This requires gratitude, admiration, commitment, and conviction, and it fosters the development of a missionary attitude.

It is up to the churches to reflect on their methods:

---

[20] World Council of Churches, "Towards Common Witness," September 19, 1997, section II.

[21] "The Arusha Call to Discipleship: World Council of Churches' Conference on World Mission and Evangelism, 'Moving in the Spirit: Called to Transforming Discipleship,'" *International Revue of Mission* (December 1, 2018), the Free Library (2018).

[22] Jean-Baptiste Siboulet, "Le Receptive Ecumenism selon Paul D. Murray," *Istina* 65 (2020): 249–70.

- What am I proclaiming? (my own group, an ideology, a model of life, Jesus, God?)
- How am I proclaiming? (through testimony, apologetics, charitable actions, direct proclamation, civic engagement?)
- Why I am proclaiming (for conversion, integration into my church, meeting, dialogue, sharing?)
- How do I react to other ways of approaching proclamation? (… by rejection, denigration, indifference, emulation, partnership, vocation?).[23]

In order to work out *a common ethics of evangelization*, a few criteria should be considered:
- Recognize the primary work of God, for the mission and for unity;
- Admit one baptism as a missionary mandate;
- Consider the good transmitted rather than the agent;[24]
- Have respect for Christ's disciples/followers and their community;
- Examine the motives of the candidate applying for membership in your community;[25]
- Deepen the hermeneutics of testimony,[26] because the way content and mode are transmitted brings either credit or discredit.

Conclusion

When the churches consider evangelization and common witness together, one spurs the other on and becomes the point of verification. A common witness that renounces evangelization no longer renders witness to Christ; an evangelization that rejects common witness produces scandal and does not bear lasting fruit. The testimony par excellence is that rendered to love, through love.

At the end of this journey, we are invited to reflect on the following points:
- In the competition among the churches, what comes from a wounded history, from lack of knowledge of the other, from fear of the future?
- What, in my context, makes me feel indifferent, suspicious, or reluctant to spread the gospel with other Christians?
- What indicates legitimate differences in belief and practice?

---

[23] Round table, "Live Mission in Christian Unity," at the Mission Congress "Heal, Baptise, and Proclaim," Paris, October 2020.

[24] "For he that is not against you is for you" (Lk 9:49–50).

[25] Cf. *Ad Gentes*, no. 13.

[26] Charles Coutel, *Témoigner, entre acte et parole. Une herméneutique du témoignage est-elle possible?* (Paris: Parole et Silence, 2017).

- Which factors can further the search for common witness in the work carried out by the churches and in my own context? Do I make sure I know them and put them into practice?

We could illustrate these different points by concentric circles, starting from the closest circle, then joining the neighboring communities and going to the places of apostolate together, where we are sent to bear witness to Jesus Christ, the power of unity, and communion for humanity.

> **Marie-Hélène Robert, OLA,** is a missiologist, full professor of dogmatic theology at the Faculty of Theology of Lyon Catholic University, and a member of the Sciences and Humanities Confluence Research Center of Lyon Catholic University. She has published numerous books and articles, and given lectures at various national and international conferences. She is a sister of the Missionary Institute of Our Lady of the Apostles.

Interculturality

Culture and the Experience of God

Tim Norton, SVD

As our religious communities become increasingly diverse with people from different ethnic and national backgrounds, age groups, and personalities, we are learning to adapt the food we eat, the houses we live in, the ministries we are called to, the ways we cooperate, and the shape of our leadership and administration. Although we share much that is common in our quest for God, we sometimes lack an intercultural focus on our lived spirituality, which includes our liturgy, retreats, prayers before and after meetings and meals, Bible, and life sharing.

As a twenty-nine-year-old member of the Society of the Divine Word, I left Australia for mission and ministry in Mexico. Within a couple of months of my arrival in Mexico City, through the excitement and fog of all that was new, I began to sense a desire to talk about my experience of God in this new place—and I wanted someone to listen.

So, I went to the local parish (staffed by the Discalced Carmelites) and found someone who understood enough of my broken Spanish to accompany me for a year. Although I found it very difficult to articulate my thoughts and feelings, that priest gently encouraged me to talk about my relationship with God, even with my limitations of language and culture. Over the next few sessions I remember the growing satisfaction of thinking about God, and relating to God in a language and culture that was not my first. Years later I learned that the priest was a well-known scholar in the area of spirituality, and that he was fluent in five languages, including English. I realized that his intention was to encourage me to renew my relationship with God in Spanish in those early conversations. He knew how critical this would be for my Christian life in a new place.

As a spiritual guide, I have been similarly active in accompanying people as they discover and try to make sense of their experiences of

God, especially during my eight years of ministry in Centro Ad Gentes in Nemi, Italy. The majority of the people there were living and working or studying away from their first culture, and their contributions to the mission of the church in the world is invaluable.

This article aims to continue our *conversations around culture and experiences of God* through the voices of some people in the spiritual accompaniment sessions. Names and personal details have been changed, and the dialogue edited, in order to maintain confidentiality. My personal reflections are offered as a way forward in thinking further about spirituality and interculturality, the relationship between them, and their impact on mission.

Learning to Pray in Another Language

Elena: Language of the Heart

Context: Elena (speaking in Spanish), forty-four years old, was born in Slovakia and speaks Slovakian, Spanish, and some English. After her final vows Elena went to Peru, where, for fifteen years, she worked with Basic Christian Communities. At present, Elena is living in Rome in her third year as the secretary general of her congregation.

> **Elena:** When I did my initial formation in Slovakia, our sung prayer, beautiful eucharistic liturgies and regular Rosary in a large community formed the basis of my growing relationship with God. It was truly precious for me and, as that was all I knew, it was more than enough.
>
> I know I have changed. I hated my new situation in Peru initially, but I couldn't help but be changed by the beauty and poverty of the people with whom I lived and worked for so many years. With time I found God enormously present in their suffering—even in my suffering. I regard it as a kind of personal conversion.
>
> As we are not a large congregation, our leadership community here in Rome is small. But I feel like I am being squeezed into a prayer space that is completely unfamiliar to me. Praying in Italian is OK as it is not so far from Spanish, but the lack of opportunities to share our spiritual journey with one another is almost suffocating me.
>
> I am so relieved that I can speak about this in Spanish, as I realize now it has become the language of my heart.

Reflection: We do not use language only for spoken conversations and songs. We also use it to think and formulate concepts and ideas. The movement in speaking and thinking and dreaming from one language to another is sometimes very subtle. For those who spend most of their ministry lives using a language that is not their own, the adopted language can gradually become their primary language. As Elena indicates, in the place of Slovakian, Spanish has become the language she uses to understand God, the language of her heart.

Learning from the Differences

Jacinta: God of Surprises

Context: Jacinta (speaking in English), thirty-one years old, was born in Lebanon and speaks Arabic, French, and English. She is a French teacher by profession. Jacinta joined an international congregation five years ago and is presently undertaking a year of preparation for her final vows in Rome with a group of seven of her sisters from Ghana, Myanmar, Cameroon, and Ukraine.

> **Jacinta:** I feel guilty about being here in Rome where I have everything I need, as my family and my country are suffering so much. Some days there is no electricity at all for normal people, and food is scarce. I often think of my former students who need to have their future opened for them, not stamped down by greed and political ambition.
>
> **Guide:** I am sorry to hear of the suffering in your home country. That is a very difficult reality for you to deal with.
>
> **Jacinta:** Yes, that is true. Yet, as I listen to the experience of my sisters in the formation community, I realize that they too suffer from being away from home and family. And some of the realities they will return to are also very tough. In some ways this helps me.
> However, beyond the suffering, there is a sense of excitement. I never dreamed of having close relationships with people who are so different from me. We struggle to understand each other sometimes because of language, and also because our cultures are so different. But through the spiritual experiences shared by my Sisters, and the

common formation we are doing, I know I am growing in Spirit. I see that God has many more surprises for me than I ever dreamed!

I now understand a little more how our cultures shape us. My sisters observe things about me that I never knew. We have a lot of differences, but we also share a lot in common. I just hope we can continue our mutual support when we live far away from one another. We already have a WhatsApp support group, and we live in the same house!

Reflection: Jacinta is on an exciting journey of discovery with her sisters from other countries. And she is clearly taking God with her on the journey. Jacinta represents many young religious who fully expect to be able to maintain healthy, life-sustaining relationships for mission through social media. I trust her congregation is ready for the journey too!

Accompaniment in Inculturation

Yakobus: The Holy Spirit in the Law

Context: Yakobus (speaking in Italian), thirty-eight years old, was born in Kalimantan, Indonesia, and speaks Indonesian, Italian, and some English. He was ordained in his diocese eleven years ago. At present, he is in his last semester of canon law studies at a university in Rome. He will return to Kalimantan to teach in his home diocese.

Yakobus: It doesn't always feel right for me to talk about God in Italian, as the words come so much easier to me in my own language, because that's where I learned about God from my family and from the people in my home parish. And my seminary training was about God who is *besar* (big). I know now that I really love my Indonesian language much more than before because I have words about God in Indonesian that help me think about him, and pray to him. I didn't know how much I would miss my Indonesian language about God.

Guide: So, it is difficult for you to think about God in Italian?

Yakobus: Yes. I am faithful to say my office and the holy mass in Italian every day. That has not changed. But it is not the same—and maybe it can't be the same for me. But there are two professors here in Italy who helped me a lot during my studies. Because of them I have come to understand that the Holy Spirit is present in the law of the church. I did not know about this Spirit of the law before, even when I studied canon law in the seminary.

Guide: Can you tell me about this Holy Spirit that you have come to know in the law?

Yakobus: Yes, I can tell you something. It is about the Holy Spirit who is compassion and understanding, the Spirit who feels the suffering of the people. We need to remember that the Holy Spirit is in the law of the church to help people live in ways that bring them close to God—and I am a little excited to tell this to the seminarians when I return to my diocese.

Guide: So, you want to tell the seminarians in your Indonesian language something that you learned about the Holy Spirit in Italian?

Yakobus: Yes, it seems strange when you say it like that, but it is true. Only in Italian did I learn about this, and it has made me happy that I came to Rome. I really have something special to take home with me.

Reflection: Yakobus articulates well the importance of our first language and culture in understanding and growing in faith. However, limiting our relationship to God to one language is not necessarily helpful. God is always willing to meet us in any culture or language. We just need to be open to find him in the "new." And sometimes we need some help on this journey.

Cooperation in Coping with Difficulties

Hortense: The God of My Language

Context: Hortense (speaking in English), fifty-seven years old, was born in the Democratic Republic of Congo. She speaks Swahili and French and is learning English. Hortense is a nurse by profession and was elected congregational leader four years ago.

Hortense: Now that I am finished passing through the shock of being elected leader, and living in Rome, I realize for the first time in my life that I am lonely. It is a strange and painful place for me to be, because they say I am an extrovert, and I think it is true. Although we have two local languages in my home, and I learned Swahili and French at school, I know that I am too old now to learn a language again. English is the common language of my leadership team so I do my best to learn it and use it. But I cannot always say what I want to in English—and this affects my leadership and my relationships with the sisters on the team. Somehow it also affects my relationship with God.

Guide: Hortense, can you say a little more about language and God?

Hortense: I shall be honest with you. I did not go on retreat for some years as I did not find a French-speaking person to listen to me. A Swahili-speaking person is too much to ask for. I know God understands us all, no matter what language. I even tell my sisters this. But how can I tell God in English what my feelings are? I feel much closer to God when I am alone.

Guide: Hortense, why not speak to God now in Swahili about your feelings? I will not understand, but you and God will understand.

Hortense: If you think that is OK, I will try *(pause)*. Oh, that is helpful because, after saying it in Swahili, it is now easier to tell you in English what I say to God. I am telling God . . .

Reflection: Hortense represents people in leadership positions who struggle with the twin culture shocks of leadership (and the associated steep learning curves in administration personnel management and mission focus) and living in Rome, away from ministerial activities. It can be a very lonely place, as Hortense mentions. Her situation is made more difficult by the fact that she is forced to think, pray, and work in an unfamiliar language. People like Hortense need those of us around her to think creatively about our cooperation in creating the best living, praying, and working environment possible for her and for her mission. We are all in this together.

Daring to Express Oneself Differently

Ernesto: Poems for God

Context: Ernesto (speaking in Portuguese), a sixty-two-year-old religious brother, was born in Brazil. He worked for thirty years with Indigenous people in various parts of his home country. At present, he is doing a sabbatical course run by his congregation in Rome.

Ernesto: I know you said I could choose a spiritual director who speaks Portuguese, but you have been with us during this course, and because of that I want to talk with you rather than to another director. I hope that is OK for you, even though you speak Spanish, not Portuguese, because it is OK for me.

Guide: It is OK for me, Ernesto, but if I do not understand well what you are saying, can I ask you to repeat it or find other words to express yourself—and you can do the same with me?

Ernesto: Yes, yes, that is a good idea. I like that. But I also want to write. Some of the Indigenous people I worked with could not write but they spoke in a kind of poetry about God that is the language of their ancestors. I learned from them how to do this, but I cannot remember all my thoughts about God, so I write them. I wrote some words yesterday after the opening prayer of the retreat, and I would like to read them to you. It goes like this . . .

Guide: During the course, you did not speak a lot. But you sounded quite emotional as you read those words today.

Ernesto: Yes, that is true. I do not speak easily, and some of the people try to make me talk in our small-group work. I always find that difficult. Perhaps you do not understand all the words I say in the poem in Portuguese. In fact, I do not understand it all either. But when I think it, write it, then speak it, I even feel like singing about God. And I can't really sing! It is just a way of saying that it makes me feel good to talk to God. Do you think I could recite one of these poems in our community mass tomorrow?

Guide: I would be happy if you say your poem at Mass tomorrow, Ernesto—perhaps after communion. And I think the group members would also be pleased to hear you.

Reflection: Ernesto is willing to take risks in his spiritual life. This is a little unusual in a person of his gender and age. He is ready to work with a guide who does not speak his language. He is also open to being vulnerable before his companions by sharing his spiritual poems. His first choice is more personal because of his previous relationship with the guide. His second choice comes from his joy at finding a way to think and talk about God. Although risky, this second choice is very likely to succeed as his companions will be given another chance to get to know their brother better.

The Message Is More than the Language

Maria Lourdes: Jesus Speaks Mandarin

Context: Maria Lourdes (speaking in English), thirty-one years old, speaks Mandarin, Cantonese, and some English. She was born in China and now lives in Macau, where her congregation works principally with vulnerable women and girls. At present, she is undertaking a Rome-based formators' course online. An online retreat is part of the course.

Maria Lourdes: It is very sad for my sister as her husband died suddenly from COVID-19 five months ago. His brother also died. I could not travel to their funerals at that time. It was a big loss for the town and for our families. Both families have young children, so I asked permission to come and spend some days with my sister while I am doing this retreat. She is not Christian, but she is so happy that I am here. The children are doing their best to understand that I can only play with them for a couple of hours each day as I have to pray, then talk to you online. I am trying hard in the retreat, Father.

Guide: I appreciate the importance of your presence with your sister and her children, Maria Lourdes. Were the scripture readings yesterday helpful to you?

Maria Lourdes: Oh, yes, Father. After I took the children to school this morning, I spent some time in the garden reading about Jesus calling Peter to come to him across the water. I used the "imaginative prayer" method that I learned in the novitiate. It was very real for me. I could see the waves on the water, and I could see the fear on the face of Peter as Jesus called to him. I could hear the other disciples calling out to Peter. They were worried about him. I was moved when Jesus held Peter firmly. Peter knew he was safe then. Even I felt some relief when he was safe, and I am sure the other disciples were relieved too.

Guide: Maria Lourdes, you said that you heard Jesus call to Peter, and you heard the disciples calling to Peter. Can you remember what language Jesus and the disciples used?

Maria Lourdes: Oh, *(pause)*, in fact, Father, they were talking in Mandarin. Oh, my goodness yes, they were using the Mandarin language. It makes sense as I was reading my Bible in Chinese characters, but I did not realize in my prayer they were talking Mandarin. Jesus speaks Mandarin! Oh, Father, I am very happy to remember that. I have not thought about it since I was a child. He understands my language. He understands me!

Reflection: When people are given opportunities on their spiritual journey to think and discern outside the box, they may find God waiting to surprise them. The Spirit does not work only in one language, even if it is the language of our founder or foundress. The spirit of God is alive and well in all cultures. This is a lesson that is sometimes hard for some of us to learn as guides.

Conclusion

These people are speaking about their experience of God during formal sessions of spiritual accompaniment. I hope that their experience highlights the intimate connection between spirituality and interculturality. I have not found any particular rule that applies to the development of our spirituality through culture; however the age-old practice of listening to one another is an excellent way for us to validate our experiences and let them be cornerstones for our spiritual growth. Experiences of family disruption, joy, loss, war, health issues (especially for women), reunion, and hope are just some of the experiences through which the Spirit of God is made known to us. And all these experiences occur within a cultural (and linguistic) context.

For the sake of mission in the world, we would do well to focus on providing individual and group forums to share with one another the experience of God that shaped, and continue to shape, our understanding of our Christian journey in mission. Hearing the spiritual experiences of others through culture also influences our own experience. This, in itself, is *interculturality at work*.

Tim Norton, SVD, was born in Sydney, Australia. He has worked in parish ministry in Mexico City, as well as in initial formation and leadership in Australia. After a seven-year term as the director of SVD courses in Nemi, Italy, Tim has been recently appointed Auxiliary Bishop of the Archdiocese of Brisbane, Australia.

Media and Mission
Staying Connected

Monique Tarabeh, RGS

Two major events in the 1960s and 1970s revolutionized life in religious communities: Vatican II, with its call for renewal in the church; and the arrival of communication technology, which changed the way we spread our gospel message.

In the 1960s, when large, cumbersome computers were used to help launch space ships and even help put astronauts on the moon, people throughout the world marveled at the power of this technology. A few years later, smaller personal computers became widely available for general consumers—computers more powerful than those used in the early, complex aerospace programs. These computers revolutionized the way work was done by many people throughout the world as new programs were designed to streamline tasks and to reduce the corresponding time needed to accomplish them, for individual users as well as major organizations.

With each decade, technology continued advancing, and its use significantly broadened. Information became more widely available with the development of a highly sophisticated communication system that is popular today—the internet! This system enables people to make connections and quickly share information across the globe. The communication method, but not the communication skills of people, changed. The internet enables us to access a vast array of information, reliable or not, within seconds. Not only do we use modern computers for accessing this system, but mobile telephones also gained the capacity to make these connections. Events that were once local now quickly become global. The internet has become part of daily life.

Among the many areas of reform addressed during Vatican II, congregations reexamined their religious life and ministry. What had been familiar and existed for years underwent enormous change. Congregations recognized and responded to the massive changes that communication technology was undergoing. When the internet became widely available, they began adapting and using it to spread their messages. Over the years, forms of media communication moved from oral messages to print, radio, and television. Now the internet helps congregations to share their true stories based on charism, connectedness, ministries, and friendships, as Jesus did. Woven together to communicate a single central theme, these messages, regardless of the media form used, are based on the deep human need of those who seek an experience of God.

We Belong to One Another and to God

In his message for the 50th World Communications Day in 2016, Pope Francis said: "Communication, wherever and however it takes place, has opened up broader horizons for many people. This is a gift of God which involves a great responsibility. I like to refer to this power of communication as 'closeness.'"[1] In 2020, we did not know that a pandemic would be the catalyst to transform us and deepen our awareness of our need for one another in very tangible ways. In the midst of the COVID-19 crisis, we are grateful for the internet, as its familiar use prepared us to enter into online conversations and reflections about what really matters to us.

Our desire for communion and connection has become much clearer as we see that the simple things of life can bring deep joy, such as neighbors who play live music loud enough for everyone to hear and see. Realizing how much we need one another, as we belong to one another and to God, we were also amazed to see many websites, which had been created to provide daily prayer and spiritual reflections, shifting from requiring monetary contributions to providing open access and creating an oasis to let people encounter God. The media is showing us how many congregations are using different methods such as blogs, video messages, and photos to share their stories and the actions that they are taking during this pandemic to maintain contact and closeness among members as well as their families. These changes in access and method have made an impact not only on the mission, but also on each person. The choice is ours to be transformed—and to be a transformer.

---

[1] Pope Francis, "Communication and Mercy: A Fruitful Encounter," Message for the 50th World Communications Day 2016.

"I Am the Way, the Truth, and the Life" (Jn 14:16)

When I started my ministry as the congregational communication coordinator, and reflected on this passage from John's Gospel, I found a way to use the available media effectively. I was given the opportunity and the responsibility *to indicate the way, to tell the truth,* and *to celebrate the life* of my congregation by using multiple communication technologies for what I publish online.

Indicating the Way

We are called to find a way to connect with one another. The internet offers us one possibility, and we cannot be grateful enough to those people who contributed their knowledge, creativity, and persistence to develop this technology. But while the use of media such as organizational websites, Facebook, Twitter, Instagram, or TikTok can be beneficial, it cannot replace the value of a face-to-face encounter that can lead to deep friendship and connectedness to others. There are many different ways to connect with people—the only *golden rule* to remember is that *we belong to God and that is what makes us belong to one another.* These days it's very easy to connect through the internet, anytime and anywhere. Thus, it is our responsibility to choose what is meaningful and useful to us to our spiritual life, in view of our mission. It is to be hoped that connections will grow into true encounters. For our communication to be effective, it ought to appeal to the imagination and passion of those we wish to invite to an encounter with the mystery of God's love.

Telling the Truth

> Communication has the power to build bridges, to enable encounter and inclusion, and thus to enrich society.[2]

Through the many forms of electronic communications and internet presence, we and our mission partners share news and circulate information. This enables us to build up connections and strengthen networks and partnerships in a way that promotes our mission and values. Care, however, is needed, as a responsible use of the various forms of media—whether audio, visual, or traditional text—also involves being sensitive to the impact of our communication on people and their reputation. It

---

[2] Ibid.

is important to remember that people, not pieces of equipment, are the source of all communication.

Congregations sometimes encounter crisis situations that may place them in an undesirable spotlight. But for the sake of mission and in an effort to build bridges, we can use these situations as an opportunity to promote our values in a highly visible way. The media is the window through which the world sees us—and how we respond. On our journey we need to pause and ask ourselves:

- Is our communication at the service of an authentic culture of encounter?
- Are we telling the real stories about our mission around the world in an authentic way?
- Are we helping others to know us in an appropriate way highlighting connectedness and friendships?
- Are we able to acknowledge our failures or weaknesses?

In my opinion, news from our religious communities is sometimes very similar to the secular press. We forget to share our experience of God's peace and wisdom with the world and open the hearts of our audience to see themselves as God sees them and invite them to be transformed and to be a transformer as well.

Celebrating Life

Many cultures have much to share regarding what is essential in life. Our mission stories can create a life-giving experience for our audience and shape relationships among us and others. Pope Francis describes this aspect of relationship very well:

> Human beings are storytellers. From childhood we hunger for stories just as we hunger for food. Stories influence our lives, whether in the form of fairy tales, novels, films, songs, news, even if we do not always realize it. Often, we decide what is right or wrong based on characters and stories we have made our own. Stories leave their mark on us; they shape our convictions and our behavior. They can help us understand and communicate who we are.[3]

When communicating, we express who we are, what is important to us, and what our values are. Our life is a story, whether good or bad. Clearly, as religious communicators, we need to ensure that our messages

---

[3] Ibid.

communicate the good news that gives life—the fundamental message we want others to know. In our relationships and connectedness we seek to build people up, not tear them down. Their dignity should never be compromised.

Internet at the Service of Mission

Last year a decision was made in my congregation to continue having an international gathering that was scheduled to occur in France in preparation for our 2021 congregation's Chapter. When the pandemic prevented us from having an in-person meeting, we had to make major adjustments. Our original plan was to have four groups of face-to-face sessions, each spread over eleven days, with a total of sixty-six hours of content. Instead, we had to have virtual gatherings that accommodated numerous time zones as well as connection challenges. Our final decision was to condense the content to what could be done in twenty hours over a five-day period. Repeating this process for eight weeks would allow us to broadcast the presentations in the various time zones and language groups in a way that encouraged much wider participation. As no one could travel, we started with an eight-month preparation process. During the early days of preparation we were energized by an encouraging letter from congregational leader Sr. Ellen Kelly, RGS, who at the peak of the pandemic wrote:

> We know that God has no limitations and God is with us on this journey and the energy of the God who is love will enable us to continue our mission as Sisters and Partners. . . . If Our Foundress Mary Euphrasia Pelletier were here today, she would be filled with joy at the collaboration and the great zeal of our partners and our sisters working together in the midst of this pandemic. This pandemic is our dark night and people like John of the Cross can lead us to a deeper understanding of our Trinitarian life calling us to live communion, interconnectedness and relationship with all people and oneness with all creation. The reality is we are ONE.[4]

To prepare for our first international event of this scope, we divided the planning team into three groups: facilitators were responsible for the content; a liturgy group handled prayer services; and the communication

---

[4] Sr. Ellen Kelly, letter, April 24, 2020 (on the occasion of St. Mary Euphrasia's feast day).

office managed all the technical elements and determined which virtual platform would be best for us to utilize. Once we had selected the platform, we began to look at the internet service available in each country and advise the sisters of the requirements needed for this type of meeting to permit them to have adequate bandwidth and capacity for livestreaming the event. Next, we trained sisters and mission partners, provided the needed equipment to our units in seventy-two countries around the world in preparation for the virtual meetings, and conducted several tests with users in different countries. During each test session and in the actual gathering, live presentations were given in English with simultaneous translations into French, Spanish, Italian, Portuguese, Japanese, and German, as needed by participating countries. Aware that internet connections are not always reliable in some countries, we also developed a backup plan that included sending pre-taped presentations ahead of time and had participants download them in case any internet issues arose during the gathering. This was to enable them to watch the video and join us for sharing. At each of the eight actual gatherings, sisters and mission partners spent five days reflecting, praying, and learning together in a sacred space.

I was very grateful that the new technology permitted us to use several platforms to facilitate these gatherings online, as they provided beneficial ways to share our insights and helped us to connect and conduct our meetings as if we were holding them face to face. Rather than limiting discussion groups to local areas, we encouraged participants to join with new people across the globe through WhatsApp, Skype, Facebook, and others. Our registration data revealed that instead of 460 participants in a physical space, we had 1,400 virtually; and as these numbers grew, we were even more thrilled knowing that the relationships and connectedness have continued spontaneously. The combined work of our preparation teams enabled us to build a sacred space in an atmosphere of openness and freedom to share our wishes, hopes, and dreams in shaping our future. Participants' feedback showed that a deeper communion and oneness with one another was achieved at a higher level than we had hoped. In addition, the process used helped participants to better appreciate the culture of diversity, which was meaningful and life-giving to them.

Close teamwork and communication during the entire planning and implementation process was critical as we organized and executed a project of this scope. Our challenges were many when we began and delivered this project, but the positive results have compensated for all the time and effort needed to ensure the success of this endeavor.

Connectedness and Friendship

It is obvious that religious at all levels use the internet creatively to accomplish their duties and help announce the mission of their congregation. Given its many constructive possibilities, particularly when it is not possible for friends to meet, the internet can help community members maintain welcome connections with one another, family, and friends. In prolonged absences friendships can grow cold or wither if contacts are not kept up.

Throughout the Gospels we see Christ among friends. *They are connected.* Who are the people he connects with? Foreigners, outcasts, tax collectors, fishermen, men and women who helped do ordinary daily tasks. Already two-thousand years ago, Jesus used the media of voice and physical presence. Today, as we use these forms and many more, something new is being born and something old is being transformed, but our need for contact and friends is nothing new; our longing is the same. Our world grows smaller as our communication methods increase, but our need for one another remains constant. Friendships are life-giving.

Conclusion

In fulfilling the mission of our congregations, the internet is enormously beneficial for evangelization and proclaiming our values, which, in turn, enable progress in all ministry endeavors. Although our communities have weaknesses and may not be perfect, as we use the available technology
- we can be the eyes that can show a *way* for the world to see connections and partnerships focusing on mission;
- we can be the voice that can speak the *truth* to the world for those who are now the voiceless, particularly those whose dignity is compromised; and
- we can be an example of people who live an authentic *life* of ministry in service.

For the success of the mission, we envision a way of living in a world where we continually strive to build friendships and partnerships that celebrate the connectedness of all God's people and where the diversity of all life is honored and protected; and we share our insights, learnings, and experiences through the internet. There is, however, one exception to using the internet. It's when we seek God in prayer. No electronic connection or password needed! Only a believing heart.

Monique Tarabeh, RGS, a member of the congregation of Our Lady of Charity of the Good Shepherd, is communications coordinator of the congregation, and also president of Multimedia International. Born in Damascus, Syria, she served in Lebanon as director of an intercultural group home for girls in addition to doing interreligious work with Iraqi refugees.

Medical Mission

Mission as Healing

AGNES LANFERMANN, MMS

Mission as healing summarizes a wish I've had since my youth to bring hope in situations of conflict, of separation (such as in East Germany and West Germany), or of economic inequity. During my theological studies I realized that it was Christians who decided in the Nazi concentration camps the fates of millions of women and men who were discriminated against due to their ethnicities or political or religious convictions. This unfathomable mystery of the Holocaust urged me to give my life for a "new" world and to work toward healing and reconciliation, because "*another world is possible*."[1]

The international Congregation of Medical Mission Sisters' understanding of mission as promoting healing and wholeness in all aspects of life, in the healing presence of Jesus Christ, prompted me to join the community in 1981 after concluding my theological studies. Since then I have become interested in the constantly evolving understanding of the charism of healing in mission and spirituality. People's life stories taught me about the dynamics in processes of healing and about long journeys toward becoming reconciled. At the moment, the idea of "*becoming one*"[2] speaks to me, that is, being deeply connected with all people and the whole of creation on the journey to being united in Christ.

In this short contribution I describe the evolution in medical mission that took place in many congregations, with my own congregation as a concrete example.

---

[1] Medical Mission Sisters, "Walking beyond Boundaries: The Society's Study on Religious Life and the Vows" (London, 2010), 10.

[2] Medical Mission Sisters, "Our Evolving Understanding of Spirituality and Mission: Renewal—A Continuous Journey" (London, 2019).

Starting from Medical Care

Healing did not generally become a topic of concern for Christian missions until the advent of medical missions in the nineteenth century.[3] By the turn of the of the century, in 1900, medical mission was deemed so essential that the Ecumenical Missionary Conference in New York proclaimed that no mission could be "considered fully equipped that has not its medical branch."[4]

At the same time, the Catholic Church was still bound by the decrees of the Fourth Lateran Council and remarkably hesitant to embrace medical missions.[5] The situation changed in 1925, when Anna Dengel, an Austrian medical doctor, founded the Catholic women congregation of Medical Mission Sisters (MMS) in Washington, DC. She gathered an international group of women who combined the professional vocations of medical doctors, nurses, and midwives with a religious vocation. The aim was to offer medical care to Muslim women who had little or no access to medical treatment.

Medical mission was understood to be the imitation of Jesus, who demonstrated healing and wholeness through the visible physical healing of diseases. People were to see the goodness and compassion of a self-giving and all-loving God reflected in the service the sisters rendered in newly built hospitals. They attended to people of all cultures and religions without discrimination and counted on everybody in engaged in healing ministries—Muslims, Christians, Hindus, and others—because, as Anna Dengle would point out, they were all working for the same purpose.

Medical mission was identified with hospitals. The work of the doctors and nurses was seen as heroic, risking the possibility of being overworked, getting sick, or even dying for the sake of the gospel.

In the second half of the twentieth century, as missionary thinking reacted to the relationship between the "giver and receiver of mission,"[6]

---

[3] Christopher Grundmann, "Mission and Healing in Historical Perspective," *International Bulletin of Mission Research* 32, no. 4 (October 2008): 185–88.

[4] *Report of the Ecumenical Missionary Conference on Foreign Missions, held in Carnegie Hall and Neighboring Churches April 21 to May 1, 1900*, 2 vols. (New York: American Tract Society, 1900), 2:199.

[5] The Fourth Lateran Council of 1215 included the study and practice of medicine. Canon 18 is aimed at preventing clerics from causing the shedding of blood in the practice of surgery. See Andreas Kjeldsen, "The Origins and Reception of the 'Medical Canons' of the Fourth Lateran Council" (April 2009).

[6] Robert J. Schreiter, "Reconciliation and Healing as a Paradigm of Mission," *International Review of Mission* 94, no. 372 (2005): 77.

this question came up: Do the hospitals still touch the lives of those most in need of healing?

Going to the Root Causes of Suffering

Analyzing the root causes of repeated sickness, constant bad health, and lack of access to medical care, healing mission widened the horizon and looked into the poor conditions caused by social and economic injustices and their impact on health and healing. As hospitals became more accessible to the poor, mission shifted from the curative model of primarily hospital-based to community-based preventive care and health education, and to complementary and holistic healthcare.

The proclamation of the reign of God and the liberation from poverty and oppression swept throughout the poor of the world. Medical Mission Sisters understood mission "as a personal and communal call to involve ourselves in the transformation of the world as we join with others who struggle for freedom, justice, and love."[7]

Including the Option for the Poor

Medical mission also became deeply connected to the preferential option for the poor, as described in Catholic social teaching documents.[8] The "poor" were the marginalized in countries of the southern hemisphere, victims of injustice, and the oppressed.

Accompaniment, dialogue, contextualization, and liberation guided and shaped medical mission activities. Living close to the poor and those on the margins, the missionaries entered their lives, being humble enough to give of themselves and open to being affected by them. Medical Mission Sisters experienced the encounters as a process of mutual growth and seeking, where all involved became more sensitive to one another and learned from the different approaches and perspectives.

In working together with the poor, the Sisters helped the poor to discover their own potential to improve their quality of life, to seek justice for health, and to take their health and well-being into their own hands.

---

[7] Congregation of Medical Mission Sisters General Chapter, 1979.

[8] See, for example, the Pontifical Council for Justice and Peace, *Compendium of the Social Doctrine of the Church* (2004), nos. 182–84; and Pope Francis, apostolic exhortation *Evangelii Gaudium The Joy of the Gospel* (2013), no. 199.

The poor and marginalized were and continue to be the ones who give their unique contribution to the evolving understanding of healing in mission and the spirituality of the Medical Mission Sisters.

Acting with a Holistic Approach

Medical mission grew into a healing mission that encompasses many aspects of human life. In addition to physical health, social, emotional, political, economic, psychological, and spiritual health began to be considered as Medical Mission Sisters shifted their mission from medical care to promoting healing and wholeness in all aspects of life. They focused on the essentials of healing and how they could embody what they believed. Learning how to "become fully human"[9] became essential, as well as relating to people in many different circumstances in such a way that Christ's healing power might act through them.

Medical missioners looked into new methods in medical care through which people could have medical treatment in a less expensive but also more holistic way. For instance, in India ministry became less defined by medical care to the sick and more defined in terms of a holistic response to health and healing for all.

Holistic health works toward the integration of body, mind, spirit, and emotions, raising consciousness to explore how healing takes place in a person and in the context of ecological and cosmic interconnections. The purpose is to assume responsibility for one's own health and that of others. In holistic health the healing of the earth is integral to the health of people. All kinds of treatment can be used in holistic healing, but the most important thing is to use them appropriately and responsibly.

Medical Mission Sisters in India began to spread awareness of holistic health and its practices in 1980 through workshops held in many areas. In 1997, the sisters inaugurated a Holistic Health Centre in Pune for training and healing with alternative systems of medicine, both in a clinic and with outreach activities designed to reach especially the poor and neglected.

Alternate healthcare methods and efforts in India broadened to include drugless therapies; therapeutic counseling; rehabilitation of victims of drugs and alcohol abuse; actions against human trafficking; protection of ecology, environment, and biodiversity; safe migration of the poor; promotion of sustainable development; enhancement of socio-economic-cultural

---

[9] Godelieve Prové, *Becoming Human: A Story of Transformation Through Conflict and Healing* (Utrecht: Eburon Academic Publishers, 2005).

determinants of health; pastoral and palliative ministry; advocacy; and social justice activities. The focus was to bring about justice and dignity to women, children, and other marginalized people in the society. The journey continues in collaboration, partnership, and networking with church, religious, government, and likeminded groups.

Embracing the Spiritual Dimension of Healing Mission

Since ancient times the spiritual dimension has been an integral part of healing mission, pointing to the relationship among faith and health and healing. Consequently, *pastoral* care became an important aspect of the new view of *medical* care.

People with theological and pastoral expertise who were involved in healing mission shared their knowledge of pastoral care in hospitals and hospices, in social pastoral work, and in education and formation. The healing of memories in ecumenical settings as well as interreligious dialogue became part of healing mission as well.

Healing mission included accompaniment of physical and spiritual growth processes, in which life-hindering images of God could be replaced by life-giving ones. Wounds of the past began to heal and became like "clay jars" that hold a "treasure" (cf. 2 Cor 4:7) of reconciliation and a promise of a fuller life. Connecting to a loving and forgiving image of God supported healing from experiences of being treated unjustly as well as healing from feelings of guilt in reaching out to forgive.

Medical Mission Sisters intensified reflection on the spiritual dimension of healing mission in the late 1990s. In highly secularized societies, religion and faith were no longer influencing people's daily lives. At the same time, people's spiritual hunger did not find the food that could nurture their spiritual desires, whether they were in situations of crisis, suffering and dying, or on their daily life journeys.

The Center for Christian Meditation and Spirituality in Frankfurt, Germany, is a concrete example of an effort to address this spiritual need. In 2007, the diocesan center opened a space for people of all Christian denominations, worldviews, and cultures, and for all those with a great desire to express their own spirituality and to grow and mature on a journey that is authentic and not necessarily church connected.

Medical Mission Sisters are part of a team at the center, offering a program with workshops and exercises for body, mind, and soul that support growing and maturing on a personal spiritual journey as well as courses in meditation, contemplative prayer, yoga, Zen meditation, and meditative archery. Classes in yoga and Qi Gong, a kind of contemplation in motion, as well as traditional meditative dance performances from different cultures and religions widen the horizon in getting to know different methods of prayer. Creating new rituals with old (biblical) stories can also help people to find a way to express their spiritual needs.

All of these efforts will help to open an inner space for becoming one with oneself and for encounter with the Eternal. Silence and contemplation play an important role, as well as exercises to awaken the senses of seeing, hearing, feeling, and smelling to help open one's heart to the Divine.

Meditative singing, songs of the heart, mantras from different traditions, listening, and lingering in silence all connect people. Reflection days, retreats, and spiritual accompaniment inspire people. Special lectures and practice on Christian mysticism, biblical themes, and spiritual city walks help participants to see social-political issues in Frankfurt from a spiritual perspective.

In Advent, a labyrinth is created in the church using twenty-five-hundred tealights. Walking the path and meditating on the mystery of light and dark touches the hearts of many.

One important pillar of the spiritual dimension of healing is studying and reflecting on different issues. For instance, during the COVID-19 pandemic the issue of personal and communal vulnerability came to the surface. Sharing about the one's own vulnerability intensifies the experience that all are like brothers and sisters; none is better or worse, greater or smaller, or inferior or superior.

The mystery of Jesus the "wounded Healer" and the discovery of the hidden face of the risen Lord and the suffering God in the wounds of people deepen the understanding of healing and lead people to focus on the potential and new life in all woundedness and suffering.

Healing Even the Earth

Healing mission recognizes the persistence of poverty and misery and of the limits of and threats to the earth's capacity to sustain human life. The need to strengthen the interrelationship of mission, spirituality, and the integrity of creation has become obvious. Pope Francis spoke about "the intimate relationship between the poor and the fragility of the planet," noting that "everything is connected."[10]

---

[10] Pope Francis, *Laudato Si' (On Care for Our Common Home)* (2015), no. 16.

Now, healing mission includes environmental concerns in all activities in order to be a healing presence to the web of life, to witness to the integrity of all creation, and to act where this integrity is threatened. Ecological justice gives a new direction to healing mission and its context of the wounded universe.

The United Nations' Millennium Development Goals (MDGs) and Sustainable Development Goals (SDGs) have become essential for prioritizing the involvement of healing mission and networking across the globe with other like-minded groups.

Some projects of Medical Mission Sisters are directly involved with organizations and movements seeking to protect natural resources like water, forests, and land, such as HEAL (Haven for Ecological and Alternative Living) in Villasis, Philippines, which responds to the needs of healing the entire community of life, or SAMANVAYA—Eco-Holistic Healing and Health Center in Pune, India, which combines care for the earth with alternative health therapies. Urban-gardening initiatives in Duisburg, Germany, and London invite migrants and refugees to help care for the earth and for their families. Together with many likeminded people and organizations, the Medical Mission Sisters witness and promote the "justice, love, and peace" lifted up in the "Prayer for Our Earth" at the conclusion of *Laudato Si'*.[11]

Becoming One for the Healing of the Nations

A further evolution within mission as healing includes uniting for the healing of the nations with a global vision of mission that does not adhere to the North-South paradigm or to Eastern-Western cultural patterns, but shares a common purpose beyond cultural, national, and religious borders and boundaries.

A concrete example is the YouTube program "'Frauen aller Länder laden ein' zum multireligiösen Online-Gebet" (women from all countries and religions invite you) in Duisburg, Germany, supported by Medical Mission Sisters, in which Muslims, Christians, Jews, Hindus, and those without any religion get to know each other, as they dialogue and evolve from strangers into neighbors.

Racial justice responds to the disparate negative treatment of and discrimination against people on the basis of race, human chattel enslavement, and the forced removal of people from their ancestral homelands. Medical

[11] Ibid., no. 246.

Mission Sisters in North America consciously include the lens of racial justice in their decisions (for example, regarding investment decisions and employment polices) in the same way they seek to incorporate concern for ecological justice, gender justice, and other justice issues.

Intercultural living as mission is a call to become one as an intercultural body with a global mission to promote healing and wholeness in a divided world.[12] The intention of the members, from different cultures and nations, is to create a new culture where no particular group or ethnicity dominates the others, and where everyone is respected and feels at home. Intercultural living holds a vision for the greater good of all humanity and for living in a more fraternal relationship with the whole of creation.

Becoming a Healing Presence at the Heart of a Wounded Universe

Nowadays many different perspectives on healing shape healing mission worldwide. The following examples witness to the diversity of these efforts.

Mission as healing in *Africa* includes health programs that are hospital and community based; education; farming; and relief of poverty. In *India*, it includes grassroots and community development that targets scarcity of water, energy, food security, and sovereignty; ministries in hospitals and holistic health centers; and advocacy efforts around environmental justice issues like deforestation and mining.

In *East Asia*, healing mission is dedicated to the care of the earth and to indigenous people's education and rights. Medical Mission Sisters in *Pakistan* provide medical, educational, and social support to the community of brick-kiln workers in bonded labor (that is, modern-day slaves).

In *Europe*, one focus area is inclusive health, which promotes the inclusion of homeless, migrants, and refugees in mainstream health policies, laws, and programming. Other initiatives accompany survivors of abuse of power, such as victims of sexual violence or of different forms of spiritual abuse on their spiritual life journeys.

In *Latin America,* medical mission is present in the barrios located in the periphery of capital cities, and in semi-rural areas. In *Venezuela*, Medical Mission Sisters feed hundreds of people through their soup kitchen, and their water filtering system provides fresh drinking water to their

---

[12] Anthony J. Gittins, *Living Mission Interculturally: Faith, Culture, and the Renewal of Praxis* (Collegeville, MN: Liturgical Press, 2015).

neighbors. In addition, a radio program there reaches thousands of people twice a week, offering encouragement, support, and motivation.

In *North America*, healing mission includes interreligious dialogue at the grassroots, dismantling artificial constructs of race and caste, and walking the talk of radical relationality. Medical Mission Sisters and Associates in their elder years see their mission in deepening the quality of their engagement with the process of life. With the wisdom of who they are now in their later years, they are touching the sacredness of the intimate relationship between spirituality and mission and discovering the spiritual quest at the heart of mission, and mission as healing at the heart of spirituality.

Conclusion

The pain and suffering of the world will continue to echo in our hearts, and healing mission will remain engaged in the brokenness of the world. More than ever before we need to support one another when responding and be witnesses of hope and salvation.

In the end, mission as healing is God's mission—a journey where finally "the whole Universe will be transformed into a Christ consciousness characterized by communion and interdependence."[13]

> **Agnes Lanfermann, MMS,** was born in Kirchhellen, Germany. She studied theology, philosophy, and pastoral psychology; served in religious formation, education of religious formation, and different roles of leadership; worked at the Jesuit Graduate School of Philosophy and Theology in Frankfurt; and currently serves as a consultant for Consecrated Life in the Diocese of Limburg.

---

[13] Constance FitzGerald, OCD, 2017 LCWR Outstanding Leadership Award acceptance remarks, Orlando, Florida, August 11, 2017.

Education

The Transforming Role of Education

Maria Antonetta Pereira, FMM

India is one of the four "valley civilizations" in the world: Egypt is in the valley of the Nile; India is in the valley of the Indus, Ganga, and Narmada; Mesopotamia is in the valley of the Tigris and the Euphrates; and China is in the valley of the Wangho, the Yangtze Kiang, and the Si.[1] India had its own system of education, which can be traced back to the time of the Aryans, who ruled from about 542 BCE.[2] The Aryans developed and practiced the *gurukula* system of education, which was very unique to India.[3] The *gurukula* system, which has seen a revival in modern times,[4] was inspired by the Vedic School of thought, where the *shishya* (student) acquired knowledge by living with his *guru* (teacher). The teacher did not receive a fee, as teaching was a vocation and education was a service. Great centers of learning existed well before the advent of Christianity and the arrival of Christian missionaries.

The way of teaching was fundamental, practical, and taught the religious way to realize *nirvana* (salvation) here and now in daily life. Life was a kind of process to learn mentally and spiritually; hence, there was a mutual relationship between religion and education.[5] However, not all were entitled to receive education. Education was reserved to the Brahmins and other upper-caste Hindus. The caste system prevented ordinary people

---

[1] H. K. Bagga and Indrani Choudhury, *A Textbook of History and Civics* (New Delhi: Jay Cee Publications, 2007), 15.

[2] Ibid., 34.

[3] Ram Ahuja, *Society in India: Concepts, Theories, and Recent Trends* (Jaipur: Rawat Publications. 1999), 215.

[4] See Madalsa Ujjwal, *Swami Dayanand Saraswati: Life and Ideas* (Jodhpur: Book Treasure Publications, 2008), 96–97.

[5] Fritz Blackwell, *India: A Global Studies Handbook* (Santa Barbara, CA: ABC-CLIO, 2004), 88.

from acquiring education or even from hearing the lessons. Thus, lack of education accounted for the lack of development among the masses, for the perpetuation of poverty, and for lives filled with superstitious beliefs.

Besides the *gurukula*, the temple and the monastery have also been sites of education in India. Colonization and the influx of missionaries opened India to the Western system of education. However, once again, this was accessible only to the elite, royalty, and the upper castes—people with land and money. A movement to establish missionary educational institutions away from the cities into the tribal areas made quality education available and affordable to the ordinary masses. Though this irked the powerful, it also angered religious fundamentalists.

The liberal Western and nationalistic ideas imparted through Western education and Christian social activities played an important role in the nineteenth-century Indian renaissance, and the Christian contribution to Indian education paved the way for the eradication of some of the social evils in India.[6]

Several studies have been done on the role of Christian missionaries and church bodies in the education system in India from the colonial era on. This essay acknowledges all those studies but presents a new reflection on the transformation *of* education and the transformation *by* education. The first part looks at three of the shifts that education has undergone in India; the second part explores three areas in which education has brought about a transformation in society; and the third part proposes some practical options to reinforce the transforming role of education.

Transformation of Education

Since nothing remains static, education too has undergone an evolution, marked by shifts in sociocultural, political, and religious viewpoints.

Shift One: From a Privilege of a Few to the Right of the Masses

As mentioned earlier, education was the privilege of a few: the progeny of the rich and the upper caste. The lower castes and the outcastes had no right or access to anything concerning learning. This was religiously ordained, culturally sanctioned, and meticulously followed by society. A

---

[6] S. M. John Kennedy, "Christian Contribution to Indian Education," *Research and Reflections on Education* 17, no. 6 (January–March 2018).

classic example is that of Dr. Bhimrao Ambedkar, the architect of the Indian Constitution. As a boy he was denied a place in the classroom at his village school because he belonged to the untouchable community. He was able to pursue his education at Elphinstone High School and later at Elphinstone College, Bombay, because these Christian institutions lived up to their motto—all are equal under God. In the early nineteenth century Christian missionaries introduced this revolutionary concept of education for all.

Furthermore, when education eventually moved from the hallowed precincts of the missionary schools to the bamboo huts or under the Banyan trees in the villages and countryside, it brought learning to the masses, including women, thanks to the efforts of pioneers like Mahatma Jotirao Phule and his wife, Savitribai Phule. They initiated education for women, especially for widows.[7] A girl child was always the property of the father, her spouse, or her son. A widow would often be burned on the funeral pyre with her husband (sati custom), as her lack of education and qualification would leave her with no means to fend for herself. The proverbial saying "educate a woman and you educate a nation" was indeed the backbone of development for women, gender equality, and bringing education to the masses.

Social reformers like the Phules, who were themselves educated, promoted values such as the removal of the caste restrictions, equality for women, doing away with harmful social customs and practices, giving women a voice in the governance of the country, and establishing democratic institutions. They regarded education as a flame or light of knowledge that could dispel the darkness of ignorance.[8]

Shift Two: From a Tool of Oppression to a Tool of Liberation

It is said that in a kingdom of the blind, a one-eyed person is king. This was true of the majority of people, who were told what to do and how to live by the few who made the laws, interpreted the religious texts, and ruled over the masses. The elite had the tool of education, which they used to subdue the masses and keep them submissive. But once the masses began to be educated, their eyes were opened and they started to question, criticize, and demand justice, equality, and their rightful place

---

[7] Namita Patil, "Role of Education in Social Change," *International Educational E-Journal* 1, no. 2 (Jan-Mar 2012).
[8] Ibid.

in society. Thus, education made those who were considered to be backward or outcaste by birth, socially forward, economically compatible, and politically capable. Education has led to the liberation of the people from ignorance, blind obedience, and superstition.

Shift Three: From the Means of Mission to Being a Mission

The missionaries had used education as a means for making inroads among the masses. This was especially true wherever the mission-compound model was adopted, in which a school and a medical facility (dispensary) were crucial components. The missionaries were engaged in imparting both practical instruction and moral values, which made their schools distinct. Even though they were an explicitly proselytizing agency, these schools were well accepted, mostly because the general moral tone was perceived to be superior in mission schools.[9]

The mission-compound model was then succeeded by government schools established at the national level. The Indian Education Commission of 1964–66 began its historical report by stating: "The destiny of Indians is now being shaped in the classrooms."[10] In more recent times the government schools have been replaced by state-sponsored schools or private institutions. Education is an important part of the development process in modern India and may well lead to widespread social transformation. Thus, the government is committed, at least in principle, to bringing literacy and education to all. Education for All, a global movement led by UNESCO, is the Government of India's flagship program for the achievement of universalization of elementary education.

Transformation through Education

Education is a key part in the process of transforming individuals. It is a continuous journey that calls for change and for the humanizing of the individual and the world. If education cannot transform, there is something wrong with it. We explore three transforming aspects of education.

---

[9] Hayden J. A. Bellenoit, "Missionary Education, Religion, and Knowledge in India, c. 1880–1915," *Modern Asian Studies* 41, no. 2 (March 2007).

[10] C. V. Myageri, *Educational Organisation Administration and Management* (Gadag: Vidyanidhi Prakashana, 2005), 354.

Education Enables

The Sanskrit word for education is *Shiksha*. According to Pundit Ram Prasad Tripathi, it derives from the root *sak*, meaning "to be able."[11] Education by nature has a mission (to enable) embedded in its meaning. As Maurice Craft noted in 1984, there are two different Latin roots of the English word *education*. They are *educare*, which means "to train" or "to mold," and *educere*, meaning "to lead out." Although the two meanings are quite different, they are both represented in the word education: one implies the preservation and passing down of knowledge through instruction; the other sees education as preparing a new generation for the changes that are to come. One calls for rote memorization and becoming good workers; the other requires questioning, criticism, thinking, and creating. Thus, education is finding the right balance between learning to read and write and mastering the ability to choose between right and wrong.[12] The mission of education is incomplete if students have only earned a certificate. Education accomplishes its mission if the earned certificate enables them to create a future for themselves and others. However, so far education has mainly enabled the ambitious, the advantaged, to outdo the rest and to remain at the top of the social and political hierarchies, enabling the rich to become policymakers and decision makers.

Education Empowers

Education is directly related to the development of an individual and a community. It is one of the most important factors for economic development as well as social emancipation. Empowerment can be viewed as a means of creating a social environment in which a person can make decisions and retain control of key aspects of life. Empowerment is the process of enabling or authorizing an individual to think, take action, and generally live in an autonomous way.[13] It is the process by which someone can gain control over his or her future and the circumstances of life. The education of women is a milestone in their empowerment because

---

[11] *Sak* is a Sanskrit word pertaining to pronunciation. In this context it refers to one of the six limbs of Vedic studies.

[12] Maurice Craft, "Education for Diversity," in *Education and Cultural Pluralism*, ed. Maurice Craft (1984; London: Routledge, 2018).

[13] Arjun Sarader, "Education as a Panacea for Empowerment of Women in India," in *Gender Perspectives in Indian Context: Critical Responses*, ed. Dipak Giri (Chhattisgarh: Booksclinic Publishing, 2021), 190.

it enables them to respond to challenges, confront their traditional role, and take control of and change their lives. And when education empowers women in this way, it brings about a positive change in attitude, which makes a significant difference in the lives of previously oppressed women. Well-educated women are "game changers" in every society, creating a better future for themselves and for others. Gender-equitable education systems empower girls and boys and promote the development of life skills—like self-management, communication, negotiation, and critical thinking.

With the arrival of the British colonizers in the early nineteenth century, education became accessible to the lower castes and Adivasis (Tribals).[14] With knowledge came the desire to be recognized and respected. It strengthened the resolve of Dalits and Adivasis to struggle against discrimination. But although education has empowered women, outcastes, the socially unseen, and the untouchables, the divide between lower and upper castes is still far from being bridged.

Education Elevates

Education is a marvelous tool for freeing a society from violence and moving toward peace, whereas the lack of education often contributes to increasing instances of poverty, social unrest, antisocial elements, and crime, in addition to violence against women. Education is a continual process that can be acquired anywhere, at any time or age, by anyone. It is a fundamental right of every citizen, which is beneficial because it promotes empowerment and ensures development. Education can bring about the betterment of society because it helps to elevate the social and economic standard of those who are marginalized. Educated citizens become aware of their rights, overcome superstitious beliefs, make informed choices, and promote a healthier and more fruitful lifestyle. Nevertheless, in certain communities in India, education has remained only a well-earned trophy that has no real power to challenge harmful social customs and violence against women, Tribals, and Dalits carried out in the name of long-entrenched social and religious practices.

The Transforming Role of Education

There is little doubt that education has played a crucial role in the transformation of societies. Yet it should be noted that it is mostly formal or

---

[14] Patil, "Role of Education in Social Change."

institutional education that tends to be regarded as the major player in the field of education. Thus, for Christian missionaries, Pope Francis asserts, our mission is "to have the necessary *parrhesía* [boldness] to leave behind superficial approaches to education and the many short-cuts associated with utility, (standardized) test results, functionality and bureaucracy, which confuse education with instruction and end up atomizing our cultures. Instead, we should aim to impart an integral, participatory and polyhedral culture."[15] In other words, access to aptitude tests and rote learning are not enough to bring about true societal transformation.

The COVID-19 pandemic has brought to light a marked disparity in educational and technological opportunities, as large numbers of children and adolescents have fallen behind in the natural progression and process of schooling. How can missionaries bridge this disparity? If the mission of education—education for all—is to be achieved, we need to think differently, especially in the post-pandemic times. Apart from the educational institutions, where those seeking education come to us, we have to bring education to the doorstep of those already marginalized due to their occupation, poverty, or traditional and cultural practices. In several countries there are now encouraging efforts to look beyond school-based systems in order to ensure that the rights articulated in global statements such as the United Nations Millennium Declaration and the World Declaration on Education for All, can be fully exercised by everyone.[16] Here are some options that have proven to bear fruit:

- creation of temporary, moving schools, especially for catering to the needs of nomads, pastoralists, and other seasonal migrants in the rural, tribal, and mountain areas;
- creation of mobile "schools on wheels" for the children of pavement dwellers, slum dwellers, construction workers, rag pickers, and so on, in the urban and semi-urban areas;
- continuation of education through a mixture of distance learning, mobile schools, and static schools;
- provision of flexible school schedules for children engaged in work;

---

[15] Pope Francis, "Global Compact on Education: Together to Look Beyond," video message on the occasion of the meeting organized by the Congregation for Catholic Education, Pontifical Lateran University, October 15, 2020.

[16] See Office of the High Commissioner for Human Rights, "United Nations Millennium Declaration," September 8, 2000; and Seretariat of the International Consultative Forum on Education for All, "World Declaration on Education for All and Framework for Action to Meet Basic Learning Need," Jomtien, Thailand, March 5–9, 1990 (New York: UNESCO, 1990).

- provision of commonly available facilities like technology and other tools for accessing online education; and
- creation of a curriculum tailored to the local context and the learner's needs.

The list can be inexhaustible. Were not these methods employed by Jesus when he was teaching and instructing his disciples and followers? He chose natural settings: mountains, plains, seashores. He went to where people were, connecting with them at homes, synagogues, funerals, and temple. He used examples from day-to-day life to which his listeners could relate, such as yeast, a vineyard, oil, bread, a friend knocking on the door, widows, a lost coin, sheep and shepherds, sparrows, and lilies. His methodology has yielded positive results. Even today such innovative strategies have shown considerable positive impact. This approach views education not as a single factor for development, but as a partner in a multidisciplinary endeavor to achieve the integral development of individuals and societies.

Conclusion

As I conclude I remember a mantra from the Brhadaranyaka Upanishad (1.3.28), *Om asatoma sadgamaya*. The translation of the entire Mantra reads, "Lead us from ignorance to knowledge, from darkness to light, and from death to immortality." Every time I hear this Mantra, I realize a desire for a transformed life in it. Education has the capacity to fulfill that desire.

Humanity today is at the crossroads of inevitable change. These changes are influencing our social institutions, such as the family, community, religion, political systems, financial institutions, and so on, besides affecting our individuality and our human relations and interactions. In such a context we are challenged to respond. Even the increasingly hostile environment toward Christians in India invites us to respond by dialoguing with these realities. Our commitment to social change through education is more crucial than ever. We must make education a mission to empower, enable, and elevate the masses in order to educate human beings to be capable of upholding life and the rights of all.

> **Maria Antonetta Pereira, FMM,** holds a diploma in nursing, midwifery, and pharmacy, and has a BTh from Vidyajyoti College of Theology, Delhi, and a Licentiate in Sacred Theology (*Summa cum Laude*) from Loyola School of Theology, Manila. She has taught theology at Institute Mater Dei and at Laity Theology, Goa, and is currently involved in formation.

Missionary Parishes

Growing as a Missionary Parish

Lazar T. Stanislaus, SVD

The church is missionary and she carries out the mission of the Father, Son, and Holy Spirit—the "trinitarian mission"[1]—this is to communicate the divine life to humanity, so that we can, by God's grace, be true children of God. The church carries out its mission in many diverse ways; parish ministry is one of these. It is a well-known fact that the highest number of priests are engaged in parish work, which makes sense given that the parish is the basic structure of the church. However, most of the men's religious congregations engage in parish ministry more than in other ministries, while only a very few women's religious congregations engage in parish ministry. Pope Francis recalled that "the parish is the presence of the church in a given territory, an environment for hearing God's word, for growth in the Christian life, for dialogue, proclamation, charitable outreach, worship and celebration," and affirmed that it is "a community of communities."[2]

Although parish ministry is one of the powerful means of building and engaging a Christian community, today the question arises: How can a parish become a missionary parish? As Francis asserts, quoting Pope Benedict XVI, "We need to move 'from a pastoral ministry of mere conservation to a decidedly missionary pastoral ministry.'"[3] A parish without a missionary dimension is a dead parish or a "toll house."[4] Pope Francis's missionary intention for September 2017 was "that our parishes animated

---

[1] See *Catechism of the Catholic Church* (Vatican City: Libreria Editrice Vaticana, 1994), 257.
[2] Pope Francis, *Evangelii Gaudium (The Joy of the Gospel)* (2013), 28, hereinafter *EG*.
[3] *EG*, no. 15, quoting *Letter of His Holiness Benedict XVI to the Bishops of Latin America and the Caribbean* (2007), 370.
[4] Cf. *EG*, no. 47.

by a missionary spirit may be places where faith is communicated and charity seen." He keeps insisting—and inspiring—that a parish is a *field hospital* and a *caring mother*. Missionary work is at the heart of being a Catholic or a parish. Every Catholic, every parish is missionary, and all are called to be "missionary disciples." In this short essay every aspect of a mission parish cannot be fully explored. Thus, we shall just outline some of its main aspects.

Importance of Renewal in a Parish

One of the concerns today is that parishes are largely meant to serve pastoral needs, but their involvement in administrative work takes up the pastoral team's time and energy. As a 2020 Vatican instruction notes: "The Parish territory is no longer a geographical space only, but also the context in which people express their lives in terms of relationships, reciprocal service and ancient traditions. . . . Any pastoral action that is limited to the territory of the Parish is outdated."[5] Therefore, renewal is needed to change the parish structure. "The conversion of structures, which the Church must undertake, requires a significant change in mentality and an interior renewal, especially among those entrusted with the responsibility of pastoral leadership."[6]

The pastoral conversion of structures also implies giving importance to the lay faithful who are missionary disciples; "therefore, when we reflect, think, evaluate, discern, we must also be very attentive" to their spiritual development and vocation.[7] And we must remember that a parish, rather than remaining focused on preserving the existing community, is called to reach out to everyone, without exception, particularly the poor. As we seek to make structural and functional changes, the ministries in the parish and the involvement of the lay faithful are also very important in this renewal process. And we must remember that the ultimate goal of the church is the eternal salvation of all people—the Catholics, the people of other faiths, the various races and cultures, the poor, the excluded, and those who are on the margins.

---

[5] Congregation for the Clergy, *Instruction "The Pastoral Conversion of the Parish Community in the Service of the Evangelizing Mission of the Church,"* Rome (2020), no. 16.

[6] Ibid., no. 35.

[7] Ibid., no. 37.

Approaches to Becoming a Missionary Parish

We are all committed to God's mission, but our approach to mission can differ according to the context. It is said that we need to open our mouths, stretch out our hands, and look at all the possibilities or alternatives in order to achieve our goal. Every parish needs to design its own approach in becoming a missionary community, but a few practical considerations are outlined below.

Hospitality

The parish is for everyone—believers and nonbelievers, members and guests, sinners and saints. Having a structure to welcome people in a parish is important; for example, "our church doors should always be open."[8] The availability of someone in the parish to attend to the needs of the people who come in the door, making them feel comfortable with a kind word and attending to their needs, taking pains to show that they are important and respected, are some basic steps for a parish.[9] Everyone should feel that there is no discrimination and that all are welcome—diverse cultures, nations, and peoples. A parish that shows *openness* to others and treats people with *respect* will help create an inviting and beneficial atmosphere. Being available to people all the time may not be possible, but one must be attentive to the local culture and customs in this regard.

Dialogue

Listening, sharing, and transparency are important for any family or community; when one listens with respect and shares one's feelings and thinking with an attitude of solidarity and love, a good relationship is established. True dialogue with respect for the other helps each person to grow with confidence. It is life giving, and it gives us the impulse to relate to more people. To grow as a missionary parish, dialogue is paramount among people. In dialogue we seek "the signs of Christ's presence,"[10] and in this process we try to overcome prejudice, violence, and hate. When

---

[8] *EG*, no. 47.

[9] Fr. Stephen Pullis, "Three Key Ways to Be Missionary at Your Parish," *Unleash the Gospel* (August 17, 2020).

[10] Pope John Paul II, *Redemptoris Missio (On the Permanent Validity of the Church's Missionary Mandate)* (1990), no. 56.

the parish pastoral team engages with people in a true spirit of dialogue, and when people of diverse cultural or racial groups are in dialogue, good understanding and true love blossom. The use of social media can play a key role in this process. A well-structured mechanism for engaging in dialogue is very important, and creating opportunities or arranging programs for creative dialogue will give people confidence.

Friendship

Friendship helps to form a community; it invites others to get involved. People look to make new friends; often all that is required is taking the first step. If there are some newcomers, reach out to them and find ways to dialogue and establish contact. One easy way to root the friendship in Christ is to share one's own experience of being Catholic and then to ask the newcomers what they love about their Catholic faith. Children and youth need friendships. A parish that can plan an itinerary or arrange some programs to create friendship would be wonderful. Creating a friendly atmosphere among families, elderly people, and the physically challenged gives a parish a reputation that it is not just an administrative house but a place where Jesus's love is being expressed. Having a "culture of encounter"[11] will enable the parish to welcome all.

Celebration

A *celebrating parish* is an inviting parish—celebrating faith, family, and mission. A parish celebrates by what it says and does; this experience gives life-giving energy. When the people come to the parish and see a *community of faith that values family and that is committed to its mission*, they too are challenged to share in this community and mission. A missionary parish has to be creative in finding ways to meet the people's spiritual, social, and material needs. This is only possible if the parish knows its *people* (their needs and concerns), its *resources* (time, talents, and treasures), and its *priorities* (signs of the times, relevance, and appropriateness). For example, some parishes invite people to take part in activities to feel more personally connected to their community and its mission. A *see and experience* approach needs forward-looking measures. Hence, know the people and create opportunities to celebrate with them. Find ways for people to share their resources and to show goodness to others.

---

[11] Pope Francis, *Fratelli Tutti* (2020), nos. 215–16, hereinafter *FT*.

Toward the Growth of a Missionary Parish

Working with the laity in the parish is of paramount importance today. They are partners in mission, coworkers, not just recipients. As Pope John Paul II notes, "The lay faithful are seen not simply as laborers who work in the vineyard, but as themselves being a part of the vineyard."[12] Pope Benedict further asserts that the laity are not considered as "collaborators" with the clergy, but as persons truly "co-responsible in the Church."[13] Training laity for leadership in society and for retreat ministry, youth ministry, media ministry, and social ministry identifies some important steps that need attention today. Creating a structure in which the laity are involved with pastoral activities, finance and administrative structures, and decision-making processes would be helpful. Only together with laity can a parish grow in its missionary approach. The following dimensions are important in the missionary life of a parish community.[14]

Kerygmatic Community

The church, being God's people, proclaims and brings God's salvation into the world. "Through her evangelizing activity, she cooperates as an instrument of that divine grace which works unceasingly and inscrutably."[15] Simple gestures—such as making a sign of the cross when passing a church, teaching a child to join its hands in prayer, teaching the values of the kingdom to the youth and adults, making known the Person of Jesus through testimonies, and saying prayers in public places without disturbing others—are signs of a *kerygmatic* (proclaiming) community. The following are some of the ways that a parish can engage in building such a community:
- Create a group or commission in the parish for guiding kerygmatic activities.
- Prepare lay mission preachers for parish feast days, Lent, and Advent.
- Organize a Bible Week or Bible Month once a year.

---

[12] Pope John Paul II, *Christifideles Laici* (1988), no. 8.

[13] Pope Benedict XVI, Address at Castel Gandolfo, August 10, 2012.

[14] This section is taken largely from the booklet *Becoming an SVD Mission Parish*, ed. Lazar T. Stanislaus, SVD (Rome: Generalate, SVD Publications, 2020). The practical aspects given are largely from Mr. Royston Braganza, Mumbai, who contributed to this booklet. He is a very active lay leader and resource person for the church.

[15] *EG*, no. 112.

- With practical training, send out parishioners (two by two) as missionaries to be proclaimers in word (where possible) and action. This can be once a week or once a month.
- Schedule a "Jesus walk" where for sixty minutes a week all the parish pastoral team members leave their office, residence, or church, and go out into the marketplaces, train stations, and street corners to "be Jesus." Be Jesus by smiling, lifting a heavy parcel, or helping someone to cross the street, and thus by consciously leaving one's comfort zone and being one with strangers.

Vibrant Prayer and Liturgy

The celebration of the Eucharist is "the source and summit of the whole of Christian life."[16] The apostolic letter *Novo Millennio Ineunte* sets seven pastoral priorities: holiness, prayer, the Sunday celebration of the Most Holy Eucharist, the sacrament of penance, the primacy of grace, listening to the word, and proclaiming the word.[17] A missionary church is characterized by a joyful collaboration in prayer and liturgy, with a humble openness to the Spirit, who blows where it wills.[18] Creative prayer sessions and participation in a meaningful liturgy help the faithful to come closer to the Lord. People are attracted to a church where the liturgy touches their lives. The challenge is to make all the spiritual activities not mere rituals and obligations, but opportunities to change people's lives, helping them to love God and to love their neighbor in concrete ways. Some of the key ways to build a lively praying community are

- building inclusive liturgy teams of men and women, the young and the experienced, with clergy;
- establishing district/neighborhood prayer meetings and Eucharist celebrations;
- finding ways to include, in an appropriate way, different languages, ethnic music, and cultural expressions of spirituality in the regular parish liturgies;
- including in the liturgy an international dimension and a focus on the plight of the poor;
- having praise and worship sessions once a week or month; and
- teaching different forms of meditation, including quiet adoration of the Eucharist.

---

[16] Pope Paul VI, *Lumen Gentium* (1964), no. 11.
[17] Pope John Paul II, *Novo Millennio Ineunte* (2000), nos. 29–41.
[18] Jn 3:8.

Social Outreach Programs

Our faith in God calls us to love God and to love our neighbor, especially those in need. The poor, the marginalized, the excluded, and the unwanted in society were at the center of Jesus's mission. He encountered lepers, the blind, the dumb, suffering women, and socially excluded people, and he healed them and gave them dignity and showed them that God loves them.[19] Their cries rise to the skies; we need to listen to these cries and respond with suitable action. Many parishes have various associations and groups to help the poor, but a well-structured, coordinated program with the involvement of the whole parish is an ideal model. Caring for the poor is an important aspect of the church's ultimate, divine mission; thus, solidarity with the poor must be seen as the essential element of Christian life.[20] Some of the ways that parishioners can support one another and truly be church and catholic (universal) are

- feeding the poor, soup kitchens;
- designating "Providence rooms" (where people leave good-quality secondhand items for those in need to take);
- providing room for gatherings of self-help groups or civil organizations;
- providing employment cells or placement services;
- offering women's health and security services;
- creating classes for coaching needy students by retired teachers;
- maintaining medical devices such as wheelchairs that can be lent or circulated;
- creating a common social fund for the parish; and
- finding sponsors for needy students in higher education.

The Eco-Parish

The encyclical *Laudato Si'* calls us to hear the cry of Mother Earth and to hear the cry of the poor. It calls for every inhabitant of the earth to become a good steward of creation. The havoc caused by global warming and the harm done to our biodiversity are playing out before our eyes. A missionary parish is also called to be a "green" parish—extolling the glory of God in his people and all of creation. The Fridays for Future movement by Greta Thunberg has shown the commitment of young people to this cause, and various nongovernmental organizations have

---

[19] Lk 17:11–19; Mt 12:22; Mt 9:32–33; Lk 8:43–48; Mk 9:14–21 and 16:9.
[20] See *FT*, no. 116.

shown the way for addressing ecological concerns. The commitment of a parish to ecological concerns shows that the gravest moral crisis can be confronted. Some ways to do that:

- Promote "environmental conversion" based on *Laudato Si'*.[21]
- Celebrate annually the World Day of Prayer for the Care of Creation on September 1.
- Form a Green Committee that creates both a tactical and strategic plan to reduce the parish's carbon footprint, ultimately moving to a zero-net carbon parish.
- Involve Sunday School children, youth, and families in tactical and practical methods of reduce-reuse-recycle at home, at school, and on the church premises.
- Encourage parishioners (and the parish buildings) to have solar panels and kitchen gardens, to collect rainwater, and to create other environmentally friendly habits.
- Encourage zero- or single-use plastics and separate waste.

Celebration of Diverse Cultures

The diversity of human cultures is a gift of the Spirit. All cultures need redemption from elements of sin and death, but they have a lot of goodness and life-giving values, too. Recognizing cultures and their diversity is to recognize diverse people in a community. As the world shrinks and becomes a global village, our parishes are likely to become more cosmopolitan and heterogeneous in nature. Thus we need to adopt diverse cultural forms in the liturgy, Catechism, and social gatherings; search for ways to recognize and appreciate diverse cultures in a community; build an intercultural community that appreciates all cultures; and learn from various cultures but also challenge what is life negating or immoral in them. Here are some suggestions for doing this:

- Have a representative of diverse cultural members on every committee or association.
- Organize programs for a deeper understanding of the richness of cultures within the parish and neighborhood through such activities as youth groups, workshops, Bible sharing, social outreach, or storytelling among people from different cultures and backgrounds.

---

[21] In the Philippines, Catholic laypeople have formed a group called Living *Laudato Si'* Philippines based on this encyclical. It helps to connect and to cooperate with many organizations and parishes and try to implement this encyclical's objectives in their daily life. See Benigno Beltron, "Earth Stewardship, Economic Justice, and World Mission: The Teachings of *Laudato Si'*," *Missiology* 48, no. 1 (2020): 39–56.

- Create an opportunity for each culture to contribute to the growth of the parish.
- Create a platform to dialogue with other cultures to enrich one another and to build an intercultural community.

Media and Ministry

The cyber age is here to stay, and the world has changed rapidly through technological advancement. Whether digital, internet, social media, artificial intelligence (AI), big data, or blockchain—technology is everywhere. The internet is neutral in itself—it is what we make of it that determines its effect. It offers plenty of opportunities to do good, effective things, but it can also harm people by pornography, cybercrime, bullying, and so forth. When a parish uses the media, its missionary efficacy can improve. Today, it is not just the young; even the elderly use social media and various other new means to catch up with the world. Thus, the question is: How can a parish use media for mission?

- Harness the potential of the media in the new ways of being church for a generation growing up with smartphones and social media (Facebook, Instagram, Snapchat, WhatsApp, and so forth).
- Provide the crook and staff needed for the sheep to know the inherent risks of the media.
- Provide good examples of the missionary church through videos, short films, and other programs.
- Create digital platforms, media teams, and networking units.

Significance of Interculturation (vs. Inculturation)

Inculturation is a matter of fidelity to, and practice of, the reality, principle, economy, truth, and grace of the incarnation of God's Word. Inculturation of the church, of the gospel, of the faith, and of Christian life is a continuation of the coming anew of God's creative Energy, of God's Word. The church keeps on learning the process, method, and implementation of inculturation. To a large extent, it has not really succeeded in this approach, for many reasons. Even today, many understand what inculturation is but do not know how to implement it locally. Thus, inculturation is always a challenge, and it can only succeed if the local laity has a deep understanding of the culture and its significance, of the faith, of the gospel, and of the realities of the local church.

In the globalized world more parishes are becoming multicultural. Thus, today we go one step further in understanding intercultural mission by looking at *interculturation*. Building intercultural communities is the first step that leads to respecting and recognizing all cultures, creating room to learn from one another and to challenge one another, which leads to enriching oneself and transforming the community.[22] "What characterizes the practice and transmission of the faith in a universal Church is not by freezing the ('inculturated') expression of the Christian message in one particular culture, but by the dynamics of 'interculturation' constituted by *kenonis* (dying), *pascha* (transition to the new life) and 'mission' (the spirit being sent and sending in its turn)."[23] Attention to the dynamics of interculturation brings about new life and vigor in a community cherishing the *pascha* of Jesus Christ. Interculturation emerges more as a holistic and complex process in comparison to inculturation, and it is also a necessary condition for the latter in a universal (catholic) perspective. Some of the practical ways to promote interculturation are[24]

- conducting seminars and analyzing the goodness of each culture as well as any bad elements;
- interpreting the goodness of the culture using the Bible, the teaching of Jesus, and church traditions;
- making efforts so that each cultural group learns, adopts, or absorbs the goodness of other cultures;
- more important still, creating a new culture where the goodness of diverse cultures is expressed and where all feel that they are part of that new cultural expression, custom, or tradition; and
- letting the sacraments, pastoral works, social works, and all ministries include aspects of local cultures that everyone understands, appreciates, and feels at home in.

Looking Toward the Future

Establishing parishes using alternative approaches will pave the way for creative involvement. As Thomas Finger asserts: "The Church's main social task, then, is to embody alternative approaches to race relations,

---

[22] Lazar T. Stanislaus, SVD, and Martin Ueffing, SVD, *Intercultural Mission*, vol. 2 (New Delhi: ISPCK, 2015), xxvii.

[23] Franz Gmainer-Pranzl, "From 'Inculturation' to 'Interculturation': An Essay in Mission Theology," in Stanislaus and Ueffing, *Intercultural Mission*, 2:151.

[24] Stanislaus, *Becoming an SVD Missionary Parish*, 17.

violent conflict, poverty, and other issues—as an eschatological sacrament. Through these societies become aware of new, transformative possibilities. . . . Whatever the approach, missional announcement of the new creation's peace and justice will hardly be credible apart from communal efforts to visibly embody these."[25] Social action mission entails winning over the people and enriching their faith lives. It "does not leave room for sentiment, prejudice, racism, or nepotism. It functions above political, economic, social, religious, and cultural bias."[26] The alternative approach of a parish involved in social action makes it distinctive and attractive.

A *vision-mission statement* for each parish is of paramount importance for guiding its activities. This will include an action plan that outlines the visible signs of the parish, while the explicit actions will speak for themselves. Hence, the methodology behind the actions is important. The people, together with the pastoral leaders, can draw up a vision-mission statement and action plan. When a parish has a dream, it can be fulfilled through this effort. Pope Francis writes, "I dream of a 'missionary option,' that is, a missionary impulse capable of transforming everything."[27] But what is the dream of a parish? Or how does the parish motivate its members to have a dream? Some of the dreams could be

- *volunteerism*—having plenty of volunteers for the newly established commissions, associations, and other various activities;
- *faith in a public square*—encouraging all the faithful to live their Christian values in their families, in their offices or workplaces, and helping them to be able to celebrate their faith publicly without offending anyone;
- *mission outreach programs*—getting everyone involved in the outreach activities toward the poor, needy, excluded, and migrants; and
- *self-reliance and service oriented*—becoming financially self-sufficient and having the resources to do charitable work;
- *establishing justice and peace*—getting members involved in promoting a corruption-free, human rights–oriented, just society, and establishing reconciliation and peace in society.[28]

In the process of becoming a missionary parish, the parish will face many challenges. Conservative Christians think of a parish only as a sacramental outlet for caring for fellow Christians. The sacraments are important; they

---

[25] Thomas Finger, *A Contemporary Anabaptist Theology: Biblical, Historical, Constructive* (Downers Grove, IL: IVP Academic, 2004), 321.

[26] Benjamin Diara and Favour Uroko, "Applying the Principles of Social Action in Contemporary Christian Mission in Africa," *Missiology* 48, no. 2 (2020): 177.

[27] *EG*, no. 27.

[28] Stanislaus, *Becoming an SVD Missionary Parish*, 37–40.

are like pillars that support our faith life. But these pillars also support the vast horizon and point it out to the others who need God's love. A sacrament is an impulse to reach out to the other, radiating the divine; otherwise, the sacraments would be merely empty rituals.

Clericalism is another challenge. Clerics tend to develop an attitude of thinking "I know everything," and "I have the power to decide." This orientation, placing the priestly service on a higher level, while others have to listen to them, are some of the faults of clericalism. This conduct does not allow the pastoral leaders and the people to assume the missionary nature of a community. When the parish leadership takes administration to be the priority, then other missionary dimensions are pushed aside. Many parishes are more inclined to run like a well-oiled machine than to have the "smell of the sheep."[29]

The impact of a parish depends on the pastoral team and how well it works with the laity. This is the key. Collective effort and collective thinking and discernment pave the way to good growth. All need to be personally committed to reach out to others—Catholics, people of another faith, the poor, needy, excluded, elderly, migrants, and so forth. This applies to all the pastoral team members and to every member of the parish. Although it is hard to involve every member, the parish community creates this atmosphere so that the parish becomes attractive. The church that goes forth, attracts. The church that shows mercy, tenderness, and forgiveness, attracts. The church that shows compassion and love, attracts. This is the simple and profound teaching of Pope Francis.[30] Through the community's life and action, the parish becomes attractive.

> **Lazar T. Stanislaus, SVD,** completed his doctorate in missiology at the Pontifical Gregorian University, Rome. He was the director of Ishvani Kendra—Institute of Missiology and Communications in Pune, India. He is currently the generalate mission secretary of the Society of the Divine Word, Rome, and gives courses and seminars on missiology, interculturality, and related subjects.

---

[29] *EG*, no. 24.

[30] See Stephen Bevans, "Pope Francis's Missiology of Attraction," *International Bulletin for Mission Studies* 43, no. 1 (2019): 20–28.

Laity in Mission

The Laity: More than a Lending Hand

Oliver Aquilina, SDC

The doors appeared huge—extremely huge—and finding them tightly shut was not exactly what the motley group of friends had ardently looked forward to. They had come a long, tiresome way, descending valleys, scrambling hills, and crossing rivers and deep seas, come rain or shine. They used the little energy they had left to knock hard on the bronze doors, first with closed fists, then with open palms. A feeble echo could be heard inside. Then, dead silence. They had left home with one definite aim: to make their way in. And there was no turning back. They had met people, heard stories, and read books. They wanted to see and touch, to live the experiences firsthand. But would someone open the doors for them? Would they get in? How? When? They dropped down, spent, resting their backs against the cold metal doors. Suddenly the church clock struck. Dozing, they almost missed it. What time was it anyway? They fumbled pointlessly for their phones, dead for weeks, months. Then it dawned on them: Maybe it was not time yet. Or was it?

From Humble Beginnings

In the last verses of the Gospel according to Matthew, we read that Jesus, before his ascension into heaven, commissions his apostles, even the incredulous, to continue his work of proclaiming the good news and baptizing: "Go therefore and make disciples of all nations, baptizing them in the name of the Father and of the Son and of the Holy Spirit, and teaching them to obey everything that I have commanded you."[1] From the early days the

---

[1] Mt 28:19–20a.

communities that the apostles formed were overwhelmed with the amount of work they had to do. In the Acts of the Apostles, Luke writes that the number of disciples kept growing, and with it their spiritual and material needs.[2] Thus Stephen and six other men were asked to lend a hand.

The churches that the apostles left behind recognized other men, chosen by the apostles, who became known as bishops (from the Greek *episkopoi*, meaning "overseers"). Since the harvest of followers proved to be abundant, as Jesus had foretold, the bishops then anointed and placed their hands on other men who were sent to proclaim and baptize. These became the present-day priests (*presbyteroi*, "elders") and deacons (*diakonoi*, "servants"). Thus were established the three holy orders—episcopate, presbyterate, and diaconate—whose ministers are ordained to minister to all the rest of the people of God, the laity (from the Greek *laos*, meaning "people"). The pyramid was complete, from top to bottom.

This mindset stuck for centuries: the term *church* referred to the hierarchy, and the term *laity* referred to their "long arm" who "helped out" a little. At the dawn of the twentieth century, Pope Pius X wrote:

> The Church is essentially an unequal society, that is, a society comprising two categories of persons, the Pastors and the flock, those who occupy a rank in the different degrees of the hierarchy and the multitude of the faithful. .. . . . The one duty of the multitude is to allow themselves to be led, and, like a docile flock, to follow the Pastors.[3]

Earlier in his pontificate, the same pope had commended the lay Catholics who

> seek to restore Jesus Christ to the family, the school and society . . . take to heart the interests of the people, especially those of the working and agricultural classes . . . to dry their tears, to alleviate their sufferings, and to improve their economic condition by wise measures . . . to make public laws conformable to justice and amend or suppress those which are not so.[4]

And it was still the same Pius X who, during a conversation with a group of cardinals, asked: "What is the thing we most need, today, to save society?"

---

[2] See Acts 6:1.
[3] Pope Pius X, encyclical *Vehementer Nos* (February 11, 1906), no. 8.
[4] Pope Pius X, encyclical *Certum Consilium* (June 11, 1905), no. 7.

The cardinals had suggested building Catholic schools, establishing more churches, or speeding up the recruiting of priests. But according to Pius X, "The most necessary thing of all, at this time, is for every parish to possess a group of laymen who will be at the same time virtuous, enlightened, resolute, and truly apostolic."[5]

The paradigm continued to shift. In a discourse to the new cardinals in 1946, Pius XII acknowledged the presence of the lay faithful "on the front lines of the Church's life," stressing that they "ought to have an ever-clearer consciousness not only of belonging to the Church, but of being the Church."[6]

To the Long-Awaited Promotion

The Second Vatican Council (1962–65), with its cry for *aggiornamento*—an adaptation of the church and of the apostolate to a world undergoing great transformation—ushered in a clear line of thought that continued to promote the laity. Material about the subject in the archives was scarce, and credit is owed here to the Dominican theologian Yves Congar, whose influence on the conciliar teaching was immeasurable. In *Lay People in the Church*, Congar distances himself from the clerical image of the church, which he labels "hierarchology," in favor of an ecclesiology focused on the laity.[7]

Lumen Gentium (Dogmatic Constitution on the Church), dedicates an entire chapter to the topic. It admits that lay people have a specific mission, that of seeking the kingdom of God as they engage in temporal affairs and, as leaven, they work for the sanctification of the world from within. It draws to the pastors' attention that it is their noble duty to shepherd lay people as they discover their ministries and charisms bestowed on them, for "in this way they may make Christ known to others, especially by the testimony of a life resplendent in faith, hope and charity."[8]

Gaudium et Spes (Pastoral Constitution on the Church in the Modern World) reminds lay people of their active role to play in the whole life of the church, which makes them responsible for penetrating the world with a

---

[5] Jean-Baptiste Chautard, *The Soul of the Apostolate* (Trappist, KY: Mission Press, 1943), 161–62.

[6] Pope Pius XII, *Discourse to the New Cardinals*, Rome, February 20, 1946.

[7] Yves Congar, *Lay People in the Church: A Study for a Theology of Laity*, rev. ed., trans. Donald Attwater (1953; Westminster, MD: The Newman Press, 1965), 51.

[8] Pope Paul VI, *Lumen Gentium (The Dogmatic Constitution on the Church)* (1964), no. 31.

Christian spirit and "called to be witnesses to Christ in all things in the midst of human society."⁹

Two decrees promulgated at the end of Vatican II, namely *Apostolicam Actuositatem (Decree on the Apostolate of the Laity)* and *Ad Gentes (Decree on Mission Activity of the Church)* echo the above-mentioned constitutions. *Apostolican Actuositatem* states: "The laity derive the right and duty to the apostolate from their union with Christ the head; incorporated into Christ's Mystical Body through Baptism and strengthened by the power of the Holy Spirit through Confirmation, they are assigned to the apostolate by the Lord Himself."¹⁰ As the council fathers suggest to all categories of lay people, from the adult to the child, what they should be active in, they reiterate the laity's vocation to become holy and sanctify the temporal order by bringing the gospel among other people in the diverse environments they live and work in: "The Gospel cannot be deeply grounded in the abilities, life and work of any people without the active presence of laymen. Therefore, even at the very founding of a Church, great attention is to be paid to establishing a mature, Christian laity."¹¹

Owing to the impetus of Vatican II and its long-awaited insights, lay men and lay women were made to understand their status in the church and in the world, bringing to light the new meaning the laity bring to the term *people of God* and the distinctive roles in their unique vocation, together with the charisms bestowed upon them through the sacrament of baptism where they share in the priestly, prophetic, and kingly ministry of Jesus. Vatican II acknowledged the laity's share in the apostolate and witness normally associated with the ordained and the religious, and thus called for a closer collaboration between priests and the laity. The hour of the laity had indeed begun, and their promotion was imminent, for they were mere followers no more, but collaborators.

Of Giants Deep Asleep?

The contribution of the post–Vatican II popes toward this swing is immense. The apostolic exhortation *Evangelii Nuntiandi* (1975) of Pope Paul VI following the synod of bishops on evangelization in the modern

---

⁹ Pope Paul VI, *Gaudium et Spes (The Pastoral Constitution on the Church in the Modern World)* (1965), no. 43.

¹⁰ Pope Paul VI, *Apostolicam Actuositatem (Decree on the Apostolate of the Laity)* (1965), no. 3, hereinafter *AA*.

¹¹ Second Vatican Council, *Ad Gentes (Decree on the Mission Activity of the Church)* (1965), no. 21, hereinafter *AG*.

world maintained the momentum. According to the pope, the laity, "whose particular vocation places them in the midst of the world and in charge of the most varied temporal tasks, must for this very reason exercise a very special form of evangelization."[12] He sees them engaged in the affairs of the world, in politics, culture, economics, sciences, international life, and in mass media, as they are involved in other realities such as in families and in places of professional work, and accompany the people of God especially through education, love, and care. Paul VI is convinced that the church and the world today are in urgent need of gospel-inspired lay people who point to the oft-disregarded transcendent dimension.[13]

In 1987, another synod of bishops took place, during the pontificate of John Paul II—Vocation and Mission of the Lay Faithful in the Church and in the World—and in 1988 the apostolic exhortation *Christifideles Laici* was published. From its outset, taking a hint from the parable of the workers in the vineyard, John Paul II reminded us that Jesus's invitation— "You go into my vineyard too" (Mt 20:4)—is addressed to everyone in the Church, and reassured the laity that they did not end up in the world by chance. "The 'world' thus becomes the place and the means for the lay faithful to fulfil their Christian vocation"[14] so that they become leaven, salt, and light for their fellow brothers and sisters in this enormous vineyard.

Since the laity are the majority in this vineyard, no wonder they were occasionally referred to as "the giant in the church," which incidentally is a whole lot better than being deemed "an elephant in the room." And ensuring that this giant does not fall asleep on the job will keep us abreast of the ongoing changes occurring around us in this fast-paced twenty-first century and the consequent doors of opportunities that are opening up.

During Benedict XVI's pontificate, his messages were music to the laity's ears. But in 2009, during the pastoral convention of the Diocese of Rome, the pope admits that there is still a long way to go because too many of the baptized come to church only to receive religious services. He reminded us that the church is the people of God, a concept that goes back to the Old Testament, where God chose a specific people "to reach, through a few, many people and through them to reach all."[15] The pope thus appeals for a change in mindset: if the church wishes to foster the consolidation of a mature and committed laity, "they must no longer be viewed as 'collaborators'

---

[12] Pope Paul VI, *Evangelii Nuntiandi* (1975), no. 70.

[13] Ibid.

[14] Pope John Paul II, *Christifideles Laici (On the Vocation and the Mission of the Lay Faithful in the Church and in the World)* (1988), no. 15.

[15] Pope Benedict XVI, *Address at the Opening of the Pastoral Convention of the Diocese of Rome*, Rome, May 26, 2009.

of the clergy but truly recognized as 'co-responsible.'"[16] New "job titles" were required, as Benedict XVI insisted on referring to the lay people as co-responsible for the church's being and action.

During the pontificates of John Paul II and Benedict XVI, the subject of new evangelization was consistently on the agenda. When they were still young, amid wars, regimes of injustice, and poverty, Karol Wojtyła and Joseph Ratzinger had to work tirelessly and study clandestinely; this made them believe that the antidote the world needs is indeed the good news of Jesus Christ with its message of hope and joy. This fundamental need will never be absolutely satisfied; neither will the invitation for the laity ever expire, that they witness to the joy of the gospel, not through indoctrination or proselytism, but through their exclusive mission in the church and in the world—from shantytowns to gated communities, from lecture halls to hospital wards, from their neighborhoods to the ends of the earth—as they live according to their charism in their daily encounters with the people of God.

Pope Francis underscores this crucial call to the laity and advocates for more involvement, support, and attraction. He invites us to emulate Jesus as we reach out to others, seek the lost sheep, and welcome the outcast, with all the heartache and decision making this requires as we "smell the sheep" we take out to graze, enduring our mission patiently, disregarding our wristwatch.[17]

In the apostolic exhortation *Evangelii Gaudium* after the Synod on New Evangelization in 2012, Pope Francis acknowledges the fact that "there has been a growing awareness of the identity and mission of the laity in the Church,"[18] although it is still a far cry from what he would hope for. The resonance with the thoughts of Benedict XVI can still be felt. Pope Francis identifies lack of formation and lack of room for lay people to speak and act, stemming from excessive clericalism, as they are kept under the clerics' wings. This chokes the laity's true vocation, that of transforming society, witnessing to it, and sanctifying it.

On Winding the Clock

It is against this backdrop that we should reflect about the lay people's state in the church and in its mission today. We have come a long way,

---

[16] Ibid.

[17] See Pope Francis, *Evangelii Gaudium (The Joy of the Gospel)* (2013), no. 24, hereinafter *EG*.

[18] Ibid., no. 102.

and forgetting our upbringing, or denying it, would not help the laity, the largest group in the church, to be who we are called to be. In a letter to Cardinal Marc Ouellet in March 2016, Pope Francis recalled the famous phrase "the hour of the laity has come," which marked the post–Vatican II general opinion on the laity in the Catholic Church. Pope Francis's immediate assessment of the catchphrase could not have been more provocative: "but it seems that the clock has stopped."[19] Reflecting on this a few months later, Cardinal Stanisław Ryłko, then president of the Pontifical Council for the Laity, insisted that we should heartily desire that this does not happen on our watch, and that we must work hard to claim the vocation and mission of the prophets.[20] From as far back as the Old Testament we start encountering these individuals who are teaching the unenlightened, warning the heedless, correcting the negligent, contradicting the arrogant, awakening sleeping consciences and memories, and constantly reminding God's people with their unwavering witness that God is present in their midst in all spheres of life. As the church today sends its missionary sons and daughters toward the peripheries of the world to make disciples, baptize, and teach, they cannot afford to do so without the burning flame that animated the life of the prophets. We, the laity, are urged to rediscover the beauty of our call to be prophets in the contemporary world.

The conciliar fathers reminded us that "the pilgrim Church is missionary by her very nature";[21] the main task of the church's missionaries is to continue Christ's own mission, that of proclaiming the good news.[22] The apostolate of the lay missionary expresses itself in all walks of life, for the rows in the field of the Lord are diverse. It is not uncommon for a lay person to be found teaching catechism to children preparing for the initiation sacraments; gathering together the Pontifical Ministry Children or the Missionary Youth Movement for Sunday mass; leading a seminar or retreat for the youth; meeting couples who wish to get married; teaching in a school, college, or university; accompanying those who seek spiritual direction; taking care of the sick in hospitals; bringing holy communion to the elderly; supporting people with special needs; reaching out to the homeless and the poor in slums; mixing with different families during the weekly small Christian Community Bible Study; in the marketplace;

---

[19] Pope Francis, *Letter to Cardinal Marc Ouellet, President of the Pontifical Commission for Latin America*, Vatican, March 19, 2016, para 4.
[20] Cardinal Stanisław Ryłko, "Homily during Holy Mass," 28th Plenary Assembly of the Pontifical Council for the Laity, Rome, June 16, 2016.
[21] *AG*, no. 2.
[22] See Lk 4:44.

in the hubbub of the city . . . and the list goes on. But yet, not one busy workshop or quiet side-street is forbidden for the lay Christian to live by words and deeds one's incarnational vocation, finding a way "to let the word take flesh in a particular situation and bear fruits of new life."[23]

This abundance in the harvest demands that the work moves on *ad gentes*, beyond one's parish, diocese, and country. The countless stories of missionary priests and religious men and women who left their homeland to travel to far-off countries to announce the good news as they founded new parishes and administered the sacraments, built hospitals and schools, and dug wells and tilled land, never to return home, captivated the imagination of many. Now the hour was ripe for the laity who admired the missionaries from afar to become actively committed and responsible in the mission field, "concerned about the needs of the people of God dispersed throughout the world, [making] missionary activity their own."[24] This saw the founding of missionary lay movements and associations who were ready to move out of their comfort zones, roll up their sleeves and "go forth," embracing the missionary call. Later on, Pope Benedict XVI would encourage the lay people to witness together with others, in associations, for this helps to shape their Christian conscience in the support they give to one another,[25] and still later Pope Francis would beg them to "go out, go out!"[26]

Still today, lay men and lay women in association with missionary religious congregations, or itinerant members of lay movements, or even groups of lay people on their own initiative—teenagers discerning their vocation, manual workers, university students, married couples, pensioners—part with their little savings and their time off and travel to other countries, particularly those associated with the church mission *ad gentes*. There they spend some weeks or months doing any kind of voluntary work needed with the poor, the disabled, the orphans, with those marginalized by a brutally discriminating society in which only the fittest survive. Notwithstanding the multiple sacrifices involved, something moves them to act in favor of their destitute brethren, to make their lives a little bit better. These generous lay persons might not have contemplated it down to its deep theological meaning, but theirs would be a testimony in flesh and blood that every person is a child of God deserving of the good news and the genuine joy it brings. For many, this becomes a life-changing

---

[23] *EG*, no. 24.
[24] *AA*, no. 10.
[25] See Benedict XVI, post-synodal apostolic exhortation *Africae Munus* (2011), no. 131.
[26] Pope Francis, vigil of Pentecost with the ecclesial movements, address at Saint Peter's Square, May 18, 2013.

experience, and they carry the missionary spirit in great joy back home, to their own communities and dioceses;[27] others even take the plunge, leave their loved ones for the sake of the gospel, and immerse themselves in the mission[28] among the people of God. Sad to say, when lay people are not made aware of these opportunities in the church, they might still travel to far-away places and do good deeds, but theirs would be merely a philanthropic vacation rather than an ecclesial action.

All this and much more has been my experience in Kenya for the last thirteen years or so, both through personal encounters and through the witness of other lay persons, locals and foreigners alike. My brothers and I, members of a lay missionary society, live close to the people in their everyday lives, in their places of work, in schools, in the busy markets, and in the crowded streets. The natives express a sense of appreciation when day after day they observe foreign or local missionaries among them, besides their presence in the church for mass and other services. The missionaries are not ashamed of crossing the threshold and walking the same roads with those they serve. We observe this constantly as we welcome into our home children, youth, and adults in their respective faith formation programs, and when we accompany them in their schools, homes, small Christian communities, out-stations, and parishes. The local lay catechists and other volunteers with whom we work side by side highly esteem our call as missionaries and encourage us constantly as they witness to us day after day with committed single-mindedness their work for all the people in the kingdom of God. Their remarkable testimony of faith, hope, and love inspires us and gives more meaning to the role of the laity in this abundant harvest. To all of you whom I have encountered in my missionary work, as we braved the horrid weather and the tough terrain, I will always remain gratefully indebted.

Conclusion

Our church is a church on mission, and all its children, the people of God, are duty bound to be missionaries, all in their own way, according to their personal vocation. Our charisms and way of expressions of mission might differ, but all of the baptized share one common vocation, that of spreading the kingdom of God throughout the earth. Now it is upon us, the laity, to heed the call and live it to transform the temporal

---

[27] See Mk 5:19 and Lk 10:17.
[28] See Mk 10:29 and Lk 4:18.

order through our witness and service to our fellow brothers and sisters. Sometimes we are afraid to take the step. Taking risks becomes harder as we grow older, and challenges from within and without will never cease. However, let us constantly keep in mind that it is through our self-giving that the whole world might enter into a relationship with Christ. Indeed, beautiful are the feet of those who bring good news, who proclaim the gospel of Jesus Christ.

> Footsteps could be heard inside. Are they coming to open the door? George and the rest couldn't contain their excitement. What shall they do? Frank and Dorothy knocked harder. Chiara and Andrea ran every which way on the parvis and around the columns, calling the others who had followed them. Emotions were high. Latches could be heard being lifted inside, and hinges squeaking, as the thrilled crowds gathered, the square nearly at its full capacity now. The huge bronze doors were opened first, so heavy but yet so light. Someone like a son of man, his face a shining sun, appeared. They all fell at his feet, as though dead. Then he spread his arms out over them and with a calm, sweet voice said: "Do not be afraid. Come in." The multitudes entered in order. "It's been a long journey, no? Do you feel cold? Hungry? Take a rest." Then he turned to the other multitude inside and told them: "Give them something to eat." As they peacefully ate the finest of bread, as sweet as manna, he read to them from the Book. After a short while he turned to them, saying: "Now go forth to the ends of the earth. Take the Book to those in distant lands and read it to them. May God bless you and the mission he entrusted to you. Till we meet again do not forget: I will be with you always, to the end of the age!

Oliver Aquilina is a member of the Society of Christian Doctrine (SDC), founded in 1907 by St. George Preca in Malta as a lifestyle for celibate lay people. Oliver graduated as a teacher from the University of Malta in 2002 and did his theological studies at the University of Notre Dame, in Indiana, in 2015. He has been in the missions of the SDC in Kenya since 2008.

Youth in Mission

Believing in Young People

Teresa Gómez and Nestor Anaya, FSC

Who Are the Young People?

There is no consensus on a universally accepted definition of youth. Approaches to the study of youth come from diverse disciplinary fields, purposes, times, and places. One criterion that unifies international efforts on behalf of young people is *chronological age*. The United Nations, since 1981, considers young people to be "those persons between 15 and 24 years of age."[1] Reports and studies on youth have taken up this criterion in order to understand and promote youth. However, as a notion, it is not a "given" but *socially constructed*.[2] It can be understood as a vital stage with distinctive features, such as the search for belonging, the active integration into society, and the personal construction of identity and meaning of life. Thus, it is possible to speak of *youth* because although there is no single way of being young, there are some shared characteristics. From an adult-centric understanding, youth is a transitional stage between childhood and adulthood. The model to be achieved is an adult who is socially and productively integrated into society. Hence, there is a tendency to standardize youth, thus obscuring its complexity and diversity, and to assign responsibility to the new generations as "bearers of change and hope for their future."[3] A synthesis of these two tendencies produces an understanding of *youth* and the young person as a *complete being* in a *trajectory to be built*.

---

[1] United Nations, "Who Are the Youth?" Global Issues (n.d.).
[2] Bourdieu Pierre, *Sociología y Cultura* (Mexico City: Grijalbo/CONACULTA, 1990), 164.
[3] Olivera Patricio and Valencia Daniel, "Identidades juveniles y actitudes en torno a la discriminación y tolerancia" (Santiago, Chile: ECLAC/SM Foundation, March 2019), 6.

The Situation of Youth in Latin America

The situation of youth in Latin America derives from the region's economic and social policies and also from young people's appreciation of them. Institutions have been key elements in social cohesion and in the configuration of belonging, identity, and collective action, as well as in the strengthening of social values. However, "in the specific case of Latin America, the increasingly fragmented state of society has limited the binding capacity of these Institutions."[4]

For many young people, education no longer improves their standard of life. This, coupled with job insecurity, has trapped young people in a vicious circle of discouragement and narrowed horizons. According to the United Nations, there are currently 1.2 billion young people in the world aged fifteen to twenty-four. They make up 16 percent of the world's population; 160 million of them live in Latin America. The Economic Commission for Latin America and the Caribbean (ECLAC) reports that within this population there is a core of excluded youth: more than 30 million young people between the ages of fifteen and nineteen who are neither students nor gainfully employed. They represent about 20 percent of the total. Of this population, 70 percent are women from urban sectors who are engaged in domestic work or are looking for their first job.[5] ECLAC is calling for the elimination of the stigma of the *nini*—young people who do not study or work—because this condition is linked to certain aspects of the context that have denied them opportunities, and recommends the development of strategies that take gender into account in order to include these young people in the educational and employment sectors.

Institutions that were traditionally reference points for identity have lost strength and relevance.[6] The importance of politics and religion in the lives of young people between sixteen and twenty-nine years of age is decreasing, but family and friends continue to be relevant, as well as leisure time and work.[7]

---

[4] Ibid., 7.

[5] ECLAC, "Jóvenes que no están estudian ni están empleados en América Latina y el Caribe" June 2, 2015.

[6] Sunkel Guillermo, "Sentido de pertenencia en la juventud latinoamericana," *Revista de Pensamiento Iberoamericano* 3 (2008): 186–87.

[7] Patricio and Daniel, "Identidades juveniles y actitudes en torno a la discriminación y tolerancia," 8–9.

According to a 2021 survey carried out in Latin American countries,[8] the young people who responded show some characteristic traits. Some were dreamers, passionate, sensitive, affective, fraternal, supportive, creative, sociable, friendly, committed, curious, impulsive, rebellious, innovative, spontaneous, adaptable, versatile, cheerful, and critical. The adults surveyed agreed and added that they are dynamic, impressionable, independent, immediate, reflective, empathetic, technological, enthusiastic, active, hopeful, fickle, and loyal. This appraisal shows that there are some cultural tensions and contradictions. Young people are seekers, and this is reflected in their participation in promoting peace, human rights, ecology, and gender equality, for example. The *form of organization* (to which they belong) is changing: 19 percent of young Ibero Americans declare that they are members of religious organizations (vs. 28 percent of adults), but they have also diversified the form of participation through social networks, "street" groups, and urban tribes or collectives characterized by horizontality, diversity, emotionality, and dynamism, compared to the traditional forms or organization, such as unions, NGOs, or clubs. However, many young people are still interested in group activities (related to sports, the arts, academics, and so forth) because they need to share their experiences, ways, and rituals, which develop a sense of *belonging* and a youth identity and outlook; they are a "nuclei of young people grouped around different trends . . . which emerge as an expression of social transformation."[9]

Youth Social Entrepreneurship

The term *social entrepreneurship* takes into consideration three variables: "innovation, the need to transform the lives of the most disadvantaged people . . . [and] social responsibility."[10]

Young people's social participation is related to their aspirations, needs, and contextual challenges. According to the SAMEL survey, young people are concerned about achieving their goals and self-fulfillment; fulfilling their dreams; finding new ways to face the world; having a professional career and a good quality of life; caring for nature; being transcendent,

---

[8] The survey was conducted for this essay in July 2021 by the Secretariat for Association and the Lasallian Educational Mission (SAMEL) of the Institute of the Brothers of the Christian Schools.

[9] UNAM, *Tribu urbana ¿cultura o moda?* (Mexico: Red Universitaria de Aprendizaje, UNAM, 2017), 1.

[10] S. Escamilla Solano, *Emprendimiento social* (Madrid: Instituto Nacional de la Juventud, Ministerio de Derechos Sociales y agenda 2030, 2017).

independent generators of change; working and earning money; traveling and enjoying friends; feeling surrounded by good company (friends, family, and so on); having fun, being happy, in solidarity and finding peace; making good decisions; seeking and building their vocation, identity and belonging; finding and building their vocation, and strengthening the spiritual, ethical and moral dimension.

The UN's 2030 Agenda for Sustainable Development states that young people need more and better opportunities in education, health, employment, and gender equality. The Youth Agenda, guided by the World Programme of Action for Youth, covers the following priority areas: education, employment, hunger and poverty, health, environment, drug abuse, youth crime, recreation, girls and young women, full and effective participation of young people in the life of society and in decision making, globalization, and information and communications technology, HIV/AIDS, armed conflict, and intergenerational issues. The UN recognizes that young people are the "architects" and "torchbearers" of the 2030 Agenda. This is why they have opened spaces for them, such as the Economic and Social Council (ECOSOC) Youth Forum. These global trends contextualize the relationship between young people and the church.

The Church and Young People Today

The church recognizes the importance of the *encounter and participation of young people* and promotes actions accordingly. John Paul II explains:

> All young people must feel accompanied by the church: this is why the whole church, in union with the Successor of Peter, feels more committed, on a worldwide level, to youth, to their concerns and requests, to their openness and hopes, to correspond to their aspirations, communicating the certainty that is Christ, the Truth that is Christ, the love that is Christ, through an appropriate development process.[11]

The World Youth Days have allowed the church to show its "young face," with a missionary spirit in faith and joy. These events, as Pope Benedict XVI notes, are a "medicine against the weariness of believing," "a new, rejuvenated way of being Christian," "a new evangelization lived

---

[11] Pope John Paul II, Address to the College of Cardinals and the Roman Curia regarding the establishing of World Youth Day (1985). Quotation in English at https://www.lisboa2023.org/en/about/how-it-emerged.

out," and a great sign of hope for the church and for the whole world.[12] Other initiatives followed in the wake of Pope Francis's encyclical *Laudato Si'*: the Generation Movement and the Global Education Pact, which commit the church to listen to the voice of children and young people, thus renewing the church's mission for the human being.

Many young people have given a practical response to these calls. Guided by parishes, educational centers, or nongovernmental organizations (NGO's), young people have strengthened the pastoral ministry of the church by participating in various group activities.

A good example of this participation is seen in *youth volunteer* programs. For example, the Lasallian Volunteer Program of the District of Antilles-Mexico South includes multiple activities for youth at the national and international level and in different modalities: short term (one week), medium term (six months), and long term (one year). The students who take part in these projects have a clear awareness of two social dimensions of youth mission: social solidarity and social pastoral ministry.

In the social dimension of solidarity they cooperate and commit themselves to venturing outside of their comfort zones to serve their communities. This "going beyond" requires their total involvement: skills, knowledge, attitude, aspirations, and beliefs. It helps them develop the faculty of thinking critically, which sets reason and one's personal context in dialogue with the reason and context of others. In addition, it favors an escalation to the spiritual dimension when proposals and actions are introduced in the dialogue that open up shared questions about the meaning and sense of life.

The second dimension, intrinsic to volunteer work, is Christian social ministry, because experience shows clearly that these activities help people to *be and to live as church*, because they are based on the values of *faith, fraternity,* and *service*. This practical *action* aims to modify a reality and improve the condition of the "other," thus contributing to a better life, a life lived by the criteria of the gospel.

In this way, being a volunteer means exercising one's will, fully and freely, with awareness and responsibility, in the context of social situations in search of the common good. This commitment invites us to participate, to go "beyond the frontier" not only geographically but in every situation that may separate humanity, and it is through willpower that this can be achieved. Volunteers are young persons who serve the Lasallian mission (which is the same as the mission of the church) freely, without

---

[12] Pope Benedict XVI, Pre-Christmas Address to the Roman Curia, December 2011.

any remuneration for their work, especially in projects among the poor that seek to improve existing conditions, and peoples' lives.

Apart from the number of people who benefit from these activities, the young people who have participated in volunteer work then integrate it into their personal and professional identity. That is why many alumni continue to support a better standard of life once they are employed, as well as in their personal projects. It is here that one can finally observe young people's involvement in the mission of the church, not only as helping hands but as Christians who are ready to give themselves to others and invite others to do so.

At the same time, it is rewarding to see that this type of program favors a transformative process. It starts with young persons who are "self-centered," but it steadily leads them to shift to a "we" mentality, and ends with mature persons who are able to see the "other" within a "collective we" who need one another.

This experience is consistent with the results of our SAMEL survey, which found that the mission of the church has its own interpretation of young people and educators, one basically focused on making known the word of the gospel and sharing the love of God with others; forming networks and communities; spreading the faith; promoting interiority and peace; offering support and service to those who need it most; promoting the doctrine and human values of the church and putting them into practice; and reinterpreting the teachings of Jesus in the light of the signs of the times.

Mission should be a place of encounter with the "other" that helps us to know ourselves as well as others; to accept, respect and love them; to live as Jesus lived, in charity, by performing small daily actions.

Roads to Travel

We start from the fact that young people like to take part in activities with innovation, creativity, joy, and solidarity. According to our SAMEL survey, young people recognize that participation in the mission of the church offers them great richness: space for self-knowledge, encounter, and integral development, as well as opportunities to know and transform the realities and needs of the world. Accordingly, four lines of action are proposed.

The first is to *consolidate and increase opportunities and experiences for youth participation based on dialogue and inclusion.* From this the second follows naturally: to *rebuild communication through assertiveness and synodality*, making youth and the hard core of social exclusion visible in order to integrate them through horizontality, equity, and justice. "Going to the encounter" becomes a way of living and doing. Third, *synodal dialogue* values listening and community discernment for the common good.[13] According to the International Theological Commission:

> The criterion according to which "unity prevails over conflict" is of particular value in conducting a dialogue, managing different opinions and experiences and learning "a style of constructing history, a vital field where conflicts, tensions and opposites can reach a pluriform unity which generates new life.". . . It is a matter of adopting "a relational way of viewing the world, which then becomes a form of shared knowledge, vision through the eyes of another and a shared vision of all that exists."[14]

Youth participation requires "a relational way of seeing the world, which becomes shared knowledge, vision in the vision of another or common vision of all things."[15] This connects with a fourth line of action: *Christian praxis in interpersonal relationships,* recovering their forms of organization through horizontality, diversity, emotionality, and dynamism in order to share experiences, practices, and rites that allow them to develop their sense of belonging. The key is providing an accompaniment that will allow them to overcome the weaknesses of these forms of organization, which are often ephemeral and fragmented.

Christian praxis also implies making visible the forms of violence that afflict young people and their families. It promotes a culture of respect for human rights and education for peace; it also cooperates in finding solutions to the problems of a region, which testify that the Christian community is a theological place that seeks to make utopia a possible dream.

Believing in Young People: A Call to Hope

The desire to journey as church must show itself in meaningful actions for all involved in this process. To do this we need to have a clear direc-

---

[13] Cf. 1 Cor 12:7.
[14] International Theological Commission, *Synodality in the Life and Mission of the Church* (March 2, 2018), no. 111.
[15] Ibid.

tion and a burning desire to shape a more synodal church. That is why we invite you to:

1. Know and accept our young people, recognizing that they are in a crucial phase with particular characteristics and that therefore they need guides who know how to listen to them and appreciate them.
2. Reach out to those young people who have no opportunities, who are marginalized or who have lost hope.
3. Be present in those places where young people gather, including the virtual world. For it is only by being with them that we can live together, dialogue, and spend quality time together.
4. Promote the social entrepreneurship of young people based on innovation, paying attention to the most disadvantaged, and social responsibility.
5. Create opportunities and experiences for youth participation in building a more vibrant church, attentive to the needs of the people.
6. Rebuild communication where it has been lost, starting from a relational mode where sincerity, listening, and horizontality are the essential premises.
7. Reevaluate Christian praxis in interpersonal relations as the place where the gospel attitudes of charity, commitment, and forgiveness are lived.

Faced with this task, there is no doubt that young people need teachers who are true mediators, motivators, and companions in all the dimensions of their lives. This means that every effort to train these teachers will be worthwhile.

Teresa Gómez is director of guidance and educational development at the Universidad De La Salle Bajío, Leon, Guanajuato, Mexico.

Nestor Anaya, FSC, is general councilor of the Lasalle Brothers and secretary of the Lasallian Educational Mission at the mother house of the institute in Rome, Italy.

Integrity of Creation
Our Work Is Loving the World

Ilia Delio, OSF

In his insightful book *At Home in the Cosmos* the late David Toolan devoted a chapter to the question, "Is there an environmental crisis?" Toolan's question is an important one. Our planet has been in peril for the last several decades due to the depletion of natural resources, the loss of species populations, the rise in global warming, the steady rise in greenhouse gases, soil erosion, the proliferation of disease-causing chemicals, species extinction, the prevalence of chemical pollutants, and deforestation, just to name some areas of decline. In 1992, a group of leading scientists called on religious communities to play a more active role in addressing our environmental problems, including especially their religious and ethical dimensions.[1] They suggested that we are committing "crimes against creation." "We are now threatened," they said, "by self-inflicted, swiftly moving environmental alterations about whose long-term biological and ecological consequences we are still painfully ignorant."[2]

In 1967, historian Lynn White published a controversial essay entitled "The Historic Roots of Our Ecological Crisis," in which he claimed that Christianity is the primary source of the environmental problem. Christianity, he indicated, with its emphasis on human salvation and dominion over nature, "made it possible to exploit nature in a mood of indifference to the feelings of natural objects."[3] White listed several factors important to Christian belief that have contributed to the environmental problems:

1. an ambivalent attitude toward creation;
2. a stance of dominion that has led to exploitation;

---

[1] See frontispiece in John E. Carroll and Keith Warner, OFM, eds., *Ecology and Religion: Scientists Speak* (Quincy, Il: Franciscan Press, 1998).
[2] David Toolan, *At Home in the Cosmos* (Maryknoll, NY: Orbis Books, 2001), 9.
[3] Lynn White, "The Historical Roots of Our Ecological Crisis," *Science* 155 (1967): 1205.

3. an otherworldly focus;
4. a preoccupation with sin and guilt that has led to intense preoccupation with self; and
5. an emphasis on personal salvation.

Christians are responsible for the ecological crisis, he insists, because they took God's command to have dominion over creation as a command to dominate and subdue it.[4] He argues that no religion has been more focused on human beings than Christianity, and none more rigid in excluding all but human beings from divine grace and in denying any moral obligation to the lower species.[5] "Christianity made it possible to exploit nature in a mood of indifference to the feelings of natural objects." We will continue to have an ecological crisis, he claims, until we reject the Christian axiom that nature has no reason for existence except to serve us.[6] White said that "the roots of our environmental problems are religious and the remedy must be religious as well. We must rethink and re-feel our nature and our destiny."[7]

Although White's thesis has been challenged, his emphasis on otherworldliness remains central to the environmental problem. He claims that "what people do about their ecology depends on what they think about themselves in relation to things around them."[8] One of the lingering sources of otherworldliness is the influence of Greek Neoplatonism on Christian spirituality, an influence that continues in Christian liturgy and prayers. Neoplatonism is a Greek metaphysical scheme that emphasizes spiritual reality over material reality, regarding the created world as weak, mutable, sinful, and fallen. Some scholars claim that the otherworldliness of Christian Neoplatonism stands behind the development of Gothic architecture, turning human attention away from the earth and upward toward the heavenly light. An anti-ecological spirit was incorporated early in Christian thought through metaphysical concepts of hierarchy and the great ladder of Being, placing God at the top. Although a priority of spirit over matter influenced a turn from the earth toward the heavens, the rise of modern philosophy and science caused an equal but opposite turn that has had no less of a devastating effect on the earth. René Descartes's quest for pure reason influenced the rise of scientific materialism and ultimately the roots of modern atheism. Descartes identified truth with the human

---

[4] Cf. Gen 1:27–28.
[5] White, "The Historical Roots of Our Ecological Crisis," 1205.
[6] Ibid., 1207.
[7] Ibid., 1205.
[8] Ibid.

mind, leaving the material world bereft of any value. The separation of mind and matter led to neglect of the natural world coupled with an otherworldly religious sense.

Shortly after White advanced his thesis, the Norwegian philosopher Arne Naess initiated an environmental movement known as deep ecology. Deep ecology is an eco-philosophy that questions the place of human life. Deep ecology is founded on two basic principles: One is a scientific insight into the interrelatedness of all systems of life on earth together with the idea that anthropocentrism is a misguided way of seeing things. The second is the need for human self-realization. Deep ecologists suggest we learn to identify with trees, animals, and plants, the whole ecosphere, developing a behavior more consistent with who we are in creation and for the well-being of life on earth.[9] New insights from scientists today support the principal tenets of deep ecology. The biological systems that have given birth to our lives are not merely physical systems, but systems where conscious life and the dynamics of energy are fully operative. Peter Wohlleben's book *The Hidden Life of Trees* tells the inside story of tree life. He writes: "When you know that trees experience pain and have memories and that tree parents live together with their children, then you can no longer just chop them down and disrupt their lives with larger machines."[10] Similarly, Merlin Sheldrake in his book *Entangled Life: How Fungi Make Our World, Change Our Minds, and Shape Our Futures* recounts how the living networks of fungi are essential to human life and function, challenging the notion of human identity in surprising ways.[11] Robin Wall Kimmerer, author of *Braiding Sweetgrass: Indigenous Wisdom, Scientific Knowledge, and the Teaching of Plants*, indicates that the awakening of ecological consciousness requires the acknowledgment and celebration of *our reciprocal relationship with the rest of the living world*. For only when we can hear the languages of other beings will we be capable of understanding the generosity of the earth and learn to give our own gifts in return.[12] Care for creation is a mutual relationship among all living things. All nature thrives within systems of mutual care.

---

[9] Alan AtKisson, "Introduction to Deep Ecology: An Interview with Michael E. Zimmerman," *Global Climate Change* 22 (Summer 1989): 25.

[10] Peter Wohlleben, *The Hidden Life of Trees: What They Feel, How They Communicate—Discoveries from a Secret World* (New York: William Collins, 2017), 3.

[11] Merlin Sheldrake, *Entangled Life: How Fungi Make Our Worlds, Change Our Minds, and Shape Our Futures* (New York: Random House, 2020), 18.

[12] Robin Wall Kimmerer, *Braiding Sweetgrass: Indigenous Wisdom, Scientific Knowledge, and the Teaching of Plants* (Minneapolis: Milkweed Editions, 2015).

Laudato Si'

In 2015, Pope Francis issued a novel encyclical, *Laudato Si': On Care for Our Common Home*, expressing the church's deep concern for the environmental crisis. The pope's profound empathy for the plight of the earth and for the poor led him to write an impassioned document that highlights the ills of Western society: individualism, consumerism, run-away technology, and unbridled greed. His paradigm of a new integral ecology draws on the insights of Franciscan theology and, in particular, of Saint Francis of Assisi, who spoke of creation in familial terms: brother sun, sister moon, sister-mother earth. Similarly, Pope Francis speaks of the need to recognize our interdependence with all creatures, emphasizing human creatureliness within a dynamic creation wherein the goodness of God radiates throughout the whole of creation. "God wills the interdependence of creatures," he writes. "Creatures exist only in dependence on each other, to complete each other, in the service of each other."[13] Just as Bonaventure spoke of creation as an expression of divine love, so too Pope Francis expounds on the beauty of creation as an expression of God's kenotic and humble love.[14] The pope brings together creation and incarnation in a way that is consonant with the thought of Bonaventure and Duns Scotus: Christ comes first in God's intention to love and to create. He writes: "The destiny of all creation is bound up with the mystery of Christ."[15]

Francis's encyclical is noble in its aim; however, the anthropology of the encyclical is not fully aligned with the principles of modern science but, instead, offers a medieval worldview of the human person. Pope Francis indicates that the human person who is "endowed with intelligence and love" is unique and central to creation. Our task is to "lead all creatures back to their Creator."[16] Although the earth was here before us,[17] and we cannot regard ourselves separate from nature,[18] still, we possess dignity above other creatures.[19] The distinction of the human person, according to the encyclical, is our ability to reason and our intelligence, as the pope writes: "Human beings, even if we postulate a process of evolution, also possess a uniqueness which cannot be fully explained by the evolution of other open systems.... Our capacity to reason, to develop arguments,

---

[13] Pope Francis, *Laudato Si': On Care for Our Common Home*, no. 86.
[14] Ibid., no. 77.
[15] Ibid., no. 99.
[16] Ibid., no. 83.
[17] Ibid., no. 67.
[18] Ibid., no. 139.
[19] Ibid., no. 119.

to be inventive, to interpret reality . . . are signs of a uniqueness which transcends the spheres of physics and biology."[20] The pope goes on to say that this human distinction presupposes a "direct action of God and a particular call to life and to relationship on the part of 'Thou' who addresses himself to another 'thou.'"[21]

At the heart of *Laudato Si'* is a medieval metaphysical paradigm of participatory being where the transcendence of God undergirds the interdependence of all creatures. Hence, while *Laudato Si'* offers an ideal goal of integral ecology, it does not reflect an adequate integral relationship between science and religion. Evolution is noted as a physical process, not a spiritual one. The ambivalence with regard to evolution gives rise to distinct forms of revelation insofar as creation and nature are not fully aligned. The church promotes "care for creation" by holding together creation and nature; nature and scripture; the divine image of God (reason, will) and creaturely dependence, in accordance with the static metaphysics of Being. Yet, an integral ecology requires an integral theology. Thomas Berry writes: "The reason for aversion to the story of an emergent universe is that the story has generally been told simply as a random physical process when in reality it needs to be told as a psychic-spiritual as well as physical-mental process from the beginning."[22] The universe story, the earth story, the human story, and the story of God must be understood as a single story.

Teilhard de Chardin: Faith and Evolution

Jesuit scientist Pierre Teilhard de Chardin knew that the separation of science and religion lay at the root of our contemporary moral confusion. Teilhard sought to bring together Christianity and evolution precisely because the core of the Christian faith is the incarnation. He understood the science of evolution as the explanation of the physical world and viewed Christian life within evolution. Evolution, he claimed, is ultimately a progression toward consciousness; the material world contains within it a dynamism toward the spirit. The human person is integrally part of evolution in that we rise from the process, but in reflecting on

---

[20] Ibid., no. 81.
[21] Ibid., no. 81.
[22] Thomas Berry, "The Christian Future and the Fate of the Earth," in *The Christian Future and the Fate of the Earth*, ed. Mary Evelyn Tucker and John Grim (Maryknoll, NY: Orbis Books, 2009), 41.

the process we stand apart from it. Following Julian Huxley, he said that the human person "is nothing else than evolution becoming conscious of itself.... The consciousness of each of us is evolution looking at itself and reflecting upon itself."[23] Thus the human person is integral to evolution, "the point of emergence in nature, at which this deep cosmic evolution culminates and declares itself."[24] It is precisely because we emerge from the process of evolution that we bear a responsibility for evolution; human life is integral to evolution.

Teilhard did not see evolution as a forward movement without resistance. Rather, the forces of history acting on humanity must either complexify and evolve humanity, or force humanity to wither. He felt that without a collective commitment to the future, the process of evolution could ultimately collapse on itself and result in cosmic death. The only solution he indicated is not "an improvement of living conditions," desirable as that might be; rather, evolution must be toward more being, that is, not only an evolution of consciousness but a new phase of life in the universe toward unification of mind by which the whole cosmic evolution progresses toward greater unity. We must come to terms with the fact that *we are in evolution*. Evolution is not a theory or an idea; it is our most fundamental reality. Teilhard was aware that a renewed planet of life will not arise if religion does not undergo a radical transformation of ideas, acquire new metaphors, and tell a new story that can harness the spirit of the earth along the lines of evolution. He devoted himself to developing a new theology of evolution in an effort to renew the vital religious dimension of cosmic life and spoke of the vitality of the church in movement. The kind of religion we seek today, he thought, cannot be found in the religious traditions of the past linked to static categories. "God has become too small to nourish in us the desire to go on living and to live on a higher plane," he lamented. Science now tells us that the cosmos has become a cosmogenesis and this fact alone "must lead to the profound modification of the whole structure not only of our thought but of our beliefs."[25]

Teilhard suggested that we need a new religion that can utilize all the "free energy" of the earth to build humankind into greater unity. He did not see Christianity as normative of religion but normative of evolution

---

[23] Pierre Teilhard de Chardin, *The Phenomenon of Man*, trans. Bernard Wall (New York: Harper & Row, 1959), 221.

[24] Pierre Teilhard de Chardin, *Human Energy*, trans. J. M. Cohen (New York: Harcourt Brace Jovanovich, 1969), 23.

[25] In Ursula King, "Religion and the Future," in *The Spirit of the Earth: Reflections on Teilhard de Chardin and Global Spirituality* (New York: Paragon House, 1989), 109.

and the building up of the Body of Christ in the universe, or what he called "Christogenesis." The further evolution of humanity toward greater unity, he said, "will never materialize unless we fully develop within ourselves the exceptionally strong unifying powers exerted by inter-human sympathy and religious forces."[26] Any religion that focuses only on individuals and heaven leads to "unsatisfied theism." People are looking for a religion for humankind and for the earth that gives meaning to human achievements, a religion that will enkindle cosmic and human evolution and a deep sense of commitment to the earth. Teilhard felt that any religion that remains detached from the earth and from the movement of evolution will lead to a rejection of religion because it is disconnected from the impulses of cosmic life. Religion should energize and activate the creative potential to build up the earth, not to inhibit people from welcoming being's new ideas and relationships. In his view, the world's religions must come together and find an axis of convergence through respect, dialogue, and encounter, meeting on the level of mysticism and action. Religion is a vital dimension of evolution, according to Teilhard, the necessary energy to catalyze the earth into a new unity. Without the vitality of religion at the core of evolution, we have no real direction and thus no real future together. From a Christian perspective, he felt, we need a theology that can speak to a world in evolution and support new forms of worship that can vitalize a world in movement.

Christogenesis

Although Teilhard was well acquainted with the biology of evolution of his time, he claimed "there is only one real evolution, the evolution of convergence, because it alone is positive and creative."[27] He recognized a unifying influence in the whole evolutionary process, a centrating factor that continues to hold the entire process together and moves it forward toward greater complexity and unity. His faith in Christ led him to posit Christ, the future fullness of the whole evolutionary process, as the "centrating principle," the "*pleroma*" and "Omega point" where the individual and collective adventure of humanity finds its end and fulfillment, and where the consummation of the world and consummation of God

---

[26] In Ursula King, *Teilhard de Chardin and Eastern Religions: Spirituality and Mysticism in an Evolutionary World* (Mahwah, NJ: Paulist Press, 2011), 193.

[27] Pierre Teilhard de Chardin, *Christianity and Evolution*, trans. René Hague (New York: William Collins Sons, 1969), 87.

converge. Through his penetrating view of the universe, Teilhard found Christ present in the entire cosmos, from the least particle of matter to the convergent human community. The whole cosmos is incarnational. In his *Divine Milieu* he wrote, "there is nothing profane here below for those who know how to see."[28] Christ invests himself organically with all of creation, immersing himself in things, in the heart of matter, and thus unifying the world.[29] Everything is physically "*christified*," gathered up by the incarnate Word as nourishment that assimilates, transforms, and divinizes.[30] The world is like a crystal lamp illuminated from within; for those who can see, Christ shines in this diaphanous universe through the cosmos and in matter.[31]

Unlike the classic views of God and world, Teilhard said that God is not found apart from matter but in and through matter. The radicality of the Christian faith claim is that God has become flesh/sarx/materiality. God and matter are not opposed to one another; they are united. Teilhard never spoke of creation because he wanted to avoid the idea that creation is gratuitous. Creation is not a gift, he said; rather, it is God's dynamic life self-actualizing itself in and through the rise of conscious materiality. He advocated a "metaphysics of union," a creation of an evolutionary type, according to which the order in which things appear temporally is the very order in which they are created; as he wrote in 1917, "Every new union to be effected increases the absolute quantity of being existing in the universe."[32] For Teilhard, divine creation is not, as in Thomism, a kind of logical relay in which any concept that does not involve a contradiction can be brought to existence *ex nihilo*. In Teilhard's view, organisms, species, and even ecosystems emerge in the course of time only because they have been *made possible* by the conditions that preceded them: "All things are born from what existed before them."[33] God's role, in large measure, is "*to make things make themselves*," and what Teilhard wanted to

---

[28] Pierre Teilhard de Chardin, *The Divine Milieu: An Essay on the Interior Life*, trans. William Collins (New York: Harper & Row, 1960), 66.

[29] Teilhard de Chardin, *The Phenomenon of Man*, 293–94; Timothy Jamison, "The Personalized Universe of Teilhard de Chardin," in *There Shall Be One Christ*, ed. Michael Meilach (New York: The Franciscan Institute, 1968), 26.

[30] Teilhard de Chardin, "My Universe," in *Process Thought: Basic Writings of the Key Thinkers*, ed. Ewert H. Cousins (New York: Paulist Press, 1971), 254.

[31] This is the thesis of Teilhard's classic *The Divine Milieu*. See also his "My Universe," 249–55.

[32] Pierre Teilhard de Chardin, *Writings in Time of War*, trans. René Hague (New York: Harper & Row, 1968), 163.

[33] Pierre Teilhard de Chardin, *The Vision of the Past*, trans. J. M. Cohen (New York: Harper & Row, 1966), 130.

show is that self-making nature makes God by bringing God to birth.[34] God undergirds the radial energy that builds ever more complex organisms from simpler ones. Following the ascent of complexification, Teilhard was convinced that he saw a direction to the evolutionary process towards supreme complexity, a personal center in which the uniqueness of all psychical centers is intensified—an Omega Point. "True union," he said, "does not fuse the elements it brings together"; rather, it renews their vitality. As one of his signature phrases states, "*union differentiates.*"[35]

Teilhard's metaphysics of union requires a more dynamic concept of the material world than what was assumed by the ancients or even by the early modern scientists, a concept more in keeping with the deliverance of the sciences that peer ever more deeply into the microscopic and subatomic worlds. He denied the existence of matter conceived as something lacking in consciousness or spontaneity.[36] He is well known for posting both a "within" and a "without" of things, envisioning multiple levels of mentality or experience as a function of the complexity of organisms. If the idea of God making things make themselves challenges traditional thinking in theology by attributing genuine creativity to the creatures, Teilhard's peculiar panpsychism—or better, pan-experientialism—is a challenge to rethink the dominant paradigm of a merely behavioristic approach to physics, biology, and psychology. What Teilhard brought to the questions of the relations of religion and science is a refreshingly new principle that can be stated this way: concepts of God and of the world are correlative; they have implications for each other. As he wrote to Fr. Pierre Leroy in 1951, a reform is needed in the very concept of God.[37]

Creative Union

The key to Teilhard's understanding of the God-world relationship is creative union. He did not hold to a separate doctrine of creation but saw creative union as the integral core of creation that includes the mysteries of incarnation and redemption. Creative union is the union of God and creation in evolution. He writes:

---

[34] Pierre Teilhard de Chardin, *Christianity and Evolution*, trans. René Hague (New York: Harcourt Brace Jovanovich, 1971), 28.

[35] Teilhard de Chardin, *Human Energy*, 63.

[36] Pierre Teilhard de Chardin, *Activation of Energy*, trans. René Hague (New York: Harcourt Brace Jovanovich, 1971), 125.

[37] Pierre Leroy, ed., *Letters from My Friend Teilhard de Chardin*, trans. Mary Lukas (New York: Paulist Press, 1976), 89.

> This theory came to birth out of my own personal need to reconcile, within the confines of a rigorously structured system, the views of science respecting evolution (which views are accepted here as being definitively established, at least in their essence) with an innate tendency which has driven me to seek out the presence of God, not apart from the physical world, but rather through matter and in a certain sense in union with it.[38]

The incarnation in the general sense of the immersion of God in the evolutionary process is coextensive with the total space-time continuum. God is found in and through matter. In "Hymn to Matter" Teilhard writes:

> A Being was taking form in the totality of space; a Being with the attractive power of a soul, palpable like a body, vast as the sky; a Being which mingled with things yet remained distinct from them; a Being of a higher order than the substance of things with which it was adorned yet taking shape within them.

> The rising Sun was being born in the heart of the world. God was shining forth from the summit of that world of matter whose waves were carrying up to him the world of spirit.[39]

While classical theology viewed creation as a free act of God, either by way of desire (Bonaventure) or intellect (Thomas), Teilhard saw creation as integral to God. He believed that without creation, something would be absolutely lacking to God, considered in the fullness not of God's being but of God's act of union. Evolution toward greater unity rests on the involvement of God in creation: the One flows from the many. The involvement of God in evolution through creative union means that everything happens as though the One were formed by successive unifications of the multiple. God reveals himself everywhere as a universal milieu because God is the ultimate point upon which all realities converge. The evolutive God rises up from the world of increasing consciousness, for if God had not emerged from the world, God could not be for the world.

Teilhard ultimately discovered what Francis of Assisi had discovered in the thirteenth century: the material world is filled with God; however, we

---

[38] Pierre Teilhard de Chardin, *Mon Universe* (March 25, 1924), Eng. trans. G. Vann, in *Hymn of the Universe* (New York: Harper & Row, 1969), 76–77.

[39] Pierre Teilhard de Chardin, *Hymn of the Universe*, trans. Simon Bartholomew (New York: Harper & Row, 1965), 68.

now know this material world to be a process of dynamic change. God is present in the sun, the leaves, the soil, the dry earth, the fish, the water, the grains of sand, the wind and the rain, the birds of the air and wolves that roam the forests—every aspect of nature is God-filled or *Christic*. The God of Jesus Christ is deeply embedded in the interstitial systems of nature. This whole process of emergent evolutionary life is *ecopoeitic*, self-making, self-organizing life, moving toward something more because divine Love itself is at the heart of the universe; the physical structure of the universe is love, in Teilhard's view. Nature is holy and intelligent; nature feels the pain of abuse. Nature is not a random physical process under the domain of a heavenly God; nature is where God is actively rising to new levels of conscious life. As God breaks through the limits of matter into higher realms of energized matter-spirit, divinity dawns within the light consciousness: Christ is born from within.

Contemplation: The Heart of Ecology

The whole of Teilhard's vision can be summed up in the act of "seeing": as we see, so we love. Love is the heart of Teilhard's vision and deepens with contemplation; however, contemplation acquires a new role in evolution. For the ancients of the first axial period, contemplation meant raising the soul to its higher identity by centering the mind on the God above. Since all things flow from God, all things long to return to God. In order to regain its divine status, the soul must free itself from its earthly bonds. Contemplation is the return to God through spiritual inwardness, as the soul ascends from multiplicity toward unity in God.[40] Teilhard wrote for a new age of conscious-material life, the second axial period of ecological, evolutionary life. His is not a reflective type of contemplation but an active one. We do not rely on the fruits of contemplation; we hand ourselves over in the act of contemplation so that contemplation is the act of mindful union. The word *econoesis* literally means "mindful relationality" (from *nous,* "mind" and *eco,* "household relationships") or "minded matter." Just as Francis of Assisi saw God's love in every creature, *econoesis* connotes conscious interbeing as life and mindful creative union. Insights from quantum physics and biology today suggest that every aspect of nature is mindful and bears within it

---

[40] For a discussion on first and second axial periods, see Ilia Delio, *Making All Things New: Catholicity, Cosmology, and Consciousness* (Maryknoll, NY: Orbis Books, 2015), 5–10.

its own sense of agency.[41] The infinite depth and breadth and beauty of nature is the dynamic presence of God.

For centuries, we were taught to find God in the realm of the spirit, which was distinct and above matter; now we are to find God in the very stuff of matter. "Matter is the matrix of spirit," Teilhard claimed.[42] God, who is Spirit, is not separate from matter but the infinite depth of matter. God is infinitely alive in every star and grain of sand. In his essays on science and Christ, Teilhard writes, "I allowed my consciousness to sweep back to the farthest limit of my body to ascertain whether I might not extend outside myself. . . . I realized that my own poor trifling existence was one with the immensity of all that is and all that is still in the process of becoming." He continues by saying, "Beneath the ordinariness of our most familiar experiences we realize with religious horror that what is emerging in us is the great cosmos."[43] Teilhard discovered that he was both in the earth and of the earth. He claimed that those who have had such an experience need to live with their whole heart in union with the totality of the world. He wrote of "holy matter," saying that without matter we would be ignorant of self and God. In his direct experience of the cosmos and the earth, Teilhard believed he found an "Absolute" that drew him and remained hidden.

Recently, I was thinking about Teilhard while meditating by the seashore. I felt the warmth of the sun and listened to the waves rushing on to the shore. I saw a small bird walking along the shoreline, and for a moment I saw myself. I was the bird wobbling across the sand, just as I was the ocean waves spilling over the shoreline. In fact, for a moment, there was no discernible "I." The waves, the sand, the small bird, the clouds and air and sun, all were I, and I was, briefly, a small moment of this cosmic life. To contemplate for Teilhard is to creatively unite with the power of matter; to be touched and cared for by matter; to be loved by matter, by the sand and the ocean and the sun. *Econoesis* means to arrive at a primordial consciousness of surrender where individual identity ceases and merges with all that it touches, experiencing the power of matter through the senses of listening and feeling the energies of matter-life, allowing

---

[41] For understanding the agency of matter, see Karen Barad, *Meeting the Universe Halfway: Quantum Physics and the Entanglement of Matter and Meaning* (Durham, NC: Duke University Press, 2007).

[42] Pierre Teilhard de Chardin, *The Heart of Matter*, trans. René Hague (New York: Harcourt, 1978), 35.

[43] Pierre Teilhard de Chardin, *Science and Christ*, trans. René Hague (New York: Harper & Row, 1968), 25.

the energy of tree matter to affect the energy of my matter so that tree matter, sun matter, wind matter, all matter is my matter, diffracted by the differences of being.

Teilhard realized that oneness with the cosmos is not a passive resignation. Nature is a dynamic and creative life, open to more being and consciousness. We are not simply to rest in nature; we are to unite with nature and become something more with nature, more conscious, more being in love, more "nature." All of nature, including every human person, longs to become something more. As Saint Paul writes: "We know that the whole creation has been groaning as in the pains of childbirth right up to the present time."[44] Life has been building ever more complex structures through the ages. We are one of its constructions or works of art; a constitutive member of the ever vital networks of life. We are called to continue building the earth in continuity with what life has been doing for billions of years; God is seeking to rise up through this magnificent process of interdependent life. We do not go to God directly; we go to God through and with the earth, Teilhard said.[45] It is the earth that gives us the energy to "ascend," to grow in higher consciousness of God, or rather, God grows in higher consciousness and spirit in and through us.

We are to give ourselves over to creation, merging with the psychic-spiritual energies of nature, receiving matter-nature within ourselves, so that the outer world is within and the inner world is without. To truly know ourselves, we must go beyond ourselves. We are the world in its becoming. Teilhard found a spiritual power in matter and realized that matter puts us in touch with the energies of love. Together with all interbeing creatures of the earth—with fungi, bacteria, trees, mycelium, earthworms, bees, chickadees—all creatures great and small, we find ourselves touching and experiencing the hidden God of love.

Conclusion

If the church truly wishes to make a difference in the world through a gospel of interdependent life, then it is time to bring theology into dialogue with the sciences. We must accept evolution as our deepest reality and understand God's dynamic activity in a world of change and complexity.

---

[44] Rom 8:22.
[45] Teilhard de Chardin, *Writings in Time of War*, 57.

Raimon Panikkar writes: "Service to the earth is divine service; just as the love of God is human love. All that remains is for us to spell it out in our lives."[46] We are to be earth members caring for other earth members; we are earth-carers and earth-bearers, attentive to the power of divine love coursing through the stars and air and water and our own lives, drawing us all into a single heart of love. This power of love is the power of God shaping the earth into the body of Christ, the light shining through all matter as the dawn of unspeakable beauty.

Teilhard's contemplation, according to Martin Laird, means to become a "human energetic," a new center of energy entangled with other energies of life.[47] The contemplative energetic does not arrive at truth; rather, one discovers truth as it unfolds through the creative process of entangled matter. We are the voice of nature; we are the trees, the sun, the wind, and the rain that give voice to the glory of God. The contemplative energetic does not rest in God; one creatively gives birth to God through the energies of love. By creatively uniting with matter, we are true to nature in all its splendor, birthing the earth that has birthed us, into a new whole.

The practice of *econoesis* invites us to experience the Absolute in the ordinariness of earth–life–matter creatures–cosmos. To contemplate God is to creatively unite with matter, to let matter touch us, speak to us, hold us, embrace us, lifting us up through the energies of love. To care for creation is not what we do *for* creation; rather, it is how we *love* creation. Do we love trees, rabbits, deer, fish, stars, and wildlife? Better still, do we allow ourselves *to be loved* by all of nature? This is what I hope we mean by care for creation—that our work, our mission, is, as Mary Oliver writes, "loving the world."[48] And we will be amazed as we begin to sense that we are loved by even the smallest of creatures, the tiny earthworm, the delicate petal of a flower, the conifer tree that rises high above us. Love is the spiritual blood of evolution, according to Teilhard, capable of uniting all living beings in such a way so as to complete and fulfill them.[49] Out of love, God is born; the world is Christified and brought into a new energy-presence. Love alone can bring about a new world; through the energies of love we participate with nature in shaping the earth's future.

---

[46] Raimon Panikkar, *The Rhythm of Being: The Unbroken Trinity* (Maryknoll, NY: Orbis Books, 2013), 278.

[47] Martin Laird, "Contemplation: Human Energy Becoming Cosmic Energy," *The Teilhard Review and Journal of Creative Evolution* 21, no. 2 (Summer 1986): 43.

[48] Mary Oliver, "The Messenger," in *Thirst* (Boston: Beacon Press, 2006), 1.

[49] Pierre Teilhard de Chardin, *Building the Earth,* trans. René Hague (New York: Dimension Books, 2000), 45, 49.

Ilia Delio, OSF, is a Franciscan sister of Washington, DC, and holds the Josephine C. Connelly Chair in Christian Theology at Villanova University. Her area of research is systematic-constructive theology with a focus on evolution, quantum physics, and artificial intelligence and the import of these for Christian doctrine and life.

Conclusion

Marie-Hélène Robert, OLA

From biblical times up to the present day, the relationship of believers to the mission that God has conferred on them corresponds to an infinite number of models and to various trends. Indeed, mission is both *one* (it is the mission that God entrusts to his people, until the end of this world) and *particularized* (God sends people to other people, in various contexts). God acts in favor of the world he creates and loves. This action of God, which varies according to time, place, and the freedom involved, motivates his envoys. Rekha M. Chennattu in "The 'Why' of Mission: Biblical Trends in Mission for our Changing Times" and Stephen Bevans in "Theological Evolution in Mission: A Theology of Mission" have shown the strength of the biblical and theological roots of contemporary mission, where God's action and human commitment are linked.

This book provides an impressive overview of how mission is understood and lived out in the contexts to which missionaries are sent. Reference to scripture, the Second Vatican Council, and the great texts of the magisterium on the mission of the church unifies the meaning of the various commitments to the proclamation of the gospel, to spirituality, to the promotion of peace, to dialogue with cultures and religions, and to justice for those left behind or maltreated. Paul Béré in "Pope Francis and Mission: A Call to Hear the Crying Existential Peripheries" gathers these various elements of Christian mission and emphasizes the importance of a church in a permanent state of mission, *ad intra* and *ad extra*.

At the end of this journey, let us step back to assess the importance of these contributions in the current and emerging mission landscape. It may be interesting to see whether a *general trend* emerges from among the authors of this book, and if so, how they explain it, and what it implies for the future. What does "doing mission" mean to them? Is it (1) a way of *transmitting* the faith and *affirming* the conditions of salvation; or is it rather (2) an *engagement* with the most vulnerable, a *dialogue* with other faiths and wanting to be a *support* for all; or is it (3) pointing to a whole *new trend* in mission?

The Self-Assured Mission: Affirming Salvation and Transmitting Faith

Self-assured mission is characterized by the missionaries' strong conviction of faith drawn from revelation, from the divine election they benefit from, and from the community that formed them and sends them out. This conviction gives them the certainty of salvation for (1) the one who is faithful, (2) the one who proclaims the faith, and (3) the one who receives it.[1] These missionaries are determined to transmit the treasure of the gospel in both good times and bad. The assurances of those sent do not prevent crises and suffering, but they overcome them by returning to the source of truth, the word of God, interpreted by tradition and lived in agreement with the community.

Missionary Assurance

In scripture the prophet Elijah, John the Baptist, and Paul of Tarsus are examples of this trend, with nuances that would be interesting to study more closely. Broadly speaking, in the First Book of Kings, Elijah engages in a relentless struggle against idolatry and impiety, with signs, wonders, and strong mystical experiences, in the ninth century before Christ. In preparation for the imminent public ministry of Christ, John the Baptist calls for conversion through his impassioned words and his example of radicalism, because the time of judgment is at hand. After Christ's death and resurrection, Paul of Tarsus, thrown from his horse on the road to Damascus, gives himself up entirely to the mission of proclaiming the gospel, building up and accompanying communities in order to guide them along the path of faithfulness. "Woe to me if I do not proclaim the Gospel!"[2]

This missionary assurance includes *self-questioning* as one progresses in faith: Elijah runs away and wishes to die;[3] John the Baptist wonders if Jesus was indeed the One who was to come;[4] Paul knows that he is only

---

[1] Cf. Rom 10.
[2] 1 Cor 9:16.
[3] 1 Kings 19.
[4] Mt 11:3.

a vessel of clay,[5] and he wonders with concern whether it is better to die or to live,[6] or if he has the right tone to speak to the Galatians.[7] These missionaries are humble servants of a God infinitely superior to them.

Most founders of missionary congregations are filled with the need to proclaim the gospel, even at the risk of their lives, here on earth. Looking forward to eternal life at the end of the road, they do not hesitate to question their former ways of serving the gospel. They find assurance not in themselves but in their vocation and in the faithfulness of God.

Affirming Salvation

It is this self-assured missionary model that dominated the history of mission until the early twentieth century. It is still important in the twenty-first century, less dominant than in the last century but very active on all the continents with very diverse expressions: some *traditional families* are keen to pass on their spiritual heritage to their children; *new converts* suddenly discover the truth of the Christian faith and understand the importance of passing it on; *new communities* throw themselves into a joyful, uninhibited evangelization; and *pastors* work to respond to the pastoral needs of their parishioners.

The self-assured mission cannot be exclusively relegated to the past or simply ignored. The zeal of this style of mission does indeed bear visible fruit, but the local church has the task to discern it in order to avoid or denounce abuses, excesses, arrogance, tension, so that the tree does not become a forest! Other models of mission are legitimate and do not bear less fruit, even if they are different.

As for the established religious congregations, which are almost exclusively represented in SEDOS, and in our book, they tend to relegate this type of mission to the time of their foundation and to cultivate the *aggiornamento* of the conciliar years. That is why no contribution in our collection follows this line of self-assured mission. It is also because it recalls the intransigent current of the nineteenth century, which very closely correlated the professed faith and salvation, and which coincided with the colonial period, with little respect for cultural differences. However, for the missionaries who are self-assured, and who tend to group themselves by self-referential affinities (sociological or spiritual), a complacency to-

---

[5] 2 Cor 4:7.
[6] Phil 1.
[7] Gal 4:20.

ward the outside world risks compromising and dulling the faith, to the detriment of the proclamation and transmission of the gospel.

Transmission of Faith

While the self-assured promote the transmission of faith in their family or reference group, one may wonder if their understanding of transmission takes into account a world that has changed a great deal. The texts in this book, written by men and women religious missionaries from all the continents and of all ages, do not emphasize the transmission and affirmation of faith as the primary form of apostolate, even though proclamation is always given pride of place in the magisterial texts on mission. Instead, the authors promote a mission of witness, dialogue, and active engagement in the world.

The Comforting Mission: Engagement, Dialogue, and Support

The turning point of the Second Vatican Council was the occasion for a new awareness: God works in every heart, in all human realities, and he saves them because he created them in love, for love. The unique mediation of Jesus for salvation is not exclusive of other mediations, derived from him. Diverse cultures, other religions, and the modern world are not obstacles to evangelization and salvation but are opportunities through which God manifests his fidelity, his power of love. It is an era of dialogue with the world and of diaconal commitment that is beginning and that most religious congregations founded in previous centuries have supported in various ways: revision of the constitutions; creation of committees for dialogue, justice, nonviolence, and ecological commitment; and promotion of actions in defense of the rights of vulnerable people, such as foreigners, women, and exploited children, including in the traditional apostolate of the institutes (education, health, and pastoral).

The comforting mission is very inclusive: no person of good will is a priori excluded from salvation. Everyone can work in his or her own way to promote a kingdom of justice and peace here below.

The second part of the Book of the Prophet Isaiah (chaps. 40–66) or the parables of mercy in the evangelist Luke are prominent biblical models for this missionary line. The question is not so much to transmit religious convictions, the content of the faith, as to witness to the spirit of the gospel.

God came into the world to show his love for it, from the first to the last hour. The missionary is one who is committed entirely to the service of this love of God and neighbor; does not fear ingratitude or misunderstanding, even if he or she suffers from it; and bears witness in deed more than in word, especially in environments where the gospel is not tolerated, seeking less to transmit and affirm than to dialogue and support the weakest.

The comforting mission's pitfall, the tree that risks hiding the forest, would be to testify to itself, its commitment, its achievements, more than to God, his Being, and his visible and invisible action in the world. The risk is also to adopt a spirit of "spiritual worldliness" or "self-referentiality,"[8] which Pope Francis denounces.[9]

At first glance it seems that the majority of the contributions of this symposium are situated in the comforting mission, in line with the Second Vatican Council. See, for instance, Joseph Scaria Palakeel, "The 'What' of Mission: Refining Our Comprehension of Mission"; Anthony Akinwale, "The 'Where' of Mission: Fifty Years of *Ad Gentes* in Africa"; and Pudota Rayappa John, "The 'How' of Mission: Going 'Outside the Gates' for the Kingdom's Sake"; as well as most of the institutes represented (see, for example, the experience of the three Comboni sisters Ida Colombo, Hélène Israël Soloumta Kamkôl, and Maria Teresa Ratti in "The 'Who' of Mission: We Are Mission"; or Tim Norton, "Interculturality: Culture and the Experience of God"). The texts of Part Three of the book emphasize the following as integral parts of the Christian mission: dialogue with believers of other religions; commitment to ecology, justice, peace, education; or care for people in difficulty. The title of the article by Gerard Hall, "Eastern Religions: Trusting Christianity's 'Incarnational' Thrust," can therefore be taken as representative of the whole section.

This type of mission reassures the recipients of their salvation, based on charity and good will, because it wants to give comfort to the other more than to challenge them. However, the exercise of this mission outreach entails also a risk, and thus requires courage and endurance,

---

[8] "This insidious worldliness is evident in a number of attitudes which appear opposed, yet all have the same pretence of 'taking over the space of the Church.' In some people we see an ostentatious preoccupation for the liturgy, for doctrine and for the Church's prestige, but without any concern that the Gospel has a real impact on God's faithful people and the concrete needs of the present time. In this way, the life of the Church turns into a museum piece or something which is the property of a select few" (Pope Francis, *Evangelii Gaudium,* no. 95).

[9] The encyclical continues with these words: "In others, this spiritual worldliness lurks behind a fascination with social and political gain, or pride in their ability to manage practical affairs, or an obsession with programs of self-help and self-realization" (ibid.).

as James H. Kroeger points out in "Peacebuilding: Peace Promotion as Integral to Evangelization." He highlights the peacebuilding of Saints Mother Teresa of Calcutta, Francis of Assisi, and Óscar Romero, whose lives were neither tranquil nor tranquilizing. The mission of this second trend is therefore similar to *the mission of the prophets*, who do not fear any hardships, and who proclaim the word of God even far in the desert, teach in good times and bad times, and watch for the promised dawn on the frontiers. These aspects allow for the construction of *an important bridge* between the first form of *self-assured mission*, the second form of *comforting mission,* and the following third form of *mission of awakening*, which is invaluable for a better understanding of the *unity of the mission* at the heart of its variants.

The Awakening Mission: Transcendence of Life and Hope

While the self-assured mission places greater emphasis on truth (transcendence of the word, of faith), and the comforting mission is based on charity (transcendence of love), the awakening mission places emphasis on freedom (transcendence of life and hope). Life, here, is understood in a very broad sense: first as gift of God; then as inalienable but often threatened dignity; as intimate, existential movement; and also as community cohesion.

The mission of awakening is more difficult to define than the other two, because it is lived out as much by self-assured missionaries as by comforting missionaries, by parishioners who are not affiliated to one community or another, as by members of communities that are somewhat atypical. What these missionaries have in common is not an affiliation to a particular group but an attitude. Faith being first and foremost a surprising action of God, the mission seeks to identify it and to make it grow. The "awakener of the dawn"[10] is the one God makes attentive to his very presence, to his mysterious action in the hearts of people. He listens, accompanies, risks a word, never withholds his support, but never leads to himself, his family, or his ecclesial group of reference. He watches for

---

[10] Pope John Paul II addressed the young people of the Diocese of Rome in 2001 as "sentinels of the dawn." See apostolic letter *Novo Millennio Ineunte* (January 6, 2001), no. 9. The expression was to be often repeated, as at the World Youth Day in Toronto in 2002, all the way up to Pope Francis, who said, "As Christians, we are called to be sentinels of the morning," during the General Audience of April 1, 2015.

the work of the Spirit in the other person and helps him to discern the voice that speaks to him in depth.

"Awakeners" like to animate parish life from within; they commit themselves without clinging to positions, they spot the living forces, and they are annoyed by institutional structures while respecting them when necessary. They like to be regularly immersed in the spiritual pulse of a monastery, a community, a group, but without becoming attached to it. They promote the strong moments of ecclesial gatherings where everyone has a proper place, as in the World Youth Days. In their family environment and the world of work, they watch for the slightest interstice through which the Spirit of God can blow, and they work to reveal it. They are wary of overly strict moral and social codes that block the encounter from the outset, but do not encourage laxity.

Among the biblical figures the awakeners are close to Joseph, the husband of Mary. His mission was fundamentally to listen to God's action in Mary and in the world, an unheard of and yet announced action in which he was the privileged partner. Joseph combines a mission of watchman, witness, protector, and companion, taking risks, letting each one follow the inner voice of God, and stepping aside when the time comes. "When fathers refuse to live the lives of their children for them, new and unexpected vistas open up. Every child is the bearer of a unique mystery that can only be brought to light with the help of a father who respects that child's freedom."[11]

Not everything can be planned in mission, since it is God who is the starting point and the point of arrival. This mission of awakening is therefore not always comfortable to live in parishes or well-structured communities. The missionary sometimes disturbs his own confreres more by his zeal than the people he meets!

Among the texts in our book, the one by Alfred Maravilla, "The 'When' of Mission: Rediscovering 'Initial Proclamation' in Evangelization," illustrates this missionary position wonderfully. I would like to highlight some of its aspects. The author relates the mission of vigilance to the unique, unpredictable state of love. In particular, he notes that "living one's Christian life permanently in a constant state of mission, always on the lookout to grab any opportunity for initial proclamation, is *like a sentinel ever ready* to give a reason for the hope that is within oneself. . . . The lover is always *vigilant to seize the opportune time* to make his or her declaration of love freely" (emphasis added). The important thing according to him, as according to this trend of mission, is not to start from dogmatic

---

[11] Pope Francis, apostolical letter *Patris Corde*, December 8, 2020.

formulas but to lead a person to the experience of the Holy Spirit and of Jesus, the Master and Lord. For this to happen, every Christian, every Christian community should create a space that favors the freedom and truth of the first or renewed encounter with God.

It is also a question of rediscovering the meaning and importance of the initial proclamation in the process of evangelization, in particular its relation to the *kerygma* (proclamation of the content of the faith, which leads to conversion), catechesis (pedagogy of commitment in the long term), and life witness (importance of interpersonal relationships, attention to the poorest, consistency of lifestyle).

The author is also attentive to contemporary challenges, such as the way in which truth is spoken and received, not so much through speech as through the imagination, interiority (John Henry Newman); in the face of the difficulty of making transcendence understood in a world that is increasingly open to the virtual, "the means of social communication are not mere instruments to enter the digital continent but means of creating and fostering a new culture in order to be a prophetic presence which reflects the face of Christ."

The text by Lazar T. Stanislaus, "Missionary Parishes: Growing as a Missionary Parish," also gives interesting insights into a mission that combines proximity, proclamation, and attention to what God is working in others. The author suggests various practical ways for becoming a missionary parish: hospitality, dialogue, friendship, celebration, kerygmatic community, vibrant prayer and liturgy, social outreach programs, being an eco-parish, inclusion of diverse cultures, media, and ministry.

As we can see from this example, the mission of the awakener does not oppose currents, as self-assured and comforting missionaries tend to do, but takes into account as many components and opportunities as possible to reach out and touch people and situations. Mission consists in being there where the Lord wants to speak, to give himself, to reveal himself. To speak of God is also to lean over his wounded image, whether close by or far away. This new trend in mission, the mission by awakening, will hopefully receive more attention in our missionary endeavors as it belongs to the emerging future of mission today.

Overall, the testimonies gathered in this collection stimulate a vision of mission that does not overemphasize words and ideals, but one that bears witness to the strength of divine Life; which transfigures our fears, our habits, our inhibitions; and which awakens in us the hope in a better world. But while pastoral ministry does indeed engage a large number of the members of our missionary institutes, our book, apart from these two examples, shows little concern with the mission of proclamation and transmission in the parish or in the family. Why? Shouldn't the question of proclamation and transmission be put back in the spotlight in our institutes?

Proclamation and Transmission of Faith: A Crisis, a Necessity

We often speak of a crisis of transmission in the twenty-first century, and more widely than in the church. It is becoming difficult to transmit the faith from generation to generation, from group to group, because of current trends such as immediacy, individualism, scandals, the fragility of families, the "rat race" that does not take history into account, the discrediting of institutions, pluralism, and so on.

Why does mission in the church today no longer consist first and foremost of transmitting the faith? Several hypotheses can be considered:
- The affirmation of the faith has weakened in certain circles, including Christians (analysis of *Redemptoris Missio*, no. 2).
- Generalized communication tends to replace transmission (analysis by Michel Bertrand[12]).
- The urgency seems to lie elsewhere than in the proclamation of salvation;
- The affirmation of past centuries was too constraining. There was too much pressure, an obligation to believe, which has given way to its opposite, total freedom and refusal to transmit for fear of impeding freedom.

Transmission is generally speaking more about the internal (family, association, parish), while *mission* is more about the external. But is it so clear cut? Mission is not achieved without transmission (content, methods, practices, values, qualifying attitudes), and transmission is the first form of mission. Moreover, it is sometimes difficult to separate the catechumenate, catechesis, and the first proclamation. The *New Directory for Catechesis* even pleads for a missionary, kerygmatic, mystagogic, and inculturated catechesis (considering the ages, the cultural contexts, the digital age, and so forth):

> Since there have been changes in the forms of transmission of the faith, the Church is committed to deciphering some of the signs of the times through which the Lord shows her the path to take. Among these multiple signs can be recognized: the centrality of the

---

[12] Michel Bertrand, "Qu'est-ce que transmettre?" *Études théologiques et religieuses* 83, no. 3 (2008): 389–404.

believer and of his life experience; the considerable role of relationships and the affections; interest in what offers true meaning; the rediscovery of what is beautiful and lifts up the spirit. In these and other movements of contemporary culture the Church grasps the possibilities for encounter and for proclamation of the newness of the faith. This is the cornerstone of her missionary transformation, which drives pastoral conversion.[13]

For all that, the mission must always be strongly committed to dialogue and to charity toward the most vulnerable. The texts in this volume bear a great witness to the fruitfulness of this commitment, which is fully faithful to the gospel and authentic.

In sum, it seems to me that we have beautiful paths here to renew our missionary commitment together, by making us attentive to what is changing without losing the beauty and grandeur of what we are already experiencing. Religious life certainly transmits its tradition to its new members, and in exchange it also receives from them the surprising movements of the Spirit always at work.

> **Marie-Hélène Robert, OLA,** is a missiologist, full professor of dogmatic theology at the Faculty of Theology of Lyon Catholic University, and a member of the Sciences and Humanities Confluence Research Center of Lyon Catholic University. She has published numerous books and articles, and given lectures at various national and international conferences. She is a sister of the Missionary Institute of Our Lady of the Apostles.

---

[13] Pontifical Council for the Promotion of the New Evangelization, *New Directory for Catechesis* (June 25, 2020), no. 5.

Appendix

The Emerging Future in Mission

Summary of the 2021 SEDOS Mission Symposium

What do we mean when we use the term *mission*—what is mission? As we saw from the talks over the five days of the SEDOS mission symposium, there is a great diversity in what mission is today. The Redaction Committee has been listening to the talks given at the symposium, along with its many participants online, and has been looking to see what major themes surfaced across the different talks that were presented. And while there are significant themes we can spell out, we do not want to take away the unique richness of each contribution.

Four Foundations

A major question for the committee has been: What are the pillars we notice that support our understandings of mission as expressed during this symposium? The 1969 SEDOS symposium focused on the significance of the roles of development in missionary activities and of dialogue, and the 1989 SEDOS symposium came up with four principal activities of the church's mission: proclamation, dialogue, inculturation, and the liberation of the poor.

Although all these activities remain present in mission today, based on the talks of this 2021 SEDOS mission symposium, we first considered what the *foundations of mission* are. These foundations might be called the nonnegotiables in mission; they are valid for all time:

1. scripture;
2. experience;
3. Holy Spirit; and
4. cry of the world.

These four foundations interconnect. This means that when we reflect on the working of the Holy Spirit in mission, for instance, its working will also be present in the cry of the world/poor (see, for instance, "The 'Who' of Mission" by Ida Colombo, CMS, Hélène Israël Soloumta Kamkôl, CMS, and Maria Teresa Ratti, CMS), in scripture (see, for instance, "The 'Why' of Mission" by Rekha M. Chennattu, RA), and in experience (see, for instance, the chapter on intial proclamation, "The 'When' of Mission," by Alfred Maravilla, SDV). This interconnectedness makes it difficult to be one-sided in talking about mission.

Missio Dei

Alongside the meetings of the Redaction Committee, different discussion groups gathered daily to do some sharing about the talks, with questions that were set beforehand. Toward the end, the conclusion of the committee was given to the groups for evaluation. There were many specifications of the proposed emerging future aspects, which are taken up in the next paragraph, but one very important remark was that "mission starts in the mind of God," as Sr. Rekha Chennattu, RA, so vividly explained from her study of the Bible. The four foundations therefore are to be taken as a unity under the umbrella of *missio Dei*, the mission of God. One can imagine the four foundations to be the four legs of a table, and the table as a whole the mind and heart of God. As missionaries we are seated at this table, eating from one or more sides of the table, enjoying the same food (= mission).

Emerging Themes in Mission

During the five days of the symposium, the Redaction Committee started to see more clearly which aspects of today's mission the different speakers had in common; those from a theological background (Parts One and Two) as well as those from a more practical background (Part Three). We did not want to come up with just one term for each theme, but to place it with another so as to give some dynamism to each of the themes. There are thus four main themes, each with two aspects that are very much related.

Synodality and Communion

Possibly one of the most significant themes that arose from the talks was the theme of *synodality*, which came to the fore right at the beginning when

Sr. Mary Barron, OLA, reflected on SEDOS and its history, in which nine missionary congregations made a significant contribution to the text *Ad Gentes*. Perhaps, after Sr. Mary's talk on Thursday, it is appropriate to add "her-stories" to the history of SEDOS, for we have heard often enough in these five days about the significant role of women in mission. The theme of synodality came through in the talk by Cardinal Tagle and his three points for SEDOS to follow up on. In the light of synodality, what he had to say was important and new. Another aspect of synodality that perhaps was named well by Sr. Mary T. Barron, OLA, is the shift from *ad gentes* to *inter gentes* as we move from a mission "to," to a mission "with and among." We heard echoes of it again in the talk Fr. Paul Béré, SJ, gave on images of Pope Francis's mission, and in the reflections of Sr. Marie-Hélène Robert, OLA, on ecumenism and the search for unity. Fr. Joseph Palakeel, MST, then asked, "What is mission, and how is mission developing?" He reminded us that our ecclesiology shapes mission and spoke of three perspectives in particular—*regno*, *communio*, and *missiological*—with the last one as a new understanding in ecclesiology. The talks spoke strongly of our call to communion. Sr. Marie-Hélène Robert, OLA, for example, said that mission is done by groups, not individuals, and reminded us of the importance of the complementarity of others. Sr. Agnes Lanfermann, MMS, mentioned that networking and cooperation are not to be done on our own. The importance of dialogue, as an aspect of synodality and communion, was reaffirmed in the reflection Sr. Maria De Giorgi, MMX, gave on interreligious dialogue, and also by Fr. John Mallare, CICM, in our dialogue with Islam and the mission of mercy. Synodality was also a central requisite for Mr. Oliver Aquilina, SDC, who referred to the need for a change of mindset from cooperation to co-responsibility when it comes to our attitude to the laity. The theme of synodality can also be heard in the enfolding paradigm shift that sees us moving from the "I" to the "we." The talks placed strong emphasis on the collective thrust of mission. It is not, "I am the missionary"; rather, we now hear, "We are mission," as Sr. Hélène Kamkôl, CMS, shared with us.

Dignity and Human Fulfillment

The second theme we heard emerging this week was the significance of *respect for the dignity of the other*. A former mission approach might have considered mission to others as mission to those who had no knowledge of or were in need of what we bring. This theme came up strongly in the talk given by Sr. Monique Tarabeh, RGS, and in the reflection of Fr. Tim Norton, SVD, on spiritual direction. We heard of the importance of honoring the God who is already present among others. Fr. Daniel Huang, SJ, quoted his superior general, Fr. Arturo Sosa, SJ, who said that one of the signs of the times today is the universal process of secularization. God speaks to us even from the heart of a humanitarianism that has no need of the transcendent. Thankfully, God goes before us on mission. As many speakers reminded us, the Spirit of God is capable of being in any place and with any people. Fr. Paul Béré, SJ, reflecting on the mission of Pope Francis and the cry of the existential peripheries, helped us to see that we are talking not about geography but about the human peripheries we acknowledge.

Maria Antonetta Pereira, FMM, reminded us that education is mission. Mission demands a certain mutuality and willingness to go to where people are. We saw a firm emphasis on the human aspects of mission—interculturality, peripheries, and women. Multiplicity of options is now a value. Again, Fr. Daniel Huang, SJ, spoke of human centeredness: putting the human at the center of mission. This is not to replace God as the foundation of mission, but rather to acknowledge the God who works within human experience. First, learn to know human feelings, then go to how Jesus felt, and then to church as a community of believers. How are we to speak of God today, of God's offer of salvation, to people who do not need God? What allows for human flourishing? Young people today are looking for identity. There is a need for a new way of communicating—identity. Sr. Rekha Chennattu, RA, and Fr. Stephen Bevans, SVD, spoke of prophetic dialogue that is respectful of the other.

Fr. Pudota Rayappa John, SJ, also spoke of the dignity of the human person when referring to the mission among Indian farmers, and of our need to go beyond the gates for the sake of the kingdom of God. He talked of the agrarian language Jesus used as the language of the local people. Fr. Gerard Hall, SM, invited us to learn to respect the inherent Christian experience that is not dominated by a culture not its own. Sr. Robyn Reynolds, OLSH, began her talk by paying her respects to the Indigenous People of her country. She drew special attention to Indigenous religiosity and leadership by Indigenous people, rather than by church ministers. The moderator called her talk "mystical." Nestor Anaya, FSC, and Teresa Gómez spoke about young people, the work of supporting them as they develop to be fully the people they are called to be, and of accompanying them in their dreams. As mentioned, Sr. Mary Barron reminded us of the importance of hearing the "her-story" of women on mission, so often omitted from the official records. She honored the feminine genius as she mentioned the qualities of sensitivity, generosity, maternity, and receptivity.

Sr. Carmen Elisa Bandeo, SSpS, speaking on the roots of "people on the move," called us into a place of respect found in deeper communion with God, with others, and with all creation. The dignity of people not wanting to be called refugees deserves our respect—they are first and foremost human beings. We all have our roots in movement. With God we are all itinerants journeying on the road to the definitive union with God. We should respect people on the journey of their life with God.

Christ-connectedness and Witness through Spirituality

Fr. Stephen Bevans, SVD, situated mission in the context of missionary discipleship, in which our connectedness to Christ enables the transformation of the world. The third theme that emerged was that of spirituality uniting the talks and expressing our being linked to God through Jesus Christ. Sr. Rekha Chennattu, RA, spoke about biblical trends in mission for our time. Mission begins in the mind of God, and we have to be of the same mind and heart. I'm reminded of Philippians 2:5: "Have this mind among yourselves, which was in Christ Jesus." We are givers and receivers on a journey together with Christ at the center. Mission has to touch the spiritual yearning of humanity, said Fr. Bevans. The church's mission is to be a covenant community. Sr. Rekha appreciated the reciprocal love that defines Johannine discipleship. We must first evangelize ourselves to be able to talk about God. The task of mission today is to evangelize ourselves, so that we become visible signs of God in the world. Fr. Joseph Palakeel, MST, pointed out that as missionaries we should not look only to be in communion with other human beings but at the same time with God, and to be open about it to others.

Alfred Maravilla, SDB, spoke of rediscovering the initial proclamation. There is the initial proclamation to new catechumens and the ongoing renewed proclamation to the faithful. *Kerygma* is the preaching or proclamation of the Christian gospel, but initial proclamation is how to come to know the Person of Jesus Christ. The *kerygma* is witnessed by a credible lifestyle, with an authentic practice of charity. A credible witness of life is an attractive invitation. We heard several times the use of the term *encounter*, which spoke to us of the initial proclamation.

Witness has many expressions. We heard of the expressions of the media from Sr. Monique Tarabeh, RGS. Dialogue gives witness, as does good inculturation in the outreach to the poor. Fr. Lazar T. Stanislaus, SVD, spoke of the parish's missionary potential. Inculturation in the parish enables the new culture of the gospel to witness to our centeredness in

Christ. Fr. Aloysius Pieris, SJ, in his reflection on the search for the real identity of religious missionary institutes, speaks of Jesus communities animated by love, whose presence and witness reflect the Trinity. From a faith aspect we are full of the Holy Spirit, and we recognize the centrality of discernment in our mission witness.

Basic themes were the sacredness of the human person, the sacredness of the human family, the shared passion to create human community, and also interrelatedness, that is, to go where the people are, to join in their struggle, to learn their language, and to respect their dignity. To respect their aspirations in mission dialogue is very important. In gathering all people and peoples into the heart of God, we are challenged to build up the communion of God's people. A new consciousness that begins with evangelizing oneself was treated by Fr. Anthony Akinwale, OP, as he reflected on the African church that has grown up in the fifty-five years of *Ad Gentes* and *Lumen Gentium*. He showed us the growth of the church in Africa, which now gives reciprocal witness by sending missionaries out to the world.

We regret that the talk "Mission among the Poor" by Sr. Marvi Delrivo, SFP, and Sr. Licia Mazzia, SFP, was canceled at the last minute. Fortunately, the text of their talk is included in Part Three of this volume. It enlightens us on how to empathize with and recognize the face of Jesus in the poor, suffering, rejected, excluded, and marginalized brother and sister.

Holistic Approach and Unity

As the final emerging theme, Fr. Stephen Bevans said that mission has to be approached in a holistic way that inspires unity. The theology of mission addresses the whole of creation. Through transforming missionary discipleship, personal transformation leads to transformation in others. As we await the completion of creation, ecology and the whole of creation—all life—are the focus of mission. We are in a new consciousness, in which we must see ourselves as only part of the whole of creation. We are not separate from but interconnect with the whole.

The holistic approach also focuses on the centrality of healing and salvation, as Sr. Agnes Lanfermann, MMS, shared in recognizing healing as mission. Healing is part of what has emerged at this time, but only lately in the church, that is, how Christ's healing power may act through us. Healing the earth is an integral part of the healing of people. To walk together to promote the culture of life means healing must be holistic, not fragmented. We also heard of interdenominational healing. Furthermore, we are requested to become vulnerable and face our vulnerability as in the wounded Christ, thus healing the whole person, remembering that *we* are mission. Sr. Anne Béatrice Faye, CIC, shared a riveting story of forgiveness that illustrated the healing power that frees and reconciles. This is the new face of reconciliation. Mission speaks to the victims of crimes against humanity who have a right to truth and justice. Forgiveness and reconciliation are acts of hope. God is the author of all reconciliation and healing of the offender. For Sr. Anne Béatrice, evangelization takes the name of forgiveness and reconciliation.

Fr. Joseph Palakeel, MST, spoke of communion with God at the heart of mission. Our walking together in unity is linked to wanting to connect with one another. We heard the African word *Ubuntu* in a number of talks. Sisters Maria Teresa Ratti, CMS, Hélène Kamkôl, CMS, and Ida Colombo, CMS, echoed this in "The 'Who' of Mission." We do not work alone. Fr. Bede Ukwuije, CSSp, encouraged working together to promote the culture of life. African Traditional Religion and Christianity have similar values, which can build on one another. A further sign of this unity and holistic approach was developed by Fr. James Kroeger, MM, in his exploration of peace promotion, which forms an integral part of the work of mission and evangelization. We also listened to Sr. Ilia Delio, OSF, who proposed a new framework that can hold the reality of creation. It demands we enter the holistic consciousness with the whole of which we are a part, but not separate. In what ways is mission evolutionary? While we are "wholes," we are becoming something more within greater "wholes." Our unity with God in creation is the very unity on which *the emerging future* depends.

The Redaction Committee:
Chris Chaplin, MSC,
Marie-Hélène Robert, OLA,
Peter Baekelmans, CICM,
Rachel Oommen, ICM.

SEDOS Member Congregations

CBS	Congregation of the Sisters of Bon Secours of Paris
CFC	Congregation of the Christian Brothers
CICM	Congregation of the Immaculate Heart of Mary (Missionhurst)
CJMJ	Congregation of Jesus Mary Joseph
CMF	Claretian Missionaries
CMM	Marianhill Missionaries
CPS	Missionary Sisters of the Precious Blood
CSJ	Congregation of the Sisters of St. Joseph of Chambéry
CSSp	Congregation of the Holy Spirit (Spiritans)
CSsR	Congregation of the Most Holy Redeemer (Redemptorists)
DMI	Daughters of Mary Immaculate
FC	Brothers of Charity
FCJ	Faithful Companions of Jesus Sisters
FDNSC	Daughters of Our Lady of the Sacred Heart
FD(L)S	Filles de la Sagesse (Daughters of Wisdom)
FMA	Figlie di Maria Ausiliatrice (Salesian Sisters)
FMM	Franciscan Missionaries of Mary
FMS	Marist Brothers of the Schools
FSC	Brothers of the Christian Schools
IBVM	Institute of the Blessed Virgin Mary (Casa Loreto)
ICM	Missionary Sisters of the Immaculate Heart of Mary
ISMC	Consolata Missionary Sisters
MAfr	Missionaries of Africa (White Fathers)
MCCJ	Comboni Missionaries of the Heart of Jesus
MEP	Paris Foreign Missions
MFIC	Missionary Franciscan Sisters of Immaculate Conception
MG	Missionaries of Guadalupe
MHM	Mill Hill Missionaries
MM	Maryknoll Fathers and Brothers
MM	Maryknoll Sisters

MMB	Mercedarian Missionaries of Berriz
MMM	Medical Missionaries of Mary
MMS	Medical Mission Sisters
MSC	Missionaries of the Sacred Heart
MSC	Missionary Sisters of the Sacred Heart of Jesus (Hiltrup)
MSHR	Missionary Sisters of the Holy Rosary
MSOLA	Missionary Sisters of Our Lady of Africa (White Sisters)
NDA/OLA	Sisters of Our Lady of the Apostles
NDS	Our Lady of Sion
O-CARM	Order of Carmelites
OFM	Order of Friars Minor (Franciscans)
OFM-Conv	Order of Friars Minor Conventual (Conventual Franciscans)
OMI	Missionary Oblates of Mary Immaculate
OP	Order of Preachers (Dominicans)
OP (P)	Dominican Sisters of Charity of the Presentation of the Blessed Virgin
OSU	Ursulines of the Roman Union
PIME	Pontifical Foreign Missionary Institute
PM	Presentation of Mary
PSA	Little Sisters of the Assumption (Petites Soeurs de l'Assomption)
RGS	Religious of the Good Shepherd
RNDM	Religious of Our Lady of the Missions
RSCJ	Religious of the Sacred Heart of Jesus
RSHM	Religious of the Sacred Heart of Mary
RSJ	Sisters of St. Joseph of the Sacred Heart
SA	Soeurs de Marie Auxiliatrices
SCJ	Priests of the Sacred Heart of Jesus (Dehonians)
SCJM	Sisters of Charity of Jesus and Mary
SCMM	Sisters of Charity of Our Lady Mother of Mercy
SDB	Salesians of Don Bosco
SDC	Society of Christian Doctrine – M.U.S.E.U.M.
SFB	Sisters of the Holy Family of Bordeaux
SFM	Scarboro Foreign Mission Society
SFMA	Franciscan Missionaries Sisters of Assisi
SFP	Franciscan Sisters of the Poor
SHCJ	Society of the Holy Child Jesus
SM	Society of Mary (Marist Sisters)
SM	Society of Mary (Marist Fathers)

SM	Society of Mary (Marianists)
SMA	Society of African Missions
SMB	Bethlehem Mission Society
SMC	Comboni Missionary Sisters
SME/PME	Societé Mission Etrangères (du Québec)
SMSM	Missionary Sisters of the Society of Mary
SND	Sisters of Notre Dame
SP	Sisters of Providence
SSC	Society of Saint Columban
SSND	School Sisters of Notre Dame
SSpS	Holy Spirit Missionary Sisters
SUSC	Holy Union Sisters
SVD	Society of the Divine Word (Steyler Missionaries)
TSSF	Tertiary Sisters of Saint Francis
UISG	International Union of Superiors General
USG	Union of Superiors General